Encyclopedia of American Women in Business

Encyclopedia of American Women in Business

From Colonial Times to the Present

Volume I
A–L

CAROL H. KRISMANN

Brooks – Cork Library
Shelton State
Community College

Greenwood Press
Westport, Connecticut • London

Library of Congress Cataloging-in-Publication Data

Krismann, Carol
    Encyclopedia of American women in business : from colonial times to the present /
Carol H. Krismann.
        p. cm.
    Includes bibliographical references and index.
    ISBN 0–313–32757–2 (set)—ISBN 0–313–33383–1 (vol. I : alk. paper)—ISBN
0–313–33384–X (vol. II : alk. paper)
    1. Businesswomen—United States—History—Encyclopedias. 2. Businesswomen—
United States—Biography—Dictionaries. 3. Women executives—United States—
History—Encyclopedias. 4. Women executives—United States—Biography—Dictionaries.
    5. Entrepreneurship—United States—History—Encyclopedias. I. Title.
HD6054.4.U6K753 2005
338.092'2–dc22   2004056065

British Library Cataloguing in Publication Data is available.

Library of Congress Catalog Card Number: 2004056065
ISBN: 0–313–32757–2 (Set)
        0–313–33383–1 (Vol. I)
        0–313–33384–X (Vol. II)

First published in 2005

Greenwood Press, 88 Post Road West, Westport, CT 06881
An imprint of Greenwood Publishing Group, Inc.
www.greenwood.com

Printed in the United States of America

The paper used in this book complies with the
Permanent Paper Standard issued by the National
Information Standards Organization (Z39.48–1984).

10 9 8 7 6 5 4 3 2 1

This book is dedicated with love to my husband, Jerry Keenan:
my mentor, my inspiration, my best friend and kindred spirit

Contents

Women in Business Entry List

Accounting
Adams, Evangeline
Adams, Harriet Stratemeyer
Adler, Polly
Advertising
Affirmative Action
African American Businesswomen
Agriculture/Ranching
Aguirre, Pamela
Ainse, Sally
Aitken, Jane
Albee, Mrs. P. F. E.
Alberty, Eliza Missouri Bushyhead
Alexander, Mary Spratt Provoost
Alliance of Women's Business and
    Professional Organizations
Alvarado, Linda
American Business Women's
    Association
American Indian Businesswomen
American Women's Economic
    Development Corporation
Anderson, Margaret C.
Andress, Mary Vail
Anthony, Michele
Apparel Industry, *see* Fashion
    Industry
Arden, Elizabeth
Arnold, Susan E.
Ash, Mary Kay
Asian American Businesswomen

Astor, Sarah Todd
Auerbach, Beatrice Fox
Automobile Industry
Avent, Sharon Hoffman
Ayer, Harriet Hubbard

Bajaj, Kavelle
Balance, *see* Work-Life Balance
Ball, Lucille
Balverde-Sanchez, Laura
Banking
Banta, Vivian
Banuelos, Romana Acosta
Barad, Jill Elikann
Barcelo, Maria Gertrudes
Barnes, Brenda C.
Barrett, Colleen C.
Bartz, Carol A.
Beach, Sylvia
Beauty Industry
Beck, Teresa
Beech, Olive Ann
Beers, Charlotte L.
Benefits, *see* Employee Benefits
Bentas, Lily
Berman, Gail
Bern, Dorrit J.
Bernard, Betsy J.
Bernick, Carol Lavin
Beverage Industry, *see* Food Industry
Birnbaum, Sheila

Introduction

For the past few years, I have had the privilege of spending my time with hundreds of fascinating women. They are all American and all have been or are now women of business. Some are entrepreneurs, some are not. Some married into the business or inherited it, others became businesswomen out of necessity, and still others chose business because they loved it or followed a dream. They all had an abundance of energy and all showed that good old American trait, guts; and with it, perseverance. Most can be categorized as women executives, women entrepreneurs, or women business owners; all have interesting stories.

This encyclopedia attempts to tell some of their stories. It also covers some of the issues and concerns that have hindered and are still hindering the success of women in many fields. Some people feel that the struggles for equality are over, and that women have finally reached parity in the United States. According to my research, this is not so. Only eleven *Fortune* 500 companies are led by women. There are other statistics indicating that true equality has not been reached. Ask almost any woman in business whether she's paid as much as her male counterpart and the answer will be no. Negative stereotypes about women, particularly ethnic women, still rear their ugly heads. Some of the issues, such as childcare and work-life balance, have become issues for men as well.

The goal of this encyclopedia is to summarize these concerns and trace the accomplishments of the women who succeeded. My hope is that the progress that has been made is very clear, and also that there is still a long way to go.

The most difficult part of this project was the necessity of choosing which women to include and which to leave out. I established some criteria, and in some cases, chose to omit entire categories. I included only those women involved in profit-making enterprises. While those founding or running nonprofit organizations worked just as hard or have ideas just as wonderful and inspiring (Clara Barton and Elizabeth Dole of the American Red Cross, Lupe Anguilano of the National Women's Employment and Education, Inc., or Juliette Lowe of the Girl Scouts), I had to draw the line somewhere and this arbitrary line was, at least, fairly clear. I also excluded women who are primarily artists such as actresses, musicians, designers of jewelry or interiors; as well as government officials, if they were not businesswomen also; and editors, but not publishers. These decisions may seem arbitrary and they are; however, because there had to a finite length to this book, they were necessary. I should note at this point that the text is based on research into secondary sources, not personal interviews. Any errors are inadvertent and my own.

There are 426 entries in the book, arranged in alphabetical order. Of these, there are biographies of 327 women, from colonial businesswomen through contemporary entrepreneurs, arranged in alphabetical order interspersed with issues and concerns such as affirmative action and financing, laws such as the Civil Rights Act of 1964, professions such as accounting and banking, and a number of industries. Each entry includes the text, cross references pointing to related topics, and suggestions for further reading indicating places where more information can be found. Full citations for items in the Further Reading sections are in the bibliography at the end of the book.

There are also many "See" entries. For example, if the user wants information on salaries for women, there is a "see" reference to compensation. After the text for the compensation entry, the user is also referred to two other related entries, employee benefits and Equal Pay Act of 1963.

Five appendices follow the encyclopedia entries. The first contains *Fortune* Magazine's annual lists of the most powerful businesswomen in the United States from 1998 through 2003. The entry "Power" explains the meaning of power to businesswomen and the criteria used by Patricia Sellers and the *Fortune* team in compiling their list every year. The second appendix lists the first thirty business women in *Working Woman*'s compilations of the largest woman-owned companies in the country from 1997 through 2001. A clear explanation of the significance of the working woman lists and the criteria for inclusion can be found under the entry "Top Woman Business Owners." Because *Working Woman*, an excellent magazine, stopped publishing in September 2001, later lists are not available. Each of the women in all of the above lists has a biographical entry in the encyclopedia. Appendices III through V identify each businesswoman by ethic group, if relevant; by historical period; and by industry or profession.

The chronology lists events important to women's advancement in the world of business. An extensive bibliography and an index conclude the book. The bibliography contains all citations listed in Further Reading sections as well as basic collective biographies and texts about women in business.

Like all authors, there are many people who helped with this book, some with hard work, others with support, and still others with listening and encouragement. My wonderful husband, Jerry Keenan, not only put up with my down times and encouraged me to persevere, but also input text, counted words, and did all sorts of other important computer tasks. Nancy Carter, my friend and editor, edited and proofed the entire manuscript and kept my semicolons and convoluted sentences under control. My long-enduring staff (Betty Grebe, Marth Jo Sani, Janet Freeman, Joseph Yue, Gene Hayworth, and a former staff member, Chris Pusateri) encouraged, identified helpful articles and new books as they came in, and carried on the work of the library without me during times of looming deadlines. My heartfelt thanks to Dean Jim Williams and Associate Director Susan Anthes of the University of Colorado Libraries for generous research leave so I could work on this project. My grown children always were encouraging and supportive. I would also like to thank my friends who listened to my latest stories of the women, were interested, and also encouraged and supported. And, last but not least, a special thank you to Lynn Araujo and the folks at Greenwood.

Chronology

1607	105 colonists settle in Jamestown, Virginia.
1612	John Rolfe plants tobacco in Virginia.
1620	Pilgrims land at Plymouth, Massachusetts, and settle.
1624	Dutch settle in New Amsterdam.
1629	Brick kiln is started at Salem and leather tannery at Lynn, Massachusetts.
1630	First Thanksgiving.
1636	Harvard College is founded.
1638	Margaret Brent is first woman landowner in Maryland.
1639	First printing press in America.
1645	Lady Deborah Moody is the first English woman settlement leader and town planner in the American colonies.
1650	World population estimated at 500 million people.
1652	Boston starts first colonial mint.
1660	Margaret Philipse is the first woman business agent in the colonies.
1664	British annex New Amsterdam and rename the city New York.
1670	Hudson's Bay Company incorporated to trade in northernmost America.
1678	Robert La Salle explores Great Lakes region.
1680	Massachusetts bans business activities on Sunday.
1681	Pennsylvania receives Royal Charter.
1692	William and Mary College founded in Virginia.
1693	Mary Spratt Provoost Alexander is born, becomes one of the most influential and powerful merchants in the colonies.
1698	Paper manufacturing begins in America.
1701	Yale University founded.
	Elizabeth Haddon Estaugh begins to develop her father's New Jersey land into plantations; one eventually becomes Haddonfield.

1704	*Boston News-Letter* is founded; first newspaper in America to survive.
1715	Sybilla Masters patents her first invention, the corn pulverizer; she is the first American woman inventor to receive a patent.
1716	Mary Butterworth is the first woman to be charged with counterfeiting in America.
1718	New Orleans and San Antonio founded.
1719	Newspapers published in Philadelphia (*The American Mercury*) and Boston (*The Boston Gazette*).
1721	Swiss immigrants introduce rifles into America.
	First insurance office opened.
1729	Benjamin and James Franklin publish *The Pennsylvania Gazette*.
1732	Mary Musgrove Bosomworth (Cousaponokeesa) establishes a trading station on the bluffs of the Savannah River.
1734	First colonial women's labor organization is formed by New York City maids to protest abuses from their employers' husbands.
1735	Ann Franklin inherits her husband's printing business, becomes the first woman printer in New England.
1738	Elizabeth Timothy is the first woman newspaper publisher in the colonies.
	Eliza Pinckney begins experimenting growing indigo.
1746	Princeton University founded as College of New Jersey.
1748	Mary Singleton Copley Pelham's first husband Richard Copley dies, she continues to operate his tobacco shop.
1750	200 merchant traders operating in Philadelphia.
1752	Benjamin Franklin invents the lightning conductor.
1763	Philadelphia is first colonial town with a population over 20,000.
1764	First permanent settlement at St. Louis.
1765	Chocolate first manufactured in America.
1767	Abigail Stonement opens The Merchant's Coffee House at the Sign of the King's Arms.
	Sarah Goddard is the first woman to publish a book in the colonies.
1770	Population in the colonies is 3 million; American Indians are not in this count.
1773	Boston Tea Party.
1775–1783	American Revolution.
1775	Mary Katherine Goddard publishes the first signed copy of the Declaration of Independence.
1778	Sally Ainse buys a house and land in Detroit with profits from her fur trading business.
1781	First pharmaceutical firm is started.
1782	Bank of North America established in Philadelphia.

1785	Sarah Todd marries John Jacob Astor, they build a very successful fur trading business with her dowry.
	First state university, the University of Georgia.
1786	First private golf course is built.
	Congress mandates a U.S. mint.
1787	The Constitution of the United States is ratified.
1789	George Washington becomes the first president.
1790	The first stock exchange is established in Philadelphia.
	Rosa Maria Hinojosa de Balli, the first cattle queen of Texas, inherits her husband's ranch.
	Samuel Slater establishes a spinning mill in Pawtucket, Rhode Island.
	Netnokwa begins her business as a wild game trapper.
	Congress passes the first patent act.
	First U.S. census: Philadelphia—42,000; New York—33,100; Boston—18,300.
1792	Catherine Littlefield Greene begins her patronage of Eli Whitney, suggests idea for cotton gin.
	Captain Gray explores Columbia River and claims what is now the state of Washington for the United States.
1800	Washington, D.C., becomes capital of the United States.
	U.S. population is 5.3 million; 5 million live in rural areas.
1803	President Jefferson approves the Louisiana Purchase.
	Robert Fulton propels a boat with steam power.
1804	The world population is estimated at one billion.
	Lewis and Clark begin exploring the Louisiana Territory.
1808	Jane Aitken prints the first English Bible in America.
	United States prohibits importation of slaves from Africa.
1810	Population of United States is 7,239,881.
1812	Elleanor Eldridge begins the first of many businesses, including weaving, soap making, painting, and wallpapering.
1815	Battle of New Orleans, last battle of the War of 1812.
1817	Rebecca Lukens is the first ironmaster in the United States and the first woman CEO of an industrial company.
1823	Monroe Doctrine.
1824	Maria Gertrudes Barcelo sets up her first gambling operation at Real Dolores de Oro in New Mexico.
1825	New York Stock Exchange opens.
	A baseball club is organized at Rochester, New York.
1826	James Fenimore Cooper writes *The Last of the Mohicans*.
1828	First day nursery opens.
	Construction begins on the Baltimore & Ohio, the first railroad to transport passengers and freight.
1829	First cooperative stores established in the United States.

1831	Nat Turner leads Virginia slave revolt.
1833	Abigail Whittelsey publishes the first magazine in the United States aimed at mothers.
1836	The Alamo falls in what is now San Antonio, Texas.
1837	Financial and economic panic caused by inflated land values, wildcat banking, and paper speculation.
	First college for women in the United States, Mount Holyoke, is established.
1839	*Godey's Lady's Book* debuts; one of the most popular woman's magazines.
	First married woman's property law is passed in Mississippi.
1840	Margaret Haughery founds the first of eleven orphanages in New Orleans with profits from her daily.
	First laws limiting hours of employment of minors in textile factories.
1841	First university degrees granted to women in the United States.
1842	Hetty Green, the "Witch of Wall Street," opens her first bank account at age eight.
1843	John C. Fremont crosses the Rocky Mountains to California.
1844	Samuel Morse invents the telegraph.
1845	Anna Ottendorfer and her first husband Jacob Uhi buy *New-Yorker Staats-Zeitung*, a German American weekly newspaper.
	First wave immigrants Irish.
1846	Elias Howe invents the first sewing machine.
1847	Gold is discovered in California.
1848	First Women's Rights Convention in Seneca Falls, New York.
	Levi Strauss designs the first pair of blue jeans.
1850	World population estimated at 1.1 billion.
	New York, Philadelphia, and Boston provide 81 percent of the U.S. publishing output.
1851	Biddy Mason, the first African American woman to own land in Los Angeles, moves to California and wins her freedom.
	The *New York Times* begins to publish.
	I.M. Singer improves the sewing machine with a continuous stitching mechanism.
1852	Mary Ellen Pleasant arrives in San Francisco and auctions off her services as a cook, she is offered $500 per month.
1857	American civil engineer E.G. Otis installs first safety elevator.
	Oberlin College is established as first coed college.
1860	Ellen Demorest is the first to create and distribute accurate patterns for dressmaking.
	Abraham Lincoln is elected president.
1861	Elizabeth Keckley first visits the White House to design dresses for Mary Todd Lincoln.

1861–1865	American Civil War.
1862	Homestead Act grants 160 acres of unimproved Western land to any citizen.
1865	Thirteenth amendment abolishes slavery.
	250,000 immigrants arrive.
1866	Margaret LaForge becomes superintendent of Macy's Department Store; she is America's first woman boss.
	Clara Brown earns $10,000 from the first laundry in Central City, Colorado, buys real estate.
1868	Myra Bradwell founds first weekly legal newspaper.
1869	Transcontinental railroad is completed.
1870	Wyoming Territory passes first equal pay law.
	Victoria Woodhull is the first woman stockbroker on Wall Street.
1871	Margaret Knight invents the square-bottomed paper bag machine.
1872	Nellie Cashman opens a boarding house in Pioche, Nevada, and begins her career as a prospector.
1875	Lydia Pinkham sells her first bottles of Mrs. Pinkham's Vegetable Compound.
1876	Alexander Graham Bell invents the telephone.
	Elizabeth Pringle begins managing her rice plantation, Chicora Woods, in South Carolina.
	Eliza Nicholson inherits *The New Orleans Picayune* and brings it out of debt.
1878	First telephone exchange put into operation.
1879	Macy's Department Store opens a ladies' lunchroom.
1881	First collegiate school of business established by Joseph Wharton in Pennsylvania.
1885	Henrietta King inherits King Ranch in Texas and builds it into the largest ranch in the world.
1886	Harriet Ayer is the first woman to make a fortune in the cosmetics business.
	Mrs. P. F. E. Albee is the first Avon lady.
1888	Elizabeth Boit and Charles Winship found the Harvard Knitting Mill in Cambridge, Massachusetts.
	Maria Montoya Martinez makes her first piece of pottery.
1889	Eliza Alberty, after her husband's death, continues running the National Hotel in Tahlequa, Cherokee Nation.
	First issue of *The Wall Street Journal*.
	Anna Bissell takes the reins of the Bissell published Company and becomes one of the first woman CEOs.
1890	Mary and Gordon Greene begin their steamship company, they eventually buy the *Delta Queen*.
	Rose and Charles Knox found Knox Gelatin and begin their advertising campaign.

1893	Sears Roebuck & Company founded.
	Financial panic of 1893.
	World's Columbian Exposition in Chicago.
1894	Freda Ehmann starts growing olives; becomes the "Mother of the California Ripe Olive industry."
1897	First Dow Jones Industrial Average published.
1898	Spanish American War.
1899	Alice Brown Davis takes over her husband's trading post and ranch in the Seminole Nation.
1900	International Ladies Garment Workers Union formed.
	First women accountants in the United States.
	Ada and Minna Everleigh open the Everleigh Club in Chicago.
	Booker T. Washington founds the National Negro Business League to promote entrepreneurism.
1901	United States Steel Company founded.
	First discovery of oil in Texas.
1902	Annie Turnbo Malone moves to St. Louis, sells her hair straightener door to door, begins her haircare empire.
	Helena Rubinstein opens her first beauty salon in Melbourne, Australia.
1903	First Ford motorcar.
	Mary Fields opens her laundry in Cascade, Montana.
	Maggie Walker is the first woman president of a U.S. bank.
	First airplane flight by the Wright brothers.
1904	Lane Bryant is first to design and market maternity clothes.
	Eartha White begins her entrepreneurship career, opening the first of seven businesses, a department store catering to the African American community.
	The U.S. Department of Commerce and Labor is created.
1905	Sarah Walker moves to Denver and begins to build her million-dollar haircare business, she eventually become the first African American woman millionaire.
1906	Congress passes the Pure Food and Drug Act, first federal standards for food and drug regulation.
1908	Bess and Ole Evinrude begin the Evinrude Detachable Row Boat Motor Company.
	Muller v. Gregson limits women's hours in the workplace.
	Harvard University founds its business school.
1909	Hattie Carnegie opens her first store, Carnegie Ladies Hatter.
	Gertrude Willis and her husband Clem found an insurance company and funeral parlor in New Orleans.
	First motion picture newsreel.
1910	Elizabeth Arden opens her first salon, beginning her cosmetics empire.

	Nearly 500,000 motor vehicles are registered in the United States.
1911	Triangle Shirtwaist Fire kills 146, mostly women and children, working in a locked factory under unsafe conditions.
	New York Herald accepts first advertisement for maternity dresses.
	First women's advertising clubs are founded.
1912	Marguerite Greenfield begins her ice business in Montana.
	Massachusetts passes the first minimum wage law.
1913	Federal Reserve System established.
	Ford Motor Company begins using mass-production assembly line.
	Associated Advertising Clubs of America adopts truth in advertising code.
1914	Marjorie Merriweather Post inherits General Foods.
	Margaret Anderson publishes *The Little Review*, an avant-garde journal.
	Kate Gleason builds the first housing development.
	Ruth Waldo becomes the first woman vice president of J. Walter Thompson, the advertising agency.
1914–1918	World War I.
1915	Blanche Knopf becomes one of first modern book publishers.
1916	Jennie Grossinger opens 9 resort in the Catskills.
	Nell Quinlan Donnelly Reed designs "dress aprons."
	Einstein proposes theory of relativity.
	Rose Blumkin leaves Russia and takes a peanut boat to America.
1917	Kate Gleason is first woman president of a national bank.
	Bertha Ronzone begins store in Manhattan, Nevada, with a large supply of socks.
1918	Mary Pickford is first woman to form her own film production company.
1919	The first women are admitted to business school, a secretarial degree program at the University of Georgia.
	Madame C.J. (Sarah) Walker becomes the first African American millionairess.
	Lena Phillips founds National Federation of Business and Professional Women's Clubs, Inc.
1919–1933	Prohibition of alcohol in the United States.
1920	Women granted the right to vote.
	Two of F.W. Woolworth's daughters are elected to Woolworth's board of directors.
1921	Nathalie Laimbeer and others found Financial Women International.
	Lila and DeWitt Wallace issue the first *Reader's Digest*.
1922	Estee Lauder begins selling skin cream.
	Sylvia Beach is the first publisher of James Joyce's *Ulysses*.

1923	A.C. Nielsen Company pioneers marketing and media research.
1924	Mary Andress is the first woman officer of a large New York City bank.
	Gertrude Muller founds Juvenile Wood Products Company to market her invention, a safe child's toilet seat.
1925	Ida and William Rosenthal incorporate their brassiere business and call it Maiden Form.
	Women's World Fair in Chicago.
1926	Nathalie Laimbeer is the first woman financial writer.
1927	Josephine Roche inherits the Rocky Mountain Fuel Company.
	World population is two billion.
	Evangeline Adams predicts stock market fluctuations.
1929	Rose Knox is first woman elected to the board of the American Grocery Manufacturers Association.
	Stock market crashes.
	Business Week publishes first issue.
	65,000 African American businesses exist in the United States.
1929–1939	Worldwide economic depression.
1930	Helena Rubinstein, Dorothy Shaver, and others form Fashion Group International.
	Harriet and Edna Adams lead the Stratemeyer Syndicate, publisher of the Nancy Drew and Hardy Boys series.
	Fortune publishes first issue.
	First home sales party.
	Eleanor Patterson is first woman to publish a large metropolitan newspaper, *The Washington Herald*.
1931	Gilbreth Medal is created by the Society of Industrial Engineers, Lillian Gilbreth is first recipient.
	Polly Adler is described as New York's most notorious vice entrepreneur.
1932	Twelve million persons are unemployed in the United States.
	Radio City Music Hall opens.
1933	Franklin D. Roosevelt begins the New Deal, a program of social reform and economic stimulation.
	Banking Act reorganizes banking system, establishes deposit insurance and other regulations.
1934	The Securities Exchange Act establishes the Securities and Exchange Commission.
	Sylvia Porter begins her weekly personal finance column.
	Congress establishes the Federal Communications Commission.
1935	Gretchen Schoenleber is elected to the New York Cocoa Exchange, the first woman member of any commodity exchange.
	Harriet Lewis inherits her father's plumbing fixtures company and builds it into one of the top woman-owned companies.

	The Social Security Act provides benefits for workers.
1936	The Douglas DC-3 revolutionizes air travel by providing passenger comfort and operating capabilities.
1937	Margaret Rudkin sells the first loaves of Pepperidge Farm bread.
	Rose Blumkin starts her discount furniture business in Omaha.
1938	Beatrice Fox Auerbach becomes president of G. Fox department store and builds it into the largest privately owned store in America.
	Rose Morgan styles Ethel Waters' hair for a concert in Chicago and begins her haircare business.
1939	Dorothy Schiff is the first woman newspaper publisher in New York City.
	World's Fair introduces regular U.S. television service.
1941	Japanese attack Pearl Harbor.
	Lanham Act provides federal funds for day care for children of defense workers.
1942	United States joins World War II.
	National War Labor Board issues General Order No. 16 which suggests equal salaries for men and women doing the same job.
	Hope Schary is the first woman cotton manufacturer and textile converter.
1943	Lady Bird Johnson buys KTBC, her first radio station.
	Rosie the Riveter appears in a Norman Rockwell cover painting on the *Saturday Evening Post*.
1944	D-Day, the invasion of Europe by allied forces.
1945	Bombing of Hiroshima and Nagasaki.
	The United Nations is founded.
1946	Catherine Clark founds Brownberry Ovens.
	First bikini is designed.
	War Brides Act results in the immigration of almost 10,000 wives from Japan, China, and the Philippines.
1947	Helen Reid takes over the *New York Herald Tribune* and turns it into a national newspaper.
	Jackie Robinson is the first African American baseball player in the major leagues.
	Dorothy Bullitt pioneers television in Seattle.
1948	Ruth Washington inherits the *Los Angeles Sentinel,* one of the first African American newspapers in Los Angeles.
1949	Diners Club begins the credit card industry.
	Helen Boehm sells two of her husband's porcelain sculptures to the Metropolitan Museum of Art.
	Hilary Button founds the American Business Women's Association.

1950	Hazel Bishop launches mammoth advertising campaign to promote her indelible lipstick.
	Liz Claiborne begins her career in fashion design.
	Cable television is introduced.
	First homeowner's insurance policies are offered.
	World population estimated at 2.4 billion.
1950–1953	Korean War.
1951	First *I Love Lucy* episode airs on television; stars Lucille Ball, the first woman to own and run a large TV production studio.
	Lillian Vernon begins her mail order business with an ad in *Seventeen* magazine.
	First network color TV broadcast.
	UNIVAC computer developed.
	Pampers are introduced.
	First Tupperware party.
1952	Ernesta Procope founds E.G. Bowman, the largest minority-owned and woman-owned insurance brokerage in the United States.
	Toy Len Goon is named Mother of the Year.
	First hydrogen bomb exploded.
	Jonas Salk invents the first polio vaccine.
1953	Congress creates the Small Business Administration.
	First open heart surgery.
1954	Lillian Gilbreth awarded the Gold Medal of the International Committee of Scientific Management (CIOS).
	Supreme Court ends school segregation.
	TV dinners are introduced.
	Beginning of rock and roll music.
1955	Bernice and Leonard Lavin buy Alberto-Culver for $400,000.
	Disneyland opens.
	9.3 million motor vehicles sold in the United States.
	Beginning of the Civil Rights Movement.
1956	Ruth Handler invents the Barbie doll.
	The Immigration and Naturalization Act erases earlier quotas for immigrants.
	The Interstate Highway System is funded.
1957	First Frisbee.
	Soviets launch Sputnik, the first effort in space.
1958	Joyce Chen opens her first restaurant introducing northern Chinese cuisine.
	Mary Roebling becomes the first woman governor of the American Stock Exchange.
	Hula hoop invented.
1959	Marian and Michael Ilitch open the first Little Caesar's Pizza.
	Alaska and Hawaii become the 49th and 50th states.

1960	90 percent of the bank clerks and tellers are women, very few women are executives.
	World population estimated at 3 billion.
	First laser demonstrated.
	First oral contraceptives sold in the United States.
1960–1970	Longest sustained global economic boom.
1961	Harvard admits first women into MBA program.
	First Presidential Commission on the Status of Women.
1962	Felice Schwartz founds Catalyst.
	Lynda Resnick begins her own advertising agency when she is 19.
	John Glenn orbits the earth.
	Rachel Carson writes *Silent Spring*.
1963	Mary Kay Ash begins her cosmetics company and builds it into the largest direct-sale multilevel cosmetics company in the world.
	Marion and Herbert Sandler form Golden West Savings & Loan and build it into a *Fortune* 500 company.
	Congress passes the Equal Pay Act.
	Weight Watchers begins.
	Betty Friedan writes *The Feminine Mystique*.
1964	Equal Employment Opportunity Commission (EEOC) is established.
1965	Barbara Proctor is the first African American person in advertising in Chicago.
	Harvard Business Review article states: 61 percent of men and 47 percent of women executives feel that the business community will never fully accept women executives.
	Congress passes Medicare and Medicaid amendments to the Social Security Act.
	Ralph Nader begins the consumer movement.
1966	National Organization of Women is founded.
1967	Muriel Siebert is the first woman to buy a seat on the New York Stock Exchange.
	First heart transplant is successfully performed.
1968	Mary Wells Lawrence takes her advertising agency public, the first woman to list a company on a stock exchange.
1969	Muriel Siebert founds her own brokerage company.
	Joan Whitney Payson's New York Mets win the World Series.
	Joan Ganz Cooney and her team debut *Sesame Street*.
	Black Enterprise launched.
	Men walk on the moon.
1970	Gertrude Boyle inherits financially ailing Columbia Sportswear and builds it into a leading outdoor sportswear company.
	"Doonesbury" debuts.
	The Environmental Protection Agency is created.

	The Occupational Safety and Health Act is passed.
1971	Romana Banuelos is the first Mexican American treasurer of the United States.
	Rose Totino sells Totino's Pizza to Pillsbury for $20 million in stock.
	Lilo and Gerard Leeds found CMP Media on Long Island.
	Katharine Graham publishes the Pentagon Papers in the *Washington Post*.
	In ruling on *Griggs v. Duke Power Company*, the Supreme Court ends discrimination in hiring.
	The voting age is lowered to 18.
1972	National Association of Female Executives is founded.
	Gloria Steinem co-founds *Ms.* magazine.
	The Census Bureau begins to count woman-owned businesses; there were 402,000, 4.5 percent of the total business in the United States.
	Title IX requires equal funding for women's sports.
1973	9 to 5 is founded.
	Vietnam War ends.
	Publishers Lunch Club admits its first woman.
	Helen Copley inherits financially troubled Copley Press, reorganizes and expands it into profitability.
1974	Donna Karan designs her first complete fashion collection.
	National Association of Women Business Owners is founded.
	Christel and Jon DeHaan revolutionize the travel industry with vacation condominium time-share swapping.
	President Nixon resigns.
1975	Equal Credit Opportunity Act makes it possible for women to obtain financing.
	Linda Sanford joins IBM and designs a color ink-jet printer.
	Nanci Mackenzie starts Lucky Lady Oil.
	Junior Achievement's Global Business Hall of Fame is founded.
1976	American Women's Economic Development Corporation begins.
	Maria Elena Lagomasino begins at Citibank as a Latin American private banking specialist.
	Steven Jobs and Stephen Wozniak found Apple Computer.
1977	Debbi Fields sells her first cookie.
	Rosabeth Moss Kanter publishes her groundbreaking book, *Men and Women of the Corporation*.
	Josie Natori begins her intimate apparel company.
	Mary Fendrich Hulman inherits the Indianapolis Motor Speedway.
	Women own 61,600 construction firms, 5 percent of the industry total.

1983	Laura Balverde-Sanchez buys El Rey Sausage Company and turns it into a profitable company.
	Irma Elder inherits her husband's auto dealership and builds it into one of the largest Hispanic-owned businesses in the United States.
	Abby Cohen originates her forecasting method of investing.
	Jenny Craig begins her diet company.
	Sally Ride is the first American woman in space.
	The compact disc is introduced.
1984	*Fortune* calls Faith Popcorn "The Nostradamus of Marketing."
	Pleasant Rowland makes the first American Girl doll.
	Deborah Wright is the first African American woman to earn a double degree from Harvard.
	Geraldine Ferraro is the first woman nominated to run for vice president.
1985	*The Oprah Winfrey Show* debuts in Chicago.
	Kavelle Bajaj founds I-Net, one of the first computer network service providers.
	Marcy Carsey and Tom Werner win an Emmy for producing *The Bill Cosby Show*.
	Stacey Snider begins her film industry career in the mailroom.
	Judy Odom founds Software Spectrum.
	Madonna dominates the music and fashion worlds.
1986	Linda Wachner engineers a hostile takeover of Warnaco, the first woman to do so.
	The term "glass ceiling" is coined by Carol Hymowitz and Timothy Schellhardt in a *Wall Street Journal* article.
	The first sexual harassment case comes before the Supreme Court.
1987	Linda Johnson Rice becomes the president and CEO of *Ebony*.
	Dawn Steel is the first woman to head a major movie production company, Columbia Pictures.
	Lois Rust takes over Rose Acre Farms.
	Amy Pascal produces *Little Women* and *A League of Her Own*.
	Stock market crashes, "Black Monday."
	World population estimated at 5 billion.
1988	Julie Nguyen Brown builds Plastech Engineered Products, an auto parts company, out of two financially troubled companies.
	Leona Helmsley is dubbed "Queen of Mean" by New York media.
	Anthea Disney redesigns *Self*, which becomes the best-selling women's magazine in the United States.
	The Indian Gambling Regulation Act allows casinos on Indian reservations.
1989	Michele Anthony joins Sony and signs Sony's first contracts with rock bands.

Pat Moran becomes president and CEO of JM Family Enterprises which became the largest woman-owned company in the country.
Rosabeth Moss Kanter is the first woman editor of the *Harvard Business Review*.
Ann Winblad founds the first venture capital firm specializing only in software.
Felice Schwartz advocates an alternative track for women; media calls her idea "the mommy track."

1990   Martha Stewart founds Martha Stewart Living/Omnimedia.
Joanna Lau buys LAU Technologies, an electronics defense company.
Dorothy Brunson is first African American woman TV station owner.
Judy Lewent becomes the first woman CFO in the pharmaceutical industry.
Americans with Disabilities Act is signed into law.

1991   Linda Alvarado is the first Hispanic woman baseball team owner.
The Glass Ceiling Commission is appointed.
Donna Dubinsky and Jeff Hawkins found Palm Computing.
Civil Rights Act of 1991 defines sexual harassment.
First class action sexual harassment case.
Executive Women's Golf League established.

1992   Brenda Barnes is named president of Pepsi-Cola South, becomes the highest ranking woman in the company.
Charlotte Beers becomes the most powerful woman in advertising when she is recruited for the chairmanship of Ogilvy & Mather Worldwide.
Betty Cohen begins planning and building the Cartoon Network.
Loida Lewis inherits TLC Beatrice, the largest African American–owned company in the United States.
Working Woman publishes its first ranked list of woman-owned companies.

1993   Carol Bartz becomes the first woman CEO of a large technology company in Silicon Valley.
Lois Quam is a senior advisor on the White House Task Force on National Health Care Reform.
Linda Yang is appointed executive director of the Asian Development Bank.
The Family and Medical Leave Act becomes law.
Phyllis Takisaki Campbell is the first woman president of a major bank in the state of Washington.
Lisa Little Chief Bryan begins selling her Indian fry-bread mix.

1994   Pamela Aguirre inherits Mexican Industries from her baseball pitcher father.

Nina DiSesa is McCann Erickson's first head of creative advertising.

JoMei Chang founds Vitria Technology and is the first to develop enterprise-integration software.

Lois Juliber becomes the first woman president of Colgate Palmolive North America.

Sylvia Rhone is promoted to chair and CEO of Warner's Electra Entertainment Group, the first African American and first woman to reach that level in a major record company.

Jenny Ming is one of the creators of Old Navy.

Larree Renda is first woman vice president at Safeway.

Marilyn Carlson Nelson becomes CEO of Carison companies and celebrates by flying in an F-16 fighter jet over the Nevada desert.

1995   Martha Ingram inherits Ingram's.

Pamela Thomas-Graham becomes the first African American partner at global consulting company, McKinsey & Co.

The Small Business Administration begins the Tribal Business Information Center program.

1996   Jill Barad is the first woman to rise through the ranks to CEO of a major corporation.

Cathleen Black is the first woman president of Hearst Magazines

Christy Haubegger launches *Latina*.

The Alliance of Women's Business and Professional Organizations is founded.

1997   Jamie Gorelick is one of three chairmen of Fannie Mae.

Shelly Lazarus succeeds Charlotte Beers as CEO of Ogilvy & Mather Worldwide.

Marjorie Scardino becomes CEO of Pearson LLC, the first woman to head a major British company.

Madeleine Albright becomes the first woman Secretary of State.

1998   Daria Moore is the first woman to have a school named for her, the Daria Moore College of Business Administration at the University of South Carolina.

Geraldine Laybourne partners with Marcy Carsey and Oprah Winfrey to launch Oxygen Media.

Felice Schwartz is inducted into the National Woman's Hall of Fame for her pioneering work with women's issues in corporations.

Patricia Fili-Krushel is the highest ranking woman in network TV as president of ABC Television Network.

Meg Whitman is recruited to eBay as president and CEO.

The National Automobile Dealers' Association has 400 women among its 19,000 members.

Fortune publishes its first list of the most powerful women in business.

1999	Carole Black is the first woman president and CEO of Lifetime Entertainment. Carly Florina is chosen to head Hewlett-Packard, the only woman to lead a Dow Jones Industrial 30 and a *Fortune* 50 company. Esther Dyson becomes chair of ICANN, the Internet Corporation for Assigned Names and Numbers. Andrea Jung becomes CEO of Avon, its first woman leader. *Barron's* calls Mary Meeker "Queen of the Net." Women own 9.1 million businesses which employ 27.5 million and generate sales of $3.6 trillion. The world population is estimated at 6 billion.
2000	Judy Estrin starts her fourth technology company. Myrtle Potter is the first African American to head a pharmaceutical division. Katharine Graham is the first woman to receive the Robie Award for achievement in industry. Anne Sweeney is president of ABC Cable Networks and Disney Channel Worldwide. Betsy Holden is director and co-CEO of Kraft Foods. Denise DeBartolo York takes over the San Francisco 49ers. Flexible work schedules are offered in 43 percent of American companies. Nine women serve in the U.S. Senate; 58 women are in the House of Representatives. President Clinton signs Executive Order 13157—Increasing Opportunities for Woman-Owned Small Businesses.
2001	Marce Fuller is president and CEO of Mirant. Rachelle Friedman's music store is an emergency command center during 9/11. Fran Keeth is the first woman to head a major U.S. chemical company, Shell Oil. Betsy Bernard is the president and CEO of the AT&T Consumer. Division and the highest ranking woman in the telecommunications industry. Colleen Barrett is the president and COO of Southwest Airlines, the only woman president in the airlines industry. Abigail Johnson is appointed president of Fidelity Management Research Company. Indra Nooyi is promoted to president and CFO of PepsiCo, the highest ranking Indian-born woman in American business. 25 million mothers work, almost 20 percent of the total workforce. Women own 51 percent of the homes in the United States. Catalyst study finds primary need of both women and men is help balancing work and personal life.

Maine enforces comparable worth for both public and private companies.

2002   Lana Corbi is one of the highest ranking minority women in Hollywood.

Linda Dillman is the first woman Chief Information Officer for Wal-Mart.

Ann Moore is the first woman CEO of Time, Inc.

Vivian Banta is one of four officers running Prudential Insurance.

Louise Francesconi is one of the highest ranking women in the international aerospace industry.

Women hold 14 percent of the board of directors' seats on *Fortune* 1000 companies.

The average pay for women is 77 percent of that of men.

Some kind of diversity program exists in 75 percent of the *Fortune* 500 companies.

2003   Anne Mulcahy becomes chairman and CEO of Xerox.

Oprah Winfrey is the first African American woman billionaire.

Ann Fudge is CEO of Young & Rubicam, the first African American to head a large advertising agency.

Pamela Strobel is appointed Chief Administrator of Excelon.

Mary Sammons is president and CEO of Rite Aid.

Patricia Russo is CEO and chair of Lucent.

105,000 fathers in the United States stay home and care for the children.

Woman-owned companies number 10.1 million, 46 percent of all businesses in the United States.

2004   Martha Stewart is found guilty of conspiracy, making false statements, and obstruction of justice.

Janet Robinson is announced as the next president of the New York Times Company.

Encyclopedia of American Women in Business

A

Accounting is one of the oldest professions in the world, dating back to the Egyptians. Although accounting has been a fact of life since the advent of numbers, it did not emerge as a profession until around 1870. In both the 1851 and 1911 censuses, accountants were lumped in with "services" rather than being counted on their own. Until about 1985 accounting was dominated by males in two ways: at first barring entry into the profession by making it difficult for women to pass the certification process and, then, once they had finally been certified, obstructing promotion and equal compensation. Barriers were built into the profession with its very long hours, huge amounts of travel, and stressful work environment especially during the "high" accounting season. This was particularly true at the large public accounting firms. The end result was high turnover rates, particularly for women. Many sought alternative routes, opening their own businesses either in their homes or an office, looking for accounting jobs in industry or the government, or leaving the profession altogether. Today, the large accounting firms are finally trying to change their culture, but it's been a long road.

In 1901 there were two women accountants in England. In the United States, 1900 saw the first attempts to admit women in a few states: Colorado, Illinois, Louisiana, New Jersey, New York, and Pennsylvania. Maryland, in 1909, passed two women as Certified Public Accountants. That same year, the Institute of Chartered Accountants in England resolved that women could practice accounting but, in 1911, rejected a motion that women be admitted to their organization. In 1913 the Institute resolved that women could establish their own association, but, in 1918, another group, the Society of Incorporated Accountants and Auditors, voted to admit women. After 1920 the number of women learning the profession grew, but the majority ended up being bookkeepers or officers of corporations rather than professional accountants. The reasons given were varied: women had problems with travel and the clients wouldn't like women representing them. A consequence of women being excluded from fieldwork (because they couldn't travel) was that they could not get certified because they did not have the required experience.

Nevertheless, in 1933, there were one hundred woman CPAs in the United States and they formed the American Women's Society of Certified Public Accountants. In 1937 the group sponsored the formation of another organization, the American Society of Women Accountants. The goal of this second group was to discuss common problems and try to solve them. They developed chapters that offered technical and vocational courses designed to provide the prerequisites needed for obtaining field experience. By 1941 the Department of Labor reported that 10.7 percent of their accountants and auditors and 23.5 percent of their accounting, fiscal, and payroll clerks were women. Women were being hired, but salaries were 62 percent of salaries paid to males in comparable positions.

In 1941 the United States entered World War II, and the men went off to fight. The following year, an editorial in the *Journal of Accountancy* stated: yes, women accountants certainly can travel and do fieldwork, let's not be silly and let's hire them, besides, the men have gone to war (Lehman, p. 263). The firms did hire women and found that the clients didn't object, the women could keep up the long hours, and the partners were also happy. When the men returned, however, they also returned to their jobs. The old arguments against employing women returned. In 1950 there were 600 women CPAs in the United States, but the old stereotypes were still there: women would marry and leave or have babies and leave; they couldn't do inventory work or travel; they were not acceptable to clients; and they were also unacceptable to their male counterparts, particularly in a supervisory position. In 1959 the *Occupational Outlook Handbook* contained a warning to women about the small amount of progress made in hiring practices within the accounting profession. In fact, many firms accepted only male applicants.

The Civil Rights Act of 1964 with its accompanying Title VII was signed into law that year. This stated that gender could not be a category for employment; that employers with more than 15 employees could not discriminate on the basis of race, color, sex, or national origin. The war surrounding hiring was over but now moved into issues of compensation and opportunities for advancement. By 1969 the profession was more open to hiring women, but they were hired for lower salaries, sometimes told they'd never become partners or supervisors and did not get the challenging opportunities or assignments.

In 1970 women earned 10 percent of the bachelor's degrees in accounting, and 24.6 percent of the employed accountants were women. The battle continued around discrimination in compensation and promotions. Several surveys taken in this decade and in the 1980s showed the same issues: women were paid less than men for the same job; they were not initially paid as much as male new hires; they were not assigned work that led to promotion and leadership; and most of the opposition came from within the profession, not from the clients. By 1979, 34 percent of all accountants and auditors were women; their earnings were 60 percent of their male counterparts. In the large accounting firms known as the "Big Eight," women were 35 to 50 percent of the new hires but only 2 percent of the partners. By 1983, of 6,000 partners in one of the large firms, sixty-two were women. Three years later, women numbered 45 percent of all accountants and auditors, but their earnings were 72 percent of the men's earnings. A survey in 1989 pinpointed some of the problems: lack of support for family issues, lack of equal compensation for the same work, and different opportunities for advancement. That year also saw change in the profession: the "Big Eight" became the "Big Six" through mergers; more dual career couples with accompanying conflict of interest problems were in the profession; the firms also moved into consulting; and accountants became increasingly specialized and thus less interchangeable. High turnover became an issue, and the professional associations began to seriously look at the reasons. Women accountants had an especially high rate of turnover. Although initially it was the same as men, by the third year, it was doubled. The women blamed long overtime hours, lack of support for family issues, unequal compensation practices, and inadequate training for future promotions, so they left to find better opportunities.

By 1994, 55 percent of all the bachelor's degrees in accounting were awarded to women, but once in the workforce, they were a dissatisfied group of people. A 1990 survey of the American Women's Society of CPAs, with a 51 percent return, showed their belief that the job demands of the profession negatively impacted members' chances for marriage or even an adequate social life and that the reasons for separation or divorce was partly job-related. By 1997, women were 13 percent of the partners, but turnover was particularly high as they left to open their own businesses or move into corporations. It was becoming clear to the large accounting firms that retention was far less expensive than replacing employees and that men were also chafing under the all-consuming workaholic culture. The 1990 survey and many journal articles written through-out the nineties suggested possible solutions: an alternative track to a partner-ship, flexible and part-time work schedules, time off for family-related problems, counseling, stress reduction techniques, publication of promotion criteria, grievance procedures, gender awareness and sexual harassment training, imple-mentation of day care programs, more female role models in powerful positions, networking and mentoring, career planning, diversity training, and a reduced travel schedule.

Two of the Big Six firms seriously pursued cultural change beginning in the mid-nineties. In 1996, Ernst & Young had 8 percent female partners and a female turnover rate of 22 percent. Late that year they hired the research director of Catalyst to direct an Office for Retention. She began four pilot programs to address internal and external networking and mentoring for women and, for all 34,000 employees, a re-evaluation of the company work routines and culture. Four years later, a variety of retention techniques were in place including telecommuting, a kinder travel schedule always including home on the weekends, no voice mail or e-mail on the weekends, and workload patrols to ensure an even load for all. Another company, Deloitte & Touche, had a 30 percent female turnover rate in 1993, so they launched a "Women's Initiative" that year. They surveyed those who had left and initiated a series of more family-friendly policies, including flexible and part-time work arrangements, job sharing, child care leave, elder care, gender awareness programs for both managers and partners, and a mandatory training program on managing people in flexible programs. Since then, woman partners have increased from 5 percent in 1992 to 14 percent in 2000, and turnover is down to 18 percent. A surprising benefit is that 15 percent of the programs' participants are men. The company says it has saved $66 million with these programs. Also, *Fortune* now consistently ranks it among the best one hundred companies to work for.

There are organizations for women in accounting: the American Society of Women Accountants (www.aswa.org), the American Woman's Society of Certified Public Accountants (www.awscpa.org), and the Educational Foundation for Women in Accounting (www.efwa.org).

Further Reading

Educational Foundation for Women in Accounting. "Statistical Survey."

Hooks, Karen L. "Diversity, Family Issues and the Big 6."

King, Teresa Tyson and Jane B. Stockard. "The Woman CPA: Career and Family."

Lehman, Cheryl R. "'Herstory' in Accounting: The First Eighty Years."

Adams, Evangeline ([1868–1872]–1932), Astrologer

Evangeline Adams was the first person who tried to predict the fluctuations of stocks traded on the New York Stock Exchange. Her heyday was in the late 1920s when the stock market was rising rapidly and everyone was buying stock hoping to make a huge fortune. She was a popular astrologer and made predictions depending on the relationships of the planets. She was "one of the first newsletter quacks, publishing and selling stock market picks for a fairly steep price during the 1920s bull market" (Fisher, p. 287).

She was born sometime between 1868 and 1872 to a prominent family. Her father died when she was only fifteen months old. Adams was educated in Andover, Massachusetts, a center for theological and academic institutions at the time. Dr. J. Herbert Smith, a professor of materia medica with a deep interest in astrology, selected her as a student. Smith believed in astrology and told her she was talented in prediction, based on a reading of her horoscope.

After studying with him, she opened an office in a Boston hotel and began her business.

In 1899 following her horoscope, Adams moved to New York City where she was immediately catapulted into the public eye through a prediction that the owner of the Windsor Hotel, where she was staying, was in immediate danger. The next day the hotel and the hotel owner's family were destroyed in a fire. The newspapers picked up the story, and she became famous.

Adam's office in the Carnegie Hall building was busy with famous people all the time. She predicted the length of time of the Lindbergh flight with only a twenty-two-minute error, the death of Rudolf Valentino within a few hours, and the 1923 devastating earthquake in Tokyo by a few days. In 1914 she was arrested for fortune telling, then against the New York City laws. The judge let her testify about astrology as a science and gave her a test to see if her horoscopes were accurate in describing a person. Rumor has it that he was so impressed that he dismissed the case. Anyway, the charges were not pressed.

In 1923 Adams married but kept her maiden name for business purposes. It was not until 1927 that she began her newsletter that predicted the vagaries of the stock market. Her clients were well-known figures like John Pierpont Morgan, the billionaire founder of the J.P. Morgan Bank, who stopped to see her on his way to work. The rich (the two millionaires who ran the New York Stock Exchange) and the famous (Mary Pickford and Enrico Caruso) used her predictions. She sold the monthly newsletter for 50 cents and received around 4,000 letters per month requesting horoscopes and stock tips. For the last two years of her life, she had a radio program three times a week. She was wildly popular and well paid for her predictions.

Although Adams did not predict the crash of 1929, she did, however, tell her broker to sell all her stock after he told her she had lost $100,000. That day she also made money commiserating with, and making horoscopes for, her clients who crowded into her office waiting to see her.

Skeptics point out that Adams had no knowledge of economics and that her predictions were always fuzzy, foretelling disaster but not specific disasters, and telling that the market would go up when in fact the country was in a period of remarkable growth in the stock market. People who believed often forgot the erroneous predictions and used the ones that happened to come true to "prove" that she was accurate. By any measure, she was colorful, and her clients believed in her. There have been many like her since, but she was the first.

See also: Finance Industry

Further Reading
Adams, Evangeline. *The Bowl of Heaven.*
Biographical Cyclopaedia of American Women, p. 240–241.
Fisher, Kenneth L. p. 287–289, 293–295.

Adams, Harriet Stratemeyer (1892–1982), Book Publisher

For over fifty years, Harriet Adams owned and ran the Stratemeyer Syndicate, a book-packaging company that churned out several mystery series: *The Hardy Boys*, *Nancy Drew*, *The Rover Boys*, *Tom Swift*, and *The Bobbsey Twins*. By the time she died in 1982, the books had sold almost 200 million copies all over the world and had been translated into eighteen languages.

She was born in Newark, New Jersey, one of two daughters of Edward Stratemeyer who founded the Stratemeyer Literary Syndicate in 1905. By age five she had begun to write stories and, after she graduated from Wellesley College in 1914, she even edited in her father's company—at home because office work was considered ungenteel for women. When she married two years later, her father would not let her continue working and ordered her to stay at home and concentrate on being a wife and mother. When he died in 1930 leaving the company to her very ill mother, she and her sister Edna took over the reins. So at age 38 Adams hired a nurse for her four children, moved the company from Newark to East Orange, closer to her home, and proceeded to take a good look at the company and its products. At that time, the series included *Tom Swift*, *Bomba the Jungle Boy*, *The Bobbsey Twins*, *The Ted Scott Flying Series*, *Nancy Drew*, and *The Hardy Boys*.

Adams and her sister decided to focus on just mysteries and cut almost half of the series to save on costs. In 1934 they developed two new series, *The Dana Girls* and *Kay Tracey*. The writers employed by the syndicate did the actual writing of the books; the Adams sisters created plots, developed detailed outlines, explained the formula (chapter-end cliffhangers, plenty of suspense and excitement, no violence, but lots of action and some humor, no profanity, and a first page that hooked the reader), chose the title and general theme of each book, and did the meticulous research required for the setting and plot. They also edited the finished manuscripts to make sure they fit the general tone of the series and dealt with the publisher.

In 1935 their mother died and the sisters officially inherited the company. Edna retired in 1942 to become an inactive partner. By 1945 Adams had only four series, due to World War II and its accompanying shortage of paper as well as the loss of one of her sons. When the war ended, she hired more employees, developed more series, doubling and tripling the output. The series then included *Nancy Drew*, *Hardy Boys*, *Tom Swift, Jr.*, *The Bobbsey Twins*, and *Honey Bunch*.

Sales boomed. In 1959 to answer criticism about literary merit and particularly about what some saw as racial slurs, Adams began a huge project to revise and update *Nancy Drew*, *Hardy Boys*, and *The Bobbsey Twins* by removing the slurs, modernizing the plots, and streamlining and simplifying the text.

The project took sixteen years. Critics saw the books as too simple, unrealistic, and middle class; but the series sold even more copies.

Adams liked Nancy Drew the most; in interviews she sometimes even called Nancy her third daughter. During the 1960s and 1970s, both her husband and sister died. By the middle of the 1970s, the books were lagging a little in sales, so she approved a television series with the Hardy boys characters alternating weekly with Nancy Drew. It ran from 1977 to 1979, was wildly popular, and also caused a major revival of book sales. By 1980 the *Nancy Drew* series had sold 70 million copies in the United States alone.

> Harriet Adams owned and ran the Stratemeyer Syndicate, a book-packaging company that churned out several mystery series: *The Hardy Boys, Nancy Drew, The Rover Boys, Tom Swift,* and *The Bobbsey Twins.*

In 1978 Harriet Adams received the annual alumna achievement award from Wellesley College; in 1979 she was named Mother of the Year by the National Mothers' Day Committee. She also received honorary degrees from New Jersey's Upsala College and Kean College. She endowed a chair at Wellesley for the study of children's literature. Her mystery series were responsible for generations of children who became excited about reading through her books. The series are still selling and are still good popular entertainment. When Adams died, the *Washington Post* called her "the Henry Luce of juvenile publishing" (March 30, 1982).

See also: Publishing Industry

Further Reading

Johnson, Dierdre Ann. "Adams, Harriet Stratemeyer." In Garraty and Carnes, p. 89–90.
Roche, Kathy Bieger. "Harriet Stratemeyer Adams, 1892–1982." In Burstyn, p. 226–227.
Suplee, Curt. "Nancy Drew's Story: Recalling the Woman Behind the Adventurer; the Woman Behind Nancy Drew."

Adler, Polly (1900–1962), Madam

Polly Adler was the most famous madam in New York City in the 1920s and 1930s. Her bordello was known across the entire country, and it became the most fashionable place to go, even for society women who dropped in for cocktails and conversation. In 1953 she wrote a book about her experiences that became an instant bestseller, was translated into eleven languages, and made into a movie.

Born in Yanow, Russia, to a fairly wealthy family, Adler was the eldest of two daughters and seven sons. At age thirteen, she traveled to America alone, landed in New York City, but went to live with relatives in Holyoke, Massachusetts. Because of World War I, her family couldn't join her but sent money to pay for her room and board. She attended school for one semester but needed money, so she went to work in a paper factory. Her relatives wanted her to marry, but she was attracted to a more glamorous life and refused. In 1915 she moved to Brooklyn and lived with cousins, obtaining a job in a corset factory and attending night school when possible. When she was sixteen, she was raped by her supervisor, became pregnant, had an abortion, and lost her job. After arguing with her relatives, she ended up in a tenement and finally found part-time work in another corset factory.

In 1920 Adler accepted the offer of an actress to share an apartment; there she learned all about the fashionable, flashy, and fast-moving life of show business, nightclubs, and bootleggers. The actress turned out to be a drug addict, so Adler moved into an apartment funded by a bootlegger-gangster. It was free to her with the condition that he could meet his mistress there when he wished. In her book she called this her first step down the primrose path. Soon she began hiring women for other men, and her home turned into a house of prostitution. In 1922, after she had been arrested and suffered the accompanying fear and humiliation, she opened a lingerie shop, determined to run a legitimate business. Unfortunately, it failed after only one year.

Adler went back to her former life, determined to be the best madam that ever operated in America. Her clients were mainly gangsters and bootleggers who persuaded her to add liquor to her offerings, a highly successful move. Her establishment was very popular, but raucous. There were many disruptions and the police came, despite frequent bribes. She had to relocate many times, using the moves as opportunities to find places that were in more fashionable neighborhoods. Because she wished to attract a better class of clients, she began a highly visible publicity campaign, regularly visiting night-clubs, dressing flamboyantly, and spending freely. She hoped to attract the attention of columnists and was successful, for her patrons began to include movie stars, theater people, business tycoons, and society folks. She also opened a place in Saratoga, the fashionable summer racing town of the time. By the late 1920s going to Polly's became the thing to do, the place to meet friends, play cards, or arrange a dinner party.

In 1929 Adler became a citizen of the United States. She had made a significant amount of money, in spite of the stock market crash that year. Her revenues kept pouring in, and the police were assuaged with liberal bribes. In November of 1930, however, she was told that she was going to be subpoenaed by the Seabury Committee, New York officials investigating the city's vice and criminal justice divisions for corruption. She went into hiding, but when she returned six months later, was subpoenaed and questioned about her relationship with a vice squad officer named O'Leary. The committee thought it was strange that she had never been convicted of operating a disorderly house even though she had been arrested fourteen times.

During the summer of 1931, Adler's name was in the newspapers constantly, described as the city's most notorious vice entrepreneur, but she refused to divulge any useful information. Her house closed for a time but was more popular than ever when it reopened. In 1934 she occupied the entire floor of a building, twelve rooms, on East Fifty-fifth between Fifth Avenue and Madison Avenue, right in the heart of fashionable New York. The following year, Fiorello La Guardia, then mayor of New York, began a cleanup campaign, and there was a raid on her house. She was convicted of operating a disorderly house and made to spend thirty days in jail and pay a $500 fine. This was the only time she spent in jail.

By now Adler was tired, and she tried once again to operate a legitimate business. Again she failed and went back to what she knew best. The next year, after yet another vice campaign, she went to California, then Chicago, but eventually returned to New York where her house prospered until 1943. Again, a case was brought against her, but it was dismissed. She retired and moved to Los Angeles where she finished high school and began college. During her last years, she completed her autobiography, *A House Is Not a Home*, which became a bestseller. She was working on a sequel but died of cancer in 1962, just before the movie was made of her book. She never married or had children.

Adler didn't seem to be troubled by the morals of her profession. She viewed her work as a business and treated it as such in her publicity campaigns, increasing the services she offered and the quality of those services (liquor, free dinners, conversation, a club-like atmosphere, long hours, etc.). She treated her employees well, offering medical care, good pay, and protection from those she saw as the real exploiters: the pimps, crooked police, and corrupt sex-trade providers. She said in her book that the only unforgivable sin of the 1920s was to be poor, and she certainly was not that. Her biggest asset was her personality; she was amiable, attractive, and had an ability to mix with people of all kinds.

See also: Immigrant Businesswomen

Further Reading

Adler, Polly. *A House Is Not a Home*. New York: Rinehart, 1953.
Hill, Marilyn Wood. "Adler, Polly." In Garraty and Carnes, p. 164–166.
"Polly Adler." *Wall Street Journal Almanac*, p. 933.

Advertising

Women have been involved in advertising since 1840 when there were several women advertising agents. In 1867 Matilda Weil began the M.C. Weil Advertising Agency, the first owned by a woman. During the 1880s and 1890s, many women began advertising their products, including Lydia Pinkham and Rose Knox with their newsletters of motherly advice, health tips, and recipes. The industry became more segregated after the turn of the century, however. In 1911 the first women's advertising club began in New York City because the Men's Advertising Club would not admit women members. Chicago women followed suit in 1917. There were about 200 women in advertising in the country then. The clubs focused on education, career guidance, and networking.

During the 1920s and 1930s, women were mostly copywriters. Advertising at the time consisted of drawings and catchy phrases encouraging the customer to buy. The 1930s and 1940s were periods of enormous growth. By 1939 there were approximately 2,000 women in advertising agencies.

In 1950 the first African American advertising agencies began advertising to the African American market. Mainstream agencies did not notice this market until the mid-1960s. Barbara Proctor was the first African American woman to own her own agency. In the late 1960s, Mary Wells opened her own very successful agency. By the 1970s, however, most of the large agencies were still reluctant to hire women as account executives or managers. One excuse was that clients' wives wouldn't like to have their husbands working late with other women. Also, agencies did not want women presenting campaigns to clients from male-dominated companies, such as the automobile industry.

When women found they were not being promoted, they started their own agencies. As of 1982 there were 14,000 woman-owned advertising agencies in the United States with receipts of $400 million. By 1985 one firm alone brought in $640 million during a period of enormous growth in the industry. Women in agencies began to make inroads in media departments and advertising sales. By 1989 they had also begun to infiltrate as account executives and also, to some extent, on the creative side. They were paid less than their male peers, however, and had to work harder for promotions. Most made it only to the middle management level. Less than 20 percent of upper management was women.

By 1995 women account executives were finally accepted by clients, and, in account management, 50 percent were women; however, 65 percent of them were in entry-level and lower management jobs. This began to change as the century wound down. The industry began to change at the same time, emphasizing brand buying and clients demanding all the new technological techniques available. It became more and more difficult to keep clients. Advertising is now moving toward a blend of advertising, public relations, and marketing. It is a high-powered, very volatile industry.

Further Reading
Dietrich, Joy. "Women Reach High."
Frederick, Christine. "Historical Introduction." In Clair and Dignam, p. xiii–xxi.
"Mad Avenue: A Star Is Reborn."
Winkleman, Michael and Mary Huhn. "The Seventh Annual Women's Survey."
"Women to Watch: *Ad Age* Special Report."

Affirmative Action

Affirmative action is a phrase that describes "a broad set of policies and programs designed to provide opportunities in education, employment, and housing to demographic groups commonly denied such opportunities by virtue of their race, ethnicity, gender, and social circumstances" (Zierdt-Warshaw, p. 2).

These policies began in the early 1960s with President Kennedy's Executive Order 11246, which stated that businesses with government contracts must hire minorities. Presidents Johnson and Nixon continued in the same vein; but Presidents Reagan and Bush disagreed, particularly with the idea of quotas, which they thought caused reverse discrimination. The controversy continues today with vociferous acrimony on both sides.

Many women and minorities have benefited enormously from these policies. Employment discrimination was prohibited, and the Equal Opportunity Employment Commission was created to enforce the Civil Rights Act. Many, many women and minorities have credited affirmative action programs for being able to go into business at all. Hiring practices and recruitment have changed from the "who-you-know" method to more formal programs. On the other hand, it is more difficult for in-company promotions; women and minorities sometimes are concerned that they don't know whether they are being hired or promoted because of their gender or ethnicity or because of their performance.

In 1998, California Governor Pete Wilson terminated all state affirmative action programs in accordance with the passage of Proposition 209, an anti-affirmative action proposal approved by the voters of the state. The case went to a court of appeals, which upheld his action. Many minority- and woman-owned businesses were negatively impacted because they did not receive government contracts any more.

See also: Diversity

Further Reading
Cahn, Steven M., Ed. *The Affirmative Action Debate*.
Deutsch, Claudia H. "Affirmative Action: Selling to Big Companies Cautiously in The Mainstream; Minorities Move Ahead as Political Currents Shift."
Nelson, Patricia M., Ed. *Affirmative Action Revisited*.

African American Businesswomen

Africans coming to America, whether as slaves or indentured servants, brought a business heritage from a complex, entrepreneurial, organized marketing economy in Africa. The women were expert traders with many different skills. In the colonies, they continued these activities on a small scale, selling herbs, produce, baked goods, services, and crafts to any who would buy. During the colonial period, a number of laws forbade business participation by African Americans. The markets flourished nonetheless because their goods and services were in demand. After the Revolutionary War, many free African Americans entered trades and opened successful small businesses in areas such as hair care, catering, dressmaking, food services, and tavernkeeping. They also bought land when they could. By 1836 property with a total worth of $2,462,000 was African American owned.

Slave women were dressmakers, midwives, and food vendors. Activities were all on a small scale because of racism, impoverished customers, and a lack of capital or credit. From the 1830s to the beginning of the Civil War, African Americans formed secret and benevolent societies to promote cooperative aid and were also the center of social and religious life. These led to the formation of African American banks, insurance companies, and funeral businesses. In 1841, one hundred African Americans in New York City established a cooperative grocery store. In 1859, 80 percent of African American women in the United States were employed in domestic work.

After the Civil War, slaves were freed, but the national economy was unhealthy. Most of the small African American businesses survived, however, and the women ran boardinghouses, catering services, laundries, food shops, and employment services. Many became dressmakers, hairdressers and wig-makers. African American communities emerged in the South, and businesses were established to serve them. Former slave women were usually more literate than the men, so they kept the company records and paid the bills. Free African Americans became increasingly professional, particularly in financial institutions, hair care, shopkeeping, and manufacturing. Mutual aid societies flourished, and women were usually the sales agents. The first survey of African American businesses in 1898 identified 1,906 such businesses.

In 1900 Booker T. Washington founded the National Negro Business League to promote entrepreneurism. By 1910 there were more than 3 million African Americans employed in 8,384 businesses, most of which catered to, and employed, African Americans. Resorts and hotels for African Americans developed, as did grocery stores, restaurants, and general merchandise stores. During the 1920s the great migration to the northern cities created markets for the businesses. By 1921, 39 percent of African American women were employed—in jobs no one else wanted. Only 18.5 percent of Caucasian women were employed.

Large-scale manufacturing began in the mid-1890s in both hair care and cosmetics products that created an African American female consumer base; African American newspapers began to appear. Growth continued in both northern African American communities and southern towns. By 1929 the estimate of African American-owned businesses was 65,000, predominantly in trade but also in groceries and retail. During the Great Depression of the 1930s, most of the businesses stayed afloat because they were small and offered needed services. The leading women's businesses were beauty shops and boarding houses. All during this time, African Americans operated, particularly in the South, under restrictive racist laws.

World War II opened up opportunities for women in corporations, but they were sent home when the men returned. From 1930 to 1960, African American women doubled their share of manufacturing jobs and increased their participation in clerical and sales jobs eightfold. The 1960s Civil Rights movement pressured for laws guaranteeing equal rights for African Americans, and businesswomen expanded into new areas such as investment firms, franchising, and financial institutions. In 1969 the phrase "Black Capitalism" was first used, and there were 100,000 African American businesses, mostly very small. The first issue of *Black Enterprise* appeared and in 1973 began to rank African American companies by sales, thus quantifying the growth and development of African American business. Legislation and executive orders aided in growth, making capital and government contracts available.

Businesses included auto dealers, then food and beverage wholesaling and retailing, followed by construction and contracting. Hair care and cosmetics manufacturing continued, as did entertainment and services. Most companies were privately owned and served minority markets. As of 1986 there were thirty-six African American–owned commercial banks and thirty-two savings and loan companies. During the 1990s the larger companies began to diversify and market to non-minority markets; also, bank credit became more available. In the 1997 Economic Census, there were 881,646 African American-owned businesses, up 108 percent from 1987.

African American women come from a long entrepreneurial tradition. The horrors of slavery required that they be independent and look out for themselves, persevere, and be ingenious. These abilities have been passed on from mother to daughter. Although racial and societal factors may impede their success, their tradition of self-help stands them in good stead. They expect to work and raise a family simultaneously, as many of their mothers did. Women traditionally held the family together, during slavery and after emancipation; frequently they are the family breadwinners. African American benevolent societies have goals that encourage nurturing the women who come after them and providing role models for younger women. One of their chief reasons for succeeding is to blaze a path for other women to follow.

The Center for Women's Business Research counted 365,000 African American woman-owned businesses in 2003. These companies had sales of $14.5 billion and employed 200,000 workers. The same survey determined that they are much more likely than other women business owners to have altruistic goals. Being a role model was important to 92 percent, and making a difference in their communities through business ownership was important to 83 percent. Their biggest problem was access to capital from banks and/or venture capital companies.

Many contemporary African American women entrepreneurs came from corporations where they felt undervalued. Like other minority women in corporations, they faced both sexism and racism. African American women call this the concrete wall. The cultural traits that help them in entrepreneurial endeavors work against them in the corporate world; their ability to speak up is seen as pushy. They must be different people on the job and in the community, a factor of high stress. They have to fight to be taken seriously and to get high-visibility assignments, which are the ones that lead to promotion. There are few, if any, mentors or role models, so they feel isolated. A 2003 study by Rutgers University and the University of Connecticut revealed many problems, despite affirmative action and diversity programs. Half of African American women workers believe that they are the most likely ethnic group to be treated unfairly, and 28 percent said they had been discriminated against in terms of promotions, additional training, networking, and special projects. The price of success is very high. A quotation by an African American woman executive says it all: "You get tired of representing your race, you do it every day" (Texeira, p. 68). Although African American women are making great strides, work life is stressful and can lead to identity loss.

See also: Appendix 3, Ethnic Groups; Minority Businesswomen

Further Reading

Bell, Ella L. J. Edmondson and Stella M. Nkomo. *Our Separate Ways: Black and White Women and the Struggle for Professional Identity.*

Collins, Sharon. *Black Corporate Executives: The Making and Breaking of a Black Middle Class.*

Gite, Lloyd and Dawn M. Baskerville. "Black Women Entrepreneurs on the Rise."

Walker, Juliet E. K. *The History of Black Business in America.*

Agriculture/Ranching

Women have been either working on the land or running the farms and plantations since the colonization of America. While most married women could not own property until the 1880s, single, widowed, and divorced women could and did. In the colonies, which were based on an agricultural economy, the entire family worked together plowing, harvesting, preserving foods and, if there was more than they needed, bartering and trading their produce for other goods. Also, men were often away from home, fishing, trapping, and hunting for the winter, leaving their wives in charge.

In the South many women managed the plantations. Women slaves often sold or traded produce in the markets, so much so that laws were enacted forbidding this practice because their prices were less than those of their competitors.

In the Southwest, before Americans arrived, Hispanic women, even after marriage, retained title to their property and also owned half of all shared property. There were several woman-owned ranches along what is now the Texas–Mexico border.

During the long years of the Revolutionary War and for some time afterward, women kept the farms going while the men were away, first fighting and later politicking. The best example of this may be seen in the letters of Abigail Adams to her husband. A Civil War example, although fictional, is Scarlett O'Hara working the fields of her family's plantation. During the nineteenth century middle and upper class women did not usually perform hard labor in the fields but were perfectly able to supervise the laborers while the men were away, which was often the case. This was regarded as socially acceptable.

The same pattern followed in the movement westward: the pioneer women worked alongside the men, and either alone or with children when the men were away. Also, men often hired out to earn money to develop the farm. The Homestead Act of 1862 allowed 160 acres of land to any "citizen or intending citizen" with no mention of gender. In Colorado, 11.9 percent of those who took advantage of the act were women; in Wyoming, the number was 18.2 percent. Riley estimates that one-third of them succeeded (Riley, p. 2). The Oklahoma land rushes of the 1890s and the early 1900s included a high number of women. Of course by this time, women had the right to hold property. A number of these women turned their holdings into cattle ranches and either worked alongside the men, or managed the ranch hands and cowboys. If there were husbands, they would often be gone on long cattle drives.

By 1900, 29 to 72 percent of the total women in the workplace in the South, Texas, Arizona, and Oklahoma worked in agriculture, while 9 to 28 percent were involved in agriculture in North and South Dakota, Kansas, Nevada, Utah, Washington, New Mexico, Missouri, Tennessee, Virginia, and West Virginia (Opdyeke, p. 67). In 1910, 12 percent of working women were employed in agriculture; by 1940 the number had diminished to 4 percent (Routledge, p. 90). In 1995 the census lumped farming with forestry and fishing in its count; women in those occupations numbered only 2 percent of the total number of working women (Opdyeke, p. 115).

See also: Colonial Businesswomen; Western Businesswomen

Further Reading
Dexter, Elizabeth. "When Eve Delved." In *Career Women of America*, p. 183–198.
Riley, Glenda. *The Female Frontier*.
Opdyeke, Sandra. *The Routledge Historical Atlas of Women in America*.

Aguirre, Pamela (1959–), Automotive Accessories Manufacturer

Pamela Aguirre was the Chair and CEO of Mexican Industries in Detroit, a position she took when her father died in 1994. As one of the original six employees, she started from the bottom, hand-checking threads on nuts and bolts. By 1999 the company employed 1,500 people at eight plants where they made air bags, head rests, consoles, cruise control assemblies, arm rests, floor mats, door panels, and interior trim for Ford, General Motors, Chrysler, and other automobile manufacturers. They were the only plant in the United States to hand-wrap leather on steering wheels.

Hank Aguirre, pitcher for the Detroit Tigers, founded Mexican Industries in 1979 as part of a minority enterprise program. He began by making automobile furnishings for Volkswagen of America. One of his missions was to provide employment for the large Mexican population of Detroit. Seventy-five percent of all workers in 1999 were Hispanic, and 86 percent of all workers were women. Pamela adhered to her father's mission and followed his lead in hiring. She also believed in offering generous benefits to the workers. She worried about the workers' reaction to a woman CEO, but she proved herself and earned the respect of both employees and customers. Because she began at the bottom and had worked in every department, they knew she knew the business. Most of the jobs were computerized. In 1997 the company changed gears and became involved in a number of joint ventures with large suppliers. These included building instrument panels for General Motors with Collins & Aikman Automotive Plastics; supplying interior components, also for General Motors, with Cambridge Industries Inc.; and producing side-impact air bags for Ford Motors with TRW Vehicle Safety Systems, Inc. These ventures enabled the company to automate and build a high-tech plastic injection modeling plant.

Mexican Industries was number 34 of the top woman-owned businesses in 1997, number 55 in 1998, and number 78 in 1999. Their 1998 sales were $167 million with 1,500 employees. It was a private company with generous benefits, including profit sharing, on-site GED training, support for further education, flexible hours, scholarships for employees' children at Holy Redeemer Catholic School, free lunches during the summer, and the opportunity to apply for a low-interest line of credit. The company received the 1998 Entrepreneurial Success Award from the Small Business Administration.

Sadly, in early 2002 the company folded due to too-rapid expansion in its operations, reduced earnings, high manufacturing costs, and problems in the upper management. Aguirre had tried to convince Ford and Daimler Chrysler to lend money to the company, but failed.

Before Aguirre married an Arizona businessman and moved to Tucson, she was involved in many community activities in Detroit, including an appointment to the Detroit School Board in 1999. She was on the board of directors of the Economic Club of Detroit and was also active in food and clothing programs at St. Anne and Holy Trinity Catholic churches.

See also: Automobile Industry; Latina Businesswomen

Further Reading

Bodipo-Memba, Alejandro. "Detroit Auto Supplier's Bankruptcy Filing Offers Sad Ending for Family Dream."

King, R. J. "Auto Supplier Shifts Gears: Mexican Industries Grows—and Changes Its Fortune."

"Pamela Aguirre: A Daughter Leads Company Synonymous with Her Father into its Own."

Ainse, Sally (circa 1728–1823), Fur Trader, Landowner

Sally Ainse was famous as an Oneida fur trader, as owner of considerable landholdings in Detroit and later in Ontario, and as a diplomat and negotiator. She was active both before and after the Revolutionary War.

Ainse was born around 1728 and raised in the Susquehanna River area in upstate New York. At age seventeen she married Andrew Montour, a Native American interpreter for the British government, with whom she had several children. Around 1757 he deserted her, leaving her with her Oneida people. Desertion was apparently a very common occurrence for American Indian wives at that time. From the Oneidas, she was deeded lands under the name Sally Montour in the area of what is now known as Rome, New York, and began fur trading.

During the American Revolutionary War in 1775, she left New York and moved to the Detroit area, which was controlled by the British. There, known as Sally Ainse, she continued to trade cider and other goods to the Indians for furs. In 1778 she bought a house and land in Detroit with the profits from her trading business. The city's 1779 census indicates she was very prosperous for that time; she had four slaves, three cows, four horses and one hundred pounds of flour. In 1783 she acquired land in Ontario from the Chippewa; and three years later she sold her holdings in Detroit and settled in Ontario. There her holdings were also large, consisting of three improved farms, an orchard, and a house.

Unfortunately, Ainse's prosperity was not to last. In 1790 the British also bought lands from the Chippewa in a sale known as the McKee Purchase. These lands surrounded her property that was specifically excluded from the contract, but the British Land Board chose to ignore that clause and took over her property as well. Many prominent persons, both American Indian and white, supported her in her petitions and letters for justice, but she was not successful and finally, in 1813, gave up the fight. By this time she had moved to Amherstburg, Ontario, where she stayed until she died in 1823.

Ainse served as a negotiator during the peace talks following the 1794 Battle of Fallen Timbers when the Indian tribes were defeated by Anthony Wayne. She also acted, on occasion, as a messenger for Chief Joseph Brant in negotiations between the tribes and the British.

See also: American Indian Businesswomen

Further reading

http://meyna/com/oneida.html

Kennedy, Patricia. "Voices in the Shadows."

Siminoff, Faren R. "Ainse, Sally [Sally Montour, Sara Montour, Hands, Hains, Willson]." In Bataille, p. 2–4.

Aitken, Jane (1764–1832), Printer, Bookseller, Bookbinder

Jane Aitken was the first woman in the colonies to print an English translation of the Bible. She was born in Paisley, Scotland, the eldest of four children. In 1771 the family immigrated to Philadelphia where her father set up a business of binding and printing books and selling stationery and books. He died in 1802 leaving $3,000 in debts, incurred by signing notes for the late husband of one of his other daughters.

At thirty-eight Aitken became the owner of the business which had already gained a reputation from the printing of the Aitken Bible of 1782, the first English Bible printed in America. She produced at least sixty publications between 1802 and 1812. The most important was the four-volume Thomson Bible of 1808, a new translation by Charles Thomson, former secretary of the Continental Congress. This was the first English Bible printed by a woman in America. Isaiah Thomas, her contemporary and a printing historian, said that this work gave her a reputation for excellence in printing (Spawn, p. 26).

She had a difficult time financially and mostly depended on the bookbinding for subsistence. Her binding output in the later years is very similar to that from her father's shop, suggesting she may have been doing the binding all along. According to Carol Spawn, she is "the only woman binder of such skill known to us from this period" (Spawn, p. 26).

Unfortunately, Aitken never did overcome the family debt. There are differing accounts of whether her father's debt was paid or not; however, the business did fail twice. In 1813 her equipment was auctioned off but leased back to her. In 1814 she went to debtor's prison. Her last binding was issued in 1815. She was not listed in the Philadelphia directory after 1819, and the next public notice was her obituary in the *Germantown Telegraph* in 1832. Aitken's reputation as one of the finest publishers and binders of this period lives on, however, as does her achievement as the first, and perhaps only, woman printer of the Bible in America.

See also: Colonial Businesswomen; Publishing Industry

Further Reading

Spawn, Carol M. "Aitken, Jane." In James, Edward T., p. 26–27.

Spawn, Carol and William. "The Aitken Shop: Identification of an Eighteenth-Century Bindery and Its Tools."

Thomas, Isaiah. *History of Printing in America.*

Albee, Mrs. P. F. E. (birthdate unknown–1914), First Avon Lady

Mrs. P. F. E. Albee was hired in 1886 by David McConnell, founder of the California Perfume Company, to sell his first product, Little Dot Perfume Set. She was from Winchester, New Hampshire, and married to a United States senator. She not only sold the five different perfumes (white rose, violet, lily of the valley, heliotrope, and hyacinth) door-to-door but also is credited with recruiting over a hundred salespeople, developing the sales network that is still the basis of the Avon company today. She successfully promoted these women as friendly neighbors rather than hard-selling salespeople. In her twelve years with the company, she recruited and trained almost 5,000 representatives. At that time, this was one of the first opportunities for a housewife to augment the family income without changing her image as the "woman next door" and fellow homemaker. Albee was the first of more than 450,000 Avon ladies in the world.

> Albee is credited with recruiting over a hundred salespeople, developing the sales network that is still the basis of the Avon company today.

See also: Beauty Industry; Saleswomen

Further Reading
Derdak, Thomas. *International Directory of Company Histories*, vol. III, p. 15.
O'Neill, p. 519.

Alberty, Eliza Missouri Bushyhead (1839–1919), School Manager, Hotelier

Eliza Alberty was a Cherokee businesswoman, school administrator, and educator in Oklahoma. She and her husband established the National Hotel in Tahlequah, the capital of the Cherokee Nation, and when he died, she continued to run it successfully. It was well known for providing comfort, hospitality, and good food.

Alberty was born in Missouri on the Trail of Tears when the Cherokees were forced to move from their home in the southern Appalachian Mountains to Arkansas and Oklahoma. She was the seventh child of the Reverend Jesse Bushyhead, a Cherokee and Baptist minister, and Eliza Wilkinson. Her father founded a Baptist mission near today's Westville, Arkansas. She attended school there and later graduated from the Cherokee Female Seminary at Park Hill, Cherokee Nation, in 1854. After teaching in two public schools, she married David Vann in 1858. He died in 1867; and three years later, she married Bluford West Alberty.

Both Alberty and her husband were appointed stewards of the Male Seminary in Tahlequah. They managed the business aspects of the school, purchased all the supplies, directed and managed the appropriations, collected and paid all the bills, and were responsible for hiring and managing all the domestic employees. They also had many of the same duties as stewards of the Cherokee Insane Asylum. In 1885 they bought a hotel in Tahlequah and named it the National Hotel. After her husband died in 1889, Alberty continued to run the hotel, which by that time was one of the most successful hotels in the territory.

Alberty was very active in the Baptist Church. Known as "Aunt Eliza," she taught Sunday school and participated in church activities. When she died, the newspaper called her "Tahlequah's most distinguished citizen" (see Further Reading). She was said to be more famous than her brother, a principal chief of the Cherokee Nation from 1879 to 1888.

See also: American Indian Businesswomen; Travel Industry

Further Reading
Foreman, Carolyn Thomas. "Aunt Eliza of Tahlequah."
Mihesuah, Devon A. "Alberty, Eliza Missouri Bushyhead." In Bataille, p. 4.
http://rosecity.net/tears/trail/eliza.html

Alexander, Mary Spratt Provoost (1693–1760), Merchant

Mary Alexander was one of the most influential and powerful merchants in the colonies. She was born in New York City, the daughter of a merchant, and inherited both her father and her mother's business sense and wealth. She married her stepbrother, Samuel Provoost and became a partner to her merchant husband, investing her inheritance in his business. They had three children. After he died, she married lawyer James Alexander in 1721. For the next thirty-nine years she not only bore seven children but also continued the Provoost mercantile business. The business thrived. She imported and exported goods and sold them in her store along with colonial goods and her husband's payments in kind. Hardly a ship docked in New York City without a consignment for her. In 1743 the family worth was estimated at over £100,000 sterling, and her mercantile business was one of the most successful in the city.

The colonies were prosperous at the time; Alexander took full advantage of that and was the leading distributor of dry goods, fine fabrics, domestic Indian blankets, and imported china, silver, glass, and wines. She worked hard; her husband wrote a letter to his brother describing her as returning to her shop within a few hours of delivering her daughter Mary.

Five of her children survived; her son William became her business partner when he was twenty-three. He expanded the business into New England, New Jersey, and Philadelphia. He also served in the French and Indian War and later in the American Revolution under George Washington.

Alexander was involved politically, as was her husband. She may have supplied General Shirley's Fort Niagara expedition during the French and Indian War, and she supported John Peter Zenger in his libel trial in 1735. James Alexander died in 1756, and she continued to run the business, first with William, then after he left, by herself. Alexander died at age sixty-seven surrounded by her daughters and grandchildren. The governors of New York and New Jersey were pallbearers.

See also: Colonial Businesswomen; Retail Business

Further Reading

Kennedy, June O. *Mary Alexander, 1693–1760.*

Kennedy, June O. "Mary Spratt Provoost Alexander, 1693–1760." In Burstyn, p. 6–7.

Varga, Nicholas. "Alexander, Mary Spratt Provoost." In James, Edward T., p. 35–36.

Alliance of Women's Business and Professional Organizations

PO Box 67183
Chestnut Hill, MA 02467

The mission of The Alliance of Women's Business and Professional Organizations, formed in 1996, is to increase the economic power, influence, and visibility of women. The alliance is a group of over forty women's business organizations. The goals are: "To set and implement an annual agenda of key initiatives by alliance members; to communicate information of mutual interest to our group; and, to partner with other organizations to leverage and support women's business issues" (www.womensalliance.org). The organization holds quarterly meetings of member representatives and two special events (a Legislative day and a networking program) each year. Its home page states that all business and professional associations are encouraged to join. Dues are $175 per organization.

Further Reading

Associations Unlimited.

www.womensalliance.org

Alvarado, Linda (1951–), Construction Executive

Linda Alvarado's construction company in Denver was ranked in the *Working Woman* list of top woman-owned companies in 1998 and in 1999. She is also part owner of the Colorado Rockies baseball team, which makes her one of a few woman executives in two different male-dominated fields, and the first and only Latina to own a baseball team.

Alvarado grew up in Albuquerque, New Mexico, the only girl of six children. Her father worked for the Atomic Energy Commission, and her mother was a homemaker. Both parents encouraged all the children to excel in both academics and athletics. She was excellent at both, lettering in softball. After graduating from Pomona College, she went to work for a California development company where she got experience in all facets of the construction business from contracts to preparing bids, to obtaining materials, to dealing with suppliers and everyone else involved. Her boss liked to play golf and take long lunch hours and left the company in her hands, telling her that she could handle it; so she did. She found that she loved the business and went to school to learn more of the basics such as estimating, blueprints, and the critical path method of scheduling.

In 1974 Alvarado moved to Denver, found a partner, and began her own construction business: Martinez Alvarado Construction Management Corporation. After two years she bought out the partner and changed the name to Alvarado Construction, Inc. At the beginning she took advantage of a U.S. Department of Transportation program that encouraged hiring women and minorities. Since then the company has won many contracts, including one for Warren Village in Denver that consisted of 106 apartments; a day-care center; a job-training center; a dental clinic; a high-energy research and technological facility at Kirtland Air Force Base in Albuquerque; a national seed storage laboratory at Colorado State University in Fort Collins; an integrated materials research laboratory at Sandia National Laboratory, also at Kirtland; a materials scientific laboratory/office facility at Los Alamos; the terminal complex at Denver International Airport; and the Ocean Journey Aquarium in Denver. In 1998 the company was named one of the contractors for Invesco Field at Mile High, the new Bronco football stadium in Denver.

Throughout her career, Alvarado has been a staunch supporter of Hispanic entrepreneurs and founded the Denver Hispanic Chamber of Commerce in 1978 with the express purpose of opening up opportunities for Hispanic enterprises, as well as adding to the number of Hispanics in leadership positions. In 1996 and 1997, she chaired the board of the Hispanic Chamber of Commerce, the first woman to do so. She also has served on the White House Initiative for Hispanic Excellence in Education.

Alvarado has been on many corporate boards, including 3M, Pepsi Bottling Company, Cyprus Minerals Inc., Lennox Industries, Pitney Bowes, Qwest, and the United Bank of Denver. She also has been on the executive boards of the Colorado Economic Development Council, the Women's Forum of Colorado, and the Governor's Transportation Round Table.

Alvarado has won several awards including the 1990 Director's Choice Award from the National Women's Economic Alliance Foundation; the 1993 Sara Lee Frontrunner Award for accomplishments in her field and her abilities as a role model and inspiration to others; Hispanic Business Woman of 1994 from the Denver Chamber of Commerce; and the Horatio Alger Award in

2001. She was one of one hundred honorees at the Diamond Salute to Women in Business sponsored by the Colorado Women's Leadership Coalition and Arthur Andersen/Arthur Andersen Consulting. In 1998 the Girl Scouts Mile Hi Council named her a Woman of Distinction, and she was also honored at the annual Women's Leadership Circle. *Hispanic Business Magazine* named her one of the most influential Hispanics in America and also one of the 2002 Hispanic business boardroom elite. That year she was inducted into the Colorado Women's Hall of Fame and in 2003 into the National Women's Hall of Fame.

Alvarado and her husband are partners in another company, Palo Alto, Inc., one of the largest owners of Taco Bell, Pizza Hut, and KFC franchise restaurants. She often speaks on the lecture circuit and is a staunch advocate for opportunities for women and minorities. She has been called a trailblazer and a wonderful role model for both women and Hispanic people. She and her husband have a son and two daughters.

See also: Construction Industry; Latina Businesswomen

Further Reading

Hopkins, Carol. "Linda Alvarado." In Telgen and Kamp. *Latinas! Women of Achievement*, p. 14–17.

Hopkins, Carol. "Linda Alvarado (1951–) Business Owner." In Telgen and Kamp. *Notable Hispanic American Women*, p. 11–12.

Klis, Mike. "Minority Owner, Major Accomplishment."

American Business Women's Association (ABWA)

9100 Ward Pkwy, PO Box 8728
Kansas City, MO 64114-0728
www.abwa.org

Founded in 1949 by Hilary A. Bufton, the mission of American Business Women's Association is "to bring together businesswomen of diverse occupations and to provide opportunities for them to help themselves and others grow personally and professionally through leadership, education, networking support, and national recognition" (www.abwa.org). Mr. Bufton wished to provide education and business training for working women and also a support organization. His daughter, an authority on workplace issues facing women, is the executive director today. The association's more than 70,000 members include women who own or operate their own businesses, women in the professions, and women employed in any level of government, education, or corporations. The members represent twenty-three different industries; 14 percent of them are from government, 10 percent from education, thirteen percent from health care, and 13 percent from service. Twenty percent are entrepreneurs. Local chapter memberships, and there are 1400 of them, are also available. An annual fee enables the "Company Connection" option with special benefits and the "PrimeTime Connection" which allows retired businesswomen to continue membership. Another membership option is the "Express Network" which is focused on professional development and is set up to network with women business leaders. The association publishes a bimonthly magazine, *Women in Business*, and offers several scholarships and awards every year. The Top Ten Business Women of ABWA recognizes outstanding achievement in a career, community involvement, and educational development. Its calendar lists one national convention, regional spring conferences, and, every September 22, American Business Women's Day. Available benefits include an ABWA Visa, various kinds of insurance, discounts on a variety of products, and free consultation with a financial advisor.

Further Reading
Associations Unlimited.
www.abwa.org

American Indian Businesswomen

The Pine Ridge Indian Reservation in South Dakota has never experienced prosperity. According to Kevin Dobbs, "Unemployment approaches fifty percent, private business is rare, education is pitiable. It is the United States' own third world country" (Dobbs, p. 56). Although Pine Ridge has been the poorest since reservations were established, other American Indian tribes have had their societies and individuality destroyed and have few opportunities for education or bettering themselves economically. During World War II many left the reservations. Women moved into clerical and service jobs. From 1950 to 1980, their participation in these fields grew 50 percent. However, 66 percent of these jobs were part-time, and unemployment was high.

American Indian women focus on passing on their culture to their children. Most have not been involved in business activities, and even their crafts have a ceremonial purpose. Women have, in some tribes, been a major part of the political workings of the tribe; but for many, business is not a priority. Stereotypes and racism are major barriers in the world outside the reservations. Even in towns on the fringes, many American Indians are turned away because of such prejudices.

The Indian Financing Act of 1974 offered grants and loans to assist in developing new reservation businesses, but it was sadly underfunded. Further legislation addressed contracting with the federal government and, most importantly, taxes. By 1985 the Bureau of Indian Affairs and tribal authorities were partners in almost 1,300 joint contracts. Entrepreneurial activities focused on domestic activities such as selling the fruits of Alaskan hunting and fishing, tourism, arts and crafts, and casinos. The last began as a result of the 1988

Indian Gambling Regulation Act, and casinos are the strongest American Indian economic engine in the country.

Arts and crafts activities are lucrative but problematic, as is tourism, because of the ceremonial aspect of many American Indian arts and crafts. Beadwork, quilts, and artwork have been the mainstay of women's entrepreneurism, however. Other businesses are hampered by the difficulty of obtaining financing, although many reservations have business-development entities; however, women are less likely than men to become entrepreneurs. By the 1997 Economic Census, there were almost 200,000 American Indian businesses with annual revenues of $34 billion. This includes the casinos, which have provided financing for start-up businesses, at least in Wisconsin and Minnesota. On the Pine Ridge Reservation, the Lakota (Sioux) Fund was started in 1986 to train those who wish to obtain a loan in money management and business basics. In 1995 the Small Business Administration (SBA) began the Tribal Business Information Center (TBIC) program. Centers are located on reservations and provide computer access and workshops on starting a business and following successful business strategies. The National Center for American Indian Enterprise Development (www.ncaid.org) is the only national organization that promotes business development and trains future businesspeople in starting a business. They offer fellowships and leadership awards and publish a directory.

The corporate world is a difficult one for American Indian women. As of 1999 only 7.9 percent of them held managerial or administrative positions, and many of those were in tribal or government agencies. They face ongoing racism and gender bias and feel that they must choose between being an American Indian and being a woman. Many are the lone American Indian in their workplace and find that white people have either romanticized or negative feelings about their heritage. This undermines their self-worth and is stressful at the same time. Corporate diversity programs are trying to alleviate the problems; but change comes slowly, particularly because there are few such programs.

See also: Minority Businesswomen; Appendix III, Ethnic Groups

Further Reading
Bataille, Gretchen M., Ed. *Native American Women: A Biographical Dictionary.*
Dobbs, Kevin. "Training: The Last, Best Hope for the Nation's Poorest?"
White, Margaret Blackburn. "The Invisible Minority: American Indian Women in Corporate America."
www.ncaid.org

American Women's Economic Development Corporation

216 East 45th Street
New York, NY 10169
www.awed.org

Founded in 1976, the goal of this nonprofit corporation is to train and counsel women entrepreneurs and executives. The corporation provides telephone and in-house counseling, courses, workshops, and special events. Topics include business plans, how to start a business, and survival tips.

Anderson, Margaret C. (1886–1973), Magazine Publisher

Margaret Anderson published *The Little Review*, a literary magazine, from 1914 to 1929, printing the best of American and European avant-garde literature. Some of her authors were Ezra Pound, T.S. Eliot, Gertrude Stein, Amy Lowell, Hart Crane, Sherwood Anderson, and Ernest Hemingway. One of the most famous was James Joyce. His *Ulysses* landed her in court in one of the most celebrated obscenity cases of the time.

Anderson was brought up in a well-to-do family in Columbus, Indiana, the eldest of three daughters of a railroad executive. She was very independent, with a yearning for beauty and a dislike for the women's social functions of the day. From 1903 to 1906, she studied piano at Western College for Women in Oxford, Ohio. In 1908 she went to Chicago with a sister and landed a job doing interviews and book reviews for a religious magazine, *The Interior*. She also wrote reviews for the *Chicago Evening Post*. She was extravagant, so she lost her allowance from her parents. To earn money, she worked for Browne's Bookstore for $8 per week. The store was connected to a literary review, *The Dial*, and she later became the literary editor of the magazine.

In 1913 Anderson became editor of *The Continent*, another literary magazine. Among its contributors were Theodore Dreiser and Sherwood Anderson. At a party, she announced that she wished to start *The Little Review*, a magazine "filled with the best conversation the world [has] to offer" (Gargan, p. 33). She found financial support for the endeavor from Eunice Tietjens and DeWitt Wing. When the magazine launched in March 1914, she was twenty-seven. The first issue carried a Vachel Lindsay poem, an Anderson article on Paderewski, and articles on Nietzsche and Gertrude Stein. It was the epitome of avant-garde and helped make Chicago the center of early twentieth century modernism. It was also a part of the Chicago Renaissance, a literary movement that attacked the conservatism of the late nineteenth century. The next issue contained an article favoring anarchism. She lost a financial backer because of it. Not to be stopped, she lived in a tent on the shores of Lake Michigan from May to December that year.

In 1916 Anderson met Jane Heap and hired her as a co-editor. They had a very close relationship over the next eight years; Heap had a strong influence on Anderson's beliefs and philosophy. They moved to Muir Woods for a brief time, then back to Chicago, then on to New York City the following year. The magazine attracted the best writers, poets, and thinkers of the day: Carl Sandberg, Ben Hecht, William Carlos Williams, Ford Maddox Ford, Amy Lowell, Emma

Goldman, and Harte Crane. Their first international contributor was Ezra Pound, who recruited William Butler Yeats. The writers received no compensation, but prestige because the journal had become the foremost literary magazine of the time.

In 1918 the March issue began the serialization of James Joyce's *Ulysses*, planned to last three years. Issues were immediately seized by the United States Post Office, declared obscene, and burned in four different episodes. In October 1920 the Society for the Suppression of Vice prosecuted but lost the case. In February 1921, however, both Heap and Anderson were found guilty, fingerprinted, fined $50 each, and prohibited from publishing any more excerpts from the book. *Ulysses* did not pass censorship laws for another ten years.

After 1921 *The Little Review* was published only four times per year. In 1922 Anderson met Georgette LeBlanc, and her relationship with Jane Heap slowly ended. Anderson and LeBlanc moved to France in 1924 and turned the magazine over to Heap. In 1929 the final issue was published. Meanwhile, Anderson became enthused about the mystic philosopher, Gurdjieff, and she and LeBlanc traveled over Europe, supported by the books they both wrote. LeBlanc died from breast cancer in 1941.

The following year Ernest Hemingway gave Anderson $400 to sail to New York City where she met Dorothy Caruso, the wife of the great singer, and lived with her until 1955. She compiled *The Little Review Anthology* and wrote the second volume of her autobiography at that time. In 1956 she returned to France and lived there in seclusion until she died from emphysema in 1973.

Her legacy, *The Little Review*, was a magazine of legendary quality. According to Holly Baggett, it not only "advanced the work of innovative Americans but exposed the United States to the latest in European art and letters" (Baggett, p. 466). Anderson was fascinated by every political, artistic, and literary movement of the time, from anarchism to psychoanalysis, feminism, cubism, and surrealism, and included them in her magazine. She published the most important modernist writers of the first half of the twentieth century.

See also: Publishing Industry

Further Reading

Anderson, Margaret C. *The Autobiography*.

Baggett, Holly. "The Trials of Margaret Anderson and Jane Heap." In Albertine, p. 465–467.

Gargan, William M. "Anderson, Margaret Carolyn." In *Dictionary of American Biography*, Supplement 9, p. 32–34.

Flanner, J. "Life on a Cloud."

Andress, Mary Vail (1877–1964), Banker

In 1935 *Fortune* called Mary Andress one of the outstanding businesswomen in America. She was the first woman officer of a large New York City bank, Chase National Bank of New York.

After graduating from Moravian College in Bethlehem, Pennsylvania, she became involved in relief work during World War I. She was one of the first eight women to be sent to France by the American Red Cross in the early days of the war, and after doing relief work there, she organized a relief unit and worked in Caucasia in 1919 and 1920 as director of an orphanage.

In 1920 when Andress was forty-three, she began her banking career. She was hired by the Paris Branch of Bankers Trust and worked there for four years. In 1924 Chase National Bank of New York hired her as an assistant cashier. She was in charge of establishing a woman's department and was the only woman officer of the bank. Her duties were to help women with financial matters, a concern of banks at that time. She later served on their board of directors, the first woman in that capacity.

Andress was also active during World War II and worked on behalf of the British War Relief, the United China Relief Drive in 1942, and the Red Cross War Fund Drive in 1941 and 1942. She received many awards as the result of her war efforts: the Distinguished Service Award (the first woman to receive this award for work in the field), the French Medaille de la Reconnaissance, and the Near East Medal. She was also a trustee for the Moravian Seminary and College for Women and on the board of directors of the Henry Hudson Hotel.

See also: Banking; Late Bloomers

Further Reading
"Mary Vail Andress." In Parshalle, p. 133–134.
"Women in Business: III," p. 83.

Anthony, Michele (1957–), Music Industry Executive

In 1997 Michele Anthony was forty-seventh on *Fortune*'s list of powerful women in corporate America because she turned Sony's music division around and doubled its sales through her contracts with popular musical artists.

Anthony is a lawyer; she graduated from George Washington University with a BA with distinction and received her JD from the University of Southern California. She belongs to the Order of the Coif. Before going to Sony, she was a partner in an entertainment law firm, Manatt, Phelps, Rothenberg & Phillips. Her clients included Guns N' Roses, Ozzy Osborne, Soundgarden, Sugarcubes, and Pixies. At the time, these were the most popular rock acts in the country. For her accomplishments, she received the Norma Zarky Entertainment Law Award. In 1989 she told the president of Sony that no rock band would sign with his company, so he hired her as an executive vice president with the responsibilities of negotiating contracts and overseeing the development of talent, touring, family entertainment, and special projects. She was, at that time, the most powerful woman in the record business.

Since Anthony joined Sony, she has been responsible for signing many of their most popular artists, including Celine Dion, Mariah Carey, Ricky Martin, Aerosmith, Pearl Jam, Rage Against the Machine, and Alice in Chains. She has also been in charge of the new Work Group label. Sales have doubled until Sony was the leader in the market in 1998 with $6.3 billion. In 1999 Sony was again in the top spot, over Warner Music Corporation, for the first time in twenty years. Her president fully credits her for this growth.

Anthony is a highly respected member of the music industry, both as a lawyer and as a music executive. She was fifth on the *Hollywood Reporter's* 2002 list of the most powerful women in the entertainment industry.

See also: Entertainment Industry

Further Reading
"Michele Anthony Appointed Executive Vice President, Sony Music."
Sellers, Patricia. "These Women Rule."

Apparel Industry, *see* Fashion Industry

Arden, Elizabeth (1878–1966), Cosmetics Executive

Elizabeth Arden revolutionized the cosmetics industry at a time when using makeup wasn't acceptable for proper ladies. As its use became more common, her business grew into more than 100 salons and 300 cosmetic items. She was the queen of the beauty industry for over fifty years. In 1977 she was inducted into the Junior Achievement National Business Hall of Fame.

Arden was born Florence Nightingale Graham near Toronto to a market gardener and his wife Susan, who died when their daughter was six. She didn't finish high school, and after a series of low-paying jobs, joined her brother William in New York City. Her last job there was for Eleanor Adair who, at Arden's request, taught her how to do facial massages. Her customers told her she had wonderful hands, and she saw potential in this field, so she and a friend, Elizabeth Hubbard, opened a salon. The partnership was doomed, for both were strong-willed people. It dissolved in 1910, and Florence,

> Elizabeth Arden revolutionized the cosmetics industry at a time when using make-up wasn't even acceptable.

with a $6,000 loan from her brother, bought Elizabeth's share. She redecorated the salon, including painting the door red. That became her trademark. She named the salon Elizabeth Arden (Elizabeth from her former partner and Arden from a popular Tennyson poem). From that day, she preferred to be called that name although she never had it legally changed. She spent the next four years perfecting a facial and searching for a light fluffy cleansing cream (the creams of the day were all greasy). In 1914 a chemist compounded her formula, and she named it Amoretta. This was the beginning of her cosmetics empire.

Later that year she opened her first branch in Washington DC, and by 1922, two more in Paris and Boston. In 1915 she married Thomas Jenkins Lewis. He was responsible for managing the wholesale department that grew to carry over 300 products sold in forty-four countries. They had no children and were divorced in 1934.

The times were right for cosmetics, formerly only for "not quite nice" girls and women. Customs and social taboos were changing, and Elizabeth Arden was at the forefront of that change. She began with facials and skin creams, but in 1917 she introduced mascara and eye shadow and later lipsticks. Respectable women began wearing makeup and using her best seller, an astringent lotion called Ardena Skin Tone and her most popular product, Velva Moisture Film. In 1932 she began selling a line of lipsticks to complement the wearer's clothing. She was meticulous with her products, mixing and trying them on herself, friends, and employees.

Arden then branched into exercises, which she offered at her salons. She was an advocate of advertising and even tried a radio program. A more successful advertisement was her sponsorship of balls for several charitable organizations. Her salons were built on prestige and luxury. She hired members of the nobility and other European ex-patriates, as well as a number of blind workers and a greater number of women than other manufacturers of the time. She was a demanding, sometimes tyrannical, employer, quick to fire, but also quick to reward. She paid top salary, and many of her employees were with her for a long time. Her famous feud with Helena Rubinstein was capped by Arden's hiring several Rubinstein employees; in retaliation, Rubinstein lured away Arden's ex-husband for her business.

In the 1930s Arden bought a farm in Maine, the Maine Chance Farm, which she turned into a luxurious spa offering low-calorie diets and luxury hair and foot services, massage, manicure, exercise, and steam baths. Expansion brought a winter spa in Arizona and another in the Kentucky bluegrass country. In 1943 she began a fashion business, with designers creating exclusive designs to be sold in the salons. Later she was the first to manufacture a line of cosmetics for men.

Arden was also active in horse racing from 1931 to the 1960s under the name Elizabeth N. Graham. In 1947 her horse Jet Pilot won the Kentucky Derby. She named a perfume Blue Grass and treated her horses with her own preparations. She was active in civic organizations and a lifetime member of the Museum of Modern Art and the Metropolitan Museum of Art, both in New York. In 1949 she was awarded an honorary doctorate by Syracuse University.

Elizabeth Arden, Helena Rubinstein, and Estee Lauder have been called the "Beauty Queens" for their role in pioneering the cosmetics industry in the United States. They were all indefatigable with an uncanny sense of timing. Arden and Rubinstein started their companies when cosmetics were just on the edge of becoming respectable and were responsible for much of that respectability. In the beginning, their customers were wealthy and socially prominent women, mostly over forty, worried about the ravages of time.

At the height of her business, Elizabeth Arden's sales were over $60 million per year and her estate was $30 to 40 million. She was the sole owner of her company. She left $4 million to long-term employees, $4 million to her sister Gladys who ran the European operations, and the rest to her niece who was also her companion. The company was sold to Eli Lilly to pay inheritance taxes, who later sold it to Faberge for $700 million, who sold it to Unilever in 1998 for about the same price. In November, 2000 FFI Fragrance bought it from Unilever for $225 million.

See also: Beauty Industry

Further Reading
Bauer, Hambla. "High Priestess of Beauty."
Harriman, Margaret Case. "Profiles: Glamour, Inc."
"I am a Famous Woman in this Industry."
Lewis, Alfred Allen and Constance Woodworth. *Miss Elizabeth Arden.*

Arnold, Susan E. (1954–), Toiletries Executive

Susan Arnold was first named to the *Fortune* list of most powerful corporate women in 2002, at thirty-second. In 2003 she was thirty-first. She is the president of Personal Beauty and Feminine Care for Procter and Gamble and the highest-ranked woman in the company.

Arnold graduated from the University of Pennsylvania and then received her MBA in 1980 from the University of Pittsburgh. She immediately joined Procter and Gamble as a brand assistant for the Dawn and Ivory Soap Group. She held increasingly responsible positions including brand manager of Gain, associate manager for the laundry products, advertising manager and general manager for deodorants and Old Spice in the United States. In February 1996 she was promoted to vice president and general manager of deodorants and Old Spice and skin care products in the United States and the following year, to vice president of laundry products. In this position, she managed Gain's marketing team and brought the product from eighth to fifth internationally. In 1999 she became vice president of North American fabric care and, in June, president of global skin care and the first woman in the history of the company to rise to the presidential level. Her challenge was to turn around the company's diminishing market share in this arena. The following year global cosmetics was added to her umbrella and in 2001 personal beauty care. Her latest promotion added feminine care products such as Tampax and Always.

Arnold attributes her success partially to good mentoring; she notes that the present CEO of the company was her first boss. Others point to her excellent leadership abilities and strong strategic thinking. She has consistently led her teams to excellent sales results, gaining market share for the company in several categories. She also makes sure to mentor new employees, passing along the benefits she garnered from her experiences.

She was named to the *Advertising Age* list of the "Marketing 100" in 1998, and their list of "21 to Watch in the 21st Century" in 1999. Arnold was also awarded the Cincinnati YWCA Women of Achievement Award in 2000. She has been on the board of Procter & Gamble and React.com and was elected to the board of Goodyear Tire & Rubber in January 2003. She also serves on the board of the Cincinnati Zoo.

See also: Beauty Industry

Further Reading
Neff, Jack. "Susan Arnold: President, P Skincare Chief Pushing P&G Forward."
Overholt, Alison. "Open to Women?"

Ash, Mary Kay ([1917–1918]–2001), Cosmetics Executive

Mary Kay Ash began her skin cream company in 1963 with $5,000 and a tanning cream she had purchased from the daughter of a friend. She was in her fifties and disillusioned with corporate America. Today, mainly because of her charismatic, inspirational, motivational leadership style, Mary Kay Cosmetics is the largest direct-sale, multilevel marketing cosmetics company in the world. It is a *Fortune* 500 company with over $1 billion in sales, over 1,400 employees, and 250,000 independent beauty consultants in nineteen countries.

Born in Hot Wells, Texas, Ash had a difficult childhood. Her father became ill with tuberculosis when she was two. He spent the next five years in the hospital, and when he finally returned home, his care was put in her hands. Her mother was the sole earner, working two jobs, often for sixteen hours per day. Her major communication with her daughter was over the telephone, saying "You can do it, Mary Kay!" She did the housework and the chores and nursed and watched over her father, as well as going to school and receiving excellent grades. She married a would-be country singer at seventeen, had two sons and a daughter. They stayed together until he returned from World War II when he informed her that not only had he been living with another woman, they also had a child, and he wanted a divorce. She was devastated.

Ash had been working for Stanley Home Products since 1938, and she continued until 1952. This meant selling on the road through parties in homes. She was their top sales producer, but in spite of this, she was passed over many times in favor of men with less experience and talent. At one of the parties, she met a woman with beautiful skin, which was unusual in Texas with its dry climate and winds. When Ash asked how she kept her skin so lovely, she explained that she used a lotion her father used for tanning hides for leather.

Even though it smelled bad, Ash tried it and was amazed at the results. In 1952 she changed jobs to work for World Gift Company, selling home accessories. In the ten years she was there, she built a sales organization that covered ten states. Again, men she had trained were promoted over her. When she asked to be a sales manager, her boss made her a national training manager instead at half the salary of the other position. She was so angry that she quit.

Ash had married again and was not as financially unstable as she had been, so she decided to write a book about male-dominated corporations and their treatment of women. Sitting at the kitchen table, she began to make two lists. One was a description of the ideal company. She liked the description so much that she decided to start a company that met these requirements. From the beginning, she wanted to provide opportunities for women to do anything they wished. Her vision would allow a working mother to earn plenty of money by following her own level of advancement on her own schedule and be her own boss.

Ash decided that the product would be skin care, and she and her husband carefully planned for four months. He would be the business administrator, and she would do the rest. With $5000 capital, she bought the rights to the tanning lotion and rented a 500-square-foot storefront in Dallas. One month before the opening, her husband died suddenly. Her son Richard agreed to be the business manager, and they opened on schedule on Friday, December 13, 1963. They had one shelf of products that she had bottled in her bathroom and nine friends who agreed to be beauty consultants. The business grew into a direct sales company with a facial care system sold through in-home consulting sessions. Emphasis was on personalized service, consultations, and follow-up visits. The rule was that only six invitees came to a session, ensuring the personalized attention that became the hallmark of the company. The independent beauty consultant was taught the rudiments of skin care which she passed on to the invitees. Ash was truly independent, buying the products at fifty percent off retail and selling them at the beauty sessions. Mary Kay incorporated contests and self-competition with prizes of diamond bumblebee pins and pink Cadillacs. There was an annual three-day motivational seminar where she spoke.

The first year's sales were $38,000; the next year, sales had risen to $650,000 with 200 on-site employees and 100,000 independent beauty consultants. The company moved into new quarters that year and again in 1969. In 1977 Mary Kay built an eight-story headquarters in Dallas. Sales and numbers of employees continued to rise. In 1966 she married Melville Ash, who died in 1980. In 1967 the company was valued at $50 million, and the next year there was a public stock offering. In 1976 the company was listed on the New York Stock Exchange. By 1981 sales were $235 million with 1400 employees and 150,000 beauty consultants. That year, fifteen of the consultants had become millionaires (Landrum, p. 179).

In 1985 the company bought back all the publicly held shares because one of the women stockholders had objected to the pink Cadillacs. Ash also began a line of men's cosmetics, Mr. K. In 1987 she named her son Richard as chairman of the board, and she went into semi-retirement to be chairman emerita, still giving her traditional speeches, however. During the 1990s the company added foreign subsidiaries as well as foreign manufacturers. It also stopped testing on animals and began an active recycling program.

Ash won many awards, beginning with the Horatio Alger Award in 1978. In 1979 she was the subject of a "60 Minutes" profile and in 1980 received the Gold Plate Award from the American Academy of Achievement. She was on all the talk shows, named the Cosmetics Career Woman of the Year, and was elected to the Direct Selling Hall of Fame and the Sales Executive Club's Hall of Fame. Ash was named one of America's top corporate women by *Business Week* and was honored as one of Texas' most influential women of the century by the Women's Chamber of Commerce of Texas. She is in the Texas Business Hall of Fame and was named to the Junior Achievement National Business Hall of Fame in 1996. She wrote three books, *Mary Kay*, *Mary Kay on Management*, and *You Can Have it All: Lifetime Wisdom from America's Foremost Woman Entrepreneur*. These clearly state her management style and vision and have been translated into several languages and made into audiotapes.

In the *Forbes* issue of December 29, 1997, the editor chose the best quotations of the year. One was from Mary Kay Ash: "The two things that people want more than sex or money are recognition and praise." She built her direct sales empire on these precepts. She was a charismatic selling and marketing genius with the vision and perseverance to realize her dream. She changed the face of direct selling forever.

Ash died in Dallas in November, 2001, after a long illness. At the time of her death, there were more than 750,000 Mary Kay salespeople in thirty-seven countries. The company's wholesale revenue was $1.3 billion in 2000.

See also: Beauty Industry; Saleswomen

Further Reading
Ash, Mary Kay. *Mary Kay.*
Landrum, p. 170–186.
MacPhee, p. 21–36.
Nemy, Enid. "Mary Kay Ash, Who Built a Cosmetics Empire and Adored Pink, Is Dead at 83."
Shapero, Albert. "Have You Got What it Takes to Start Your Own Business?"

Asian American Businesswomen

Asian Americans originally immigrated from many different cultures and many different countries, such as China, Japan, Korea, Vietnam, India, and the Philippines. With the exception of more than 8,000 Chinese girls who were tricked or kidnapped and sold to American brothels, women arrived after the men had established themselves in cultural enclaves in cities or on farms. When they began arriving in the late 1800s, they worked, mostly unpaid, in the family businesses. In 1907 an agreement with Japan allowed Japanese "picture brides," young women whose families had arranged marriages with Japanese American young men, to immigrate but only if they were healthy and educated women. Again, they worked in family businesses or in the clothing industry. Asian Indian men did not wish to bring their wives during the early years.

The War Brides Act of 1946 opened the gates to women who married World War II servicemen. Almost 10,000 wives came from Japan, China, and the Philippines. There was another influx of thousands of Asian American wives after the Korean and Vietnam wars as well. By 1950, 42 percent of these women were employed as domestic laborers or in manufacturing. The 1956 Immigration and Naturalization Act erased earlier quotas, and more men sent for their wives. Many of these women were highly educated. Women from India began to arrive after 1970, usually sponsored by a relative.

In 1980 the Refugee Relief Act opened the doors to Vietnamese and Southeast Asians. From 1980 to 1990, most Asian immigrants were poor, spoke little English, and worked at low-paying as well as unpaid jobs in family businesses. Even if they were educated, many of their professional degrees were not accepted in the United States. Second-generation Asian American women began to work outside their cultural enclaves, however, and became well educated. One-third of the Chinese Americans, both male and female, were employed in managerial, administrative, or professional positions. Japanese American women had a higher median income. Korean American women, though working, were usually in low-paying or blue-collar jobs. By 1990, 50 percent of the women from India had bachelor's degrees and were also in managerial or professional positions.

By 1998 there were almost 5 million Asian American women in the United States, nearly 4 percent of the population. More than 60 percent were in the labor force, and this group was the least likely to be unemployed. Although educational attainment is highly valued, it varies among the groups, with the Japanese the highest and Hmongs from Cambodia the lowest. In the late 1990s many Asian women came to the United States for MBAs and then returned home. The Asian culture in general does not place as high a value on women; husbands have authority, and women are expected to be the nurturers. Also, women were taught to be submissive and to defer to men in traditional Asian American families. The women's movement helped some of these women to become more assertive.

Asian Americans have been called the model minority because of their high level of education, a tendency to choose professional occupations, a relatively high income level, stable family, and low crime rate. This is a stereotype and true of some, but the statistics vary from group to group, and many struggle. For Asian women, other stereotypes abound. They are assumed to be passive, quiet, and hard working with poor language skills. Because their culture values harmony, they are thought not fit to be leaders. Even if they are highly educated, they only know the technical arena. Like all stereotypes, these assumptions are ridiculous.

In corporations both Asian males and females hit the glass ceiling, but it is particularly true of females; in fact, Shirley Hume, the Associate Dean of Graduate Programs at UCLA, said: "The glass ceiling for Asian American males is a cement floor for Asian American women" (Gall and Natividad, p. 422). Negative stereotypes and traditional values work against them, particularly in earning promotions in management. They are hired easily, but promotions are difficult. Culturally, given the Asian emphasis on self-effacement, they cannot promote themselves, and there are few role models or mentors. "Asian American women are the most occupationally segregated of all groups (male and female) and . . . have the least chance of improving their situation through mobility up the job ladder" (Giscombe, p. 105). In a 1997 to 1998 Catalyst survey, 46 percent of the Asian American women polled agreed that stereotypes still exist. Like many women, they felt they had to work twice as hard to get half as far up the corporate ladder. Many companies have instituted diversity programs to combat the stereotypes and to foster executive development and promotion for all qualified employees.

From the beginning, Asian American women have been involved in entrepreneurship. The immigrants started in service businesses, often in Chinese, Japanese, and other ethnic communities. The women worked in the businesses, sometimes without pay. They came to this country determined to succeed and worked hard to do so. The communities and families financed new businesses through rotating credit associations, thus overcoming one of the major obstacles for entrepreneurs. According to the 1997 economic census, there were 305,700 Asian American woman-owned businesses in the United States, employing 787,200 people, with $95.2 billion in sales. This figure is 4 percent of all woman-owned businesses and 36 percent of all Asian American-owned companies. From 1987 to 1996, their growth rate was 138 percent. Almost half are service businesses. Entrepreneurship offers obvious benefits: an escape from subtle racism and stereotypes, the opportunity to succeed based on hard work and perseverance, and a chance to control assets and make business decisions.

There are several organizations dedicated to helping Asian American women succeed in business: Association of Asian American Advertising Agencies (www.3af.org), Asian Pacific American Women's Leadership Institute (www.apawli.org), Asian American Business Development Center (www.aabdc.com), Asian Women in Business (www.awib.org), Indian Business and Professional Women, Asian American Manufacturers Association (www.aamasv.com), and the U.S. Pan Asian American Chamber of Commerce (www.uspaacc.com).

See also: Immigrant Businesswomen; Minority Businesswomen

Further Reading

Gall and Natividad, p. 133–150.
Loos, Barbara. "For Women, Getting Hired Is the Easy Part."
Ramirez, Anthony. "America's Super Minority; Asian Americans Have Wasted No
   Time Laying Claim to the American Dream."
Women of Color in Corporate Management Three Years Later.
www.awib.org

Astor, Sarah Todd (1762–1832), Merchant

The *Dictionary of American Biography* says, under the entry for John Jacob Astor, "he married Sarah Todd who brought him $300 in cash, a clear head for business, and an especially keen sense in the valuation of furs" (p. 367). She was not only responsible for setting him up in business but also helped amass one of the most formidable fortunes in American history.

Astor and her mother, descendants of Dutch settlers, were running a boarding house in New York City when John Jacob Astor arrived from Germany. He decided to board there, and he and Sarah married in 1785. He later said he married her because she was so pretty, but probably her dowry of $300 was a nice bonus. They used the money to open a flute and piano store; the instruments were made and shipped to them by John's brother in England. They lived over the store and bought fur pelts with the profits. After processing them, they sold the furs and, as time went on, they both became shrewd judges of quality. Her husband was often away on fur-buying trips, so Astor ran the store and between 1788 and 1802 also managed to bear eight children, five of whom lived.

She assessed the quality of the furs and priced them; she was much more skilled than he at this and, for a joke, said he should pay her. They decided that $500 (in 1998 dollars, over $5,000) per hour would be fair; the pay shows how valuable her skill was.

As they began to accumulate wealth, they first bought a house and then, at Astor's suggestion, blocks of real estate, always just beyond the borders of the city. By 1800 her husband was one of the leading businessmen in New York; he had branched out into the China market aided by her relatives who were traders there. Even though the fur trade eventually declined, his real estate holdings were considerable. By the time she died, their fortune was probably the largest in the United States.

Astor was behind the accumulation of the family fortune. She provided the start-up money, scrimped and saved during the early days, tended the store, and bore children while her husband was off buying furs. She provided business alliances with her trader relatives and was the originator of investing in New York real estate.

See also: Retailing Industry

Further Reading
"Astor, John Jacob." In *Dictionary of American Biography*, vol. 1, part 1, p. 397–399.
Brands, p. 1–11.
"Family Business." In Bird, p. 41–43.

Auerbach, Beatrice Fox (1887–1968), Retail Executive

Beatrice Auerbach was the president of G. Fox & Company, a Hartford, Connecticut, department store and the largest privately owned store in the country from 1938 to 1965. She was born into the business; both grandfathers owned dry goods stores, one in Hartford and one in Newburgh, New York. When her father, Moses Fox, took over the Hartford store, she inherited a large portion of stock shares. She and her sister attended public and private schools, mixed with extensive travel in Europe.

In 1911 she married George Auerbach whose family also owned a department store in Salt Lake City. They had two daughters. In 1917 G. Fox and Company was destroyed in a fire. Her father decided to rebuild and asked the Auerbachs to move to Hartford and help in the business. Her husband became secretary-treasurer of the company. Auerbach, meanwhile, was active in community affairs. After her husband died in 1927, she began working at the company, and when her father died in 1938, she became president.

Auerbach increased the business until Fox was the largest privately owned store in the country. She also pioneered several labor programs including a five-day week, retirement plans, medical and nonprofit lunch facilities, and an interest-free loan program. Fox was the first large department store to hire African American employees in other than menial positions. She also inaugurated innovative merchandising techniques such as toll-free telephone ordering, free delivery, and automated billing. In 1959 she built an $8 million addition, which included free meeting space for nonprofit organizations. Her daughters' husbands both became executives in the company. In 1965 she resigned as president, and the family sold all the privately held stock for $40 million worth of stock in May Department Stores Company.

Auerbach was widely known for her philanthropy as well as her merchandising. She sat on the boards of several schools, hospitals, and cultural organizations. She ran a retailing and allied arts program at the Connecticut College for Women from 1938 to 1959. In 1941 she established the Beatrice Fox Auerbach Foundation to finance a variety of educational and civic activities and in 1945 established a service bureau for women's organizations. Although she never went to college, she received several honorary degrees.

See also: Retailing Industry

Further Reading
Leavitt, Judith A. p. 15–16.
Lipson, Dorothy. "Auerbach, Beatrice Fox, July 7, 1887–November 29, 1968." In Sicherman and Green, p. 15–16.

Automobile Industry

The automobile industry can be divided into two segments: operations that sell and lease, or operations that manufacture vehicles or parts. Both areas have historically been male-dominated. "Car guys" have been in the United States since Henry Ford rolled his first car off the assembly line. Since the late 1980s, however, women have entered this previously all-male realm.

In the area of dealerships, in 1998 the National Automobile Dealers' Association counted 400 women among its 19,000 members. Although women buy 50 percent of all cars (as of January 2003), only 4.9 percent of the dealerships are owned by women. Females are 7.1 percent of all general managers and hold 7 percent of the jobs, according to CNW Market Research (LeBeau, p. 4). Of General Motors' 7,400 dealerships, 226 or 3 percent are owned by women; while Ford Motors has a slightly better record: 5 percent or 278 of 5,165 businesses. CNW also notes that 39 percent of women would rather deal with another woman in the showroom.

Owning a dealership or even working in one often poses difficult problems. Considerable financial capital is needed, and often when a dealership becomes available, another large dealership will immediately buy it. Long hours and as well as evening and weekend hours, with little flexibility, also often discourage women. In the late 1990s, automobile manufacturers instituted programs designed to attract women. General Motors began the first minority dealer program in the early 1970s, but it didn't attract women until they renamed it The Women's Retail Initiatives Program in 2001. By June 2003 there were 233 woman-owned dealerships. Ford and Toyota instituted similar programs. The largest woman-owned dealership is Pat Moran's Florida-based JM Enterprises, which she inherited from her father. She has said many times that she had to work very hard to prove herself, and that it took twelve years to assemble a management team that trusted her.

The manufacturing side has been even more difficult for women to penetrate, although those who have, have found the challenge exciting. During World War II, women welded and riveted but were sent home when the war ended. In the late 1960s the big three automobile companies began hiring women, but movement has been glacial. In 1971, out of 7,000 engineers at Chrysler, three were African American and two were female. By 1985 the Society of Automotive Engineers had 300 women members. Of these, one worked as a designer at Chrysler.

In 1987 Toyota in the United States hired its first woman assembly-line worker, a move that required the company to build a ladies' restroom. By 1993 she had risen to plant manager. In 1987 out of 986 automobile executives, twelve or 1.2 percent were women. The following year that number rose to 1.7 percent. By 1997 Ford, General Motors, and Chrysler each had one female vice president. In lower ranks, General Motors numbered 410 women executives out of 3,916 worldwide; Ford had two women vice presidents out of forty, and General Motors had three vice presidents out of sixty-nine. Chrysler had one female vice president. In 1998 Cynthia Trudell became the first woman to head a car division at any domestic or foreign car manufacturer. By 1999 there were fourteen women executives at Ford, Chrysler, and General Motors, 7.1 percent of the total. The emphasis on diversity helped throughout the hierarchy: in 2001 out of 7,000 engineers, thirty were African American or female. All the manufacturers now have programs that emphasize hiring minorities or women.

Women working in both branches of the industry definitely see the challenges, but believe they are making a difference, not only in the corporate cultures, but also in the cars themselves. They all talk of having to work harder, though most feel the final results are worth the effort.

Further Reading
Bott, Jennifer. "Big Three Automakers Find Few Qualified Women to Fill Top Posts."
"In High Demand; Automakers Roll Out the Red Carpet for Talented Minority and Women Engineers."
LeBeau, Christina. "As Car Dealers, Women Are Scarce but Successful."
Sawyer, Arlena. "More Women Running Stores with GM Brands."

Avent, Sharon Hoffman (1946–), Office Supplies Manufacturer

In July 1998 Sharon Avent succeeded her mother as CEO of Smead Manufacturing, maker of over 2,500 office filing products and records management software and one of the top woman-owned companies in the United States. She had been at the company for thirty years and moved up from senior vice-president. Her mother, Ebba Hoffman, remained chairman of the board and co-owner until she died in 1999.

Avent was brought up in the business. She and her brother John took business trips with their mother and learned all about the plant and the products. She left Hamlin University to work at Smead. The previous summer she started as a secretary in the administrative area while John became involved in the production end and building new plants. In 1966 she began to work full-time as an assistant in the credit department and in 1969 became assistant to her mother, the president. John died in 1986, and Avent was appointed executive vice president and really ran the company while their mother dealt with her loss. From 1995 to 1998, her official title was senior executive vice president until she became president and CEO in 1998.

During the nineties, profit margins tightened as office superstore chains became part of the mix. Avent dealt with this by automating the plants, farming out some of the manufacturing to Mexico with its lower labor costs, and buying a software company that made electronic records-management software. After she took over as president, she also bought a Dutch office products manufacturer with an eye to moving into the European market. She also intends to work on new product development.

Avent is known as a fair, approachable manager, one who takes the time to know her employees and to listen to them. She also has a reputation for integrity and places great value on customer service. Her plan for Smead is to keep it as a family-owned company and continue the tradition of retaining a large number of long-time employees.

Avent sits on the boards of Shattuck-St. Mary's School, the Regina Health Care Center, and the Minnesota Historical Society. Her hobby is Tennessee walking horses; and in 1997 she won the championship in the amateur class. She is married with two stepsons.

See also: Hoffman, Ebba

Further Reading
Peterson, Susan. "Smead Manufacturing Stays in the Family; Following in her Mother's Footsteps, Smead President Takes Leadership Role."
"Smead Manufacturing Company Announces New President, CEO: Mother/Daughter Team Continues Leadership."

Ayer, Harriet Hubbard (1849–1903), Cosmetics Manufacturer

The life of Harriet Hubbard Ayer reads like a Gothic novel: ugly-duckling child, married, wealthy-socialite beauty, loses child in Chicago Fire, divorced and bankrupt, business success, suits and counter suits, incarcerated for insanity by ex-husband and daughter, freed, success as a public speaker and newspaper beauty columnist. In the business world she is remembered as the first promotional genius and the first to found a major U.S. cosmetics company.

Ayer was born into a wealthy but unhappy Chicago family. Her father died when she was eight, and her mother was a semi-invalid. She grew up thinking she was ugly, married at age sixteen, and had three children. She had become an acknowledged and well-traveled beauty and socialite Then one of her daughters died of smoke inhalation in the Chicago Fire of 1871. She and her husband grew apart, and in 1882, Ayer and her surviving daughters moved to New York City. After the divorce and her husband's bankruptcy, she became a furniture salesperson at an upscale store. She soon branched out into consulting and buying trips to Europe for her customers. It was on one of those trips to Paris that she bought a formula for face cream from M. Mirault, a chemist. He told her that his grandfather had prepared the cream for Mme. Recamier.

With borrowed money, she began manufacturing the cream under the name Recamier Preparations and put her name and family coat of arms on the jars.

This very public act created a scandal, as did her pamphlets promoting the beauty cream that claimed endorsements and testimonials by many famous ladies. One endorsement, by Lillie Langtry, was real, however, and business success followed. It was not to last; in 1890 one of her stockholders sued for mismanagement, and she counter sued. Ayer eventually won, but in 1893 her ex-husband and one of her daughters put her in a mental institution, and she lost all rights to the company. After fourteen months, her lawyers were able to secure her release.

She then traveled the lecture circuit telling about how the insane are treated and organizing legal help for other innocent victims. In 1896 she began writing a beauty column for the *New York World* and continued until she died in 1903 of pneumonia. She also wrote two books and invented other formulas for antiperspirants, cold creams, and a hair straightener; however, she never patented them.

Harriet Hubbard Ayer is a wonderful role model for sheer determination and perseverance. She was a pioneer in the cosmetics industry, a genius in advertising and promotion, and one of the first to establish a "woman's section" in a newspaper. When she died, the newspaper flew the flag at half-mast, explaining that she was the best man on the staff (Ayer, p. 284).

See also: Beauty Industry

Further Reading

Ayer, Margaret Hubbard and Isabella Taves. *The Three Lives of Harriet Hubbard Ayer.*
"Harriet Ayer (1869–1903)." In Oppedisano, p. 24–27.
Vare and Ptacek, p. 61–66.

B

Bajaj, Kavelle (1950–), Network Service Provider

Kavelle Bajaj was among the first to found a computer network service provider company at a time when the industry was in disarray. The company, I-Net, was eighteenth on *Working Woman*'s top woman-owned companies list in 1994. By the time she sold the company to Wang in 1996, revenues exceeded $300 million.

Bajaj was born and raised in India. Her father owned a construction company, and the family traveled with him all over the country. She graduated from Delhi University with a BS in home economics. Her marriage to Ken Bajaj was arranged by the couple's families, according to local custom—they had met only a few times. He was working at Wayne State University in Detroit, and she accompanied him back to the United States where their two sons were born.

In the early 1980s she decided to start a business. Bajaj chose computers because she understood that this was a wide-open field and one in which she could excel. She founded I-Net in 1985. The company provided services for computer-based networks, filling an empty niche in the industry. Her husband loaned her $5,000, with the proviso that she try it for six months; and she started in her basement with eight employees. The following year, I-Net was certified as a disadvantaged minority enterprise by the Small Business Administration, giving her special access to government contracts. Bajaj's first large project was a $130,000 office integration project for the Federal Railroad Administration. The company grew swiftly, and she hired Ken in 1988 as executive vice president. He handled business development, operations, and some technical work; she concentrated on contracts and financials. Her success was mostly due to timing; there were many different brands of computer equipment at the time, and her firm facilitated the integration of these various machines. With a reputation for problem solving, by 1991 I-Net had 500 employees at sixteen locations. Its revenues in 1990 were $30 million, mostly from government contracts. By 1992 sales were $95 million; and by 1994, over $200 million, with 2000 employees in 38 cities in 22 states.

These successes were tempered, in 1995, when the Government Accounting Office accused Bajaj of misrepresenting herself as a minority owner. Prosecutors said that she had claimed to be a U.S. citizen four months before her naturalization was final and that she had overstated her educational credentials. She defended herself, claiming that the charges were unbalanced and unfair. Shortly thereafter, Bajaj sold the company to Wang for $206.7 million. Ken Bajaj stayed on as president of the new Wang subsidiary.

Bajaj won several awards, including the Woman of Enterprise Award from Avon and U.S. Small Business Administration in 1993; and the Entrepreneur of the Year Award from *Inc.*, Ernst & Young, and Merrill Lynch in the woman-owned business category. I-Net was named one of the top 10 minority businesses by *Government Computer News* in 1993, and *Computer Week* ranked it among the top ten small businesses dealing with information technology in 1994. *Federal Computer Week* named her to the Fed 100—people who have had the most impact on federal information technology. She was very active mentoring other women entrepreneurs at national conferences and in a county mentor/protégé program.

See also: Immigrant Businesswomen; Information Technology Industry

Further Reading

Dasgupta, Shamita Das. "Kavelle R. Bajaj." In Zia and Gail, p. 13–14.
Franklin, Mary Beth. "The Dream Lives On; Immigrant from India Founds a Business and Finds Herself."
Meer, Aziza K. "I-Net's Bajaj Built Company from Basement Up."

Balance, *see* Work/Life Balance

Ball, Lucille (1911–1989), Television Producer

Lucille Ball was the first woman to own and run one of the most important television production studios in Hollywood. She not only starred in her own television show, but also ran the studio, seeing to every detail, while raising two children. She was a Hollywood legend and the first woman to be named to the Television Academy Hall of Fame.

She was born to a former concert pianist and an electrician/telephone lineman. Her father died when she was four and her mother remarried, sending Ball and her brother to live with step-grandparents. She quit high school in

1926 at fifteen and went off to drama school in New York City. After a stint as a showroom model for designer Hattie Carnegie, she became the 1933 "Chesterfield Girl," and then moved to California and dyed her hair red.

Ball made many movies; her first big role came in 1937 in *Stage Door*. She was best known for her television series: *I Love Lucy*, 1951–1955; *The Lucy Show*, 1962–1968; *Here's Lucy*, 1968–1973; and *Life with Lucy*, 1986.

> Lucille Ball was the first woman to own and run one of the most important television production studios in Hollywood.

She was also an astute businesswoman. Ball and husband Desi Arnaz co-founded Desilu Productions in 1950. It became one of the most important companies in television history. They made the *I Love Lucy* pilot program themselves, and then went on to shoot the series on film in front of a live audience. They were the first to use this technique, and were also the first to use the films for reruns, a lucrative idea. The peak of that show was the birth of their baby boy on television. There were 44 million viewers that night. In 1958 Arnaz bought RKO and enlarged it to thirty-five sound stages. Desilu went public the following year. In 1960 Ball and Arnaz divorced and two years later Ball bought Arnaz's shares for $2.5 million. She was the chairman of the board, and although she always said she was a reluctant businesswoman, Ball managed everything, including final approval of every project. She had a reputation for being tough, shrewd, and bossy, but appreciative of employees' efforts.

When she took over Desilu, it was the largest film and television studio in the world, but also in financial trouble. Ball was determined to set it on its feet again, and succeeded in five years. In 1967 she sold it to Gulf & Western for $17 million. While starring on Broadway in *Wildcat*, Ball met and married Gary Norton. After she sold Desilu, they started Lucille Ball Productions with Ball as president and Norton as vice president. They produced the *Here's Lucy* series, several movies, and developed programs for HBO and other cable channels. Ball and her businesses dominated television for more than twenty years. She received many honors and awards: the Emmy for best comedienne in 1952, 1955, 1967 and 1968; the Golden Apple Award in 1973; the Ruby Award in 1974; and Entertainer of the Year in 1975. In 1984 she was the first woman named to the Television Academy Hall of Fame and to the *Working Woman* Hall of Fame in 1986. She won the 1989 Television Academy of Arts and Sciences' Governors Award—another first for a woman. In 1996 *TV Guide* called her one of the 50 greatest TV stars of all time. She was posthumously honored with the Presidential Medal of Freedom. When she died, New York City's Museum of Broadcasting held "A Tribute to Lucille Ball" which ran for one month.

See also: Entertainment Industry

Further Reading
Ball, Lucille. *Love, Lucy*. New York: Boulevard Books, 1997.
Brady, Kathleen. "The CEO of Comedy."

"Lucille Ball." In O'Dell, p. 21–39.
Sanders, Coyne Steven. *Desilu: The Story of Lucille Ball and Desi Arnaz.*

Balverde-Sanchez, Laura (1951–), Food Manufacturer

Laura Balverde-Sanchez bought an almost-bankrupt sausage company and completely turned it around in five years through a series of management and marketing initiatives. As a woman in a male-dominated industry, meat packing, her success was due to her business acumen, perseverance, and working seventy-hour weeks.

She was born to immigrants from Mexico who lived in Los Angeles. Her family life was imbued with not only a hard work ethic but also the highest respect for an education. Balverde-Sanchez's mother was a sewing-machine operator and Laura helped her at night after dinner. Her father was a machinist. The family moved to Monterey Park, California, in 1959. She attended California State in Los Angeles for one year, and then transferred to UCLA, earning a degree in psychology in 1973 as well as an MPA at the University of Southern California.

To pay for her education, Balverde-Sanchez worked four jobs while carrying a full load of courses. From 1974 to 1982, her night job was teaching English as a second language for the Los Angeles school system. During the day, her first job was in the labor relations department of General Telephone of California. Her goal there was to be a manager in three years, but she resigned after being passed over in favor of a male co-worker. She then went to work as personnel director for Foremost Foods.

In 1981 she was diagnosed with a tumor. It was benign, but nevertheless, this led to a re-examination of her life and career. Because she had always wanted to own a shop, she bought an antique store. The following year she married Joe Sanchez, owner of a chain of grocery markets. In 1983 she and Joe and two other partners bought the El Rey Sausage Company. The company was almost bankrupt, losing money, the product was off the shelves, and credit was nonexistent.

The board asked Balverde-Sanchez to run El Rey, and she began the turn-around. She hired accountants, cut staff from nine to three, packed sausage herself, designed new packaging, changed the logo, and proceeded with sales and marketing grocery store by grocery store. Her creditors demanded that she pay the bills immediately, and it took almost two years for the sausage to be accepted by wholesale distributors who had member stores. She built the business back up through in-house visits and demonstrations with free samples. She encouraged employees to develop chorizo recipes inserted in each package. It was a rough time, but by 1987 she had sales of $3.1 million and thirty-seven employees. By 1988 sales were $4.5 million, she had renovated a

60,000 square foot plant, complete with a tasting and sanitation lab, and had 51 employees. By 1990 El Rey products were sold in fifteen western and southern states, labeled in English and Spanish with plans to include an Asian-language format as well since Koreans were buying her sausage in great numbers.

Balverde-Sanchez's future goals included expanding sales territory and developing new products. Unfortunately, however, the California recession in 1995 was the beginning of the end. In April 1996 the company closed primarily because of a weak economy and large increases in insurance costs.

Balverde-Sanchez is highly respected in Los Angeles and California. She was honored for her contribution to the advancement of the status of women at the Woman of Achievement Luncheon at the 1987 California Governor's Conference on Women in Business, and also was named the Small Business Person of the Year by the Small Business Administration office in Los Angeles. In 1992 she was on a blue-ribbon panel to choose finalists for the chief of police in Los Angeles and she was the first Latina to serve on the Los Angeles Chamber of Commerce board. She was also the chair of a workers' compensation task force of the Council on California Competitiveness.

See also: Food Industry; Latina Businesswomen

Further Reading

Berry, Pam. "Laura Balverde-Sanchez." In Telgen and Kamp. *Notable Hispanic American Women*, p. 48–49.

Brooks, Nancy Rivera. "Business a Grind for Chorizo Queen."

"Southern California Woman: On the Job; Making It; The Personal Stories of Six Women Who Have Found Success in Individuals Ways; Laura Balverde-Sanchez; Sausage Entrepreneur."

Banking

The first woman bank officer in New York City was Virginia Furman, who was hired by Columbia Trust Company to start a woman's department in 1919. Other New York banks discovered that women had money to deposit and they followed Columbia's example of hiring women as assistant secretaries in charge of the woman's department. These women, six in all, were untrained and had little idea of what they were supposed to do. The bank executives didn't either. Because they were not allowed to join the American Bankers Association, the six women formed the National Association of Bank Women in 1921 to exchange ideas and to instill professionalism in their positions. By the end of the following year, there were fifty-nine members in eighteen states and twenty-eight cities. The criteria were that members be officers—from president to assistant cashier. By the end of 1925, 2,134 bank women were members, including ninety-three cashiers and 1,885 assistant cashiers. In 1929 the number of eligible members had grown to 4,000, two-thirds of whom were assistant cashiers. The Great Depression caused the closing of most of the women's departments and many women officers lost their jobs. After 1941 banks employed women by the thousands to fill jobs vacated by men serving in World War II. A 1944 report showed that the employee ratio shifted during this time to six females for every one male. A 1946 National Association of Bank Women survey stated, "In banks with job evaluation programs, the prejudice against employing women in most bank jobs had disappeared by the end of the war." Banks even began to promote women to executive positions. By 1960 women made up 90 percent of the bank clerks and tellers, but very few of the bank executives. Also, banks seldom provided loans to women without a man's signature.

In the late 1960s and early 1970s, the civil rights and women's movements pushed for equality. Part of both movements was inclusion in all levels of business and society. Legislation and changing attitudes opened up opportunities. A 1971 study by the Council on Economic Priorities noted that women in banks were primarily tellers or cleaners. Banks rationalized that not enough women were trained for executive positions. The reality was that women were not encouraged to be a part of training programs that led to these positions. By 1974, 827,000 women were employed in banks, 25 percent of whom were officers and managers. Not one was an executive, although thirteen of the top banks had women on their boards of directors. Women's banks evolved as one result of bankers' discriminatory practices. The first women's bank was formed in 1919; however in 1926 it merged with a bank run by men.

In the 1970s at the height of the women's movement, women's banks became a viable way around sexist lending practices. Prominent women activists in New York City started the first in 1975. It was called The First Women's Bank. Its goal was to serve the needs of women depositors and woman-owned businesses. At the time banks often refused to lend to women entrepreneurs on the grounds that it was too risky. Other women's banks followed; at the height of the movement in the 1980s, there were fifteen spread across the country, mostly in large cities: Los Angeles, San Francisco, Atlanta, Washington DC, and Denver.

They were small, with a small loan portfolio, usually conservatively run, and not profitable for several years. Eventually, as other banks began to change their outlook, instigated marketing programs aimed at women, and stopped discriminating against women needing loans, the need for women's banks disappeared. They either merged with larger banks or were subsumed by them. All changed their names to better reflect their management and customer base. The last female-run bank was Denver's Women's Bank of Colorado, which became the Colorado Business Bank in 2002.

In the later 1980s and 1990s, as banks went through a series of mergers, downsizing, and reengineering, they saw growth as important for survival. The burgeoning number of women entrepreneurs was a potential customer base. The growing numbers of women in undergraduate and graduate business programs meant a growing pool of women employees, often in management and upper management positions. Federal legislation also encouraged hiring women. By 1996 a Catalyst report showed 8.4 percent of the executives in commercial banks were women, 22 percent of the executives in savings banks, and women accounted for 70 percent of the entire banking workforce. The largest banks began to write diversity into their mission statements and policies and to look at family-friendly benefits.

Countering these gains, a 1999 Financial Women International survey of the top 100 community banks found no women CEOs and only 16 percent of all executive management positions were held by women. Three years later 67 percent of the workforce in commercial banks and 69 percent in savings banks were women. In the fifty largest publicly held banks, only 13 percent of the top executives were women.

Outright discrimination has diminished, but the glass ceiling still exists. In many cases, women who have succeeded credit a strong male mentor. Some women left to begin their own businesses. One part of the industry where women have excelled is private banking. In ten of the largest private-banking and wealth-management companies, women are executives. *Business Week* explained: "The nature of private banking plays to women's strengths" (February 4, 2002, p. 98). Private banking success hinges on establishing successful long-term relationships with clients, and developing trust and rapport.

See also: Finance Industry; Financial Women International

Further Reading

Allison, Melissa. "Women in Banking's Upper Ranks Still Rare, But They Prefer to Focus on the Future."

Council on Economic Priorities. *Women and Minorities in Banking: Shortchanged Update.*

Gildersleeve, Genieve. *Women in Banking: A History of the National Association of Bank Women.*

Holliday, Karen Kahler. "Breaking into the Old Boys' Club."

Banta, Vivian (1950–), Insurance Executive

In March 2000 Vivian Banta was appointed executive vice president and CEO of the U.S. Consumer Group at Prudential Insurance Company of America, earning her the number 45 spot on the 2000 *Fortune* list of the most powerful women in corporate America. In February 2001 she was named an executive vice president of Prudential Financial, Inc. In 2002 she rose to number 27 on the *Fortune* list when she became vice chairman, insurance.

She was at Chase Manhattan Bank for ten years. Banta's final position there was executive vice president and group executive of global investor services, responsible for the bank's growth in the global custody business. She was replaced as a result of a merger with Chemical Bank in 1996, so she became an independent consultant. One of her jobs was as a one-day-per-week consultant with Prudential. That company, in financial straits because of a very large settlement granted to disgruntled policy holders, wished to rebuild and construct a strategy for individual financial services. Banta not only built the strategy through teamwork involving the entire company, but also eventually became the head of that department, appointed senior vice president of individual financial services—the division she had reorganized. She was responsible for finance, communication, and business development.

The following March Banta rose to her present position where she oversees salespeople, developers, and life, property, and casualty insurance. The division has $15.6 billion in revenues. In February 2001 she was also appointed executive vice president of the entire company. In September 2002 the company reorganized under four vice chairmen who comprise the CEO function. Banta is one of the four, in charge of the $16 billion insurance division. Her management style focuses on teamwork. As a consultant, she was able to motivate and meld a large number of employees into a team working together to improve the company. Banta's strategy was to listen carefully to everyone, both about their concerns and what they saw as opportunities for change and growth.

Banta is married with two stepsons. In February 2003 she was honored by the National Council for Research on Women at its annual Women Who Make a Difference Awards Dinner.

Further Reading

Fitzgerald, Beth. "CEO of Prudential's Financial Services Unit Started as Part-Time Consultant."
Holliday, Karen Kahler. "Breaking into the Old Boys' Club."
Ress, David. "Prudential Taps Executive to Lead Financial Service Unit."

Banuelos, Romana Acosta (1925–), Food Manufacturer

Romana Banuelos founded and managed a nationwide tortilla company in 1949, founded the Pan-American Bank in 1965, and served as treasurer of the United States from 1971 to 1974, the first Mexican American to hold that position.

She was born in 1925 in a small Arizona mining town but grew up in Sonora, Mexico, where her mother made and sold empanadas to local restaurants and bakeries, teaching Banuelos the important lesson of working with what she had.

By the time she was nineteen, Banuelos was divorced with two sons. In 1944 she moved to Los Angeles, married, and in two years saved $400 by working in a laundry and clothing factory. She bought a tortilla machine, a grinder, and a fan and opened her downtown business in 1949, making $36 the first day. She named it Ramona's Mexican Food Products, Inc. after a California folk heroine, and soon she was selling to restaurants and stores. Thirty years later the company had 400 employees, twenty-two different products, and sales of $12 million. By 1990 it was the largest independent food-processing plant in California.

With the business prospering, Banuelos turned her attention to the Hispanic community. She established a company scholarship and in 1965 co-founded the Pan-American National Bank whose mission was to help Hispanics start businesses and to increase the community financial base. Banuelos was chair of the board, the first of three terms. In 1969, the same year she was named Outstanding Business Woman of the Year. Ten years later, the bank's deposits were over $38 billion with assets over $41 billion.

Shortly after President Richard Nixon nominated her as U.S. treasurer in 1971, immigration agents arrested thirty-six suspected aliens in a well-publicized raid on her factory. Banuelos's claim that this was politically motivated was confirmed. In December, she took the oath of office and served until February 1974.

In 1975 she received an honorary doctorate of business administration from the City University of Los Angeles. The American Bicentennial Research Institute listed Banuelos as a "Valuable Resource" in 1976. The next year the East Los Angeles Community Union gave her the Board of Directors Woman Achievement Award.

All three of her children work in Ramona's Mexican Food Products, Carlos Torres as a vice president. Banuelos is president of Ramona's and the Pan-American National Bank as well as manager of Ramona's Mexican Food Products Scholarship foundation, which annually awards three full scholarships to Mexican American students.

See also: Food Industry; Latina Businesswomen

Further Reading

Garcia-Johnson, Ronie-Richele. "Romania Acosta Banuelos (1925–) Businesswoman, Former U.S. Treasurer." In Telgen and Kamp, p. 49–51.

Meier, Matt S. *Mexican American Biographies*, p. 25.

Barad, Jill Elikann (1951–), Toy Manufacturer

Jill Barad, one of three women CEOs in *Fortune* 500 companies from 1997 to 2000, was the first woman to rise through the ranks and become president and CEO of Mattel Inc. In the first *Fortune* list of the most powerful women in corporate America in 1998, she was sixth. Her tough management style, combined with an ability to anticipate consumer trends in popular culture, made her a success. Due to a particularly bad acquisition decision combined with large losses, however, Mattel's board of directors asked her to resign in February 2000.

Barad was born in New York City; her mother was a pianist and artist, and her father a television and film director and producer. She was raised to believe that she could be anything she wanted to be, but had to earn it, whether it was respect or money or prestige. Dreaming of being an actress, in high school she modeled bell-bottoms and focused on makeup. With an interest in selling, she worked as a beauty consultant for Love Cosmetics while at Queens College, graduating in 1973 with a BA in English and psychology.

While assisting Dino de Laurentiis on a film, Barad spent one day in a bit part then decided against acting. She worked for Coty Cosmetics in 1976 and 1977, first as an assistant product manager of marketing, then as product manager. In 1978 she married Thomas Barad, moved to California, and worked for the advertising agency Wells, Rich and Greene, where she was assigned Max Factor as a client. Barad quit in 1979 prior to her son's birth.

She returned to work as the product manager of marketing in Mattel's novelty department in 1981, but her first project, "A Bad Case of Worms," failed. Barad asked for another job and became the marketing director for Barbie from 1982 to 1983. One of her creations was She-Ra in the Masters of Universe line, the first action figure for girls. Barad progressed in marketing until she transferred to product development in 1986 when Mattel retrenched due to lagging sales and profits. She earned a reputation as a rejuvenator of brands and a person with a flair for anticipating trends. Barad's successes included the launch of a new doll line, Li'l Miss Makeup; and the skyrocketing sales of Barbie, which became the major part of Mattel's profits. She developed Day-to-Night Barbie, whose clothes converted from daywear into elegant evening clothes, 'career' Barbies with the slogan, "we girls can do anything," and expanded the Hot Wheels line.

In 1989 Barad was promoted from executive vice president of marketing and worldwide product development to the president of the girls and active toys division and, in 1990, to the co-president and board member of Mattel USA. As president and COO of Mattel Inc. in 1992, she sought assurance that she would succeed CEO John Amerman. She did in 1996, becoming one of two female heads of a *Fortune* 500 company. Amerman remained as chairman of the board.

Barad painted the office in bright colors, instituted benefits to domestic partners, and extended Christmas vacations to sixteen days. Barbie sales reached $1.9 billion, 38 percent of Mattel's sales. Her major initiatives were partnerships with companies such as Disney, Nickelodeon, and McDonald's. She also attempted to broaden the market globally, acquiring companies including Pleasant Rowland's American Girl Company. To compete in the high-tech division of toys, she launched Barbie computer games and high-tech toys for boys, but the Learning Company software division incurred major losses. After a particularly heavy loss in the fourth quarter of 1999, Barad resigned as CEO of Mattel on February 2, 2000. Her severance pay, with stock options and insurance, was $47 million.

Barad's management style focused on communication and teamwork. She was an inspirational and motivational hands-on manager who expected, and got the best from her staff, through a combination of charm, toughness, and talent. She had a reputation for knowing and following the trends in popular culture with a sharp sense of style in both packaging and product. She loves challenges and truly believes there's no such thing as "can't." She rose to power through unceasing hard work in Mattel's gender-bias-free atmosphere. Barad was pregnant with her second son when promoted to head the toy division and, although her family was important to her, continued working. Her husband chose to stay home with the boys. She found the travel requirement was the most difficult part of raising a family and running a company.

Barad won many awards, including her place on the *Fortune* most powerful women list (moving to number 25 in 1999 because of Mattel's decrease in sales). In 1992 she was one of *Business Week*'s fifty top women in business. She won Sara Lee's 1994 Frontrunner Award, was called "the toy industry's Princess of Power" by *USA Today* in 1988, one of the ten smartest women in America by the *Ladies Home Journal* in 1993, and one of the world's most beautiful people by *People* magazine in 1994. She also received an award from Girl Inc. She has served on the board of directors of BankAmerica, Microsoft, Reebok, Arco Toys, Pixar, Claremont University Center, Town Hall of California, Leap Wireless International, the advisory board of Children Affected by AIDS Foundation, the UCLA executive board for the Medical Sciences, the board of governors of Children's Miracle Network, and the board of trustees of Queens College.

Further Reading
"Barad, Jill Elikann." *Current Biography Yearbook 1995*, p. 35–38.
Maters, Kim. "It's How You Play the Game."
Morris, Kathleen. "The Rise of Jill Barad."

Barcelo, Maria Gertrudes (1800–1852), Gambling Enterprises Operator

Maria Gertrudes Barcelo, or La Tules (a diminutive of Gertrudes), was, according to Janet Lecompte, "the only woman in Santa Fe and perhaps New Mexico to start a business, continue it, improve and develop it, and succeed with it" (Lecompte, *La Tules*, p. 10). She was famous in the 1830s and 1840s for her most fashionable and elegant gambling house that was visited by all the important men of the era before, during, and after the Mexican-American War.

She was born in the province of Sonora in 1800, one of four siblings, all of whom were educated—her brother became New Mexico's superintendent of schools. In the early 1820s the family immigrated to Valencia. Barcelo married Don Manuel Antonio Sisneros in 1823, but kept her maiden name, her property, and the right to enter into contracts and institute legal proceedings, as was common in her culture. What was not so common was the privilege of entertaining her friends in whatever manner she wished.

Her first recorded gambling operation was in 1824 at Real de Dolores de Oro, the first mine in New Mexico. Although illegal, gambling was a Mexican pastime, and only small fines were assessed against operators, even in New Mexico. During 1825 La Tules was fined forty-three pesos and, in 1826, twenty-five pesos. There are no records of her activities from 1826 to 1835, when she was well established in Santa Fe as the best monte dealer.

In 1837 General Manuel Armijo, governor of Santa Fe and a close friend of La Tules, changed the assessment to fees instead of fines, thus legalizing gambling by passing an ordinance authorizing its licensing and taxing. In 1839 La Tules opened her own establishment at Number 37, Calle de Muralla, the most opulent, elegant, and fashionable in town, and she proceeded to enjoy her position as a favorite in Santa Fe high society. With a considerable reputation and fortune, she was renowned for her business acumen, shrewdness, and sense of fashion. Many rumors surrounded her. She appeared in court records suing to collect gambling debts and also suing for slander. La Tules also became involved in trade, sending $10,000 to the United States to buy goods to sell to traders and settlers.

General Stephen Kearny occupied Santa Fe during the Mexican War of 1846–1848 and established a civilian government after General Armijo fled. La Tules was one of the first to welcome the Americans, however, the immigrants who followed looked upon her as a disreputable loose woman, dealing in sin. Her fashionableness waned although the soldiers used her gambling services. Because the Americans levied higher fees, the other games closed, and La Tules operated without competition, and rumors resurfaced. Some say she loaned a substantial amount to the occupational forces for supplies in return for attending a military ball. Another credited her with revealing a Mexican plot to overthrow the American government.

Although Mexicans and New Mexicans respected La Tules's business acumen and skills, Americans, viewing gambling as a sin, were shocked at her activities and her acceptance and renown in Santa Fe's high society. Her will shows that she died a wealthy woman, owning two houses, jewelry, furniture, a carriage, many mules, and enough money to educate, clothe, and support two adopted daughters. La Tules's own two children had died in infancy. Her funeral, which cost over $3,000, was elaborate and attended by nearly the entire city of Santa Fe.

See also: Entertainment Industry; Entrepreneurs; Latina Businesswomen, Western Businesswomen

Further Reading

Foster, Sally. "Maria Gertrudes Barcelo (1800–1852) Entrepreneur." In Telgen and Kamp, *Notable Hispanic American Women,* p. 51–52.

Lecompte, Janet. "La Tules: The Ultimate New Mexico Woman." In Glenda Riley, p. 1–21.

Lecompte, Janet. "La Tules and the Americans."

Barnes, Brenda C. (1954–), Food Industry Executive

Brenda Barnes became the highest-ranking woman executive at PepsiCo when she was named president of Pepsi-Cola South in 1992, the same year that she appeared in *Business Week*'s list of the top fifty women in business. *Fortune* named her the forty-fourth most powerful woman in corporate America in 1998, even though she resigned the year before. They felt that her power came from her position on five corporate boards: Starwood Hotels and Resorts Worldwide, Inc.; The *New York Times* Co.; Avon Products, Inc.; Tyco International; Sears, Roebuck and Company; and Lucas Arts and Entertainment.

She was raised in Chicago by her factory worker father and homemaker mother. Barnes credits them with teaching her the value of a strong work ethic and the importance of listening to other people and respecting and valuing everyone's ideas. After graduating from Augustana College with a degree in business and economics in 1975 she sorted mail, waited tables, and sold clothes. In 1976 she joined PepsiCo at $10,000 per year as a business manager for its subsidiary, Wilson Sporting Goods, a male bastion where everyone was expected to know about sports paraphernalia.

She quickly moved up in the company. In 1981 Barnes became vice president of marketing for Frito-Lay; in 1984 group director of marketing for Pepsi USA; in 1985 vice president of marketing for Pepsi-Cola Bottling Group. On a mentor's advice, she switched direction to become vice president of on-premise sales for Pepsi East the next year, and vice president of national sales and marketing for PepsiCo in 1988 before being promoted to senior vice president of corporate operations three years later.

In November of 1992 Pepsi went through a restructuring effort called Right Side Up, and Barnes, president of Pepsi-Cola South, became the chief operating officer (COO) for the Western division, reporting to the president and CEO. By 1994 she was the COO for Pepsi-Cola North America, and in 1996 she became the president and CEO when the company had sales of $7.7 billion and 30,000 employees.

After twenty-two years at PepsiCo, she resigned in September 1997, saying that she was missing her children growing-up, and she couldn't balance career and family while committing 100 percent to the company. She continued with numerous speaking engagements and served on the boards of PepsiAmericas, Staples, and Primark Extel; the board of trustees of Augustana College; and supported charities including Rosie O'Donnell's Kids Foundation.

See also: Food Industry

Further Reading
Alioto, Maryann. "Brenda Barnes; Former President and CEO of Pepsi-Cola North America."

Coolidge, Shelley Donald. "Trading 30,000 Staff for 3 Kids."
Jabbonsky, Larry. "What Makes Brenda Run?"

Barrett, Colleen C. (1944–), Airline Executive

Colleen Barrett began her working career as a secretary at Southwest Airlines. Becoming president and chief operating officer in June 2001 made her the industry's top-ranked female and only female president. She ranked number 20 on the 2001 *Fortune* list of the most powerful corporate women, rising to number 13 the next year by retaining profits during turbulent times.

She was born in Vermont, the oldest of three children of an alcoholic father and a mother who worked a six-day week at a tool-and-die company. Barrett learned from her mother to respect people and their differences and to have a sense of pride without arrogance. Because the family couldn't afford a four-year college, she attended Becker Junior College, graduating in 1964, the same year she married an airman who soon went to Vietnam. They had one son and divorced in 1970. When they were stationed in San Antonio, Texas, she worked at a law firm, aiming to be the world's best legal secretary. After three months, she became Herb Kelleher's secretary, and, by 1968 she was executive assistant to the president and corporate secretary.

After ten years of planning, Kelleher left to found Southwest Airlines, with Barrett as his executive assistant in 1971. As his right-hand person, she was promoted in 1985 to vice president of administration, responsible for customer relations, employee communication, and employee relations as well as activities related to the president's office. In 1991 she was named corporate secretary and vice president of customers. As one of three executive vice presidents in 1994 Barrett oversaw marketing, government affairs, personnel, customer relations, public relations, the frequent flyer program, and employee communications.

Southwest Airlines' unique corporate culture reflected Barrett's characteristic combination of getting the job done and an irreverent attitude. Customer satisfaction was a top priority, and in 1992 the company was number 1 in this area. It regularly recorded the fewest reports of mishandled baggage, best on-time performance, and the lowest number of customer complaints—the Triple Crown of airline performance. Barrett founded and heads the formal culture committee. In spring of 2001 Kelleher announced his retirement, although he still chaired the board and the executive committee, and Barrett became president and COO. Her role is to ensure that the culture of Southwest focused on customer satisfaction, collegiality, and high performance.

Because of a cash cushion of $1 billion, Southwest Airlines survived the decline in air travel better than most carriers after September 11. To help even more, 4,000 employees agreed to donate part of their pay to shore up the company. Barrett went on television in a series of spots designed to reassure the public and condole the grieving. Southwest was the only airline to report a profit for the fourth quarter of 2001.

She has a wonderful sense of humor and describes herself as not career-oriented, seeing herself as an ideal number-two person. With her leadership skills and talent for building consensus and a shared vision, Barrett is the people person in the company. *Wall Street Journal* named her the top-ranked woman in the airline industry, *Fortune* chose her as one of seven "Women to Watch," and *Travel Agent Magazine* called her one of the "100 Most Powerful Women in Travel." In September 2001 she and Vice Chairman James Parker were named "strategists to watch" by the *Journal of Business Strategy*. The next year Woman's Leadership Exchange gave her a Compass Award and *Business Week* named her and Parker best managers.

Further Reading
Allen, Margaret. "Southwest Airlines Head Takes Flight with Ground Control."
Gittell, Jody Hoffer. *The Southwest Airlines Way: Using the Power of Relationships to Achieve High Performance.*
Goldberg, Laura. "Southwest's New Co-Pilots; As New President, Barrett Plans to Keep Helping Airline Customers."
Woodward, Chris. "There's Something Familiar about Kelleher's Successors."
Zellner, Wendy. "Holding Steady."

Bartz, Carol A. (1948–), Software Manufacturer

Carol Bartz became CEO of Autodesk, one of the leading personal computer software manufacturers in the world in 1992. As one of two female CEOs in the high-tech industry, she was included that year in *Business Week*'s top fifty women in business. In 1998 *Fortune* listed her as one of the fifty most powerful women in the United States.

Although born in Minnesota, Bartz was raised by her grandmother on a dairy farm in Wisconsin. After attending William Woods College for Women and graduating from the University of Wisconsin with a BS in computer science, she started work in 1976 with 3M as a field systems analyst. She quit after learning that 3M didn't want women managers and went to Digital Equipment Company where she became the highest-ranking woman. In 1983 she joined Sun Microsystems, then a young company, as a customer marketing manager, and moved up to head the Federal Systems Division in 1987, tripling sales within her first year. She then became vice president of customer service in charge of 12,000 employees, half of the company workforce.

In April 1992 she joined Autodesk as the CEO, president, and chair. It had good solid computer-aided design products but floundered because of low morale, poor management, and weak marketing. The challenge of the situation appealed to Bartz. She quickly opened the lines of communication through brown-bag gatherings and team building. She eliminated unprofitable divisions, made a series of strategic acquisitions, and diversified the product lines, including digital maps and entertainment software. By 1995 Autodesk, the world's fourth largest software developer, saw revenues rise from $285 million to $455 million. In 2000 and early 2001 sales slumped, but by April the company was the fourth largest manufacturer of personal computer software. Its software was instrumental in creating the visuals for all three films nominated for 2002 Oscars in the special effects category.

As a strong advocate for women's health, education, and career issues, Bartz started internships at Autodesk so teenage girls could work on actual programming projects and encouraged employees to volunteer, on company time, at local schools. She supported telecommuting and flexible work schedules, adoption assistance, and mentoring. Teamwork and shared responsibility is her preferred management method, and she is known for her persuasive techniques and use of employee involvement in decision-making.

Bartz has won numerous awards. In 1994 she was one of two women on the *Industry Week* list of 50 R&D stars to watch and won the Donald C. Burnham Manufacturing Management Award from the Society of Manufacturing Engineers. *Vanity Fair* called her one of 200 most influential women in America in 1998, and the company was named one of the 100 best companies for working mothers by *Working Mother*. In 2001 she was the Northern California Ernst & Young Master Entrepreneur of the Year for guiding and sustaining a prosperous and innovative business. She has honorary doctorates from Worcester Polytechnic Institute and William Woods University and was appointed to President Clinton's Export Council and President Bush's Council of Advisors on Science and Technology. She served on the corporate boards of AirTouch Communications, BEA Systems, Technet, Cadence Design Systems, Cisco Systems, and Network Appliance; as well as on the board of the National Breast Cancer Research Foundation, the University of Wisconsin Business School, the Foundation for the National Medals of Science and Technology, the advisory committee of the National Association of Securities Dealers, and the California Chamber of Commerce. She is a member of the Committee of 200.

See also: Information Technology Industry

Further Reading

"Bartz, Carol." *Current Biography* (July 1999): 6–8.
"Carol Bartz: Taking AutoDesk to the Top." In Marquardt, p. 85–97.
Lewis, Peter H. "Sound Bytes; She Defines AutoDesk and Women's Issues, Too."

Beach, Sylvia (1887–1962), Publisher, Bookseller

Sylvia Beach opened the first English-language bookstore and lending library, Shakespeare and Company, in 1919 during the height of the American literary movement in Paris. It became the meeting place for such literary lions and would-be writers of the era as Ernest Hemingway, Archibald MacLeish, F. Scott Fitzgerald, Sherwood Anderson, Katherine Anne Porter, T. S. Eliot, and James Joyce. One of her greatest achievements was being the first publisher of *Ulysses*.

She was born in Baltimore to a Presbyterian minister and his artist and musician wife who was much younger. When Beach was fifteen, he became assistant pastor of the American church in Paris, where Beach formed a lifelong passion for France. Three years later the family moved to Princeton, New Jersey, but she and her mother returned many times. Her extensive knowledge was due mainly to her voracious reading and traveling, and her literary friendships. From 1907 to 1916, she traveled to Italy and Spain, finally settling in Paris where she met Adrienne Monnier, her business mentor, friend, and lifelong companion. She volunteered on a farm in Touraine in 1917 and worked for several months with the Red Cross in Serbia during World War I.

Beach opened her first bookshop in 1919 in Paris. By 1921 she had a larger store across from Monnier's bookstore on the Left Bank and specialized in experimental and avant-garde books. The many English and American expatriates used Beach's bookshop as a gathering place and lending library. Up to 90 members paid five to twelve francs per month, depending on how many books they borrowed; although she didn't charge writers who couldn't pay. Many of the influential writers all knew and loved Sylvia Beach for her endless hospitality, appreciation of their work, generosity, loyalty, and charming manner. She had a quick and playful wit, common sense, a charismatic personality, and she loved books.

After meeting James Joyce in 1920, Beach almost single-handedly supported him and his family for two years while he wrote *Ulysses*. She also hired typists, pre-sold subscriptions, intervened with the printer, published and reprinted it for eleven years when Joyce could not find another publisher because the book was considered obscene. After a judge finally decided that it was not obscene, she gave up her rights, so the book could be published by Random House. Neither Joyce nor Random House ever paid her for those rights. It was, however, her greatest contribution to literature, and her bookstore is remembered as a center for Joyce studies and the home of avant-garde literature in the early twentieth century. She also published two other works by Joyce and one by Samuel Beckett.

Beach barely made a living from the bookstore, which operated on the edge of bankruptcy for most of its twenty-two years. She and Monnier accepted food and money from their families. In 1935 Andre Gide formed Friends of Shakespeare and Company, with contributions from Andre Maurois, Archibald MacLeish, Helena Rubinstein and others, just to keep the store open. Sales remained poor into early World War II, although tourists, students, and professors bought books.

During the occupation, a German officer offered to buy Beach's last copy of *Finnegan's Wake*, which was exhibited in the window but not for sale. When she refused, he threatened her, so she closed the shop, painted out the sign, and hid all her books in an apartment upstairs. When the United States entered the war, the Germans interned her as an enemy alien for six months. After that, she lived under an assumed name as a member of a youth hostel. In 1944 when Paris was liberated, Hemingway personally liberated the shop, but because of ill health and lack of funds, she never reopened. Beach did, however, stay in Paris and lend books until she died. Her last official act was to dedicate the James Joyce Library outside Dublin, Ireland.

There is a small plaque outside 12, Rue de l'Odeon in Paris commemorating the bookstore. For Beach's services to the world of literature, she received the French Legion d'Honneur in 1938 and an honorary doctorate from the University of Buffalo. She is described on page thirty-five of Hemingway's *A Moveable Feast*.

See also: Publishing Industry

Further Reading

Beach, Sylvia. *Shakespeare and Company*.

Fitch, Noel Riley. "Sylvia Beach: Commerce, Sanctification, and Art on the Left Bank." In Susan Albertine, p. 189–206.

Fitch, Noel Riley. *Sylvia Beach and the Lost Generation: A History of Literary Paris in the Twenties and Thirties*.

McDougall, Richard. "Beach, Sylvia Woodbridge." In *Dictionary of American Biography*, Supplement 7, p. 40–41.

Beauty Industry

Although women used handwritten recipes for herbal care lotions and hair preparation from colonial times, it was not until after the Civil War that shops and beauty salons began to appear. Chemists, perfumers, drugstores, and patent-medicine hucksters sold beauty products during the 1880s, but the Victorian era, focusing on clean, natural beauty, was not conducive to artificially enhanced good looks. Many women who used beauty products were thought to be "not quite nice" or, worse yet, prostitutes.

In the 1900s with the advent of Harriet Ayer, Elizabeth Arden, Helena Rubenstein, and their skin creams and cosmetics, beauty became an important industry, offering great opportunities to women. Sarah Walker and Annie Malone began their hair-care and skin-care empires about the same time. They focused on serving the African American community and employed and trained thousands of African American women in all aspects of the business; otherwise, their only alternatives were domestic service or working in laundries.

During the 1920s the beauty entrepreneurs benefited from the new large department stores, big urban markets, and the growth of advertising. A 1912

Vogue magazine article suggested that looking healthy required lipstick and rouge; and in the 1920s women wanted to look modern with bobbed hair, short dresses, and painted faces. The Victorian standard of beauty disappeared, and the beauty magnates thrived.

In 1930 retail sales of cosmetics totaled $556 million. There were thousands of face powders, rouges, and lipsticks, and magazine articles that focused on their proper application. Because users questioned the safety of such ingredients as lead, mercury, and hormones, the Food, Drug, and Cosmetic Act was passed in 1938. Lauder, Arden, and Rubinstein's upscale, exclusive beauty salons catered to the wealthy, but their products also sold in department stores. Walker and Malone saleswomen sold door-to-door and opened beauty shops in African American neighborhoods.

During World War II the government tried to ration cosmetics, but women reacted strongly, so the order was revoked. Advertising urged women to continue to use lipstick, so they could still look feminine while working in manufacturing plants. After the war, products proliferated and improved, including deodorants and toothpastes. Kiss-proof lipstick was developed, and Estee Lauder produced bath oil. By 1948, 80 to 90 percent of women wore lipstick. When adolescent girls discovered cosmetics, the customer base expanded, and advertising blossomed into mass-market magazines for them.

During the 1960s feminists decried the use of cosmetics and other beauty-enhancing products as the objectification of women. African Americans had mixed feelings about their beauty products, particularly bleaches and hair straighteners, which represented a loss of ethnic identity. For them, the "beauty culture has been simultaneously a source of opportunity, self-expression, and controversy" (Ploski and Williams, *The Negro Almanac*, p. 100).

Cosmetics and sexuality became linked. Flower power brought a surge to flowery perfumes, and Mary Kay Ash began her company, run by women for women. During the 1980s licensing was an answer to increased competition as designers developed cosmetics. Dying one's hair to look younger became commonplace. The 1990s trends were disinfection, aromatherapy, obsession with youth, and advanced sun protection.

The beauty industry, one of the major entrepreneurial accomplishments of women, grew out of traditional women's work. It was, as Drachman says, "[a] woman's enterprise that provided unique opportunities for women" (p. 78).

Cosmetic Executive Women (www.cew.org), an organization that serves women in the cosmetic and related industries, sponsors several awards and holds an annual trade show.

Further Reading
Banner, Lois W. *American Beauty*.
Drachman, Virginia G. p. 75–97.
Peiss, Kathy Lee. *Hope In A Jar: The Making of America's Beauty Culture*.
Shaw, Anita. "Celebrating 75 Years."

Beck, Teresa (1954–), Retail Industry Executive

Teresa Beck ranked number 49 on *Fortune*'s 1998 list of most powerful women in corporate America when she was president of American Stores, the second largest food and drugstore chain in the United States. It included the Osco, Lucky, and Jewel chains with revenues of $19 billion.

Beck has lived her whole life in Utah, receiving a BS in finance and a masters degree in accounting from the University of Utah; then becoming a certified public accountant. Before joining American Stores in 1982, she was an audit manager at Ernst & Whinney and the controller at Steiner Financial Corporation.

After three years as vice president and controller of Alpha Beta Company, a subsidiary of American Stores, Beck was promoted in 1989 to senior vice president of finance, assistant secretary, and controller of the parent company, and in 1992 to executive vice president of administration. Two years later she was the executive vice president of finance; and the next year became chief financial officer and a member of the Executive Council, responsible for financial accounting, tax, audit, cash management, risk administration, and public and investor relations. She also served as treasurer, before becoming president in 1998.

After the company merged with Albertson's a few months later, Beck announced her decision to pursue personal interests. As part of the merger, she joined the Albertson's board of directors, continuing in that capacity and also as a consultant.

Beck has a reputation for financial savvy and skill in management, strategic planning, and financial and business analysis. She served on the board of directors for Textron Inc., Questar Corp., and Lexmark International Group, Inc. She has also served as a trustee of Intermountain Health Care and on the boards of the Children's Center in Utah and the Utah Partnership for Educational and Economic Development, Inc.

See also: Retailing Industry

Further Reading
"Teresa Beck Is Elected to Board of Lexmark International."
"Teresa Beck Joins Textron's Board."

Beech, Olive Ann (1903–1993), Aircraft Manufacturing Executive

"She married the boss, which was lucky for him. . . If it weren't for Olive— shrewd, ambitious, tough—the Beech Aircraft Corporation probably wouldn't have made it past the 1930s" (*Fortune*, April 4, 1983, p. 145).

Olive Mellor, born in a Kansas farm community, chose a short business course instead of high school and started work. At the newly formed Travel Air Company, a light airplane manufacturer, she quickly became office manager and secretary to the president, Walter Beech, a former barnstormer and designer of airplanes. In 1929 it merged with Curtiss-Wright, and he became vice president. In 1930 they married, and he returned to Wichita, and founded Beech Aircraft in 1932. Beech was the secretary-treasurer and in 1936 joined the board of directors. After two years the company, with sales over $1 million, led the market in 285- to 459-horsepower private and commercial planes.

Beech's husband was hospitalized in 1940 for encephalitis when their second daughter was born. During his long convalescence, Beech took over the company and led it for the next forty years. He recovered, but she handled all the business matters including obtaining $50 million in loans from thirty-six banks in order to manufacture bomber, training, and other military planes for World War II. Known for her positive and persistent attitude, Beech was president from Walter's death in 1950 until 1968, and chairwoman until 1982. Business boomed during World War II and the Korean War, and she eventually built up the commercial side to offset the slumps after each war. Later the company also expanded into missile and space contracts. From 1963 to 1975, sales rose from $74 million to $267 million. In 1980 when she sold the company to Raytheon, revenues were $600 million. She served on its board of directors and was a member of the executive committee until her death in 1993.

Known as the "First Lady of Aviation," Olive Beech won many awards, beginning in 1943 as one of the *New York Times* twelve most distinguished American women. The Women's National Aeronautical Association named her Woman of the Year in Aviation in 1951, and in 1956 she was on the cover of *Business Week*. In 1980 she was the first woman and first general aviation leader to win the Wright Brothers Memorial Trophy. The next year she was named to the Aviation Hall of Fame and in 1983 to the Hall of Fame for U.S. Business Leadership, later to be known as Junior Achievement's Global Business Hall of Fame. She also received a trophy for achievement in aerospace science and technology in 1993 from the National Air and Space Museum. Although she never went to high school, Beech was awarded honorary degrees in business administration and law.

See also: Junior Achievement's Global Business Hall of Fame

Further Reading
Bird, Caroline, p. 196–199.
Drachman, Virginia G., p. 143–147.
Jeffrey, Laura, p. 26–35, 104–105.
Leavitt, Judith A. *American Women Managers and Administrators*, p. 19–20.

Beers, Charlotte L. (1935–), Advertising Executive

In 1992 when Charlotte Beers was recruited by Ogilvy & Mather Worldwide, the fifth largest advertising agency in the world, to become its chairman and

CEO, she became the most powerful woman in advertising. She is credited with the company's turnaround and a 60 percent increase in billings. In 1999 she was ranked number 49 on *Fortune*'s list of the country's most powerful businesswomen.

Born in Beaumont, Texas, she moved to Louisiana and then Houston. Her father was an entrepreneur oilman and engineer. Growing up Beers always wanted to make a difference, not just get married. With a BS in math and physics from Baylor in 1958, she taught algebra for one year before becoming a group project manager and consumer research supervisor from 1960 to 1969 for Uncle Ben's in Houston, launching long-grain and wild-rice varieties. She moved to their advertising agency in 1969 as their first woman senior vice president; and later worked as director of client services for Sears, Kraft, Oscar Mayer, and Gillette. In 1979 she was recruited by Tatham-Laird and Kudner, an advertising agency in Chicago, as CEO and managing partner. In 1982 she was named CEO and in 1986, CEO and Chair. During this period, revenue grew from $100 million to $325 million. After the agency was acquired by the French RSCG Group Roux Seguega Cayzac and Coward in 1988, Beers remained as vice chair.

> In 1992 when Charlotte Beers was recruited by Ogilvy & Mather Worldwide to become its chairman and CEO, she became the most powerful woman in advertising.

In 1992 Beers was recruited by Ogilvy and Mather Worldwide in New York City to be chair and CEO, the highest position ever held by a woman. The 7,000-person agency was in trouble, having lost key accounts and many employees in a hostile takeover. She revitalized the company through her brand of stewardship methodology and greater focus on clients, including IBM, Shell, American Express, and Jaguar.

When Beers retired in 1996, Shelly Lazarus became CEO, the first time in American business history that one woman succeeded another as CEO of a major corporation. Beers remained chairman emeritus and in 1999, came out of retirement to chair J. Walter Thompson, another agency in need of help. Her goal was to teach brand strategy and inspire a new mission.

In 2001 at Secretary of State Colin Powell's suggestion, President George W. Bush appointed Beers Undersecretary of State for Public Diplomacy. Again, it was a challenge she could not resist, that of image-maker for the Bush administration. She featured Muslim Americans in a series of advertisements aiming to reverse anti-Americanism in Muslim countries. Unfortunately, the strategy proved unsuccessful, and in March 2003 she resigned for serious health reasons.

Beers, one of the most charismatic, client-focused executives in the advertising industry, is glamorous, with a love for drama, while at the same time, charming and business-like. She has a well-honed sense of humor and thinks charm is simply good business. A famous incident occurred during a client presentation for Sears, when she took apart and reassembled a complex drill bit, flashing her long red fingernails in the process, mesmerizing the Sears board.

Beers won several awards, beginning with National Advertising Woman of the Year from the American Advertising Federation. In 1992 the Advertising Women of the Year presented her with their Silver Medal Award, and *Business Week* listed her in the fifty top women in business. In 1997 she was inducted into the Alliance of Sales and Marketing Executives' National Sales and Marketing Hall of Fame and received the first Lifetime Achievement Award from the Advertising Women of New York. She is a fellow of the International Women's Forum Leadership Foundation and is commemorated by The Charlotte Beers Award for Brand Strategy.

See also: Advertising Industry

Further Reading

"How World's Top Woman Ad Executive Hit the Heights; Marketing: Ogilvy & Mather's CEO Charlotte Beers Is Smart, Has Rapport with Clients and Gives Her Staff Credit, Observers Say."

Neuborne, Ellen. "Mad Ave: A Star Is Reborn."

Sellers, Patricia. "Women, Sex and Power."

Benefits, *see* Employee Benefits

Bentas, Lily (1940–), Grocery Store Owner

In 1989 Lily Bentas became chairman of the convenience store chain, Cumberland Farms, which her parents had co-founded fifty years before as a door-to-door milk-sales company. After some rough years, the company has been on the *Working Woman* list of the top woman-owned companies since 1998, placing number 12 in 2001.

One of eight children, Bentas was born in 1940 to Vasilios and Aphrodite Haseotes who had immigrated to Rhode Island in 1900 and bought a small farm in Cumberland. In 1956 they opened a store in Massachusetts, gradually adding other grocery products and gas pumps, as well as processing, manufacturing, and distributing. By 1990 Bentas was chair of Cumberland Farms, the country's largest private convenience store chain, with 1100 stores employing 9,000 people in twelve states. After filing for bankruptcy in 1992, due to financial difficulties and a family feud, she reorganized in 1993 with 950 stores and 7,000 employees. By 1998 the company was number 15 on the *Working Woman* list. That year a Texas company, Suiza Foods Corporation, bought the fluid dairy division but continued to supply milk to the stores. Unfortunately, the family feud persisted, with two older brothers suing her amid claims and counterclaims.

Cumberland Farms sponsors a number of local and national charities and raises money for muscular dystrophy and cystic fibrosis.

See also: Food Industry

Further Reading
Mulvihill, Maggie. "At the Bar: Legal Actions Fueling Feud within Family."
Seneker, Harold, et al. "Great Family Fortunes."

Berman, Gail (1956–), Television Executive

Due to her phenomenal success in programming for the 2002 season, Gail Berman, president of entertainment at Fox Broadcasting, was ranked number 25 on *Fortune*'s 2003 list of the most powerful businesswomen in the United States. She was responsible for the most popular shows on television that year, *Joe Millionaire* and *American Idol*.

After graduating from the University of Maryland, she began her career in Washington, DC, in 1979 by producing *Joseph and the Amazing Technicolor Dreamcoat*, which subsequently had a two-year Broadway run. After producing other Broadway plays, Berman became executive producer for Comedy Central, the cable TV channel, producing *Sweet Life* and *Mystery Science Theater 3000*. In 1991 she became a vice president at Sandollar Television, formed by Dolly Parton and Sandy Gallin, and worked on several sitcoms and movies, becoming president in 1995. Her most successful endeavor there was *Buffy the Vampire Slayer*, a project she championed with gusto, believing that teenage girls needed a strong role model. Although she became the president of Regency Television, a Fox affiliate, in 1998 she continued to be *Buffy*'s executive producer. While at Regency, she was responsible for *Roswell*, *Malcolm in the Middle*, and *Angel*.

In May 2000 Fox, then in decline and losing ratings, recruited Berman to rebuild the company and have day-to-day oversight of program development and scheduling, marketing, and promotion. She liked the challenge of turning the network's fortunes around and, by November, ratings were up. In March 2003 she was in the midst of reality television, with Fox thriving due to *American Idol, Joe Millionaire,* and *Temptation Island*.

Her management style is down to earth, but she is very passionate about her projects and will champion them to the best of her ability. With a strong belief in a diverse workforce; one of Berman's first actions was to hire a senior vice president of diversity.

She has been named to TV's Power 50 and to *Hollywood Reporter*'s Women in Entertainment Power 50 (number 8 in 2000 and number 4 in 2001). She won the RP International Women of Vision Award in 2001, was named to *Electronic Media*'s 2002 list of the most powerful women in television, and was a Lucy Award Honoree from Women in Film in 2003. She and husband Bill Masters have twins, a son and a daughter.

See also: Broadcasting Industry

Further Reading
Adalian, Josef and Michael Schneider. "Berman Braves Dangers at Fox Top."
Katz, Richard. "Regency on Hot Streak."
Zamora, Dulce. "Gail Berman: TV Topper Choreographs Own Fox Trot."

Bern, Dorrit J. (1950–), Retail Executive

Dorrit Bern revived Pennsylvania-based retail apparel company, Charming Shoppes, bringing the company from near-bankruptcy to number 11 on the 2001 *Working Woman* list of the top woman-owned companies in the United States.

She was born in 1950. Her mother, a very successful career woman, was a buyer for the retail company, Bon Marché, and the first woman promoted to every position she held. Bern graduated in business in 1972 from the University of Washington. In 1973, she joined Allied Stores as a buyer, and in 1977 was promoted to division merchandise manager. In 1979, she moved to Dallas to be a buyer for Joske's Department Store, a division of Allied Stores. Two years later, she moved to Seattle to Bon Marché, another Allied division. In 1987 she joined Sears as the special assistant to the vice president of women's apparel and then was promoted to group vice president for women's apparel and home fashions. By 1992 she was the vice president of women's apparel at Sears.

In August 1995 she became the CEO, vice chairman of the board and president of Charming Shoppes. The company was about to fail, but Bern turned it around by closing 251 stores, cutting staff, refinancing debt, and overhauling inventory systems. She also added junior sportswear and petite sizes. By June 1997 the company was solvent and Bern was one of the ten highest-paid CEOs in Philadelphia. She was elected chairman of the board in February 1998 and is credited with saving the company.

Since then Charming Shoppes has grown through the acquisitions of Modern Women, Catherine Stores, and Lane Bryant. It is now the largest plus-size specialty apparel retailer in the country with nearly 2,500 stores. Bern has also expanded the junior and teen apparel as well as sportswear. In February 2002 the company went public company on the NASDAQ stock exchange. One year later, there were 2,242 stores in forty-eight states, under the names Lane Bryant, Fashion Bug, Fashion Bug Plus, Catherine's Plus Sizes, Monsoon, and Accessorize.

Bern is a strong believer in corporate social responsibility; she regularly donates new winter coats to children who need them in the areas where she has stores and also gives new career outfits to women in job training programs.

Her advertisements focus on social messages such as child poverty, abuse, and gun control. She is a member of Business for Social Responsibility and the Committee of 200; and sits on the boards of Southern Company and Brunswick Corporation. She was named one of Pennsylvania's Best 50 Women in Business in 1997 and received the 1998 Women of Distinction Award from the *Philadelphia Business Journal*, NAWBO, and the Forum for Executive Women. In 2001 she was named the Ernst & Young Retail Entrepreneur of the Year.

Bern is married with three sons. Her husband was the CFO for a computer company, and later became a consultant working from home. They live in Illinois and she commutes to Charming Shoppes headquarters in Philadelphia during the week. The family is dedicated to Sunday family dinners.

See also: Retailing Industry

Further Reading
Lublin, Joann S. "How One CEO Juggles a Job and a Family Miles Apart."
Wilson, Marianne. "Thinking Big."
www.charmingshoppes.com

Bernard, Betsy J. (1956–) Telecommunications Executive

In March 2001 Betsy Bernard became the president and CEO of the AT&T Consumer Division, and in that position, the highest-ranking woman in the telecommunications industry. She was named the twenty-third most powerful businesswoman in the United States on the 2001 *Fortune* list and, in 2002, number 16. In December 2002 she was appointed president of AT&T Corporation.

She is a native of Holyoke, Massachusetts; her mother was a radio and television personality in the state; her father owned an equipment-making company. She graduated from St. Lawrence University with a degree in political science in 1977. During her college years, Bernard spent time studying in Kenya and holding summer internships in the Massachusetts legislature and, after her junior year, at AT&T. The latter led to a job in management following graduation. Her other degrees were an MBA from Fairleigh Dickinson University in 1983 and an MS in management as a Sloan Fellow at Stanford in 1988.

She stayed at AT&T for eighteen years, holding a variety of executive positions in marketing, sales, product management and customer service. In the early 1980s she developed a marketing strategy for the company that led to 75 percent of American businesses choosing it for their long-distance telecommunication needs. In 1996 she became president and CEO of Pacific Bell Communications, in charge of the company's entry into the long distance business.

It was a time of upheaval for the telecommunications industry, with a change in the entire infrastructure. In April of 1997, Pacific Bell merged with SBC

Communications and she resigned. The following month she joined a telecommunications start-up, Avirnex Communications Group, as president, CEO and board member. One year later Bernard became president of the U.S. West long distance division with responsibility for all retail markets. The following month her title became executive vice president of marketing, making her the senior woman on the executive team and the highest-ranking woman in any former regional bell company. Her responsibilities were enormous for both U.S. West and, after the takeover, Qwest.

In January 2001 Bernard retired, saying she needed a sabbatical. It lasted three months. In March of that year, she became the head of AT&T's consumer division. Her job was running the long-distance business with its more than 60 million customers and annual revenues of $18.9 billion. In an October 2002 reorganization, she was appointed president of AT&T Corporation. Her responsibilities include the business services division, network services, international operations, and AT&T laboratories.

Bernard is known for great leadership with the ability to inspire, tackle challenges, and have a vision for the company. She is very aggressive in recruiting, hiring, and promoting women and minorities, making sure other women receive opportunities for growth. She is said to be fun to work with and energetic, with a high degree of optimism and a deep understanding of the complex technologies in the industry. When asked about the difficulty of her job, she said that she is attracted to jobs outside her comfort zone (Backover, p. 3B). She is single with no children and likes to run and ski.

In 1996 Bernard was named one of the San Francisco Bay area's "Most Influential Business Women," and in 2000 was a finalist for the Colorado Women's Chamber of Commerce Athena Award. In December 2002 she was included on *Network World's* list of the most powerful people in the network industry. She sits on the board of directors of Zantaz.com, Principal Financial Group, Serco Group, PLC, and Astracon. She is an active member of Women's Forum West and the International Women's Forum.

Further Reading
Backover, Andrew. "AT&T Consumer Chief Loves a Challenge."
Bronikowski, Lynn. "Woman of Vision."
Smith, Jerd. "Shattered Glass; Talented Qwest Exec Credits Federal Order for Women's Advance."

Bernick, Carol Lavin (1952–), Toiletries Manufacturing Executive

Carol Bernick is the vice president of Alberto-Culver and president of Alberto-Culver USA. She is the daughter of Leonard Lavin who built the company into the worldwide toiletries company it is today. The company has been on the *Working Woman* list of woman-owned companies since 1998; in

2001, it was number 7. Bernick and her mother, Bernice Lavin, are the principal stockholders. Her husband is the CEO and president of the company.

She was born and raised in Chicago and graduated from Tulane University in 1974. In college, she worked as a counselor for disabled children. In 1974 she interviewed at Alberto-Culver without her father's knowledge; he didn't believe women should go into business even though he and his wife built the company together. Carol did get a job on the marketing staff. One of the first products she created and developed was Static Guard anti-static spray. In 1975 she met and married Howard Bernick who joined the company in 1977. From 1979 to 1981 she was director of new products; her new product during that time was Baker's Joy baking spray. In 1981 she was promoted to director of new business development and developed Mrs. Dash. In 1984 she joined the board of directors with the position of vice president. In 1988 she became a group vice president and Howard was the chief operating officer; and in 1990 she was promoted to executive vice president of worldwide marketing. In this job she added the identification of worldwide marketing opportunities to her responsibilities for new business development, marketing research, and advertising.

Her father retired in 1994 as CEO and president of the company. Her husband took over these positions and created a new position for her, the president of Alberto-Culver USA. She was responsible for the four domestic divisions, toiletries, household/groceries products, professional services and food services. In 1996 the company bought St. Ives hair care products and the following year launched a new line of shampoos called Cortexx. The company's sales increased substantially with these changes. In 1998 Bernick was promoted to vice chairman of the company and president of Alberto-Culver North America which subsumed Alberto-Culver USA and included Alberto-Culver Canada and Cosmetic Laboratories of America. By the end of 2000 revenues were up 7.7 percent; and net income, 3.9 percent. In September 2002 the Consumer Products Worldwide unit was added to her responsibilities.

Carol and Howard Bernick complement each other. Howard is known as the numbers man and she is known for her creative and innovative ideas. They have turned the company around since her father retired, beginning with a change from his top-down management style, improving compensation problems, and looking for acquisitions. The office atmosphere is friendly; Carol believes in celebrating sales victories, promotions, and anniversaries. She has cut turnover in half; her goal is to have the company included in *Fortune*'s annual list of the 100 Best Companies to Work for.

Bernick is a dedicated fund-raiser for charitable causes. Because she experienced two difficult, high-risk pregnancies, she was the founder and driving force behind the establishment of the Prentice Women's Hospital and Maternity Center of Northwestern Memorial Hospital. She also influenced the Alberto-Culver executives to pledge $1 million to the cause. She won the Leadership in Business Award from the Chicago YWCA in 1992 and was the commencement speaker at Tulane in 1994. She sits on the board of directors of Northwestern Memorial Hospital Corporation, the women's board of the Five Hospitals Elderly Program and the Boy's and Girl's Clubs of Chicago, and is a trustee of Lincoln Academy in Illinois.

See also: Beauty Industry

Further Reading

Bernick, Carol Lavin. "When Your Culture Needs a Makeover."

Freeman, Laurie. "Carol Bernick; Alberto VP Stays Busy with Product Development, Helping Raise Funds for Chicago Women's Hospital."

Tode, Chantal. "Alberto-Culver: Doing it Quietly; Health and Beauty Aids Report."

Weimer, De'Ann. "Daughter Knows Best."

Beverage Industry, *see* Food Industry

Birnbaum, Sheila (1940–), Product Liability Lawyer

Sheila Birnbaum was named to the 1998 *Fortune* list of the most powerful women in corporate America because of her expertise in product liability cases. She speaks on the intricacies of the issues frequently and is regularly quoted in newspapers such as the *New York Times* and *Wall Street Journal*.

She was born in New York City and wanted to be a lawyer from an early age. Birnbaum was educated at Hunter College of City University of New York, earning a BA in 1960 and an MA in 1962. She received her law degree from New York University Law School in 1965, was invited to join Phi Beta Kappa in law school, and was admitted to the bar in 1965. Immediately after graduation, she joined Berman & Frost as an associate and became a partner in 1970.

In 1972 Birnbaum began her teaching career as an associate professor at Fordham University. She became a pioneer in the field of product liability, writing a book on the subject in 1975. She taught at Fordham until 1978 saying that she'd never had a woman professor in law school and wished to do something she had not seen a woman do. She moved to NYU in 1978 as a full professor and associate dean, their first woman dean.

In 1984 she went back to private practice as a partner at Skadden, Arps, Slate, Meagher & Flom. Birnbaum was recruited to be the head and founder of their sixty-person product liability practice. In 1996 she was made a senior partner. Her cases since 1984 have dealt with a variety of issues: anti-nausea drugs for pregnant women, the Dalkon shield, asbestos, hazardous waste materials, silicone breast implants, and tobacco.

Birnbaum is a member of the New York City Bar Association where she is on the Executive Committee, and the American Bar Association, where she chairs the product liability committee. In 2000 the *National Law Journal* ranked her among the 100 most influential lawyers in America. She holds the 2000 Margaret Brent Women Lawyers of Achievement Award, given by the American Bar Association Commission on Women in the Profession to honor outstanding women lawyers who have achieved excellence in their specialty and who also have paved the way to success for other women lawyers.

Further Reading

Birnbaum, Sheila. *Product Liability: Law, Practice, Science.*

Wechsler, Pat. "How Do You Get to Skadden? Practice, Practice, Practice."

Bishop, Hazel Gladys (1906–1998), Inventor, Entrepreneur

In 1950 Hazel Bishop invented and introduced what she called "Lasting Lipstick" and the press dubbed "kiss-proof lipstick." She founded Hazel Bishop, Inc., which was initially very successful. Four years later, she lost the company due to a hostile stock takeover and, in litigation, lost the right to use her own name on products. Undaunted, she went on to develop a leather cleaner, a perfume, and a salve for protecting tired feet. In 1962 she became a registered stockbroker with Bache and Company, specializing in the cosmetics industry. Bishop was the first woman to be on the cover of *Business Week.*

She was born in New Jersey, one of two children. Her father was a small businessman, once having seven businesses at one time. He was a pioneer motion picture exhibitor and her mother was involved in the business as well. The family discussions centered on ethical business practices and the best way to run businesses. Bishop graduated from the Bergen School for Girls in Jersey City and entered Barnard College in 1929, planning to become a doctor. The Great Depression made it necessary for her to get a job as a hospital technician instead. Bishop continued her education through night classes.

She worked as a chemical technician, first at New York State Psychiatric Hospital and Institute from 1930 to 1935, then for a renowned dermatologist, Dr. A. Benson Cannon, from 1935 to 1942. For the next eight years Bishop worked as a senior organic chemist for Standard Oil Development Company and did petroleum research for Socony Vacuum Oil Company studying aviation fuels and oil products.

During those years she began experimenting with and testing lipstick formulas. By 1949 she had decided on a package and was ready to go to market. Bishop introduced her lipstick at a fashion show given by the Barnard College Club of New York. She hired Raymond Spector, an advertising company to repackage the lipstick and launch an advertising campaign, which cost $1,410,000, the largest amount ever spent on a lipstick. It was a resounding success (Lord & Taylor sold out its supply in one day) and revolutionized the lipstick market.

In the next three years over fifty other lipsticks hit the market. In 1950 sales were $49,527; and by 1953, they were $10 million. Eventually, however, Bishop lost the company. Spector had become the majority stockholder and she had to resign as president in November of 1951. The following year she sued, charging mismanagement and diversion of assets. The suit was settled in February of 1954, which resulted in selling her remaining stock for $295,000 and agreeing to cut all connections with the company.

Bishop went on to found three other companies: H. B. Laboratories, Inc., which produced concentrates for cleaning leather and a salve for protecting tired feet; H. G. B. Products Corporation; and Perfemme, Inc., which developed a solid perfume concentrate in four lipstick cases. In the 1960s she became a stockbroker with Bache & Company, specializing in the cosmetics industry and was often quoted in the financial pages. In 1978 she became an adjunct professor at the Fashion Institute of Technology; she was the first holder of the Revlon Chair of Cosmetics Marketing.

Hazel Bishop had three careers and a weakness for hats. She was an active member of the Society of Woman Engineers, the Society of Cosmetic Career Women, the Barnard College Club, and the American Chemical Society, serving on the editorial board of *Chemical and Engineering News*. In 1951 she was elected to the Society of Cosmetic Chemists, and in 1954 to the New York Academy of Science and as a fellow of the American Institute of Chemists. In 1957 she received the first "Women of Courage" award from the Brooklyn Jewish Women's Organizations honoring "her courageous endeavors as a woman leader in industry, business, and civic affairs" (*Current Biography 1957*, p. 56).

See also: Beauty Industry; Finance Industry; Inventors

Further Reading
"Bishop, Hazel (Gladys)." In *Current Biography 1957*, p. 56–58.
Tannen, Mary. "Hazel Bishop, 92, An Innovator Who Made Lipstick Kissproof."
"Woman Chemist Hits Lipstick Jackpot."

Bissell, Anna (1846–1934), Carpet Sweeper Manufacturer

Melville Bissell, Anna's husband, developed and improved the first carpet sweeper, so that she could pick up the tiny sticky packaging sawdust particles that covered their small crockery shop in Grand Rapids, Michigan. When customers saw her using it, they wanted one, too; so in 1876 the Bissells began their carpet sweeper company in a room above the shop. After Melville's death, Bissell turned it into an international company. It is still run by a Bissell today, more than 125 years later.

They began by employing Grand Rapids residents to make the brushes from materials that Bissell delivered to them in clothes baskets by horse and buggy. Melville supervised the assemblers who fitted the brushes into wooden boxes made of walnut. The price was $1.50. Anna went door to door to retail stores. By 1883 sales were enough to buy out two other carpet sweeper manufacturers to acquire their managers, their organization and their volume, and to build a factory.

Unfortunately, two tragedies happened that almost killed the business before it had really started. First, the factory burned down as soon as it began producing, and the Bissells had to mortgage their home and personal belongings to build it again. Then the new model proved defective and they had to recall the sweepers and destroy them all. The cost was $35,000, an enormous sum for that time. The latter event proved a blessing in disguise, however, for it established their reputation for integrity.

In 1889 Melville Bissell died of pneumonia and Anna Bissell took over, becoming one of the first women CEOs. She managed the company well into the 1920s and was the chairman of the board until her death. She paid close attention to trademark and patent requirements, then took the company into the international arena. The greatest success came when Queen Victoria endorsed the sweeper for her palace, and "bisselling" became a common word in England. Turkish sultans and Arabian sheiks also recommended the machine for their Oriental carpets because it was gentle on the beautiful rugs.

Meanwhile, Claude C. Hopkins, one of the bookkeepers, suggested changing the advertising to focus on the "woman's" market and use fewer technical details and more "woman talk." He also suggested a line of sweepers with exotic woods and pushed it as a Christmas gift. (He went on to Chicago to become one of America's advertising greats.) These plans proved very successful and, by the early 1900s, Bissell was the undisputed leader in carpet care.

This changed when the electric vacuum cleaner made its debut in the next decade. Bissell decided to co-exist with the new product based on three reasons: (1) most folks feared electricity at the time; (2) the cleaner was hard to handle and harsh on carpets; and (3) it was sold door to door and needed both demonstration and explanation. The Bissell sweeper was sold in retail stores, easy to use, and didn't require electricity. The vacuum cleaner didn't become established in retail stores until the 1930s. When the depression hit, people couldn't afford to buy a vacuum, so Bissell's decision turned out to be the right one.

She died in 1934, but the company still continues with a Bissell family member at the helm. By 1976, 60 million sweepers had been sold. The company has branched out into light vacuum cleaners. In 1997 the Little Green portable cleaner won a bronze award in the consumer products category of the 1997 Industrial Design Excellence Awards.

See also: Inventors

Further Reading
Simley, John. "Bissell, Inc." In Derdak, vol. 9, p. 70–72.
Powers, p. 13–18.
McGrath, p. 124.

Black Businesswomen, *see* African American Businesswomen

Black, Carole Lynn (1944–), Television Executive

Carole Black is the president and CEO of Lifetime Television Networks and, because of her position, was first named to *Fortune's* list of most powerful women in business in 2001 and again in 2002, ranked at number 35.

She is a native of Cincinnati and received a degree in English Literature from Ohio State University. She married right out of college. Black's first job was brand management for Procter & Gamble's toothpaste and shampoo, Crest, Gleem and Head & Shoulders. She gave birth to a son in 1969 and, in the early 1970s, worked from home for Trans-American Press and wrote articles covering the transportation industry.

In 1983 she divorced, moved to Chicago, and began her career at advertising agency DDB Needham. She was an account supervisor for Sears and later a senior vice president and management representative. She went to Walt Disney in 1986 as the vice president of worldwide marketing for the home video division. While she was there, the division rose from sixth place in the home video market to first. In 1988 Black became the senior vice president of marketing for television and conceptualized and launched *The Disney After-noon*, a highly successful program.

From 1994 to 1999 she was the president and general manager of NBC4 in Los Angeles, the first woman to run a commercial television station in the city. She refocused the station on the Los Angeles community, hired a chief of workforce diversity, and improved the programming. Black is credited for taking a station with low morale and turning it into the dominant station in Los Angeles.

She became the president and CEO of Lifetime Entertainment in 1999 where she is in charge of Lifetime Television, Lifetime Movie Network, and Lifetime Online, the first woman to hold this position. She is credited with leading the network to the number one slot in cable prime time entertainment in 2001. This was accomplished through increased marketing, public affairs and original programming, original primetime series, a daily live information program, and several advocacy projects focusing on issues such as breast cancer and childcare needs. Black also enhanced the Internet site and developed partnerships with *Ms Magazine* and women.com. The channel was number one with women of all ages in 2001.

Black is known as a savvy marketer and highly creative team builder. Her ability to develop and implement strategic visions and to motivate people has been one measure of her success. Her commitment to community outreach, both to her Los Angeles viewers and to the largely female Lifetime audience is evident through programs that mentor or deal with women's issues such as breast cancer, violence against girls and women, and self-esteem.

Black has won a large number of awards. She was one of America's 100 Most Important Women in the 1999 *Ladies Home Journal* list and has repeatedly been one of the "Top Women in Entertainment" named by *Hollywood Reporter*. In 1995 she was honored by American Women in Radio and Television, and in 1997 was named a Greater Los Angeles Leader. In 2000 she won the Corporate Leadership Award from the National Breast Cancer Coalition, the Muse Award for Outstanding Vision and Achievement from the New York Women in Film and Television, and was named to the Women in Entertainment Power 50 list. In 2001 she was honored by Women in Cable and Television for leadership for women in the industry, was named to the National Association of Women Business Owners of Los Angeles Hall of Fame, and was honored by the National Organization of Women (NOW) as one of the 25 most influential women in business. She won the Cable Television Public Affairs Association 2001 Presidential Award for the network's strong advocacy on behalf of women and appeared on *People* magazine's list of the "50 Most Beautiful People." In 2002 she was awarded the Matrix Award for Broadcasting by New York Women in Communication, Inc. and was named one of the most powerful women in television by *Electronic Media*. That November she was inducted into the Broadcasting & Cable Hall of Fame. In 2003 she was named to the board of the National Association of Television Program Executives.

See also: Broadcasting Industry

Further Reading
Black, Carole and Coeli Carr. "Executive Life: The Boss; Risks Are Allowed."
Finn, Robin. "The Woman Behind Lifetime's Surge."
Larson, Megan. "Job of a Lifetime."

Black, Cathleen Prunty (1944–), Magazine Publisher

Cathleen Black is the first woman president of Hearst magazines. She has been among the most powerful women in corporate America and on *Fortune*'s list since 1998. One of her magazine launches was *O, The Oprah Magazine*, one of the most successful in magazine history. She says her success is due to a combination of determination, perseverance, and love of her career.

Black was born and grew up on the south side of Chicago, the youngest of three children. Her parents sent her to Catholic schools. The family discussed news issues of the day at the dinner table, so newspapers were a part of her life from the beginning. Her father became blind when she was twelve, but continued to work and be productive as a private investigator in spite of his disability. She calls him the role model for her determination to succeed and persevere in the face of adversity. She graduated from Trinity College in Washington, DC, with a degree in English, and headed to New York City.

Her first job was selling advertising space in *Holiday Magazine*. She spent the next six years as an advertising representative for different magazines. In 1972 she left *New York Magazine* to be the advertising director for the newly launched *Ms Magazine*. The job was a challenge, but she managed to garner good sales and became associate publisher. In 1977 she moved back to *New York Magazine* as associate publisher and later publisher, restoring the magazine to profitability along the way. Black was the first woman publisher of a major general interest magazine. In 1983 she was named the president of *USA Today*, which had just been launched. The following year she became responsible for the coordination of national advertising sales and promotions, which successfully made the newspaper a national presence with a circulation of 1.8 million. In 1992 she was named executive vice president of marketing at *USA Today's* parent company, Gannett, and also to Gannett's board of directors. From 1992 to 1995 she was the president and CEO of the Newspaper Association of America. In this role, she was a spokesperson and lobbyist for the industry.

In 1996 Black became the president of Hearst Magazines, the first woman to occupy that position. She took over just after the company raised advertising rates, but quickly managed a turnaround, despite several editorial changes and angry advertisers. She focused on raising circulation, communicating more with both advertising agencies and clients, and introducing new magazines. Her outstanding accomplishment was the launching of Oprah Winfrey's magazine, *O, The Oprah Magazine*; other launches included *Talk*, *Cosmogirl*, and *Lifetime*.

Black is performance- and results-oriented; she also loves challenges and taking risks, the results of which clearly show her ability to manage turnarounds. She has a legendary flair for marketing and sales and is personable and outgoing with a great sense of humor. She also believes strongly in sharing the glory with her staff and colleagues. She hit the glass ceiling several times, but remained persistent and determined.

> In 1996 Cathleen Black became the president of Hearst Magazines, the first woman to occupy that position.

Cathleen Black has received many accolades. She has eight honorary doctorates and sits on the boards of Hearst Corporation, IBM, and Coca-Cola. She also serves on the Advertising Council and the Newspaper Advertising

Bureau, and in 2000 was the chairman of the board of Magazine Publishers of America. Her awards range from being named "Outstanding Communicator" by the Los Angeles Advertising Women to the 2000 *Advertising Age*'s Publishing Executive of the Year. *Folio*, in 1996, named her one of the forty most influential people in the publishing industry, commenting on her establishment of two ground breaking publications (*Ms* and *USA Today*), and quoted L. Mark Stone, a managing director at Broadview Associates, who called her "a pioneer who takes on tough assignments" ("40 for the Future," April 1, 1996). In December 2001 she appeared in spot advertisements for the "I Love New York" campaign aimed at assuaging tourist fears about terrorism in that city.

She is married to Thomas Harvey, a lawyer, who is staff director of the Veterans Affairs Committee in the U.S. Senate. They have two adopted children, a dog, homes in New York City and Washington, D.C.

See also: Publishing Industry

Further Reading

"Black, Cathleen P." In *Current Biography Yearbook*, 1998, p. 59–61.

Grande, Carlos. "Publisher with a Strong Penchant for Oprah: Interview with Cathleen Black, Hearst Magazines."

Kuczynski, Alex. "Building on Borrowed Cachet: Cathleen Black Shakes Up the Culture at Hearst Magazines."

"The Queen of Hearst."

Blumkin, Rose (1893–1998), Furniture Retailer

Rose Blumkin's motto was: "Sell cheap, tell the truth, don't cheat nobody" (James, Frank, p. 1). She put this to use in the Nebraska Furniture Mart for sixty-three years.

Blumkin was born in Russia, one of eight children. Her father was a rabbi and her mother ran a small grocery store to augment the family income. They were poor, lived in a log cabin, and slept on straw mattresses. She worked in the store from age six, leaving home at age thirteen to obtain employment elsewhere. By the time she was sixteen, Blumkin was a store manager supervising six men. She married Isadore Blumkin when she was twenty. He left Russia soon after their marriage to avoid the Russian Army. Three years later she joined him in Fort Dodge, Iowa, after convincing a guard at the Chinese–Siberian border that she would bring him a bottle of vodka when she returned from her shopping trip. Instead, she took a peanut boat to America where the Red Cross and an immigrant organization helped reunite her with her husband.

In 1919 the Blumkins moved to Omaha where there was a community of Russian- and Yiddish-speaking immigrants. Within three years she was able to bring the rest of the family to America. Her husband opened a second-hand store and Blumkin joined him, after the birth of four children. During the Depression, they printed 10,000 circulars offering to dress a man from head to toe for $5.00.

Blumkin became interested in furniture and began taking customers to furniture wholesalers. After they picked out what they wanted, she bought the items, marking them up 10 percent, foregoing the usual 40 to 50 percent commission. In 1937 she borrowed $500 from her brother, rented the 3,000 square-foot basement underneath the secondhand store and started her own furniture business. The Omaha wholesalers refused to sell to her, so she went elsewhere, always marking up by only 10 percent, depending on volume to make a profit. Her decision to sell a lot, make a little, and bend over backwards for customers made her business successful, and earned many repeat customers.

Her son Louis became active in the store after World War II. Both worked hard seven days a week, for seventy hours each week. During the Korean War there was a slump in business that forced Blumkin to take out a ninety-day loan for $50,000 to pay suppliers. To repay it, she rented the Omaha City Auditorium and held a massive three-day sale, making a profit of $250,000. Blumkin never owed money again, always dealing in cash.

In 1983 Warren Buffett of Berkshire Hathaway, Inc. bought 80 percent of the store for $55 or $60 million. By this time the store had grown to 250,000 square feet. The Blumkins continued to operate it, however, and Rose remained the chairman and ran the carpet department. In 1989 a quarrel with her grandchildren led her to stalk out and quit the operation. She was ninety-five, but rather than retire, she started another store across the street called Mrs. B's Warehouse which became Omaha's third-largest carpet outlet. Blumkin still put in long hours, zipping around the store in a golf cart. By her ninety-eighth birthday in 1992, the feud was over and Warren Buffet bought Mrs. B's store also, for $5 million cash. This time, however, he asked her to sign a lifetime non-compete clause.

Rose Blumkin was only four foot ten, but stood very tall as a businesswoman. By 1994 the Furniture Mart covered sixty-four acres and was an all-in-one store stocking carpets, furniture, appliances, and electronics with sales of $18 million. There were no mortgages or debts since she always paid cash. The Blumkins collected credit payments themselves, had very few managers and no secretaries, thus making their operating expenses half those of department stores. The customers came from all over for the huge selection and low prices.

Blumkin built her empire with hard work and by selling quality products at lower prices. She received two honorary doctorates and was the first woman to receive an honorary doctorate in commercial science from NYU. She was inducted into the Nebraska Hall of Fame in 1997. She also financially supported a home for senior citizens. She died in 1998 at the age of 104. Warren Buffet said of Blumkin, "Put her up against the top graduates of the business schools or chief executives of the Fortune 500 and, assuming an even start with the same resources, she'd run rings around them" (James, Frank, p. 1).

See also: Immigrant Businesswomen; Retailing Industry

Further Reading
Feder, Barnaby J. "A Retailer's Home Grown Business."
Hartnett, Michael. "Rose Blumkin: Retailing in the 90s Means Something Different."
James, Frank E. "Furniture Czarina, Still a Live Wire at 90A Retail Phenomenon
    Oversees Her Empire."

Board of Directors, *see* Corporate Board of Directors

Boehm, Helen F. (1920–), Porcelain Retailer

The Edward Marshall Boehm Porcelain Company, co-founded in 1949 by Helen Boehm and her artist-sculptor husband Edward, is thought of by many as the finest creator of limited edition hard-paste sculptures in the world. Boehm porcelains are famous worldwide and were, for many years, the gifts American statesmen gave to visiting dignitaries. Edward was the artist; Helen was the businessperson, promotional genius, and saleswoman behind his art.

She was born in Bensonhurst, New York, to an Italian immigrant couple, the sixth of seven children. Boehm's family life was poor, noisy, and loving. Although her cabinetmaker father died when she was thirteen, her mother raised all the children to have discipline and the motivation to want the best and do the best they could. Boehm made extra money during high school from designing and sewing dresses for her friends.

After graduating from high school, she worked for an optometrist who paid for her schooling at the Mechanical School of Optics where she became a registered ophthalmic dispenser. She met Edward Boehm while visiting her brother who was recuperating from pneumonia at the Air Force Base Convalescent Center in Pawling, New York. Edward was stationed there as a member of the Air Force animal husbandry division during World War II. She noticed him showing a patient how to model animals in clay, was fascinated, and introduced herself to him. Three months later, they were married.

Before the war, Edward had bred Guernsey cattle and sculpted animals in his spare time. The farm burned down during the war, so he became a veterinarian's assistant. Boehm firmly believed he could make a living from his sculptures, so they decided to found their own company. The vet lent them $500 to start but, when they did not immediately sell something, he wanted his money returned; so Boehm, who had joined a large optical firm in New York City and had her own clientele, sold the idea to one of her clients. He committed $10,000 and sent $1,000 right away. They opened a studio in Trenton and Edward developed a process for hard-paste porcelain, a process that had been secret and known only to the Chinese and Europeans.

Boehm kept her job and tried to sell the pieces during her lunch. One day, she decided to go to the top, so she called the curator of the American wing of the Metropolitan Museum of Art. Just by chance, he answered the phone and she talked him into coming to the studio and looking at two sculptures, a very large and lifelike Hereford bull and a Percheron stallion. He was so impressed that he bought them both for $60 each. She then immediately contacted the *New York Times* who wrote a story about the sale that appeared on January 20, 1950.

That was the beginning of the Boehm's success in business using Edward's creative genius and her promotional genius. They kept selling the sculptures, and by 1953 they owned the company with no debts. She persuaded him to sculpt some smaller pieces, so he began to do birds. She also decided they needed national recognition, so she gave a porcelain Hereford bull to President and Mrs. Eisenhower in 1954. This led to friendship, and in 1957 when Queen Elizabeth and Prince Philip came to Washington on their first visit, she suggested to the Eisenhowers that their gift be a porcelain mounted polo player. Edward had never done anything that large or complicated before, but it was a great success, and was the first of many such gifts to foreign dignitaries; giving a Boehm porcelain became a tradition. When President Nixon went to China, he took a gift of Boehm Birds of Peace to Mao Tse Tung; Boehm also gave another of these to Pope Paul VI when he visited America.

To sell the sculpture, Helen traveled the country, placing Boehm pieces of porcelain in major department stores, giving slide lectures which showed the Boehm studio, their home with its aviaries, and the farm with the prize cattle and racehorses. Sales increased so dramatically and she was so busy traveling that they hired Frank Cosentino to handle the business. He later became president while she was the chairman. Edward remained the shy artist and she was, in her own words, the aggressive salesperson.

Edward died suddenly in 1969, but she determined that the company would not die with him. Artisans trained by him continued the artwork, and she became part of the design team. Also in 1969 President Nixon toured the NATO countries, presenting each head of state with a Boehm porcelain. When he returned, she gave him a collection of Boehm birds. The ceremony took place in the White House on August 21, which would have been Edward Boehm's 56th birthday. At the ceremony, she suggested that a new symbol of peace be created. Nixon agreed, and the ensuing publicity reassured the public that Boehm's porcelains would go on even without Edward. The company prospered and by 1990 their sculptures were in 127 world art institutions, Boehm galleries in London, New York, Chicago, Los Angeles, Dallas, and Trenton, and a porcelain studio in Wales. Revenues were over $35 million.

Boehm is very active in society and also in several charities. She sits on the Fine Arts Committee of Blair House, the Council of Concilium of the Vatican, and the Horatio Alger National Executive Committee. She is a benefactor of the Scheie Eye Institute of Philadelphia, the National Audubon

Society, and the Adam Walsh Center of Florida (the center's home is named for her). She is also a founding member of the World Wildlife Association. She has won the Horatio Alger Award and the Star of Italian Solidarity Award. Honorary degrees have been bestowed by Rutgers University, St. Peter's College in Jersey City, Jacksonville University, Kean College, and Rider College. Boehm was probably the first businesswoman to be invited to the People's Republic of China. She was also the first to own a polo team.

See also: Retailing Industry

Further Reading
Boehm, Helen F. *With a Little Luck–An American Odyssey.*
MacPhee, p. 49–65.
Mansfield, Stephanie. "The Porcelain Powerhouse: Helen Boehm, Riding Her Birds to Riches and High Places."

Boit, Elizabeth Eaton (1849–1932), Textile Manufacturer

It was said that "the smartest man in Wakefield (Massachusetts) was a woman" (James, Edward T., p. 191). This was Elizabeth Boit, whose Harvard Knitting Mill kept Wakefield's economy strong for over forty years. She was born in Newton, Massachusetts, the second of six daughters. Her father was a janitor and a sexton. At age eighteen, she began working as a timekeeper in the Dudley Hosiery Knitting Mill, and by 1872 was appointed forewoman, a rarity in those times. In 1883 she was hired as superintendent of the new Allston Mills.

At the same time, Charles Winship moved from Dudley to Allston Mills and, five years later, they decided to become partners. They formed a company, Winship, Boit and Co. and set up the Harvard Knitting Mill in Cambridge, Massachusetts. Charles, with his inventive and mechanical ability, was in charge of production, and Boit managed the office and financial matters. The mill's specialty was women's underwear; they began with three knitting machines, five finishing machines and twenty-five employees, producing 240 garments per day.

In 1889 they moved to one floor of a building in Wakefield where the company flourished into the 1950s. The employees, mostly girls and women, were paid $5–12 per week and many did finishing crochet work in their homes. By 1896 they had 160 in-mill employees, plus 200 on the outside producing 3,000 garments per day. Their business grew to $250,000 annually, so it was necessary to build a larger plant. They also expanded into men's and children's underwear. All products used the trade names Merode and Forest Mills.

The plant was enlarged four times; at its peak it had a floor space of eight and a half acres with 850 employees, 500 knitting and 500 sewing machines, and an output of 24,000 garments per day. In 1909/1910 the company was fifth in employee numbers among knitting mills in the state. In 1920 Boit began a profit-sharing plan that lasted until 1927. In the late 1920s Boit turned over her share of the business to Charles. The business continued under Winship until 1956.

Elizabeth Boit never married; the mill and her extended family were her life. Even after retirement, she made daily visits to the mill as long as she was able. She was said to be personally interested in her employees and their welfare; there are several stories about her caring and generosity. At that time, she was the only woman to be actively engaged in a successful textile business. She died of diabetes and circulatory ailments.

See also: Fashion Industry; Manufacturing

Further Reading
Ciccarelli, Barbara L. "Boit, Elizabeth Eaton." In Garrity and Carnes, p. 118–119.
Ingham, John N. *Biographical Dictionary of American Business Leaders*, p. 81–82.
Lovett, Robert W. "Boit, Elizabeth Eaton." In James, Edward T., p. 190–191.

Book Publishing Industry, *see* Publishing Industry

Bosomworth, Mary Musgrove (1700–1760), Trader, Rancher

Mary Musgrove Bosomworth was an important interpreter, merchant, and trader in the Creek Nation in Colonial Georgia. To some, she was known as Empress of the Creeks.

She was born Cousaponokeesa to a Creek mother and an English trader father. Her mother was said to be the sister of Old Brim, Emperor of the Creeks. When she was seven, either her father took her or she was sent to a white family in South Carolina to be educated and also taught to be a Christian. In 1716 she returned to Indian country.

Soon after returning, she met and married John Musgrove and took the name Mary Musgrove. In 1722 they went back to South Carolina, but in 1732 she again returned to the Creeks and established a trading station on the bluffs of the Savannah River. Her annual sales were estimated to be £1,200. She also had a plantation on which she raised food crops. In 1733 when Sir James Oglethorpe founded the colony of Georgia, Bosomworth acted as his interpreter and emissary to the Creeks and helped to maintain peaceful relations between the Creeks and the British.

About this time she founded Mount Venture, a second trading station with the added purpose of watching for threats from Spanish Florida. After 1737 her relatives transferred their holdings to her. When John died in 1739 she owned a 500-acre plantation, many cattle, ten indentured servants, and a thriving deerskin trade. That same year she married Jacob Matthews, a British army captain. He died in 1742 the same year that Indians allied with the Spanish destroyed Mount Venture and its settlement.

In 1743 James Oglethorpe gave her £200 and a diamond ring and left Georgia, but she continued to interpret for the colony. The following year, she married Rev. Thomas Bosomworth, a minister of the Church of England, who had a reputation as an unscrupulous fortune seeker. He became the South Carolina agent to the Creek Nation and he and Mary went into the cattle business. Part of her land consisted of three islands: Sapelo, Ossabaw, and St. Catherine's. Thomas stocked St. Catherine's with cattle, while she claimed the other islands from both the colonial and English governments. Some of the Creeks backed them and were arrested, but later released. In 1754 both Bosomworths went to England to assert her claims, though it would take five years for a settlement. Mary received St. Catherine's plus £1,200. The couple subsequently built a house and continued developing their ranch.

See also: American Indian Businesswomen

Further Reading

Bois, Danuta. "Mary Musgrove (Cousaponokeesa)" www.DistinguishedWomen.com/biographies/musgrove-m.html.

Coulter, E. Merton. "Musgrove, Mary." In James, Edward T., p. 605–606.

Bostrom, Sue (1960–), Information Technology Executive

Sue Bostrom is the Senior Vice President of the Internet Business Solutions Group, an internal consulting services division in Cisco Systems. She was number 36 on the 2000 *Fortune* list of the most powerful women in corporate America.

Bostrom was born to a hard-working family; her father was a farmer who later became a custodian. She credits him for teaching the value of working hard and persevering, and her mother for how to dream of making the world a better place. She received her undergraduate degree in business administration and marketing from the University of Illinois, and her MBA from the Stanford School of Business.

She began work in 1984 at AT&T Information Systems and moved on to McKinsey & Company, a consulting firm, as a senior engagement manager in electronics consulting in 1987. She was there until 1994 when she went to National SemiConductor as director of strategic planning. She spent a year at FTP Software as Senior Vice President of Global Marketing and Strategic Planning before moving to Cisco Systems in 1997. In 1998 she reached her present post, a newly created position for the company. She was responsible for conceiving and planning the implementation of the group, an internal consulting group that teaches corporate executives how to use the Internet to its fullest capacity. The group now hires 150 people and is really a small company within Cisco. In 2000 it hosted 800 companies in its customer-briefing center for workshops.

She has a reputation for being articulate and direct but warm and personable. Bostrom is clear about her direction and communicates in a way that inspires trust. She has been on many panels discussing the Internet and the latest developments in the high-tech industry. She was named one of the top 20 visionaries in the United States by VARBusiness in November of 2001, citing her main accomplishment as being responsible for Cisco becoming a trusted name among corporations.

See also: Information Technology Industry

Further Reading
Angell, Mike. "Cisco: Net's Productivity Potential Uptapped."
Corcoran, Elizabeth. "Goodwill Ambassador: Cisco's Fastest-Rising Star Brings in Business but Doesn't Sell Routers."
"Top 20 Visionaries."

Boyle, Gertrude (1924–), Sportswear Executive

Gertrude Boyle took over Columbia Sportswear in 1970 after her husband died suddenly from a heart attack. She eventually turned the company into the leading maker of rugged sportswear with 30 percent of the market in the United States. It was one of the *Working Woman* top companies from 1993 through 2001.

She was born to a Jewish family in a small town near Munich, Germany. The family fled from the Nazis in 1938 and emigrated to Oregon. There her father, who had owned one of the largest shirt companies in Germany, began a wholesale hat company. Boyle graduated from the University of Arizona with a BA in sociology. She met her husband during college and they married the year after she graduated. He joined her father's company and she stayed at home with the three children, a boy and two girls. Her husband died suddenly in 1970 from a heart attack, leaving the company, which he now ran, heavily mortgaged and almost bankrupt.

Boyle found herself with a financially ailing company and three children to feed. She was advised to sell the company, but the offered price, which decreased as time passed, was insufficient to cover a small business loan the collateral for which were her house, her mother's house, and their insurance policies. Although she had not been involved with the company before, she decided to try to make it a success instead of selling.

Ten years earlier she had designed a fishing vest with many pockets, the result of listening to fishermen sitting around the living room talking. Then she designed rain pants and made the two items part of the business. The times were right; the fly fishing craze was just beginning, and people were starting to wear sportswear for more than just sports. When she took over, Boyle says she pretended she knew what she was doing. The business was run by good old boys, and she had to fire some of the best of them because they wouldn't listen to her. She hired her son Tim, a senior at the University of Oregon, and together they ran the company. She introduced the Bugaboo coat, the bugaboot, and children's wear. She also launched an unusual advertising campaign featuring herself as a tough grandma. The ads said: "If you think our fabric is tough, you should meet our chairman." The accompanying photo of her shows her peering over her glasses with a frown on her face (Bamford & Pendleton, p. 483–484).

Boyle took companies that tried to copy her ideas to court; between 1989 and 1994, there were thirty lawsuits. In 1994 Tim became president and CEO; her daughter Sally ran four outlet stores. In 1994 the CBS Winter Olympics staff wore Columbia outerwear. Sales continued to boom, and in 1998 the company went public with the majority of the stock in company hands. By 1999 it was the number one skiwear maker in the United States In 2002, sales were $784.4 million.

The Oregon Chapter of Women's Forum awarded her Woman of the Year in 1987 and, in 1994, *Business Week* named Boyle one of the best managers of that year. In 1997 the Columbia advertising campaign won the Marketing Innovation Award at the Super Show. The previous year she won the Astra Award for the Outstanding Oregon Woman-Owned Business. In 1998 she won the Golden Plate Award from the American Academy of Achievement. The company won the 2002 Northwestern Master Entrepreneur from *Inc.* magazine for its community service, financial performance, and innovation.

Boyle sits on the business advisory board of Oregon State University and has been on the boards of the Oregon Chapter of the American Diabetes Association, Lewis and Clark College, the Oregon Ballet Theatre, Sapporo Sister City, and the Oregon Ski Industries Association.

Boyle is the mother of three, grandmother of five. Her son Tim is the CEO and major shareholder of the company. He is also the president and straight man in their advertisements.

See also: Fashion Industry; Immigrant Businesswomen

Further Reading

Albrecht, Brian E. "One Tough Mama Builds a Business; Making a Success from Outerwear."

Holmes, Stanley. "Gert Gets the Last Laugh!"

Kaplan, James. "Amateur's Hour: Who Says it Takes Years of On-the-Job Experience to Run a Business?"

Yang, Dori Jones. "This Grandma Wants to Keep the World Warm."

Bradwell, Myra Colby (1831–1894), Newspaper Publisher, Lawyer

Myra Bradwell was not only the first woman lawyer in the United States, but also when she was not allowed to practice, she pioneered the first weekly legal newspaper. She founded the *Chicago Legal News* in 1868 and built it into a publication that every lawyer had to have to keep current with legal decisions and developments. She was also very influential in women's suffrage as well as legal reform. In recognition of her efforts, she was inducted into the National Women's Hall of Fame in 1994.

Bradwell was born in Manchester, Vermont, to an abolitionist family who moved west, first to western New York State and later to Illinois when she was twelve. She first went to school in Kenosha, Wisconsin; then to a female seminary in Elgin, Illinois, and became a schoolteacher. In 1852 she married James Bradwell and they moved to Memphis. They had four children. In 1854 they moved to Chicago and James became a lawyer, and eventually a circuit court judge and legislator. During the 1860s after the death of two of the children, Bradwell studied law under her husband's tutelage. She passed the bar exam with distinction, but when she applied to practice law, the state supreme court refused her application as did the U.S. Supreme Court when she applied there.

In 1868 she founded the Chicago Legal News Company, the first weekly law newspaper in the area. She was the owner, manager, and editor. The company also was a printer of forms, documents, and stationery. Bradwell's goal for the *Chicago Legal News* was to be essential reading for every lawyer in what was then the Northwest, and she succeeded. James' influence helped her obtain the right to make and sign contracts under her own name. He also lobbied special acts in the state legislature which declared that the publication of laws, acts, and resolutions in the *Chicago Legal News* made them legally binding. She not only published these legal documents, but also opinion pieces about the laws, attacks on incompetent lawyers and judges, and suggestions for regulations and reforms. Many of her suggestions later became laws or were put into effect in other ways. She gained enormous influence on the decision-making process. Two of her most influential suggestions that were turned into law were the Illinois Married Woman's Property Act of 1861 and the Earnings Act of 1869.

In 1871 the Chicago Fire decimated the company with the exception of the subscription book that was saved by her daughter Bessie. The newspaper came out on time, however; Bradwell took the issue by train to Milwaukee to be printed there. In 1872 she was admitted to the Illinois Bar Association as an honorary member and went on to serve as vice president for four terms. Finally in 1890 her application to practice was approved by the Illinois Supreme Court, and two years later she was approved to practice before the U.S.

Supreme Court. Two years after that, she died of cancer. Her daughter continued the newspaper until 1925 while her husband and son ran the printing company.

Bradwell was very active in the women's rights and women's suffrage movements. She was also responsible for a number of other reforms and improvements including the codification of professional standards, better treatment of witnesses, the regulation of large corporations, compulsory retirement of judges, and Chicago's first zoning ordinances. Her newspaper was the primary publication read by lawyers and other people involved with laws and legislation. She is also credited with influencing the decision to release Abraham Lincoln's wife, Mary Todd Lincoln, from an insane asylum. There is a drama about that event, *Mary and Myra*, written by Catherine Filloux.

See also: Publishing Industry

Further Reading

Drachman, p. 62–69.

Friedman, Jane M. *America's First Woman Lawyer: The Biography of Myra Bradwell.*

Mezey, Susan Gluck."Bradwell, Myra Colby." In Garraty and Carnes, p. 389–391.

"The Professionals: Myra Bradwell, Lucy Taylor, Elizabeth Blackwell." In Bird, p. 106–110.

Brandt, Jan (1951–), Information Technology Executive

Jan Brandt was the president of marketing for America Online and has been credited with the company's rise to the number one spot in the Internet linking business. She has a reputation as the most innovative marketer in her field and was named to *Fortune*'s list of most powerful corporate women in both 1999 and 2000. In September 2002 a top-down reorganization prompted Brandt to leave the company.

After graduating from college at Boston University, she attended the Graduate School of Business Administration at the University of Connecticut. Brandt's job history includes a stint as the president and CEO of RPA Direct Agency, whose clients included Greenpeace, Ted Kennedy, Ron Dellums, and the California Democratic Party. From 1984 to 1988 she was the president and founder of Brandt Direct Marketing with several magazines as clients as well as the American Museum of Natural History. In 1988 she joined the corporate world as the vice president of advertising for Newfield Publications where she gathered new members to the My Weekly Reader Book Club through sending the potential members a free book.

In 1993 Brandt became the senior vice president of marketing for AOL Networks. It had 250,000 members at the time, third after CompuServe and Prodigy. It was Brandt's idea to blanket the country with free America Online disks. The strategy worked, and within six years the company rose to be number one with eighteen million subscribers.

She was a pioneer in this kind of mass marketing. In 1997 she was promoted to president of marketing. Her chief accomplishment during that time was a 1999 alliance with eMachine PCs, which integrated AOL software into all its computers. By 2000 the subscribers numbered 27 million and AOL was named Marketer of the Year by *Advertising Age*. In January 2001 Brandt was promoted to chief marketing officer and vice chairman but left the following year.

Brandt is known for her marketing strategies using all available media to add to AOL's subscriber base. The company's slogan, "AOL Anywhere," was her idea and she meant absolutely everywhere, including radio, cable television, network television, giveaways at banks, in bars, on software, in amusement parks, direct mail, and cereal boxes. She believes that if something is convenient, people will try it and become loyal customers if the product is good quality.

Brandt's awards include the 1997 Top Sales and Marketing Executive from *Upside Magazine*, the 2000 Direct Marketer of the Year, the Direct Marketing Association's Echo Award for Excellence in Direct Marketing, and the Folio Gold Mailbox Award. She is on the national board of the Direct Marketing Association.

See also: Information Technology Industry

Further Reading
Gilbert, Jennifer. "AOL's Marketing Builds Service into Powerhouse."
Swisher, Kara. *AOL.com: How Steve Case Beat Bill Gates, Nailed the Netheads, and Made Millions in the War for the Web.*
www.corp.aol.com/whoweare/who-bios/brandt.html.

Brent, Margaret (1601–1671), Land Proprietor, Lawyer

Margaret Brent owned more land than any other colonist in Maryland. She grew tobacco and raised cattle and hogs on more than 1,000 acres and lived in the feudal manner. She also lent money and represented herself and others in court. While not a lawyer per se, she was an "attorney-in-fact," according to the custom of the times. Because of this activity, she has been called the first *de facto* woman lawyer in America.

She was born in Gloucester, England, one of thirteen children, to a wealthy family. Brent's father was Lord of Amington and Lark Stoke while her mother was descended from King Edward III. She was raised a Roman Catholic and received education at home. In November of 1638 she and her sister Mary, two brothers, and several servants came to Maryland, then a colony of only four years which had begun as a refuge for wealthy Catholics. The proprietor was Lord Baltimore, an early absentee landowner, and he was either a friend of the family or, according to some sources, married to one of Brent's sisters. The women carried letters from him guaranteeing land grants to them. They received seventy acres in the middle of St. Mary's, the capital city, and called it "Sister's Freehold." Because it was in Brent's name, she was the first woman in Maryland to hold land in her own right.

Both Brent and her brother Giles became very involved in the politics of the colony. They were close friends of the governor, Lord Calvert, brother of Lord Baltimore. Giles was a member of the council, acting governor, and commander of Kent Island. In 1642 Margaret received 1,000 acres of land from her brother containing a mill and a house in payment of a debt. She used the farm to raise cattle, hogs, and tobacco. She also began a lending business and went to court several times for debt payment. Raising the matter in court in effect made the debt a legal one as was customary in the colonies. Between 1642 and 1650 Margaret Brent appears in the court records 134 times, more than anyone else during those years, and won her cases most of the time. She had a reputation for being a shrewd businesswoman, and, unusual in the colonies where there was a scarcity of women, remained unmarried and independent. She signed her name: Margaret Brent, Gentleman.

> While Margaret Brent is famous for saving the colony of Maryland, being the first woman to demand a vote, and, by many sources, being the first woman lawyer in America, she was also an astute businesswoman.

In the late 1640s she became famous. An insurrection led by Protestants William Claiborne and Richard Ingle had decimated the colony; Governor Calvert had fled to Virginia but returned in 1646 with mercenary soldiers recruited there. He regained control of the colony, but died in May of 1647. As he lay dying, he made Brent his executrix, telling her to "take all, pay all." Unfortunately, this included the soldiers who had not been paid and who had each been promised 1500 pounds of tobacco—the coin of the colony— and three barrels of corn. The governor had pledged both his estate and that of his brother, Lord Baltimore, for payment. The governor's estate did not cover this payment, so Margaret Brent went to the Maryland Assembly and asked to be granted power of attorney to sell some of Lord Baltimore's cattle. She also asked for two votes in the Assembly, one for herself as a landowner and one in her role as power of attorney. The Assembly refused to grant her voting rights because she was a woman. They did consider the questions of power of attorney, however.

All of this took a great deal of time; meanwhile, the soldiers were on the verge of mutiny. She used patience, diplomacy, promises, and borrowed corn to assuage the hungry soldiers. Finally the Assembly acted, and she sold the cattle and paid the soldiers, thus saving the colony from further depredation.

Lord Baltimore was not happy that his property had been sold, but the Maryland Assembly stood up for her in this instance. He kept on complaining and made it clear that he saw the Brent family as rivals, so they all moved to Virginia. There, she amassed 11,000 acres of land between 1651 and 1666 in the Northern Neck, developed the area, managed the plantation, and imported numerous settlers. The last time Brent appears in Maryland records was to secure an inheritance from her friend Thomas White who left her his entire estate stating that he had asked her to marry him several times. She wrote her will in December 1663; it was probated in May 1671. The exact date of her death is unknown.

Margaret Brent is famous for saving the colony of Maryland; being the first woman to demand a vote; and according to many sources, becoming the *de facto* first woman lawyer in America. She was also an astute businesswoman, an independent householder who raised cattle, operated a mill, loaned money, and was able to act as attorney for herself and others. She was completely in charge of her own affairs and able to stand up for herself. She never married although there is evidence that she was asked many times. Colonial records show her as a woman of great ability and resourcefulness.

The American Bar Association's Commission on Women honored her in 1991 with the Margaret Brent Award, given annually to five women lawyers who have achieved excellence while opening doors for other women lawyers and women in general. There is a Margaret Brent League that works on issues concerning women lawyers. A bas-relief on the old courthouse in Old Alexandria, Virginia, honors her achievements.

See also: Colonial Businesswomen

Further Reading
Baker, Beth. "First Lady to the Bar."
Carpenter, Stephanie A. "Brent, Margaret (1601–1670)." In Garraty and Carnes, p. 483–484.
Spruill, Julia Cherry. "Mistress Margaret Brent, Spinster."

Brinkley, Amy Woods (1953–), Banker

In the *Fortune* list of the most powerful women of 2002, Amy Brinkley ranked number 17, a jump from her previous rank of number 31. Her promotion to the position of president of the consumer products division of the Bank of America with its 1.5 million online customers put her on the list for the first time. In July of that year, she was promoted again, to chairman of Credit Policy. In June 2002 she became the head of risk management. Her CEO, Hugh MacColl, has publicly identified her as a person who could possibly be his successor some day (Weil, p. 1).

Brinkley was born in North Carolina, received her college degree from the University of North Carolina at Chapel Hill where she was elected to Phi Beta Kappa. She joined NationsBank as a management trainee in the commercial credit department in 1978 and held increasingly responsible positions through the years. She first was a credit analyst, was promoted to banking officer and senior credit analyst in 1979, to vice president and commercial lending officer in 1983, to senior vice president and credit policy executive in 1988, and in 1990 to marketing executive.

In 1998 NationsBank merged with Bank of America, and although many of the top managers left, Brinkley stayed and was named Consumer Products Executive the following year. This was a newly created position responsible for card services, consumer finance, interactive banking, and the mortgage company. She was, during the merger, largely responsible for the smooth integration of the two banks and in developing the new company's retail business plan. She was focused on making it easier for customers to negotiate and use the variety of products the bank offers. She is also a member of the Operating Committee. In June 2002 she became the head of risk management. Due to her position, she sits on the Risk and Capital Committee, the most senior committee of the bank.

Brinkley is married with two children. She has a reputation as an extraordinarily hard worker and a capable strategic thinker. One of her more memorable accomplishments was giving a presentation to the CEO while in a body cast due to an automobile accident. She sits on the boards of the Carolinas Healthcare Systems, Bassett Furniture Industries, and Presbyterian Hospital Foundation. She is also the chairman of the board of trustees of the North Carolina Dance Theatre.

See also: Banking

Further Reading

"Brinkley, Amy." http://www.hoovers.com/officers/bio/4/0.3353.58444_12940162.00.html.
Martin, Pamela and Beverly Foster. "Bank of America's New Look at Risk: An Interview with Amy Brinkley."
Weil, Dan. "B of A Products Chief Seeks to Orchestrate Offerings."

Broadcasting Industry

The broadcasting industry consists of radio, broadcast television, and cable television. All three came of age during the twentieth century, including radio, which was dominated by ham radio operators before World War I and taken over by the government during the war.

Radio did not become a profitable industry until the 1920s. In 1926 the National Broadcasting Company was formed and advertising was used to finance programming.

Television was not a viable industry until after World War II when the U.S. economy was booming, and everyone wanted a television set. In 1950 3 million households owned a television set. By 1978 the number had grown to 18 million. The first postwar RCA television set cost $352 and weighed ninety-five pounds; 43,000 sets were sold that year (www.tvhistory.tv).

Cable television began as a way to bring television to mountainous regions. In 1950 there were seventy cable systems with 14,000 subscribers; by 1962 there were 800 systems, with 850,000 subscribers. Between 1979 and 1989, subscribing households leaped from 15 million to 53 million. The number of networks also multiplied from 28 to 74 (www.tvhistory.tv).

Women began as secretaries in the broadcasting industry and worked their way up through promotion and public relations departments. Until recently, men dominated sales, news, and programming. A 1992 survey for American Women in Radio and Television (www.awrt.org) showed that women held 26 percent of the top managerial positions at television stations and 45 percent of station promotion directors.

The 1994 Glass Ceiling Commission noted that it was urgent to put women and minorities into decision-making positions and that diversity would reduce stereotyping and improve programming quality. The commission considered both programming and the business operations. On the business side, women pioneers such as Geraldine Laybourne, Dawn Steel, Marcy Carsey, and Kay Koplovitz were working their way up and were in powerful positions by 1997. Early in 1998 most had left, but others who had been in middle-management positions moved into higher echelons. The trailblazers had made their lives easier; the newcomers now felt a part of the team unlike their predecessors.

A 2001 Annenberg Public Policy Center report of women executives in broadcasting states that women represent 14 percent of the top executives at the ten major entertainment companies and 13 percent of corporate board members. The report points out that there are fewer executive positions due to the current consolidation of companies and thus, fewer women in management positions. The report recommends mentoring, career planning, constant dialogue, and higher visibility assignments. The report also stated that there are about the same percentages of women managers at the local level.

Further Reading
Alley, Robert S. *Women Television Producers: Transformation of the Male Medium.*
Chunovic, Louis et al. "Most Powerful Women in Television."
Lowe, Denise. *Women and American Television: An Encyclopedia.*
Rathbun, Elizabeth A. "Woman's Work Still Excludes Top Jobs."
www.earlyradiohistory.us
www.tvhistory.tv

Brown, Clara (1803–1885), Real Estate Investor, Mine Owner, Laundry Operator

---

Clara Brown was a former slave who operated a laundry in Central City, Colorado, during the gold rush years; she also invested in real estate. One of the earliest philanthropists in the state, Elizabeth Schafer said of Brown: "Her friendly empathetic, and generous nature earned [her] the honorary title 'Angel of the Rockies'" (p. 66).

She was born in Virginia in 1803. When she was three, Brown was sold to Ambrose Smith, who moved to Kentucky. She married another slave and bore four children, a boy and three girls. After Smith died in 1835, she and her family members were sold to several different owners. George Brown eventually bought her and gave Clara his name. After a succession of owners, she was finally able to buy her freedom at age fifty-seven.

She was in St. Louis operating a laundry when she learned that her husband and three of her four children were dead. Her surviving daughter, Eliza Jane, she also learned, had been taken west.

She arranged transport for herself and her laundry equipment in return for cooking jobs, joining a gold prospecting wagon train bound for Colorado. First Brown opened a business in Aurora, Colorado, then another in Central City, where she charged fifty cents per garment. It was the first laundry in the mining town. She also cooked, catered, cleaned, and was a midwife. By 1866 she had earned $10,000 through her various business interests.

She invested some money in Denver real estate and more in Central City gold mines and later in real estate there as well. Brown was one of the first African American women to own land. She decided to return to Kentucky to continue looking for her daughter. Although she did not locate Eliza Jane, she did find several newly freed relatives and friends and paid for their journey west. She returned to her business and properties in Colorado and continued to bring African Americans to the territory.

During all of these years she was a generous member of the community, feeding and clothing the poor and hungry, and helping to establish churches. Brown helped two Methodist ministers begin the Union Sunday School in Denver, and also helped to build the St. James Methodist Church in Central City. In 1880 she moved back to Denver because of its milder climate and lower altitude. In 1882 a friend told her about a freed slave named Eliza Jane who lived in Council Bluffs, Iowa. Further questioning found that this woman was indeed her long-lost daughter. During a trip to Council Bluffs, mother and daughter were finally reunited.

Clara Brown died in 1885. She had been asked to join the prestigious Colorado Pioneers Association in 1881 and was buried with honors by that association. There is a bronze plaque honoring her in St. James Methodist Church in Central City and a stained glass window depicting her in the state capitol building in Denver. She also has a chair in the Central City Opera House. In July 2003 an opera about her life, *Gabriel's Daughter*, was performed there.

See also: African American Businesswomen; Mining Industry; Real Estate; Western Businesswomen

Further Reading

Bruyn, Kathleen. *"Aunt" Clara Brown: Story of a Black Pioneer.*
Noel, p. 13–16.
Schafer, Elizabeth D. "Brown, Clara." In Salem, p. 66–67.

Brown, Julie Nguyen (1950–), Automobile Parts Supplier

Plastech Engineered Products and its owner, Julie Brown, have been listed in *Working Woman*'s top fifty woman-owned companies for two years: number 43 in 1999 and number 37 in 2000. She grew Plastech from a purchase of two financially troubled companies in 1988 to a powerhouse, with sales of over $400 million and 800 employees. Plastech, with its home office in Michigan, supplies plastic parts for automobiles for both large and small automobile manufacturers.

Brown was born and grew up in Saigon, South Vietnam, and attended French schools before coming to the United States in 1967 to spend her senior year of high school in Ypsilanti, Michigan. Her English was not very good, but she earned a scholarship to Tulane University in New Orleans and graduated in 1972 with a BS in computer science. Unfortunately, her visa was not renewed and she had to return to Saigon. The timing was bad; President Nixon had just announced that the American troops would be pulling out of Vietnam. Brown taught there for two years until the Viet Cong troops were within thirty miles of the city. Because her sister-in-law's father was a high ranking officer of the military, she received word of a troop plane evacuating South Vietnamese civilians; and she her brothers and sister-in-law were able to board the last plane leaving Saigon. They was interned in a refugee camp in Arkansas, but her roommate from Tulane was able to get the family released.

She moved to California to work as a market analyst, then married her Ypsilanti high school sweetheart, Jim Brown. They moved back to Michigan, she to an engineering trainee program at Ford Motor, he as one of Ford's corporate attorneys. Brown spent eleven years at Ford, moving up through the ranks to the title of product-design manager for the front and rear bumper systems on Ford's F-series pickup trucks. She gained great experience, particularly in dealing with suppliers and decided that she could do the supply side better.

In 1988 Brown began to build her company with the help of personal savings, bank loans, and $500,000 in loans from the minority direct-loan program of the Michigan Strategic Fund. First she bought Caro Plastic Corporation, maker of plastic automotive components, then the assets of Dynaplast Corporation. She merged the two into Plastech Engineered Products. Neither of these original companies was in good financial shape, but since then she has bought several other companies and merged them into Plastech.

She is totally committed to quality service; also to minority employment. Seventy percent of her employees are either women or minorities. She is also involved in joint ventures with other automobile parts suppliers.

Brown has won acclaim from her customers. She received two citations for quality: Ford's "Total Quality Excellence" and Chrysler's "Good Pentastar" awards. The company was voted Supplier of the Year by the Michigan Minority Business Development Council, and she was named Entrepreneur of the Year in 1994. She sits on the board of the Minority Business Roundtable.

See also: Asian American Businesswomen; Automobile Industry; Immigrant Businesswomen

Further Reading

Barkholz, David. "An American Success Story: Ex-Refugee Now Hires Others."

Sherefkin, Robert. "Plastech Is Moving to Dearborn: Parts Supplier Wants to Be Close to Ford."

Brunson, Dorothy E. (1938–), Broadcasting Executive

Dorothy Brunson was a radio pioneer who developed the urban contemporary format. She was the first woman broadcasting company general manager. She founded the Afro-American Association of Advertising Agencies, as well as the Association of Black-Owned Television Stations, serving as its first president. She is one of the six women in the *Working Woman* Hall of Fame.

Brunson was born in rural Georgia, the eldest of five children. Her father died when she was young, and her mother was a laundress. The family moved to New York City where she graduated from the New York High School of Industrial Arts. She attended Tennessee State University in Nashville, married James Brunson in 1964, and later received a degree in business and finance from Empire State College. The couple had two sons and later divorced.

Her first radio job was as assistant controller for WWRL, a radio station in New York City. Three months later Brunson became controller, then assistant general manager, then general manager. In 1968 she rose to be corporate coordinator and liaison director. In 1972 she entered the world of advertising, co-founding Howard Sanders Advertising, Inc., one of the first African American–owned agencies. She was not happy with the arrangement, however, and sold her share for $115,000 that she used to buy a plus-sizes clothing store. Unfortunately, Lane Bryant opened a competitive store next door.

Brunson's career as a revitalizer of radio stations began in 1973 when she became the corporate vice president of Inner City Broadcasting. She expanded the company from one to seven stations, turning it into the sixth-largest radio station in the United States by changing the format and restructuring its debt. She wanted to own a station though, so she bought Webb-Radio in Baltimore and transformed it from number 35 to number 10 in seven years. It was in financial trouble for the first four years, so she didn't take a salary. Brunson eventually turned it around, again through changing the format to appeal to more people. In 1986 she bought two more radio stations, WIGO-AM in Atlanta and WBMS-AM in Wilmington, North Carolina. Her company was called Brunson Communications.

Her next venture was into television. Brunson received a license to operate a television station in Philadelphia. She sold her three radio stations in 1990, and after a two-year court battle, purchased WGTW-TV 48 in Philadelphia, making her the first African American female television station owner in the United States. In 1997 the station generated $7 million and in 1999 began to produce original programming. By May 2002 the station claimed 900,000 weekly viewers, ranking sixth in Philadelphia.

Her success in both radio and television was due to her new programming formula, which aimed to appeal to all ethnic groups. Brunson's target audience was ages twelve to thirty-nine, and she thoroughly researched this group's buying habits before embarking on program changes.

She has been described as having hard-headed realism blended with gritty determination (Simpson, p. 46) and is blessed with good business skills as well as vision. She is widely known as a talented marketer and manager and a workaholic who always keeps an eye out for opportunities.

She has been active in a variety of community activities: Brunson was on the board of directors of the Harlem Commonwealth Council, the president of HUB in Baltimore, a church fund-raiser, and the Jefferson Bank Advisory Board. She founded the two organizations mentioned above and wants to "be remembered for the jobs and opportunities I've created for others" (Taylor, p. 109). She received an honorary doctorate from Clark Atlanta University in 1989 and was one of the *Black Enterprise* "25 Black Women Who Have Made a Difference" in 1994. She has written articles for *Vogue*, *Black Enterprise*, and *Newsweek*. Her role model is Mary McLeod Bethune.

See also: African American Businesswomen; Broadcasting Industry

Further Reading

"The Leader as Transmitter: Dorothy Brunson, Brunson Communications." In Helgeson, p. 177–215.

Simpson, Peggy. "The Revolutionary of Radio; Dorothy Brunson; Women Who Have Changed the World."

Taylor, p. 105–109.

Bryan, Lisa Little Chief (1967–), Food Industry Entrepreneur

Lisa Little Chief Bryan, a member of the Rosebud Sioux tribe, runs a specialty foods business selling homemade jellies and fry-bread mix. She has also collaborated on an entrepreneurship course featuring American Indian enterprises.

Bryan grew up on the Rosebud Sioux Indian Reservation in South Dakota and graduated from Black Hills State University in Spearfish, South Dakota. She made Indian tacos out of her fry-bread recipe for college fundraisers and the students liked them; so she did some research, subscribed to specialty food magazines, and went to the Tribal Business Information Center (TBIC) to look up data. She arranged to sell her Indian fry-bread mix wholesale to specialty stores in 1993. By 1996 sales were almost $100,000, and she added jellies and chokecherry pudding to her list. In 2001 her products were distributed in almost 300 stores in three states and have been featured on the Home Shopping Network.

In 2001 Bryans collaborated with Michele Lansdowne on an entrepreneurship-training series. The two textbooks and sixteen videos focus on seventeen American Indian entrepreneurs on the Montana Flathead Indian Reservation, as well as the Pine Ridge and Rosebud Sioux Reservations in South Dakota. The project is particularly useful because there are very few American Indian role models. The series uses a case-study approach and deals with problems unique to American Indian businesses, such as fitting in with tribal goals and values, how to gain support from the tribal council, and finding financing when land cannot be used as collateral.

See also: American Indian Businesswomen; Food Industry

Further Reading

Fisk, Holly Celeste. "With Relish."

"New Guides to Help Lead the Way for Growth in Entrepreneurship Among American Indians."

Bryant, Lane (1879–1951), Clothing Manufacturer, Fashion Designer

Lane Bryant was the first to design and market ready-to-wear maternity and large-size clothes. She was born Lena Himmelstein in Lithuania, and according to one account, was brought to New York City in 1895 by relatives as a bride for their son. She did not like him, so she went to work as a seamstress of fine lingerie in the same garment district sweatshop where her sister worked for $1 per week. By the end of four years, she had not only taught herself English, but also because of her skill as a seamstress, her salary was raised to $15 per week, which was astounding for that time. In 1899 she married jeweler David Bryant and had a son, Raphael. David died from tuberculosis soon after, leaving her with nothing but a pair of diamond earrings. She pawned the earrings to put a down payment on a sewing machine. She made lingerie and became known for her fine work.

In 1904 Bryant opened a shop on Fifth Avenue; she lived in the rear. Needing to open a bank account, she went to the Oriental Bank in Manhattan where they misread her name, thinking it was Lane. She was too timid to dispute it, so she kept the name and used it for her shop, and her subsequent businesses.

That year she also made her first maternity dress at the request of a society matron who wished to keep entertaining while in an "interesting" condition. At that time pregnant women did not go out and the idea of a maternity dress for street wear and even home wear was revolutionary. Bryant used draping to hide the pregnancy and charged $18 for the dress.

In 1909 she married Albert Malsin, another Lithuanian and an engineer who adopted her son. They had three other children. She continued designing while he took over the business operations, which had grown to $50,000 per year. At Malsin's suggestion, she concentrated on maternity wear; specialization was a trend in businesses of the time. After two years of frustration, in 1911 the *New York Herald* accepted the first advertisement for Bryant's maternity dresses. The entire stock sold out by the end of the first day for a total of $2800. That year they also began a mail order business. In 1912 they moved to a larger store and their winter catalog grew to thirty-two pages. In 1916 the business was incorporated as Lane Bryant Inc., and advertising expanded to national women's magazines such as *Vogue*, *Ladies Home Journal*, and *Woman's Home Companion*.

By 1917 sales were $1 million with maternity wear the bulk of the business. With her experience in tailoring for women, Lane realized that the ready-made clothes of the day didn't fit many women, so she began making clothes in larger sizes. Her husband did a survey of sizes by measuring 4500 individual customers in the store and obtaining data from insurance companies for total statistics from 200,000 women. He discovered that 40 percent of women were large sized and could be sorted into three general types: overall stout, full-busted but normal hipped, and flat-busted but large-hipped. Bryant, with her skill at draping illustrated in her maternity clothes, turned her attention to flattering the larger sizes. By 1923 stout clothes outsold maternity dresses with annual sales of $5 million.

In 1920 the company incorporated in Delaware; Bryant was vice president and on the board of directors. Malsin died in 1923, and Harry Liverman was president from 1923 to 1938, followed by her son, Raphael. New lines were introduced: layettes, clothing for tall women, and large-size clothes for girls. By 1951 the special size business was 95 percent, and maternity had shrunk to 5 percent. Annual sales were $50 million. The mail order business was the sixth largest in the United States. There were 3500 employees who had profit-sharing and pension plans which included health and disability insurance. In 1946 the company built a ten-story building on Fifth Avenue.

Bryant's charity work took the form of practical help. After World War II her stores were collection stations for donated clothing to send to refugees. Any Lane Bryant customer who lost her clothing in a disaster of any kind was offered a new outfit through the Red Cross. She helped the Texas City fire victims in 1947; as well as Illinois and Indiana tornado victims in 1948. She instituted the Lane Bryant Annual Award of $1000 to go to a group or individual whose voluntary efforts benefited the American home. Some recipients have been the United Association for Retarded Children, Danny Kaye, Eartha White, and Operation Crossroads Africa.

Lane Bryant died in 1951, but her stores live on. Her sons ran the company, with Arthur Malsin following Raphael as president in 1970. In 1980 the two brothers quarreled over policy, and Raphael gave up his position on the board. In 1982 Arthur Malsin sold the company to The Limited where it operates as a separate private subsidiary. As of 1997 sales were estimated at $340 million with 5,000 employees. In July 2001 the company was sold to Charming Shoppes.

See also: Fashion Industry; Immigrant Businesswomen

Further Reading
Mahoney, Tom. "$49,000,000 Business in Round Figures." *National Cyclopedia of American Biography*, p. 60–61.

Bullitt, Dorothy Stimson (1892–1989), Broadcasting Executive

Dorothy Bullitt was a pioneer of television in Seattle who built a radio and television empire, King Broadcasting, from a small entity in 1947 into a company worth an estimated $650 million in 1990.

Bullitt was a native of Seattle where her father was a pioneer lumberman who made his fortune in real estate. She attended Briarcliffe College and then married Scott Bullitt, a lawyer and politician, in 1918. He died in 1932 of cancer, leaving her at age forty with three children and her father's real estate company. She managed the real estate interests through the Depression and was president from 1929 through 1955. In 1947 she bought the smallest Seattle AM/FM radio station, KEVR, and renamed it KING. The next year she bought Seattle Channel 5 from Palmer Leberman who had built it himself and had obtained the first license for television in the city. She paid $375,000. Because of an FCC temporary ban on the establishment of new stations, Bullitt had a five-year monopoly and hers was the only TV station west of Minneapolis and north of San Francisco.

Bullitt had watched Palmer's first television broadcast of a high school football game, a messy transmission at best, and saw the future. She had no experience in broadcasting and very little in business, but her philosophy was: tell the truth and lots of it. She started one of the first local news operations and was perhaps the first in the nation to broadcast television documentaries, showing many programs on a variety of controversial topics. The first was *Lost Cargo*, an exposé of the Seattle docks. She also pioneered news editorials and commentaries. She had a knack for hiring good people and a reputation for integrity, innovation, and public service.

By the time of her death in 1989 the company had grown to six television stations in Seattle, Portland, Spokane, Boise, Twin Falls, and Honolulu; six AM and FM radio stations; a cable company broadcasting in Minnesota, California, Idaho, and Washington; television and radio sales companies; and a mobile-broadcasting facility. Bullitt was president until 1961, chair of the board of directors until 1967, and still active until she died. Her son, Stimson, took over as president until 1972. She promised that he would have absolute control and she kept her word, even when he made some unwise decisions. Her two daughters were officers on the board until they decided to sell the company in 1990.

Dorothy Bullitt was very involved in the community throughout her life. For many years, she served on a variety of boards for institutions such as the Seattle Public Library, the Seattle Art Museum, Children's Orthopedic Hospital and the Board of Regents of the University of Washington. She was on the governor's emergency relief administration in 1932 and 1933, was the state chair for the National Women's Committee Mobilization for Human Needs in 1933, and chaired the board for the Service Women's Club during World War II. She headed the Bullitt Foundation from its inception and oversaw the funding of many civic projects. She received an honorary degree from Pacific University in 1960 and community service awards from the Seattle Business and Professional Women's Club and B'nai B'rith Women.

> Dorothy Bullitt, a pioneer of television in Seattle, built King Broadcasting from a small entity in 1947 into a radio and television empire worth an estimated $650 million.

At age eighty-five she was rafting down the Colorado River, sitting in the bow. Bullitt died at ninety-seven, and in her obituary in the *Los Angeles Times*, she was called the "grande dame of Pacific Northwest television" (June 29, 1989, Part A, p. 3); and when her daughters were selling the company, the *Seattle Times* described her as an iconoclast: "She enjoyed the unusual, she respected people's rights to be different, and she honored her own word" (Watson, p. B1). The entire city mourned her and also mourned the passing of her broadcasting empire. The Woman's Funding Alliance named the Dorothy Bullitt Women of Achievement Award in her honor.

See also: Broadcasting Industry

Further Reading
Corr, Casey O. *KING: The Bullitts of Seattle and their Communications Empire.*
Haley, Delphine. *Dorothy Stimson Bullitt: An Uncommon Life.*
Watson, Emmett. "Dorothy Bullitt Placed KING-TV in a Class by Itself."

Burns, Ursula M. (1959–), Office Products Executive

Ursula Burns is the a senior vice president at Xerox, which ranked her number 28 in *Fortune*'s 2002 list of the most powerful black executives in the United States. In October 2003 *Fortune* ranked her forty-fourth in its list of the most powerful businesswomen in the United States.

Burns was born in New York City and educated there, earning a BS in mechanical engineering at the Polytechnic Institute of New York and an MS in mechanical engineering from Columbia University. She began as a summer intern at Xerox in mechanical engineering and continued after graduation. She entered engineering management in 1987, where she garnered experience in leading a team. In 1990 she realized that an engineer would not climb into top management, so she became the executive assistant to CEO Paul Allaire. From 1992 through 2000, she led several business teams, the office and fax business, the network copying business where she spent two years in London, and as vice president and general manager of the departmental business unit.

In 1998 Burns became a corporate vice president and joined the group of policy decision makers. She was the youngest person, at age thirty-nine, to attain that level of power within the company. The following year she became vice president of worldwide manufacturing, and in April 2000 the senior vice president of corporate strategic service where she was responsible for worldwide product and supplies manufacturing and environment, health, and safety operations. She was promoted to President of the Document Systems and Solutions Group in October 2001.

Burns has an incredible array of experience including, unusually, engineering and design development and manufacturing. These skills have been her allies as well as the knowledge of what it takes to rise in the ranks. She has said that, because she is black, she was viewed as a novelty at first and received attention because of her color. She attributes her rise in power to working harder and gaining a vast variety of experiences.

She married a Xerox researcher in 1989. He has many patents in his name and is a respected scientist. He retired early to spend time with the children and organize their daily lives because her job demands so much time and travel.

Burns sits on six corporate boards: Hunt Corporation, Banta Corporation, Dames and Moore, PQ Corporation, Boston Scientific Corporation, and Lincoln Electric Holdings. She is also on the boards of the National Association of Manufacturers, the University of Rochester Medical School, and the Industrial Management Council of Rochester. In January 2003 she received the 2003 ATHENA Award from the Women's Council of the Rochester Business Alliance.

See also: African American Businesswomen

Further Reading
Carter, Joan Harrell. "Commuter Marriages."
Hayes, Cassandra, Ed. "Ursula M. Burns: Vice President and General Manager, Departmental Copier Business, Xerox."
Zawacki, Michael. "Aces not Faces."

Business and Professional Women, USA

2012 Massachusetts Ave., NW
Washington, D.C. 20036
www.bpwusa.org

Founded in 1919 the organization works toward women's equity in the workplace. It provides networking, career guidance, and educational programs. A foundation was established in 1956 that supports scholarships, loans, grants, and fellowships for education and career advancement. It also researches issues affecting women in the workplace, and has been particularly active on pay equity issues throughout their long history.

Business Travel

In 2000, 17 million businesswomen traveled, 40 percent more than in 1995. Expectations in the industry were that, within a few years, women would be 50 percent of all business travelers. A flurry of journal articles appeared in 2000 describing concerns articulated by businesswomen travelers. In a New York University survey, both men and women agreed that flight attendants, gate agents, and hotel desk clerks were more deferential to men.

Other studies show that security is the top priority for women and includes well-lit entrance areas and corridors in hotels, as well as lighting above room doors. Adequate lighting is important in hotel and rental car parking lots, as are security guards. Added and much appreciated safety amenities include in-room safes, escorts, or limousines for late-night arrivals and trips to and from nearby restaurants. Some hotels even offer a partner for early morning jogging. Some rental cars include global positioning systems.

Service quality is a second priority for businesswomen. Hotels have added skirt hangers, and makeup remover and bubble baths are included with complimentary toiletries. Other examples of service upgrades include a white blouse available for immediate delivery, personal greetings, express check-out, a re-design of the bathrobes for women, and pantyhose and fruit juices in mini-bars. Conference hotels have also improved restroom lighting. Many hotels have advisory boards of businesswomen who suggest service improvements.

Businesswomen tend to use room service twice as much as men. They prefer menus offering more salads and soups and fewer heavy entrees. If dining in a restaurant, businesswomen prefer on-site restaurants. Many hotels now include a communal table where businesswomen can network or just have a meal with company. The Heritage Park Hotel in San Diego carried this idea one step further and offers a parlor where businesswomen gather for popcorn and a classic movie. In today's world, fax machines and Internet hookups are a must for all business travelers.

A 1999 New York University survey showed that women are more likely to incorporate leisure activities into their business trips than men, and they enjoy business travel more. Women want hotels with an upscale reputation and excellent service.

Further Reading
Daniel, Jo Beth. "To Serve and Protect."
Koss-Ferber, Laura. "Road Rules."
www.journeywoman.com

Butterworth, Mary (1686–1775), Counterfeiter

Mary Butterworth was called "the colonial period's female scoundrel" (McKerns, p. 186). She was a highly successful counterfeiter (although never successfully prosecuted) of several kinds of Rhode Island bills of credit. She controlled this cottage industry in her kitchen, enlisting several family members to help make the bills and then pass them.

She was born in Plymouth Colony, later Rehoboth, Massachusetts, to an innkeeper in 1686, the eldest of four girls and five boys. In 1710 she married John Butterworth, Jr., who was a well-to-do housewright. In 1716 Butterworth invented a counterfeiting method that did not use a copper plate, thus eliminating any tangible evidence in case she was caught. Instead, she transferred the images on the bill to a piece of blank paper using a wet piece of muslin and a hot iron. Then she, her brother Nicolas, and sister-in-law Hannah, filled in the letters and designs using a variety of crow-quill pens. Eventually she produced eight kinds of bills, which she sold to people who passed them for half price. This circle included quite a few of the citizens of Rehoboth, including the town clerk who was also a justice of the Bristol County Court of General Sessions.

By 1722, however, the other justices had become suspicious, and sent the sheriff to search the house of one of Butterworth's accomplices. They found nothing, but questioned several of the passers. In August 1723 Nicholas Campe confessed in Rhode Island to passing bills. His wife agreed to testify in court. In Massachusetts the sheriff read Campe's confession and arrested Mary Butterworth, her husband and five others including her brother. They searched all the houses, found nothing, and dropped charges against her husband and brother.

The rest were assigned to the grand jury where they denied everything. Because there was no evidence and there were no other confessions or witnesses, the grand jury refused to indict. Charges were dropped and everyone was freed. After that James says, "she returned to the obscurity of a respectable housewife" (James, Edward T., p. 274). Butterworth had seven children, and lived many more years, dying in Rehoboth at age eighty-nine.

See also: Finance Industry

Further Reading
James, Sydney V. "Butterworth, Mary Peck." In James, Edward T., p. 273–274.
McDowell and Umlauf, p. 499.
Macksey, p. 134.

C

Cable Industry, *see* Broadcasting Industry

Campbell, Phyllis Takisaki (1951–), Banker

Phyllis Takisaki Campbell, president of the U.S. Bank in Seattle until May 2001, was the first woman president of a major bank in the state of Washington. She went on to chair the newly formed Seattle bank board for U.S. Bank.

She was born in Spokane, the eldest of five children. Her father, an internee during World War II, ran a dry-cleaning business, and her mother was a medical technologist. Campbell was influenced by her grandfather's combination of Eastern and Western philosophies as well as her father's sense of compassion for victims. She earned a BA in business administration from Washington State University in 1973, a professional degree from the Pacific Coast Banking School in 1981, and an MBA in 1987 from the University of Washington. At Stanford she attended the Executive Marketing Program in 1992 and the Executive Management Program in 1997. She is married and is careful to balance her work with her home life.

After working for her father, Campbell began her professional career in 1972 as a management trainee for Old National Bank in Spokane and in 1980 was promoted to vice president and area manager. After U.S. Bank of Washington acquired Old National Bank in 1987, she continued as senior vice president and area market manager of Eastern Washington. From 1989 to 1991 she was executive vice president and manager of retail branch banking and area president of Seattle/King County in 1992 and 1993, serving as president and regional manager of U.S. Bank, responsible for all U.S. Bank of Washington retail and business banking. In May 2001 she resigned but consulted for a year on diversifying the workforce.

Campbell was raised as a humanitarian, believing strongly in volunteerism and helping the less fortunate. As a manager she ensured that community service combined with business service and encouraged employees to volunteer, with time off to do so. An avid mentor, she tries to ensure that every employee feels appreciated. Success to her means leaving a person or place better because of her involvement. She is a lifelong learner, known for her positive, can-do attitude and willingness to try different solutions.

Campbell has served on boards including SAFECO, Puget Sound Energy, Alaska Air Groups, the Pacific Science Center, and the Board of Regents of Washington State University. She has been a leader in United Way, Washington Roundtable, Washington Athletic Club, Seattle Foundation, and the National Center for Nonprofit Boards. She encouraged her bank to donate $10,000 to the Hanford Relief Fund.

See also: Asian-American Businesswomen; Banking

Further Reading
Nelson, Robert T. "Banker Leaves with a Deposit of Goodwill."
"Phyllis J. Campbell." In Mikaelian, p. 320–324.
Tyler, Francine Thistle. "Successful Exec Makes Every Moment Count."

Career Planning

Women in corporations or starting their own businesses need to plan their careers. Entrepreneurs who educate themselves on the rudiments of management, finance, communication skills, marketing, and constructing a sophisticated business plan, improve their chances for success. They also must construct extensive networks for encouragement, advice, and financing. Perseverance is important, but careful planning is a necessity for starting and growing a business.

Women seeking top management positions need to network, but they also need to choose both their industry and company carefully. Promotions are more likely in an industry where women hold a high percentage of line positions and in a company with a strong female customer base. A knowledgeable mentor can explain the corporate culture, but the aspiring manager needs to position herself for higher levels by looking for jobs with authority that allocate resources and assign responsibility to others. She also should seek opportunities that offer breadth of experience or are cross-functional.

A Catalyst study suggests how corporations could support career planning: integrate career planning into yearly evaluations and include employee input and dialogue; develop women's networks; implement a formal mentoring program and foster a mentoring culture; provide rotational opportunities; and recognize that accommodating customized careers is a retention tool (Cracking, p. 126).

The goal of the National Association of Career Women (NACW) is to enhance women's personal and professional development through education, networking, and monthly meetings. Information is available at www.nacwonline.org.

Further Reading
Advancing Women in Business-The Catalyst Guide.
Burke, Ronald J. and Debra L. Nelson, Eds., *Advancing Women's Careers.*
Davidson, Marilyn J. *The Black and Ethnic Minority Woman Manager: Cracking the Concrete Ceiling.*
Moore, Dorothy Perrin. *Careerpreneurs: Lessons from Leading Women Entrepreneurs on Building a Career Without Boundaries.*

Carnegie, Hattie (1889–1956), Fashion Designer

Hattie Carnegie revolutionized the fashion industry in the United States by providing high fashion at affordable prices. A marketing and advertising genius, she set the tone of American fashion for many years and was one of the first to teach and support young American designers.

Born Henrietta Kanengeiser, the second of seven children, she left Austria with her family for New York in 1897, where her father worked in the garment industry until his death in 1913. Her name, and possibly that of the family, was changed to Carnegie. After working from age thirteen as a messenger for Macy's Department Store, she opened her own business, Carnegie-Ladies' Hatter, in 1909 with a neighbor, Rose Roth. Roth made the dresses that Carnegie designed and sold (she never did learn to sew).

In 1913 they incorporated, moved to then-fashionable Eighty-sixth and Broadway near Riverside Drive and sold expensive clothes; dresses started at $75. Carnegie was their best advertisement, wearing her own designs to New York high-society functions. At the end of World War I, she bought out her partner and changed the emphasis to restyling and redesigning Paris originals to suit the American woman's taste. Between 1919 and 1942 she made 142 trips to the European fashion market and bought original models. In 1923 she opened the shop at 42 East Forty-ninth Street, which became the foundation of her fashion empire. Her own designs reflected her preferences, simple and elegant with classic lines, that became known as "the Carnegie look." Her influence on affluent American women of fashion was great; the "little Carnegie suit" was a status symbol in the 1930s and 1940s.

Initially, Carnegie's clothes were expensive and designed for the wealthy. By 1929 sales were $3,500,000 per year, but during the Depression even the wealthy could not afford her clothes, so subsequently she also began to market a less-expensive ready-to-wear line and introduced Spectator Sports, an elegant, low-priced wholesale line that sold countrywide.

The business prospered during World War II and the 1950s; by 1942 she had a retail shop in New York for both ready-to-wear and custom-made clothes; resort shops in Palm Beach and Southampton, New York; two wholesale businesses, several factories, and a line of cosmetics. Carnegie, involved in every facet of the business, hired all her family members for key positions. She mounted four shows per year. Once, three weeks before a show, her head designer stole an entire collection, but Carnegie managed to design and manufacture a replacement collection in time. She died in 1956, leaving an $8,000,000 fashion business.

Hattie Carnegie was the arbiter of fashion in the United States for more than twenty years. With her ability to spot new talent, she encouraged many designers. She won the Nieman-Marcus Award in 1939 and the American Fashion Critics' Award in 1948 and dressed prominent women including Mrs. Randolph Hearst and Mrs. Walter Chrysler as well as many actresses. The *New Yorker* article said, "Hattie Carnegie is a clever business woman in every way, but the driving force in her soul is her love for clothes" ("Profiles: Luxury, Inc.," p. 27).

In 1927 Carnegie married for the third time, to Major John Zanft, who she had known since she was thirteen.

See also: Fashion Industry; Immigrant Businesswomen

Further Reading
Bauer, Hamble. "Hot Fashions by Hattie."
Kenney, Alma L. "Carnegie, Hattie." In Sicherman and Green, p. 135–136.
"Profiles: Luxury, Inc."

Carsey, Marcy (1944–), Television Producer

Marcy Carsey is co-founder and co-owner of Carsey-Werner Studio City, producer of top-rated television programs since the 1980s. Her company has been on *Working Woman*'s list of top woman-owned companies since 1993.

Born in 1944, the daughter of a shipyard worker and a homemaker, Carsey grew up in Quincy, Massachusetts, watching a lot of television. She graduated cum laude with a BA in English literature from the University of New Hampshire in 1966, the first one in her family to earn a degree. After being a tour guide at NBC and a go-fer on *The Tonight Show*, she became executive story editor to *Tomorrow Entertainment* in Los Angeles in 1971.

In 1974 Carsey joined ABC as a comedy programming executive, working on *Happy Days* and *Laverne and Shirley*. Within two years she was in charge of comedy, supervising *Mork and Mindy* and *Taxi*. From 1978 to 1981 she was the senior vice president for primetime series but realized that she could rise no further. As she said when interviewed, she received "a near-fatal blow to the head from a heretofore invisible ceiling" (Schmuckler and Collingwood, p. 40).

As a result she founded Carsey Productions and by 1982 had persuaded Tom Werner, also at ABC, to join her as co-owner and co-chair of the new Carsey-Werner Company. With money from second mortgages rather than financing from a studio, they preserved their independence. In 1984 she and

Werner persuaded NBC to commit to 13 episodes of *The Cosby Show,* which became one of the biggest moneymakers, grossing $1 billion and began a series of hits. In the 1988 and 1989 seasons, the company produced the three top shows: *The Cosby Show, Rosanne,* and *A Different World.* Unlike many others, it has sold shows to all four major networks, including *Cybill, You Bet Your Life with Bill Cosby, Grace Under Fire, Third Rock from the Sun,* and *That '70s Show.* Hollywood's largest production house, it had estimated sales of $199 million in 1999 and its own syndication division.

The Carsey-Werner programs are known for sympathetic and creative formats for established comedy talents. The company has an eye for talent and good scripts and attracts gifted writers and producers. The company is very selective, focusing on a few shows that it loves, and nurturing them to completion by paying close attention to all the details. The partners look at every script, are involved in most story meetings, and supervise all actual production. Carsey concentrates on judging material and shaping a series during the early stages, while Werner oversees post-production and network relations. They are both involved in every step from negotiating with the network to offering script and filming suggestions.

> Marcy Carsey, co-founder and co-owner of Carsey-Werner Studio City, has been producing some of the top-rated television programs since the 1980s.

The partners have won an Emmy for *The Cosby Show* in 1985, the NAACP Image Award for Best Episode of a Comedy Series for *A Different World,* and two Golden Globe Awards for *Cybill.* Carsey served on the executive committee of the Academy of Television Arts and Sciences in 1983. She and Werner were inducted into the Academy of Television Arts and Sciences Hall of Fame in 1996, the Broadcasting and Cable Hall of Fame in 1997, and honored by the Museum of Television and Radio in 1999. Carsey won a Lucy Award for innovation in TV in 2000 and they both received a David Susskind Lifetime Achievement Award in TV in 2001. The following year, *Electronic Media* named her to their list of the most powerful women in television.

Carsey is married with a daughter, a son, and three stepchildren. She is not a workaholic and seems to have successfully blended motherhood and a demanding career. In the early 1970s she brought her babies to work and let her employees do the same. Her latest venture is as chief programmer, in partnership with Geraldine Laybourne and Oprah Winfrey, for Oxygen Media, the cable channel aimed at women and owned by women.

She is active in the community and particularly proud of her work with the Women's Enterprise Development Corporation that helps budding women entrepreneurs (Bergman, p. B20).

See also: Broadcasting Industry

Further reading

Bergman, Anne. "Honoree Profile: Marcy Carsey: Television Honoree."
"Carsey, Marcy." In *Current Biography 1997,* p. 84–85.

Carter, Bill. "Cadillac-Sized Hits by the VW of Producers; Carsey-Werner Keeps its Independence and Still Picks Television's Winners."
Schmuckler and Collingwood, p. 40.

Cashman, Nellie (1851–1925), Miner, Restaurateur

Nellie Cashman was one of the more fascinating women of the Western frontier. She paid for her prospecting by running boarding houses, restaurants, supply and equipment shops, and grocery stores. She was known in mining camps all over the West for her expertise in mining matters as well as for her courage, fearlessness, compassion, and generosity.

Born in County Cork, Ireland, Cashman emigrated to Boston with her sister Fannie and their widowed mother. In 1869 they went by train to San Francisco where she married the following year. In Pioche, Nevada, she first attempted mining and opened a boarding house in 1872. She was also active in fundraising for the Catholic Church. After two years she returned to San Francisco before going with a party of 200 miners over the Chilkoot Pass to the Cassiar gold-placer grounds in British Columbia. There she opened another boarding house, worked her claim, and developed a reputation for fearlessness and compassion. On her way to another camp, she heard that her fellow Cassiar miners were snowed in without supplies

> Over fifty years Nellie Cashman made several fortunes in mining and various businesses from Mexico to the Arctic Circle. She appears on a U.S. stamp in the Legends of the West Series.

or medicine and were dying from scurvy. She purchased 1,500 pounds of supplies, medicine, and sleds, hired six men, left Victoria, and sailed to Fort Wrangell, Alaska. Heading inland, she finally reached the miners after sixty-six days in snow with just two blankets for warmth. The miners, suitably grateful, began calling her "the angel of mercy."

She moved to Tucson in 1879 where she opened a restaurant but soon left for Tombstone, just in time for its heyday. Although she stayed there for almost twenty years, she made brief forays to various mining strikes in Baja California, Mexico (1883), Kingston, New Mexico (late 1880s), Montana, and Harqua Hala, Africa (one month in 1889). During this time, her widowed sister Fannie and her five children lived with her. Fannie died in 1883, and Cashman took care of the children. When she went off to prospect, she supported them financially, placing them in Catholic institutions.

In Tombstone Cashman's entrepreneurial activities included a food and supply store, a hotel, and a restaurant where an indigent miner could always find a free meal. Her most famous establishment was Russ House at the corner of Fifth and Toughnut Streets. She also did charitable work for a Catholic church, a hospital, and the first school in the town.

In 1898 Cashman returned to her beloved Alaska, this time with a nephew, going south every five years or so to visit the children and her friends. She continued her pattern of staking claims, opening boarding houses, restaurants, and stores while living in Fairbanks, Dawson, and even within the Arctic Circle around 1905. In 1922 she formed the Midnight Sun Mining Company, printing shares for $2 each. Her last trip south was in 1923. The next year she contracted pneumonia and died in Alaska the following January.

Although Cashman mined for over fifty years, from Mexico to the Arctic Circle, she was known as a genuine lady with a spotless reputation. A United States postage stamp features her image in the 1994 Legends of the West Series; a park in Phoenix is named for her, as is the Nellie Cashman Woman Business Owner of the Year Award. Since 1981 it has been given to a female business owner in western Washington who has made an outstanding contribution to the status of women entrepreneurs through achievements in both business and community leadership. The trophy is a bust of Cashman.

See also: Immigrant Businesswomen; Mining; Western Businesswomen

Further Reading
Chaput, Don. *Nellie Cashman and the North American Mining Frontier*.
Rochlin, Harriet. "The Amazing Adventures of a Good Woman."
Zanjani, Sally, p. 25–59.

Castagna, Vanessa (1951–), Retail Executive

Vanessa Castagna, the executive vice president, chair, and CEO of J.C. Penney's Stores merchandising and catalog sales, is credited with Penney's retail transformation. She was on *Fortune*'s list of the most powerful businesswomen in 2000 and 2002 and ranked number 41 in 2003.

She began her retail career in 1972 at Lazarus, a division of Federated Department Stores, working there for thirteen years, rising to senior vice-president and general merchandise manager. In 1985 Castagna moved to Target as vice president of women's merchandising. From 1992 to 1994 she was senior vice president and general merchandise manager for women's and junior clothing at Marshalls Stores.

In 1994 Castagna helped Wal-Mart launch a product and brand development program to identify fashion trends and upgrade its image. As senior vice president and general merchandise manager, she had responsibility for products in its 2,500 stores.

In August 1999 she joined J.C. Penney as executive vice president and CEO of J.C. Penney Stores, Merchandising and Catalog Sales, the first woman in that position, and served on the company's management committee. With responsibility for all department store activities, Castagna started by redecorating each location, centralizing the buying decisions, holding three-day strategy sessions, and forming Home Office Merchandising Action Teams, resulting in more fashionable items. She changed the company culture, offered bonuses contingent on total company performance, and made strategic alliances with manufacturers. Overall, she focused on the customer.

Castagna has broad experience and strong leadership skills. She regularly works 100-hour weeks, is tough, and demands much, but in a nice way. She is married to Neil Castagna. In 1999 she won the HUG (Help Us Give) Award from Intimate Apparel Square Club for her "dedication and hard work to support the launch of the [Association's] $6 million campaign for the new Rusk Pediatric Wing" at the New York City Medical Center.

See also: Retailing Industry

Further Reading
"A Conversation with Vanessa Castagna."
Halkias, Maria. "Wal-Mart Exec Becomes J.C. Penney's CEO."
"J.C. Penney Names Vanessa Castagna Exec VP and Chief Operating Officer of J.C. Penney Stores, Merchandising and Catalog."

Catalyst

120 Wall Street
New York, NY 10005
www.catalystwomen.org

Catalyst is a non-profit organization with a two-fold mission: "To enable women in business and the professions to achieve their maximum potential and to help employers capitalize on the talents of their female employees" (www.catalystwomen.org). Founded in 1962 by Felice Schwartz, it has grown into a highly respected source of research and reports on women's progress in companies. The organization has a speakers' bureau and a library, researches and publishes its own reports, and consults with corporations. Its corporate board placement service assists in locating qualified women for board seats.

See also: Schwartz, Felice

Further Reading
www.catalystwomen.org

Catz, Safra (1962–), Software Executive

Safra Catz, executive vice president and chief of staff at Oracle, was ranked number 49 on the 2000 *Fortune* list of the most powerful women in corporate America. She is the highest-ranking woman officer at Oracle.

After various investment banking positions, she joined Donaldson, Lufkin, & Jenrette in 1997 and rose to managing director. As senior technology banker, one of her accomplishments was to finance Softbank, a Japanese company. In April 1999 Catz joined Oracle as a senior vice president and part of the management team. The following November she became executive vice president and chief of staff, responsible for global business practices and corporate development. CEO Larry Ellison has said the job was the same as that of a chief operating officer, but that Catz didn't want the title because of the publicity. She has served on its board of directors and that of the Oracle Help Us Foundation.

Catz, married with two children, has said that she couldn't handle such an intense job without her husband at home caring for the children. (Sellers, p. 160).

See also: Information Technology Industry

Further Reading

Barranechea, Mark J. *E-Business or Out of Business: Oracle's Roadmap for Profiting in the New Economy.*

Sellers, Patricia. "The 50 Most Powerful Women in Business," p. 142, 160.

www.oracle.com

Center For Women's Business Research

1411 K Street, NW, Suite 1350, Washington, DC 20005-3407
Phone: 202-638-3060 Fax: 202-638-3064
www.womensbusinessresearch.org

Since 1989 the Center For Women's Business Research has provided original research about the economic and social contributions of woman-owned firms around the world. It provides services to all sorts of corporations, institutions, government agencies, and organizations. Publications include statistical reports, surveys, audio-visual materials, a quarterly newsletter, fact cards, and a Web site. The organization's representatives also consult, give speeches, and run seminars about issues concerning women business owners. In 2003 the National Foundation for Women Business Owners was folded into the Center.

Further Reading

www.womensbusinessresearch.org

CEO, *see* Chief Executive Officer

CFO, *see* Chief Financial Officer

Chang, JoMei (1953–), Software Developer

JoMei Chang was named one of the top entrepreneurs of the year by *Business Week* in the first month of 2001. Her company, Vitria Technology, pioneered BusinessWare, an applications integration software that allows companies to do business on the Internet, but still use their own software. In 1998 *Red Herring* magazine named her one of the top ten entrepreneurs of the year, and the company was one of the top 50 private technology companies in both 1998 and 1999. *Fortune* called her one of the new breed of CEOs in 1999, and *Business Week* named her one of the top entrepreneurs of 2000.

Born in Taiwan to a Taiwanese bureaucrat, Chang received her BS in computer science from Chaio Tung University there and a PhD in database management systems from Purdue in 1978. In her first job as a senior research scientist at AT&T Laboratories, she developed and patented the first reliable multicast protocol for efficient scalable information distribution across communication networks. In 1984 she was appointed senior engineer at Sun Microsystems, the only woman engineer on the research team.

In 1986 she married Dale Skeen, and they both joined Teknekron Software Systems, a startup company; he as the engineering architect, and she as a project manager. The company team developed a breakthrough system for bond trading at Fidelity Investments. Over time, relationships within the team and with clients became stormy, so when Reuters bought the company in 1994, both Chang and Skeen left with their share of the proceeds, $10 million.

With their own money they started Vitria Technology, a pioneer in the development of enterprise-integration software. Chang was the company CEO and Skeen, the chief of technology. After three rounds of outside financing, the company went public in 1999 at $16 per share, selling three months later at $273, but the 2001 to 2002 stock market problems lowered the per-share value to $5.00. The company continues to develop software, including a new category of products in 2002 called Collaborative Applications. Chang insists that new products are not announced until they have been successfully tested.

Chang is noted for her soft voice, disarming smile, and boundless ambition. Emert quotes her at a company orientation: "What is our goal? Our goal is worldwide dominance" (p. E1). She is dynamic, highly intelligent, and always beautifully dressed. She is a leadership-style manager, persistent, but less abrasive than when she was younger. She listens to everyone before making decisions.

See also: Asian American Businesswomen; Information Technology Industry
Further Reading
Emert, Carol. "JoMei Chang: Boundless Ambition."
Pilgrim, Kitty. "Vitria-CEO, CNNFN."
www.vitria.com/home/management.html

Chen, Joyce (1917–1994), Restaurateur, Food Industry Entrepreneur

Until Joyce Chen introduced Northern Chinese cuisine to the United States, Chinese food was thought to be chop suey and chow mein, neither of which was authentic. She opened a restaurant, wrote a cookbook, starred in a PBS television program, and began two companies selling Chinese cooking equipment and stir-fry sauces. For her efforts, she was named by *Nation's Restaurant News* as one of the fifty most influential people in the history of the food service industry.

Chen was born in Beijing, where her father was a high-ranking official. The family had servants, but her parents encouraged her to learn household skills, including cooking. They moved to Shanghai when she was sixteen. In 1943 she married Thomas Chen, an importer and dealer of leather goods, and they had two children. In 1949 with the Communist Revolution threatening, they escaped on the last boat out of Shanghai and settled near relatives in Cambridge, Massachusetts. The community, known for its numerous universities, had many Chinese students who were regularly invited to traditional Chinese dinners at the Chens' house. One day, instead of the traditional American cupcakes, she sent egg rolls to her daughter's class bake sale. They sold out in the first five minutes. This solidified an idea to open an authentic Chinese restaurant.

In 1958 Chen and her husband opened a restaurant in Cambridge, one of the first to serve northern Chinese cuisine. Customers initially wanted the familiar chow mein and chop suey and French bread. In fact, one customer stomped out of the place when there was no bread. To help customers gradually become acquainted with real Chinese food, Chen served a buffet of American turkey, roast beef, and chicken, with authentic Chinese dishes such as moo shu pork, hot and sour soup, Peking duck, steamed buns, and pan-fried dumplings (which she called Peking ravioli) at the end of the table. Gradually, the American food disappeared from the menu, and the restaurant became one of the most popular in Cambridge and its environs. In fact, by the 1960s, it was the most famous Chinese restaurant in the United States. All three children (a third child was born in Cambridge) participated.

In 1960 Chen began teaching Chinese cooking at the Cambridge and Boston Adult Education Center, and in 1962 published a book that included recipes, cooking techniques, and informative pieces about Chinese culture and traditions. It quickly became the standard for Chinese cooking. In 1966 she was invited by PBS in Boston to have her own cooking show, *Joyce Chen Cooks*. Two years later, she opened a second restaurant. During the 1970s, she helped many Chinese chefs to enter the United States by obtaining visas, sometimes going to Washington and knocking on Senate doors. Then she trained the chefs and encouraged many of them to open their own restaurants.

Chen's belief was that Chinese food and Chinese culture go together and that many Chinese restaurants would be just that many more places to promote Chinese culture. She also inaugurated culinary events featuring a Chinese meal and lectures on Chinese traditions and heritage.

While teaching cooking, she recognized the need for Chinese utensils and equipment, so she began selling them through Joyce Chen Products. She modified some of the equipment to suit American stoves, inventing the Peking pan, a flat-bottomed wok. Then she began bottling and selling stir-fry sauces in yet another company, Joyce Chen Specialty Foods. During the 1970s and early 1980s, she modified traditional recipes, incorporating healthier ingredients to aid with heart problems and dietary restrictions.

Joyce Chen was a successful businesswoman and a cultural envoy. Because her brother was a popular Communist hero in China, she was granted freedom to travel there unescorted and was invited to advise the Chinese Board of Trade. PBS later broadcast her film of this trip. In 1983 Boston's mayor appointed her the city's cultural ambassador to its city sister, Hanzhou, China. In 1984 President Reagan invited her to a dinner for the Chinese premier where she led the party in a traditional Chinese toast. Soon after that, she contracted Alzheimer's disease that led to her death. Her daughter Helen, who continues the cookware company, tells of the many people who remember her as a wonderful friend and great lady. Chen was proud of her heritage; her mission was to share her culture.

See also: Asian-American Businesswomen; Food Industry

Further Reading
Brattain, Michelle. "Chen, Joyce." In Garraty and Carnes, p. 773–774.
Chen, Helen. *Helen Chen's Chinese Home Cooking.*
Chen, Joyce. *Joyce Chen's Cookbook.*
Weiland, Jeanne. "Joyce Chen."

Chief Executive Officer (CEO)

The CEO, the highest-ranking executive, manages the company on a day-to-day basis and is responsible to the corporate board of directors for carrying out the company's policies. The corporate board sets the CEO's compensation.

Chief Financial Officer (CFO)

The CFO is the corporate executive in charge of the company's financial operations, and reports to the CEO. The CFO is responsible for the accuracy of the company's financial reports and for the forecasting and budgeting process.

Childcare

Childcare is one of the most pressing issues for businesswomen mothers, regardless of their income bracket. According to a National Institute of Child Health and Human Development estimate, only 9 percent of childcare programs for children under three met high quality standards in 2001.

During the nineteenth century in the United States, children of working mothers got little care during the day, unless relatives or friends looked after them. Children who were old enough to dress and feed themselves usually stayed home while their mothers and fathers worked. The first day nursery opened in 1828, but by 1880 there were still only six. Although 500 existed by 1912, they were only open to mothers who had to work, and child abuse was common. Some mothers committed their children to almshouses. In 1911, Missouri passed the first Aid for Dependent Children law, and by 1935 forty-six states had passed similar laws.

The 1920s saw an increase in working mothers. Upper class women hired servants, while the others relied on relatives, neighbors, and day care. By 1923 there were sixteen nursery schools that combined care with education, and in 1928 there were 108. Poor women received Mothers' Pensions, but day nursery employees treated these mothers disrespectfully, so they stopped bringing their children, and day nurseries gradually disappeared. During the New Deal era of the 1930s, day nurseries reappeared and were federally funded. The 1941 Lanham Act provided federal funds for day care for children of defense workers. Although some companies began their own on-site facilities, most eventually closed, leaving 1,504 still operating in 1946 (Schneider, p. 43–44).

Twenty years later childcare again became a concern as women flocked to the workplace. Congress passed the Comprehensive Child Development Act in 1971, providing day care for all children, but President Nixon vetoed the bill. By 1973 day care centers could accommodate 700,000 children; but 6 million pre-school children had working mothers. The Tax Reform Act of 1976 and Revenue Act of 1978 provided tax relief. By 1979, 51 percent of three- to five-year-old children were in preschool and only 25 percent of American families had stay-at-home mothers, 33 percent of school children came home to an empty house, and childcare was the fourth-largest family budget item (Schneider, p. 45). The Bureau of Labor Statistics that year counted 29 million children whose parents, or only parent, worked. Half of these children were taken care of by relatives, and the others were in day care.

The business advantages for providing some sort of childcare benefits became obvious by the mid-1990s: it reduced absenteeism and turnover, enhanced recruitment and retention, reduced stress for employees, improved morale, and enhanced community and public relations. There are numerous options for companies: on-site childcare centers with parental access; provision of resource lists and referral services; childcare allowances; childcare vouchers; emergency childcare programs for holidays and vacations; back-up care; near-site childcare centers; investment in community childcare centers; pre-tax set-asides; a dependent care fund; sliding-scale fees or direct subsidies; and sick-child care. Flexible hours and part-time work care can also facilitate childcare. There are pluses and minuses to each of these options, of course, with expense at the top of the negative list. Other disadvantages are a feeling of inequity by those with no children, the lack of high quality centers in many locales, and the administration of such programs. Each company and business must assess its own needs and decide which kind of program meets those needs.

There have been many studies on the effect of day care on children. A wide variety of conclusions has been reached, ranging from increased aggressiveness to better social skills. Guilt for mothers is still a part of the equation in spite of the need for many mothers to earn a living. Women wrestle with this issue and use a variety of solutions, including nannies and stay-at-home husbands as well as day care.

Two national organizations work to promote quality childcare: The National Childcare Association (www.nccanet.org) and the Childcare Action Campaign.

See also: Employee Benefits; Husbands/Fathers

Further Reading

"Childcare." In Schneider and Schneider, p. 43–45.

Sher, Margery Leveen and Madeline Fried. *Childcare Options: A Workplace Initiative for the 21st Century.*

Sprague, Peg. "Weighing Your Childcare Options."

Cholmondeley, Paula (1947–), Accountant, Executive

As vice president and general manager of the residential insulation division, Paula Cholmondeley (pronounced "Chumley") was the highest-ranking minority executive at Owens Corning and the highest-ranking female officer. In 1996 *Fortune* named her one of six hot young managers with the experience, vision, and personality necessary for leadership; and she has proved that forecast through her performance at Owens Corning. In July 2000 she became vice president and general manager of specialty products at Sappi Fine Paper North America in Boston.

Cholmondeley was born and raised in the Caribbean, first in Guyana and then Jamaica. She has often said that this was a positive experience because she saw no limitations caused by race; in that region black people achieved in all the professions and high positions because they were the majority. Both parents motivated her to be a high achiever; her psychiatrist father believed in teaching his children all the time, even at the dinner table, and her mother was a social worker. She came to the United States in 1966, graduating from Howard University with a BS in accounting in 1970 and from Wharton School of Finance with a masters in accounting the next year, before becoming a Certified Public Accountant.

Cholmondeley has worked for Arthur Andersen, as comptroller of Zebra Associates, as manager of general operations with International Paper, as regional general manager with Westinghouse Elevator, and in other positions. In 1986 Blue Cross of Greater Philadelphia recruited her to be senior vice president of finance and chief financial officer. She left to become FAXON's vice president and director of the international division.

In 1992 Owens Corning created a new position, vice president of business and strategy, and appointed Cholmondeley, including her on the senior management team with responsibility for identifying and developing the global market. She was appointed president of the Miraflex Fiber Products Division and corporate vice president in 1994. In this position she made her mark, responsible for the development and launching of a new, softer insulating fiber, a top secret scientific discovery. It was an exciting product, and she led the project's team who developed it in two years, half the usual time for this sort of venture. Her leadership role was to inspire the team and to champion the technology and the product. She compared the process to Star Trek—"going where no one has gone before." (Martin, Justin, p. 76–78). Because of her success with the launch, in 1996 she was appointed general manager of Owens Corning's largest division, the $800-million general insulation division. In July 2000 she moved to Sappi Fine Paper North America, responsible for four of the company's paper businesses.

Cholmondeley was named a White House Fellow in 1982, one of fourteen chosen from 1200 applicants, spending a year in Washington DC as a special assistant to the U.S. Trade Representative. She has served on the board of directors at Armco, Gifts in Kind, Dentsply International, and the Center of Science and Industry in Toledo, Ohio. She is also an active member of the Executive Leadership Council, the Conference Board's Council of Division Leaders, and the Council on Foreign Relations. She married Thomas S. Watson Jr., founder of the largest black accounting firm in the United States and advisor to Presidents Reagan and Bush. Until he died in 1998, they had a pact not to live more than a two-hour flight apart. She attributes her success to her willingness to grow and change and also "believing that there was nothing I couldn't learn how to do." ("Paula Cholmondeley...," p. 62).

See also: African American Businesswomen; Immigrant Businesswomen; Manufacturing

Further Reading

Martin, Justin. "Tomorrow's CEOs: Meet Six Young Managers Who Have What it Takes to Lead in the 21st Century."

"Paula Cholmondeley; Vice President and Residential Insulation, Owens Corning."

Christopher, Doris (1945–), Kitchen Utensils Saleswoman, Entrepreneuer

Doris Christopher began The Pampered Chef, now a $500-million kitchen utensils business, in 1980 with a $3,000 loan and inventory in her basement. She sells directly though home parties and has been on the *Working Woman* list of top woman-owned companies since 1996.

She married Jay Christopher, a friend since high school, in 1967 and was a home economics teacher until she had two daughters. In 1980 her children were still small, so she decided that any career she had would need to be flexible and part-time. Her goal was to spend most of her time with her family and have a career that she loved and was good. She knew she could teach, and she loved to cook. Her husband, a marketing executive, suggested selling through home parties. Although she didn't like the idea at first, Christopher decided to try selling kitchen tools at friends' homes, giving a demonstration and a taste of the delicious and fragrant food made at the party, combining education, social contact, and fun.

Armed with a $3,000 loan from a life insurance policy, Christopher went to the Chicago Merchandise Mart and bought twelve dozen different utensils. At her first party, she prepared a pizza on baking stones and a fresh vegetable tray (a novelty at the time) using her favorite slicers, parers, and dicers. The attendees spent $175 on kitchen gadgets, and four of the women offered to host parties. For most of that first year, Christopher was everything: buyer, saleswoman, warehouse worker (in her basement), shipper, and bookkeeper. In the first three months she had made $10,000. When one of her friends offered to sell, Christopher called her a kitchen field consultant and hired her on commission. By the end of 1981 sales were $50,000, and she had twelve field consultants.

In 1986 she joined the Direct Selling Association; she now had fifteen employees, and the workers filled orders with shopping carts. Christopher's husband was the full-time executive vice president from 1987 to 1992, and she brought in her first outside vice president in 1993. Later she said that it took her too much time to realize that more managers were needed. From 1989 to 1993 sales increased by 4,000 percent due to the major increase in kitchen consultants and articles in *Woman's Day*, *Family Circle*, *Success, Inc.*, and *Working Woman*. By 1994 the company had a full team of managers and tapes so that field consultants could train their recruits. It also built a 220,000-square-foot warehouse, office, and testing kitchen and installed an online order filling system and centralized shipping.

In 1996 over 20,000 field consultants sold 128 products in all fifty states. The next year there were 37,000 field consultants and expansion into Canada. By 1998 sales were almost $500,000 from 42,000 field consultants, and each week there were 15,000 home demonstrations. An average day saw 3,000 orders. Two years later there were 60,000 kitchen consultants, and the company expanded into the United Kingdom. In September 2002 Warren Buffett of Berkshire Hathaway bought the company for an undisclosed price. Christopher continues to run it. A new headquarters opened in October 2002.

The culture of The Pampered Chef reflects the values of its owner. Christopher is a firm believer in the importance of family time, especially at dinner. She started her business with the idea that meal preparation should be easy and that her kitchen utensils would save time that working women could enjoy with their families. Her motto is "the kitchen store comes to your door." Her field consultants work either full- or part-time; the cost of a starter kit is around $100, and an experienced consultant from the area trains, supervises, and mentors the beginner. Videos, audiotapes, and books are also available for the trainee. Almost all of the consultants are women. The commission structure is similar to all multi-level marketing firms, and Christopher says the company will never telemarket. She has written two books: a collection of recipes and a 1999 publication, *Come to the Table: A Celebration of Family Life*, which contains reminiscences about her own experiences.

In 1998 The Pampered Chef was named one of the 500 fastest-growing companies in the United States by *Inc.* magazine and received the Better Business Bureau Torch Award for its highly ethical treatment of customers, suppliers, and employees. The company has donated money to several philanthropic entities. During the RoundUp from the Heart Campaign every September through February, the company gives $1 for every kitchen show to America's Second Harvest Food Bank Networks and the Canadian Association of Food Banks. The field consultants ask their customers to round their total purchases up to the nearest dollar, with the excess earmarked for charitable causes, and they sell a stone cookie mold made exclusively for the company proceeds from which also go to charities. The 1998 gift was $650,000, totaling over $3 million in eight years, with the company absorbing all related administrative costs. Every April there is a similar program for the Women's Opportunity Fund that offers loans and assistance to women in developing nations. For this, $2 per show is given and note cards dedicated to the project are also sold. Christopher and her husband gave Concordia University, a Lutheran college, $15 million in 1999 for a new building housing the College of

Education and its Early Childhood Center, the largest gift it had ever received. Husband Jay Christopher is on the board of directors, and his father was the company's legal council. The Christophers also donated $15 million to Valparaiso University for a new library and $10 million to the University of Illinois at Urbana–Champaign for a building to house an undergraduate program on strengthening families. The company has supported America's Second Harvest, the American Cancer Society, and the Women's Opportunity Fund. Doris Christopher is a member of the Committee of 200.

See also: Food Industry; Saleswomen

Further Reading

Check, Dawn Lynn. "Easy Does It: Products from the Pampered Chef Eases Meal-Making for Busy Families."

Christopher, Doris. *Come to the Table: A Celebration of Family Life.*

Ericksen, Gregory. Doris Christopher—The Pampered Chef, LTD. "The Kitchen Store That Comes to Your Door," p. 109–130.

Mamis, Robert A. "Master of Bootstrapping Administration."

Civil Rights Act of 1964

The Civil Rights Act of 1964 authorized federal action against segregation in public accommodations, public facilities, and employment, resulting in affirmative action and the creation of the Equal Employment Opportunity Commission. Title VII of the act was amended by the Equal Opportunity Act of 1972 and the Pregnancy Discrimination Act of 1978.

Title VII prohibits discrimination in employment on the basis of race, color, religion, national origin, or sex, except for private companies employing less than fifteen people. It covers processes such as recruitment, hiring and firing, promotion, compensation, training, benefits, work assignments, and classified advertisements. It also prohibits discrimination on the basis of pregnancy, maternity, or the possibility of becoming pregnant. Sexual harassment is also prohibited.

This law has helped thousands of women obtain jobs and promotions. In many cases, their pay has improved. The courts have continued to define and refine the issues through the many cases that have been tried. Women from all races and ethnic backgrounds have benefited.

The Civil Rights Act of 1991 extended Title VII protection to American citizens working abroad for American-owned or American-controlled companies. It also limited the amount of money awarded in a suit to $50,000 for employers of one hundred or fewer and $300,000 for employers of more than 500.

A 1985 article in *Harvard Business Review* assessed the impact of this law through two surveys, one in 1965 and a second twenty years later. In 1965 neither men nor women believed that the law would speed up the progress toward equal opportunity for women at all levels in companies. In 1985 84 percent of the men and 74 percent of the women believed that, although laws cannot change attitudes, this one did change behavior and that helped change attitudes, at least a little. Most of the women felt that women's advancement would not have happened at all without the Civil Rights Act of 1964 (Sutton and Moore, p. 52).

See also: Equal Opportunity Commission; Sex Discrimination; Sexual Harassment

Further Reading
Landmarks in Modern American Business, p. 436–442.
Sutton and Moore, p. 52.
"The Civil Rights Act Prohibits Discrimination in Employment." In Kaliski, p. 139–141.

Claiborne, Liz (1929–), Fashion Designer

Liz Claiborne was a fashion pioneer who not only revolutionized the clothing of professional women but also dominated the industry for more than fifteen years. She and her husband, Arthur Ortenberg, started their own company, Liz Claiborne, in 1976. She designed stylish, casual yet sophisticated, moderately priced clothes aimed at career women. Ortenberg handled the business side. In 1987 *Fortune* called her America's most successful female entrepreneur. She is in the National Sales Hall of Fame, and in 1990 they were both inducted into Junior Achievement's National Business Hall of Fame.

She was born in Brussels, Belgium, to American expatriate parents. Her father was a banker who loved art and history, and her mother was a homemaker who taught her to sew. In 1939 as the Nazis were about to invade, the family moved to the United States. After the war, they returned to Brussels, where Claiborne attended parochial schools and an art school then a private school in Nice, France. She won a *Harper's Bazaar* national design contest and went to live with an aunt in New York City, where, in 1950, she worked in the garment district. That year she married Ben Schulz and had a son, taking only two weeks off when he was born. They divorced in 1957, the same year she married Arthur Ortenberg.

In her first job as an assistant to Tina Lesser, she sketched, modeled, and picked up pins, learning the trade with Lesser as her mentor. From 1954 to 1960 Claiborne was a designer for Juniorite, then went to Rhea Manufacturing in Milwaukee. She spent the next sixteen years at Youth Guild, Inc., where she saw a need for moderately priced clothes, but the company was not interested.

By 1975 she had developed a reputation for solid quality and performance. Her son and stepson had finished college, so she and Ortenberg formed their own company, Liz Claiborne, Inc. with him as secretary-treasurer. As designer, president and chair, Claiborne pursued her own idea: affordable, quality career clothes. She added casual sportswear and quickly became a "bellwether for other American designers to serve the new market needs of the rapidly expanding woman's work force" (Claiborne, Liz, p. 110). During its first year, sales exceeded $2 million, and the company was profitable.

> Liz Claiborne, a fashion pioneer, not only revolutionized the clothing of professional women, but also dominated the industry for more than fifteen years.

In June 1981 it went public at $19 per share, rising to $31 per share within six months. She added petite sportswear, shoes, accessories, cosmetics, men's sportswear, and perfume. In 1989 Claiborne and her husband retired from active management but remained on the board. That year the company ranked number 299 on the *Fortune* 500 list, with $1.2 billion in sales. Her designs and clothing had dominated the fashion industry for fifteen years.

Liz Claiborne's awards include designer of the year for 1976 and 1978, the 1980 Entrepreneurial Woman of the Year, the 1985 Annual Distinguished in Design Award from Marshall Field's, and the One Company Makes a Difference Award from the Fashion Institute of Technology. In 1987 the company was number 2 on the list of the *Fortune* 500's most admired corporations and number 2 on the *Business Month* list of the five best-managed companies. In 1991 she won the Frederick A.P. Barnard Award from Barnard College. She was also nominated to the National Sales Hall of Fame and was given an honorary PhD by the Rhode Island School of Design. Claiborne and her husband established a foundation that focuses on conservation issues, with beneficiaries including the Wilderness Society, the Greater Yellowstone Coalition, wildlife preservation, and a nature series on PBS. They also supported restoration of the 1857 Fire Island lighthouses.

See also: Fashion Industry

Further Reading

"Claiborne, Liz." *Current Biography Yearbook 1989*, p. 110–113.
"Liz Claiborne–Persevering Pioneer." In Landrum, p. 15, 206–222.
Sellers, Patricia. "The Rag Trade's Reluctant Revolutionary."

Clark, Catherine Taft (1906–1986), Food Industry Executive

Catherine Clark founded Brownberry Ovens and its extraordinary bread in 1946. Because the bread contained no preservatives or artificial additives and tasted great at a time when Wonder Bread was the only choice at the grocery, the company was a success. By the time she sold it for $12 million in 1972, she was making twelve kinds of bread, six kinds of dinner rolls, several kinds of croutons, and stuffing.

She was born in Wisconsin to an entrepreneur father who ran a bicycle repair shop, the first movie house in town, and a garage. The family had the first automobile in town. He died of Bright's disease when she was young, and her mother took in washing to support the family. She was the middle child with two brothers. Clark worked at summer jobs throughout high school, was very athletic, and graduated top of her class. She moved to Milwaukee and worked on the personnel staff of a department store through the Great Depression. After meeting her future husband on a blind date and exchanging letters for two years (he was in Chicago) they married in 1931. Her mother lived with them and later babysat their children.

After mortgaging their home and borrowing $500 from friends, Clark officially began Brownberry Ovens in 1946. She had bought the recipe for freshly ground whole-wheat bread from a local bakery. She then rented a shop, bought an old beer delivery truck and used equipment from the baker, and began production with her first mixer that made twelve loaves. She pioneered whole foods long before they were popular. She priced each loaf at 22 cents, three cents higher than Wonder Bread. Clark and her husband marketed to stores on Saturdays. During the first year, operations outgrew the equipment twice. In 1951 she began advertising in the *Milwaukee Journal,* and by 1960 her net income was $180,000. In 1972 annual sales had reached $16 million, and she was marketing a variety of products to forty states. That year she sold the company to Peavey Corporation, remaining chairman of the board until her retirement in 1979.

When Clark began her company, most women did not work and certainly did not own a company. She hired mostly women, partly because few men would work for a woman. She was very intelligent with a well-honed sense of humor. Her mother raised her two children, but they came to the shop after school. She was very strong and focused on selling high-quality products for a higher price than Wonder Bread. When she retired, she kept the Wisconsin home but moved to California and bought a vineyard.

See also: Food Industry

Further Reading

"Ceres and Chardonnay: Catherine Clark." In Rich-McCoy, p. 49–72.

"Clark, Catherine Taft." In Hamilton, p. 92–93.

MacDonald, James R. "Catherine T. Clark." In Editors of *The Wall Street Journal,* p. 56–65.

Clothing Industry, *see* Fashion Industry

Cohen, Abby Joseph (1952–), Investment Advisor

Abby Cohen, the chief market strategist and former partner at Goldman Sachs and Company, has been on *Fortune*'s list of most powerful women in corporate America since 1998. Because of her perspicacity in predicting the twists and turns of the stock market and her reputation for using hard economic facts, she became one of the most respected analysts in the country. In fact, before the stock market crash of 2001, people believed that what she said affected the fluctuations of that market.

She was born and raised in Queens, New York, to parents who both worked in corporate financial departments. In high school Cohen won two Future Scientists of America Awards but fell in love with economics at Cornell, graduating in 1973 with a double degree in economics and computer science. At that time the only computers were large IBM mainframes. After graduation, she married David Cohen, moved to Washington where she received an MA in economics from George Washington University and he, a law degree. During that time, she was a junior economist for the Federal Reserve Board. In 1980 they had their first daughter.

Cohen's first corporate job was as an economist/analyst for T. Rowe Price, a mutual funds company in Baltimore. In 1983 she moved to New York City as an investment strategist at Drexel Burnham Lambert where she originated her forecasting method of focusing on the United States and global economic indicators, as well as company finances combined with securities valuations, the economic environment, and fund flows in and out of the market. She became chief strategist in 1987, but the company declared bankruptcy in 1990.

After a brief stint at BZW, Cohen joined Goldman Sachs whose clients include the world's largest corporations and governments. One of the strongest periods of stock market activity in recent times began in 1990. Her predictions, painstakingly based on all her economic facts and formulas, were always positive, and the people who relied on them saw their investments grow at a rapid rate. She also became known for her ability to explain her forecasts plainly and understandably to laypersons, and began to appear on television and in magazine and newspaper interviews.

During the 1990s Cohen was the most influential analyst in the country with an astounding record of successful predictions. She was promoted to managing director in 1996 and became the chief equity strategist and co-chair of the investment policy committee. In 1998 just before the company went public, she became a partner. The crash of the stock market in 2001 caused Cohen's influence to wane. While her analyses are still highly respected, her forecasts do not affect the vagaries of the stock market in the same way.

Cohen combines a calm and even-tempered management style with a reassuring, but compelling, way of speaking. She lives in Queens, not far from her childhood home, widowed father, and extended family. Although she travels a lot, she manages to attend all major school events for her two daughters. Even during the height of her power in the market, she never took credit for her forecasts, pointing out that she was just recognizing and summarizing the analysis.

Cohen has an honorary doctorate from Tel Aviv University and has served on the board of governors of the New York Society of Security Analysts and the National Economist Club. She has chaired the boards of the Institute of Chartered Financial Analysts and the Association for Investment Management and Research. Other recognition includes Woman of the Year Award from the New York City YWCA in 1989, *Smart Money*'s number 1 financial analyst in 1997, the best analyst of the year (also 1997) from *Institutional Investor*, and was named to the "Wall Street Week with Louis Rukeyser" hall of fame. In 2000 *Money* named her one the fifty smartest women in the money business. She has taught finance seminars at Cornell, Wharton, Harvard, and Dartmouth and is a trustee/fellow of Cornell University.

See also: Finance Industry

Further Reading

Bianco, Anthony. "The Prophet of Wall Street."
Boland, Vincent. "Bull in a Bear Market Remains Undeterred: The Interview."
"Cohen, Abigail." *1998 Current Biography Yearbook*, p. 111–113.
Usborne, David. "She's Got It Made; Abby Cohen Lives in Queens and Goes to Work on the Bus, but She's the Wonderwoman of Wall Street."

Cohen, Betty Susan (1956–), Television Executive

Betty Cohen was instrumental in beginning, building, and establishing TNT's Cartoon Network as a force in children's television programming, for which *Fortune* ranked her number 50 on the list of powerful corporate women in 2000.

She was raised in Racine, Wisconsin, with an older brother who read *MAD*, the humor magazine that influenced Cohen's tastes. After graduating from Stanford University, Phi Beta Kappa, Cohen worked in San Francisco writing public service announcements for Public Media Center. In 1982 she moved to New York to be a writer-producer for Cable Health Network, later known as Lifetime Television, and in 1984 for Nickelodeon and Nick-at-Nite, which she helped launch.

In 1988 Cohen joined TNT as general manager, and later, senior vice president. She became the executive vice president of Cartoon Network in 1992, then in the planning stages. Ted Turner had just bought the Hanna-Barbera library including *Bugs Bunny*, *Tom & Jerry*, and *Scooby-Doo* cartoons and wanted to re-play them on television. Since its launch in October 1992, the network has succeeded. In 1994 she was promoted to president of Cartoon Network Worldwide and the Turner Learning Market, marketing products tied to the series and concentrating on expanding into international markets. She also oversaw the creation of original cartoons, including *Cow & Chicken*, *Johnny Bravo*, and *Powerpuff Girls*, that were aimed at ages six to eleven. By March 1998 the network reached 50 million homes and was seventh among cable TV channels.

Cohen began a major marketing effort with toy giveaways, a joint promotion with Kraft foods; a Cartoon Network superstore, plus CDs and comics. By November 1999 the channel was seen in 60 million households with profits of $50 million. The following year she inaugurated a Web site and acquired some Japanese animation series. The merger of TNT with Time Warner also made available a library of Looney Tunes cartoons, and a full-length movie on the Powerpuff Girls was released in 2002.

In June 2001 Cohen stepped down as president of the Cartoon Network. She continued as the head of Turner Learning and planned to develop television and Internet programs and services for young adults and teens. The change was her idea; she sees herself as an "entrepreneurial builder" (*Business Wire*, April 29, 2001). One year later she left Turner Broadcasting to develop and sell a multimedia television project for teens and young adults.

Cohen's awards include the Promax International Marketer of the year in 1997, the 2000 Vanguard Award for programmers, and the Promax Pinnacle Award in 2001. The Cartoon Network received the 1998 cable TV marketer of the Year from *Advertising Age* and *Powerpuff Girls* was nominated for an Emmy in 1999. She has served on the board of AOL Time Warner Foundation and the executive committee of National Cable Television Association's "Cable in the Classroom."

See also: Broadcasting Industry

Further Reading

"Betty Cohen Stepping Down as President of Cartoon Network Worldwide to Pursue Next Venture within AOL Time Warner/Turner Broadcasting Family."

Kaplan, James. "The Queen of Cartoons."

Littleton, Cynthia. "An Animated Conversation with Betty Cohen."

Colonial Businesswomen

When the colonists settled in America, they brought their own laws. The English settled in New England and along the seacoast and brought English common law, under which an unmarried woman, or "femme seule," could own property and enter into contracts until marriage, when everything she owned became her husband's property and he spoke for both. When he was away from home, however, the wife became the "deputy husband" and could sign contracts and bills of sale, in fact, conduct business in his name. After a husband died, the widow ran the business or farm until she remarried, and the next husband received everything she had inherited.

The Dutch settled New York City and the Hudson River valley. Dutch women were equal to their husbands before the law, kept property in their own names, and operated businesses as well. The Dutch family economy was based on every member's increasing the family fortune, with the women known for their business acumen.

There were also African American women in the colonies, both slaves and freeborn. Their businesses catered to the demand for food and domestic services, and were usually single proprietorships, owned by a man or woman. The emphasis was on selling a skill such as sewing, cutting and dressing hair, cooking, baking, or selling produce in outdoor markets.

Latinas settled in Florida and the Southwest, often managing large estates or ranches. Their laws allowed them to purchase and own land, sign contracts, and own businesses. Some established small flour or sugar mills. American Indian women, like African Americans, also relied on their skills and shared their crafts with the colonial settlers.

Despite the restrictive laws, colonial women engaged in a wide variety of businesses. A woman's place was in the home, but it was a family economy; everyone worked, whether the family business was a shop or plantation. Because men were away so much, wives became adept at managing the land or farm or running the business. Society at that time expected women to work if it was necessary; it also expected single women and widows to support themselves and their children. Angel Kwolek-Folland stated: "They participated more fully in the economic life of their day than women have done since, even in our own century" (Kwolek-Folland, p. 31).

Women who lived in the towns kept shops of all kinds; the literature speaks of advertisements from women tobacconists, barbers, bakers, milliners, seamstresses, and weavers. Rural women managed the farm or plantation. Women ran inns and taverns, and some traded for furs with the Indians. They were merchants who exported and imported goods. Some were printers. Many printers' widows carried on the business and became famous: one of them, Sarah Goddard, printed the Declaration of Independence.

By 1776 the colonial economy had become more complex with the growth of towns, cities, and bustling seaports. There were many more inns and taverns and even rudimentary manufacturing. During the Revolutionary War, the women kept the businesses going. Afterwards there was no money, so both men and women worked at anything they could. Soldiers were given land grants in lieu of money and moved their families west. Early factories began to replace household industry.

British ships brought luxury goods as well as ideas of ladylike behavior. The status of women deteriorated, as status-conscious American women "eagerly assimilated" the British concept of "women as helpless, useless, dependent appendages" (DePauw, p. 36). It was fifty years before women began to demand equal rights and a voice in political matters. Although some continued to work and run businesses, they were not considered socially equal by the late eighteenth century.

See also: Fashion Industry; Retailing Industry; Travel Industry

Further Reading

DePauw, Linda Grant. *Founding Mothers: Women in the Revolutionary Era.*

Dexter, Elisabeth Anthony. *Colonial Women of Affairs.*

Kwolek-Folland, Angel. *Incorporating Women: A History of Women and Business in the United States.*

Pierson, William D. "Colonial America, Slave Market Women," and "Colonial New England, African Economic Survivalisms." In Juliet Walker, p. 155–159.

Williams, Selma R. *Demeter's Daughters: The Women Who Founded America, 1587– 1787.*

Committee of 200

625 N. Michigan Ave., Suite 500
Chicago, IL 60611-3108
www.C200.org

Begun in 1982 primarily as a support network for woman entrepreneurs and corporate executives, the Committee of 200 has broadened its goals to include scholarships and mentoring programs for women MBA students. In 1986 it established a foundation to fund outreach, research, and mentoring activities. The group also devised the C200 Business Leadership Index that measures businesswomen in comparison to their male counterparts. Early members include Muriel Siebert, Lillian Vernon, Sherry Lansing, Ellen Gordon, and Katherine Graham. As of 2002 membership was over 440.

Further Reading

Capell, Kerry. "It Sure Ain't the Ladies' Auxiliary."

Gutner, Toddi. "Progress? Not As Much As You Thought."

"Turning Points: Frank Talk from Top Execs About The Moments That Changed Their Careers Forever."

Communication

"In business, communication is the critical backbone of an organization's ability to operate internally and externally as well as nationally and internationally" (O'Neil, p. 149). There are two categories of communication, verbal and non-verbal, and of the former, two types: formal and informal. Communication today takes place everywhere in many, many modes: meetings, e-mail, telephone, fax, computer groupware, presentations, and conversation. Nonverbal communication consists of body language, gestures, dress, and the distance between two speakers. The grapevine and rumors are also methods of communication. O'Neil discusses four basic styles of communicating: direct or authoritative, analytical or fact finding, amiable or coaching, expressive or flamboyant. Each style is individual and each can be suited to a particular occasion.

Because men and women communicate and converse differently, it is important to try to avoid barriers to understanding. Women are seen as nurturing but sometimes indecisive, due to communication styles. Tina Flaherty points out several ways women can undermine their authority: seeming to be asking a question rather than making a statement (voice up at the end), beginning with a disclaimer, apologizing, over-speaking to fill the silence, speed-talking, and gushing. These traits sabotage communication and credibility. Many times, women in corporations are excluded from informal communication because this takes place in the men's room or during male social occasions such as golfing, hunting, or fishing.

In a corporation, communication begins at the top with leaders who effectively describe the vision and mission. Senior and middle managers need to reinforce that message along with frequent news updates and feedback to all employees in multiple ways.

Further Reading
Flaherty, Tina Santi. "Gender Communication: Mute Issue?"
O'Neil, Sharon Lund and D. Gaye Perrin. "Communications in Business." In Kaliski, p. 149–152.
Tannen, Deborah. *Talking from 9 to 5: How Women's and Men's Conversational Styles Affect Who Gets Heard, Who Gets Credit, and What Gets Done at Work.*

Comparable Worth, *see* Compensation

Compensation

"Compensation is composed of the base wage or salary, any incentives or bonuses and other benefits" (Lee, p. 295). Until 1875 U.S. law made woman's wages the property of her husband or father, in the belief that a woman's place was in the home. A woman's wages were based on this assumption, rather than on her skills, performance, or need and were half as much as men in the same job. In 1870 Wyoming Territory was the first state to pass any kind of equal pay statute for men and women in public employment. Massachusetts passed the first minimum wage law in 1912. It referred only to women and children, and, between 1912 and 1920, fourteen other states passed similar laws. In 1938 the Fair Standards Act guaranteed a minimum wage regardless of sex. The National War Labor Board issued General Order No. 16 in 1942, which stated that equal salaries should be paid to women and men doing the same or similar jobs; however compliance was voluntary.

In 1963 the Equal Pay Act forbade wage discrimination based on gender. When this act was signed, women made fifty-nine cents for every dollar earned by men. More than 200 court cases were filed by 1971. The Equal Pay Act of 1972 extended the former law to include executives, administrators, professionals, and outside sales persons. By 1991 more than 1,900 charges of wage discrimination based on gender had been filed with the Equal Employment Opportunity Commission.

Despite all of this legislation, however, there is still a gap between the salaries of men and women. In 2002 women, on average, earned seventy-seven cents for every dollar earned by men. Men and women who belong to ethnic minorities earn even less. Equilar, a data analysis firm, found that the median compensation of female executives was 24 percent less than that of males in 2003.

During the 1980s and 1990s, the issue of comparable worth was discussed at length. Proponents advocated evaluating jobs on the basis of skill, effort, responsibility, and working conditions, and awarding equal pay for similar jobs. Some state and local entities use this method, but private and federal employers oppose it. They feel that it might lower men's wages rather than raise women's wages, and that it might cause labor conflict. They also believe that it is very difficult to measure a job fairly. In 2001 Maine became the first state to enforce comparable worth for both public and private companies.

An ideal compensation plan is composed of "policies, procedures, and rules that provide clear and unambiguous determination and administration" (Lee, p. 295). It should be fair to all workers in the same company and in comparison to the outside market and must be proportionate to the employee's qualifications and contributions. A systematic analysis and comprehensive job description should determine base wages. Compensation can also include incentives, bonuses, stock awards, and stock options.

The National Committee on Pay Equity (www.pay-equity.org), a national coalition of labor unions, women's and civil rights organizations, commissions on women, state and local pay equity coalitions, individuals, and other organizations, works to eliminate sex- and race-based wage discrimination and to achieve pay equity.

See also: Employee Benefits; Equal Pay Act of 1963

Further Reading
Berger, Lance A. and Dorothy Berger, Eds., The Compensation Handbook.
Larson, Chris. "The Fight for Fair Pay."
Lee, W. Lee. "Employee Compensation." In Kaliski, p. 295–299.

Computer Industry, *see* Information Technology Industry

Construction Industry

The construction industry has long been famous for macho attitudes and hostility toward women workers. By the late 1970s women finally began making inroads, but then it was as company owners, not as workers. Strong unions, sexual harassment, hard physical labor, the temporary nature of the work discouraged women. Monetary and emotional rewards are high, however, for those who persevere. In 1983 there were 79,000 women construction workers. That figure doubled to 153,000 by 2002.

Women are still rare at a construction site. Because of union barriers, many began their own companies. In 1982 there were 61,600 woman-owned construction firms, 5 percent of the industry total of 1.26 million. The Center for Women's Business Research estimated 212,916 woman-owned construction firms in 2002, 8 percent of the 2.6 million total.

Most women in construction believe that any progress made is due mainly to affirmative action requirements that stipulate that to be eligible for government contracts, firms must have women as 6.9 percent of their workforce. Woman-owned firms have been able to bid and win as subcontractors under these requirements. Another trend favoring women is the growing need for professional, financial management, computer technology, and engineering skills in the industry. The physical labor is still there, but new regulations, diminishing profit margins, and high labor costs are requiring different skills. For subcontractors, just putting together a winning bid calls for sophisticated estimates not possible in the past.

There are opportunities in this field for women, given the changes in the industry and the softening of union hostility. The availability of apprenticeships and training opportunities has led to an increase in the number of women entering construction. Two organizations focus on educational opportunities, the National Association of Women in Construction (NAWIC, www.nwac.org) and Women Construction Owners and Executives, U.S.A. (www.wcoeusa.org.)

Further Reading
Johnson, Steve. "Women Building Toward Respected Role in Construction."
Mayer, Caroline E. "Women, Building Careers One House at a Time."
Touby, Laurel. "Contracting Women."

Consulting

A consultant is "a person qualified to give expert professional advice" (*Oxford Large Print Dictionary*, p. 173). The 2003 *Consultants and Consulting Organizations Directory* lists more than 27,700 companies and individual consultants. Experts in almost every realm of business offer advice and guidance on a specific goal or on problems in the entire organization. They also will take on a task and act as an outside department or division of the client's business. Many consultants have had years of corporate experience, but prefer to run their own businesses. Some consultants specialize in finance management, marketing, sales, manufacturing, industry, and transportation, with expertise in processes ranging from strategic planning to re-engineering to benchmarking. Their business is to solve problems.

It is a world dominated by men; most consultants are men and most of their clients are men; however, there are successful women in the field, like Faith Popcorn in consumer marketing and behavior and Lillian Gilbreth and Rosabeth Moss Kanter in management. Felice Schwartz, the founder of *Catalyst*, was one of the first woman consultants. Orit Gadiesh, CEO of Bain & Company, one of the top consulting firms, has said that women have had a harder time than men; if a woman and man who are consulting partners walk into a room, the client will talk to the man. This situation is slowly changing as clients become more accustomed to businesswomen consultants.

Further Reading

Harrison, Roger. *Consultant's Journey: A Dance of Work.*

Kidding, Matthias and Lars Engwall, Eds., *Management Consulting: Emergence and Dynamics of a Knowledge Industry.*

Cooney, Joan Ganz (1929–), Television Producer

Joan Ganz Cooney, president and co-founder of Children's Television Workshop, conceived and produced *Sesame Street, The Electric Company*, and several other children's educational television programs. She was an original inductee into the *Working Woman* Hall of Fame and the pioneer in early educational television.

Cooney was born in Phoenix to a banker father. She was raised a Catholic, with the Christopher movement greatly influencing her goal of making a difference in the world. After receiving her BA cum laude in education from the University of Arizona in 1951, she worked in Washington D.C. for the government for a year, as a journalist for the *Arizona Republic* for a year, and then moved to New York City at age twenty-three.

After one year as a publicist for NBC-TV, Cooney became the publicist for the *U.S. Steel Hour* for CBS-TV. At a dinner party one evening in 1966, she sat next to a vice president of the Carnegie Corporation of New York who was interested in education delivered by television. He invited her to study the possible use of television for early education, particularly for disadvantaged children. She submitted the report, "The Potential Uses of Television in Preschool Education," to the corporation in November of that year. It verified that 96 percent of families in the United States owned television sets; that in homes with young children, the TV set was on sixty hours per week; and that children need to begin education before they are five.

Cooney convinced not only the Carnegie Corporation, but also other foundations and government agencies to fund the Children's Television Workshop for $8 million. The work began in 1968. She researched children's viewing habits and the kinds of programs they enjoyed most and discovered that fast action, catchy music, and cartoons captured their attention. With this knowledge, her sixty-person team created *Sesame Street*, which debuted on November 10, 1969. It was a success, attracting 7 million preschooler viewers by the end of the first season. In April 1970 the Children's Television Workshop incorporated as a nonprofit with Cooney as president, and later chair and CEO from 1988 to 1990. She then became the chair of the executive committee, and vice chairman of the board.

Just because it was a nonprofit corporation did not mean that funding wasn't necessary. Cooney had to learn the basics of running a business and put a major effort into finding funding. The government and foundations helped, but she began exploring other ways to support the programs. Overseas distribution brought in some money, but the real support came from licensing agreements: i.e., Oscar the Grouch, Cookie Monster, Big Bird, and other characters' dolls, books, records, puppets, and other products. By 1981 the company was supporting itself this way, and she had become a shrewd businesswoman as well as a creator and producer. In 1995 there were 250 employees and revenues were $55 million. The Children's Television Workshop changed its name to Sesame Workshop in 2000.

Cooney is an inspired creator with the ability to get things accomplished. She combines idealism with practicality and managed to set the standard for educational television. *Sesame Street* was her first program, followed by *The Electric Company* for eight- to twelve-year-olds, *3-2-1 Contact* about science for pre-teens, and *Square One TV*, a math program. *Sesame Street* has been beloved by preschoolers for more than thirty years and has won more than that number of Emmy awards. It not only gave children a head start in reading and counting, but also focused on such difficult issues as death, child abuse, and sibling rivalry in a nonthreatening and positive way.

> Joan Ganz Cooney, combining idealism with practicality, set the standard for educational television with her first program, *Sesame Street*, a perennial Emmy winner that preschoolers have loved for over thirty years.

Cooney married twice, once in 1964 to Timothy Cooney, a dedicated feminist and civil rights worker. After a 1975 divorce that made her one of the first women to pay alimony, she married Peter Peterson, a former U.S. Secretary of Commerce and investment banker. She now has five stepchildren. One of her strongest beliefs is that the "secret to a happy life is finding some balance between work and emotional relationships" (Gilbert, p. 298).

Cooney is in the National Women's Hall of Fame, the Academy of Television Arts and Sciences Hall of Fame (the first female non-performer), and was the *Ladies Home Journal* Woman of the Year in Education in 1975. She received the 1988/89 Daytime Emmy for Lifetime Achievement, the AAUW Educational Achievement Award in 1984, the Frederick Douglass Award from the New York Urban League in 1972, and the Presidential Medal of Freedom, the nation's highest civilian honor, in 1995. She also holds a Franklin Institute Award honoring individuals who have transformed entire fields of knowledge. In 2001 she was awarded the Lambchop Award from KIDSNET, and in 2003 she was honored by the New York Council for the Humanities. Her honorary degrees are from Harvard, Notre Dame, Smith, Princeton, Georgetown, Brown, Oberlin, and Columbia University among others. She has served on the board of directors of Johnson & Johnson, May Department Stores, Metropolitan Life Insurance, and Xerox where she was the first woman director in 1975. These positions, she said, helped her enormously in learning business methods. Her civic activities include an appointment in 1991 by President Bush to the New American Schools Development Corporation, a group exploring ideas to revamp the nation's schools. She is also a trustee of the Museum of Television and Radio, the Presbyterian Hospital of New York, and WNET/Channel Thirteen.

See also: Broadcasting Industry

Further Reading
Gilbert, Lynn and Galen Moore, p. 293–299.
Morris, Michele. "The St. Joan of Television."
O'Dell, Cary, p. 67–78.

Copley, Helen Kinney (1922–), Newspaper Publishing Executive

Helen Copley inherited the Copley Press, a newspaper publishing company, from her husband in 1973. Though it was in financial trouble, she decided to make the company profitable. It has been on *Working Woman*'s list of the top woman-owned companies since the first list in 1992.

She was born in Cedar Rapids, Iowa, the daughter of a railroad man and his wife. She dropped out of Hunter College in 1945. She started work as James S. Copley's secretary in 1952 and married him in 1965. After he died in 1973, Copley inherited the company, although his two children from a previous marriage received 5 percent of the stock. The next year she took over as CEO and chairman of the board, selling the unprofitable newspapers to pay the $16 million inheritance tax and expanding the remaining publications. The chain, run as a political forum, had a conservative slant that Copley continued for a while as she balanced the books, reduced staff, and reorganized the company.

During the 1980s she expanded the editorial scope to include women's and minorities' rights and got rid of the ban on letters criticizing the newspaper. By 1984 she controlled almost 90 percent of the company, estimated to be worth $225 million. In 1991 she bought a television joint venture and merged the failing evening *San Diego Tribune* with the successful *San Diego Union*. She expanded into newspapers in Los Angeles and Illinois and three cable systems by 1995. The next year she sold 50 percent of her stake in the latter for about $50 million. By then Copley had left the day-to-day operations to her son David but remained as chair of the board. The following year she named David CEO, and in 2001 she retired after thirty years but stayed on the board.

Copley, a shy woman who hates publicity and rarely grants interviews, was so uncomfortable giving public speeches that she took speech lessons. She was the driving force behind luring the Republican 1996 convention to San Diego and supporting the bid for the 1998 San Diego Super Bowl. She has honorary degrees from Coe College, Pepperdine University, and the University of San Diego. In 1974 she was the first woman elected to the board of directors of the California Chamber of Commerce. The next year President Ford appointed her to the National Commission on the Observance of International Woman's Year, and in 1978 Governor Jerry Brown named her to the Commission on Government Reform. She was vice chairman and a director of the American Newspaper Publishers Association Foundation and a director of the International American Press Association. In 1976 she won the Golden Plate Award from the American Academy of Achievement and in 1981 the Excellence in Achievement Award from the Golden West Regional Chapter of the International Toastmistress Clubs, Inc. The VFW gave her the U.S. News Media Award in 1982. She has chaired the board of the James S. Copley Foundation and is a life member of the La Jolla Friends of International Center, the Museum of Contemporary Art, the San Diego Hall of Science, Scripps Memorial Hospital Auxiliary, and the San Diego Opera Association.

See also: Broadcasting Industry; Publishing Industry

Further Reading

"Helen K. Copley Steps Down as Chairman, Publisher; Son to Succeed Her."

Macdonald, J.R. "Catherine T. Clark." In Editors of the *Wall Street Journal. New Millionaires and How They Made Their Fortune*, p. 57–65.

Schmuckler and Collingwood, p. 36.

Corbi, Lana (1955–), Television Executive

In October 2001 Lana Corby was appointed CEO of the Hallmark Channel, the year that *Fortune* ranked her number 35 on its list of the most powerful black executives in the United States. She was one of the highest-ranking minority women in Hollywood. Unfortunately, that October she was asked to resign.

She was born in Los Angeles, received her BA in journalism from the University of Southern California, and attended graduate school in film and television at California State at Northridge. Her career began when she developed a marketing business. In 1989 Corbi became vice president of marketing for the Association of Independent Television Stations and two years later, vice president of Midwest affiliate relations for Fox, becoming actively involved in Fox Sports. One of her accomplishments was setting up business with the minority-controlled Blackstar Communications. In 1994 she was promoted to senior vice president of network distribution, then to president and COO of Blackstar LLC, an entity backed by Fox, in September 1995. She was responsible for strategic acquisitions and station operations. The following April, she returned to Fox as executive vice president of network distribution, becoming division president in June, 1997. She continued as the liaison between Fox and its affiliates and oversaw network programming distribution strategies.

In March 1999 she moved to Odyssey as the chief operating officer, responsible for a distribution agreement with TimeWarner Cable. The following June she became executive vice president and chief operating officer for CrownMedia. In October 2001 she was named CEO of the Hallmark Channel, just launched that August. Her goal was to increase both original programming and the number of viewers. Audiences did increase but only by 1 percent of total television viewers. Corbi focused on family entertainment, initiated a series on adoption, bought family movies as well as *MASH*, and *Touched by an Angel*, and reran *Roots*. By August 2002 subscribers had increased by 13.7 million to 46.2 million with strong ratings, but advertising revenue had declined, causing cash flow problems. As a result the channel reorganized, and Corbi was asked to resign but remained as a consultant until the end of the year. In January 2003 she started her own consulting company, CorbiCo.

Corbi is married with twin girls. She thrives on spending time with her family. *Cablevision* named her one of the "Women to Watch" in 2000; and the following year, *Hollywood Reporter* ranked her number 49 on its list of Hollywood's Women of Power. In September 2002 the Hallmark Channel received a National Angel Award from the Congressional Coalition on Adoption Institute.

See also: African American Businesswomen; Broadcasting Industry

Further Reading

Chunovic, Louis. "Plugging Hallmark into Cable Market; President and CEO Lana Corbi has Sights Set on a Higher Brand Profile."

Rice, Lynette. "Fox's Corbi to Rejoin Loesch."

Satzman, Darrell. "Crowning Achievement: Armed with Family Fare, Veteran TV Exec Leads New Hallmark Channel into Competitive Cable World."

Corporate Board of Directors

The board of directors makes the major decisions, sets policies of the corporation, and in a public company, represents the shareholders who elect them, in board deliberations. The board's primary responsibility is oversight, but the directors give advice and counsel, are expected to anticipate problems, and watch for any risk to the stability of the company. They are heavily involved in corporate strategy, management succession, evaluating the CEO, and determining compensation practices.

Forbes commented, on June 12, 1920, when two of F.W. Woolworth's daughters were elected to Woolworth Company's Board of Directors, "wouldn't the advent of women as directors be in line with the trend of the times?" ("Flashbacks Census of Women Directors of the *Fortune 1000*," March 20, 2000, p. 32). Women were agitating for the vote, which came two years later. Some women began serving on boards, but they were mostly socialites, heiresses, or wives of CEOs. It was not until the 1960s and 1970s that women were appointed in any numbers at all. Even then most were from the public sector, that is, nonprofit organizations, academia, or high-profile community leaders.

In 1977 Catalyst took its first census of *Fortune* 1000 board members and found forty-six women. The following year, 262 seats were filled by women, but many occupied seats in more than one company. Unfortunately, most were seen as ornamental rather than as contributing members. By the early 1980s, however, women board members were taken more seriously, invited to serve because of their business knowledge, and to expand board awareness of women's issues. Board members continued to be recruited through the old boys network and the tendency, when a member left, was to fill the position with someone like him.

The 1980s mania for mergers did not help, since CEOs wanted rubber-stamp boards who would approve decisions without asking unfortunate questions. Most boards were peopled by two inside (from the company itself) directors for every independent outside director. They were compensated lavishly with fees for meeting attendance, stock options, free company products, and sometimes benefit plans.

It was not until the advent of technology in the 1990s, coupled with shareholder pressure to focus on equity, increased earnings, and tighter accountability regulations, that boards began to change their makeup and recruitment criteria. They needed experts, particularly with strategy experience, and ones who were unafraid to ask uncomfortable questions. Diversity became a priority for both ethnic minorities and women. The 1993 Catalyst Survey showed women held 721 of 11,715 seats of *Fortune* 1000 Companies. Of the *Fortune* 500, 69 percent had at least one woman on the board, a great improvement over 1985, when only 45 percent did. Despite a belief among CEOs that women in senior management positions were scarce, two years later, 81 percent of the *Fortune* 500 had at least one woman on their board, and 33 percent had more than one.

By 1998 a director's job changed, not only in terms of oversight duties, but also in compensation. Benefits disappeared as did large dollar amounts. There was more shareholder focus on accountability, with the accompanying threat of lawsuits. The number of meetings per year increased. Coziness with the executive was frowned upon. Diversity and expertise were the emphases for finding new board members, and the ratio changed to two outside independent directors for every insider. By 1999 *Chief Executive* said "Board diversity, in terms of women and minority directors is now almost taken for granted as a desirable feature" (Lear and Yavitz, October 1999). The proliferation of high technology and dot.coms exhausted the ranks of CEO board candidates, allowing for more women and minority appointees who were experts, particularly in the Internet and strategy, but not at the CEO rank.

Following the dot.com collapse and the Enron scandals, boards began to be more closely scrutinized and questioned. Shareholders felt that the boards should have foreseen problems, asked harder questions, and in the case of Enron, found fraud much earlier. Strict new governance rules emphasized the importance of independent directors and board members who were paid in stock, so their compensation was tied to the company's health—with mixed results. Many companies added board members. The old boys, "do-little" director network had mostly disappeared. In its place came possibilities for expert women and minorities but also new challenges and the risk of litigation.

CEOs and boards oversee diversity, conflict of interest guidelines, and formal board performance evaluations. The Catalyst 2001 Report showed that women held 735 seats at 434 of the *Fortune* 500 companies, 12.4 percent of the total seats. Catalyst estimated that it will be 2027 before that figure reaches 25 percent. At the end of 2002 women held 14 percent of all directors' seats in the *Fortune* 1000 companies. In 2003 only Golden West Financial showed parity: five men and five women on the board.

Women's Leadership Forum and the Kellogg School of Management at Northwestern University run two of the many training programs for potential board members. Women's contributions are important to a board because they bring diversity. Women are also said to be more people oriented and more aware of subtle discrimination and dehumanization. Their experience in business can bring a fresh viewpoint, particularly into the minds of half of the customers. Experience has shown that women in the boardroom dramatically alter the board dynamic.

Further Reading
Census of Women Directors of the Fortune 1000.

Hymowitz, Carol. "In the U.S., What Will It Take to Create Diverse Boardrooms?"
Krotz, Joanna L. "All Aboard."
Lavelle, Louis. "Angling for a Board Seat?"
Tifft, Susan E. and Janet Bamford. "Board Gains; Corporate Boards of Directors."

Corporate Culture

According to *The Human Resources Glossary*, corporate culture is "the atmosphere or environment surrounding an organization, which influences and shapes the behavior of its people and the quality of interpersonal relationships within it" (Tracey, p. 109). Terrence Deal and Alan Kennedy call it "a cohesion of values, myths, heroes, and symbols that has come to mean a great deal to the people who work there" (Deal and Kennedy, *Corporate Cultures*, p. 4).

The elements of culture include the business goals and mission, the organizational and top management values, the history of the business, social rites and rituals, and both formal and informal means of communication. Deal and Kennedy also point out that newcomers who are different are outsiders to the corporate culture (p. 78), and that unless mechanisms are in place to welcome and accept these persons, they are excluded from support that is a part of the culture. A strong culture provides expectations for work habits, time management, communication, and sometimes even dress.

A recruit can find out about company culture through its homepage presentation, mission statement, benefits, various policies, annual report, and a search for newspaper and journal articles through various databases. A talk with company employees is very helpful as well. Rutherford outlines expressions of company culture: management style, philosophies about work, language, formal and informal communication, dress, physical facilities, history, informal socializing, time management, as well as gender and diversity awareness. Employees become attached to the company's culture, which helps explain why it has been so difficult for women and minorities to rise to the top in male-dominated companies.

Further Reading

Deal and Kennedy. *Corporate Cultures: The Rites and Rituals of Corporate Life.*
Deal and Kennedy. *The New Corporate Cultures: Revitalizing the Workplace after Downsizing, Mergers, and Reengineering.*
Rutherford, Sarah. "Organizational Cultures, Women Managers and Exclusion."
Tracey, William R., Ed. *The Human Resources Glossary.* 2nd ed.

Cosmetics Industry, *see* Beauty Industry

Covey, Joy (1963–), Information Technology Executive

Joy Covey was the chief financial officer and de facto co-chief strategist for Amazon.com when *Fortune* named her to its 1999 list of most powerful corporate women. Earlier that year she had been appointed chief of strategy but since 1996, had worked alongside the founder, Jeff Bezos, in assuring the company's future through funding opportunities.

She grew up in San Mateo, California, the younger of two daughters of a doctor and a nurse. Covey learned self-reliance particularly from her mother, who had survived two years in a World War II Japanese prison camp. Although Covey quit high school, deciding that it was not worth her time, she graduated at age 19 summa cum laude with a degree in business administration from California State University and then passed the CPA exam with the second highest marks in the country. After working a year at Arthur Young & Co., she went to Harvard in 1982 and earned a law degree magna cum laude and an MBA as a Baker Scholar.

After an eight-month stint at Wasserstein Perell & Co. as a mergers and acquisitions associate, Covey became the CFO of Digidesign and increased the value of the company through sales growth, managed a successful public offering, and negotiated a merger with Avid Technology. In December 1996 she joined Amazon.com as its CFO, responsible for finance, planning, administration, and human resources. She also shepherded the company through one of the most successful public offerings in the e-commerce business while serving as the chief spokesperson for the company with the shareholders. One of her main accomplishments was convincing the shareholders to accept no profits and huge losses while the company built itself into a viable online profit-making company, which took several years. Covey's greatest achievement was a $125-billion bond offering. In September 1999 she was named the chief strategy officer, a job she was already doing. In April of the following year, she decided to take a sabbatical from the business world and left Amazon.com to do some rock-climbing, skiing, and traveling.

Covey has a reputation for being intense, resourceful, persuasive, and a very hard worker. The pace of the e-commerce world was well suited to her talents and love of risk and fast change. She is a sports fanatic. She married a cardiac anesthesiologist in Park City, Utah, arriving by snowmobile for the mountain-top ceremony. When she left Amazon.com, she indicated that she was not finished with the business world, just taking a little time off.

See also: Information Technology Industry

Further Reading

"CFO's Faith in Future Worth Millions: Joy Covey Must Convince Investors to Accept Losses for Several Years while Amazon.com Inc. Rebuilds its Role on the Internet."

Koselka, Rita. "A Real Amazon."
Sellers, Patricia. "These Women Rule," p. 130.

Cox, Carrie Smith (1956–), Pharmaceutical Executive

Carrie Cox, on *Fortune*'s list of the fifty most powerful women in business for the first time in 2001, is the executive vice president of Pharmacia and the president of Global Prescriptions, an $11 billion operation.

After graduating from the Massachusetts College of Pharmacy, she was a pharmacist in research and development for Sandoz Pharmaceuticals where she had previously been a summer intern. In ten years there Cox held positions in marketing research, sales, and product management. Her major accomplishment was the development of a distribution and monitoring system for Clozaril, a drug to treat schizophrenia. In 1990 she became vice president of woman's health care at Wyeth-Ayerst Laboratories, in charge of very successfully marketing Premarin, the most prescribed hormone replacement drug. She also developed an innovative direct-to-consumer program for the company's products.

Cox joined Pharmacia in the newly created position of senior vice president and head of global business management in 1997, assigned to turn the company around and build the international market. In 2001 she became executive vice president and co-president of the global prescription business, then worth $11 billion. Her job encompassed marketing worldwide, consumer communication and e-commerce, medical affairs, business planning and pricing, and good communications between sales operations and research and development. Her invention of a seamless product flow system that involved continuous input throughout a product's life cycle was an important step in building brands for the company.

The goal of her work, she has said, is to help people and work with patients. In her initial pharmaceutical practice, she helped people on a small scale; in the company, Cox is doing patient counseling in a much larger arena. One of the important facets of her marketing efforts is the pharmacy-based educational programs that she plans to emphasize more. In 2001 she was named Woman of the Year by the Healthcare Businesswoman's Association who cited her accomplishments in Pharmacia's turnaround into one of the industry's top performing companies.

Further Reading
"Pharmacia and Upjohn Appoints New Head of Global Business Management."
West, Diane. "HBA's 'Woman of the Year' Remembers Her Retail Pharmacy Roots."

Craig, Jenny (1932–), Diet Industry Entrepreneur

Although Jenny Craig had been in the fitness business for twenty years, she didn't begin her diet company until 1983. Jenny Craig, Inc. reached its height in 1992 and the number 4 spot on the *Working Woman* list of top woman-owned companies in the United States.

She was born in Louisiana, the youngest of six children, during the Depression. Her father worked at three part-time jobs while her mother raised chickens to feed the family. As a teenager, Craig worked in a dental clinic and wanted to become a dental hygienist but dropped out of high school to marry a race-boat driver. They had two daughters. During her second pregnancy, she gained forty-five pounds, which she was unable to lose. She joined a New Orleans gym, watched what she ate, and lost the pounds. She began working for the gym, one of a chain, and worked her way up to manager, learning the business along the way. Her ambition was to own a franchise. She joined Sid's Body Contour, owned by Sid Craig, which had just opened. To get a franchise, she had to work there two years, and she soon became national director of operations. Meanwhile, she divorced, as, coincidentally, had Sid. In 1979 they married, with a blended family of seven grown children.

Craig and her husband built the company into 200 centers nationwide. She wanted to offer nutritional guidance along with exercise, but his partners refused. In 1982 Sid sold Body Contour to Nutri-System. Since the agreement included a two-year non-compete clause, the Craigs went to Australia and used the profit from the sale to begin Jenny Craig. After surveying Australians about a name and developing a line of low-fat foods, they opened their first center. By the end of the first year, they had fifty centers; by 1985, their income was $50 million with profits of $10 million. Their non-compete clause expired that year, so they came back to the United States and opened fourteen centers in the Los Angeles area. Although competition had intensified, they were successful and kept expanding, using company revenue from Australia.

Jenny Craig built a highly successful worldwide diet business introducing the idea of good health.

By 1990 Jenny Craig was named by *Inc.* as the sixth fastest-growing private company in the United States. It had 444 centers offering nutritional advice, weekly counseling sessions, prepackaged food, exercise and activity suggestions, as well as behavior modification guidelines. The next year it went public. Craig was the vice chair and president, and her husband was the CEO and chair. He did the marketing and finance, she developed the prepackaged food, wrote a cookbook, and planned the programs. With continued expansion, by 1994 revenues peaked at $465 million. By 1997 it had 800 centers worldwide with revenues of $336 million.

The 1990s were not good years for the diet business. Competition was strong, the Federal Trade Commission complained about false advertising, and potential clients were beginning to distrust the results, learning that the pounds returned soon after they had disappeared. By March of 2000 the company was down to 548 centers. In June 2001 the stock was delisted because of the declining stock price, and the Craigs tried to sell the company. The following January ACI Capital Company and DB Capital Partners, an investor group, bought it in partnership with Craig and her husband.

Craig was highly successful with her diet business before dieting became popular. Her personal goal was to help overweight people break the fat cycles, and she was successful for many years. In 1990 she was invited to address a Harvard Business School seminar on entrepreneurship. Later she was named the New England Entrepreneur of the Year.

See also: Food Industry

Further Reading
Berman, Phyllis. "Fat City."
Ericksen, Gregory K. "Jenny Craig—Jenny Craig, Inc.," p. 25–43.
Hallett, Anthony and Diane. "Jenny Craig, Sid Craig," p. 128–129.

D

Davidson, Janet G. (1957–), Telecommunications Executive

Janet Davidson was promoted in 2001 to Group President, Integrated Network Solutions at Lucent, the year *Fortune* ranked her number 47 on its list of the most powerful women in American business. She manages 20,000 employees and is responsible for Lucent's non-wireless products.

She was born in Short Hills, New Jersey, and earned a BA in physics from Lehigh University, an MSc in electrical engineering from Georgia Tech, and a masters in computer science while working at Bell Laboratories.

In 1978 Davidson joined the technical staff at Bell Laboratories, saw it through name changes and the spin-off of Lucent from AT&T working in software design and development, research and development, global product strategy, marketing, product management, and sales. Her first administrative position was as the vice president of broadband access program management. In 1996 she became product manager and vice president of Lucent's access business and later, vice president of North American sales and services, responsible for sales to Sprint, MCI, Worldcom, and all the other service providers in the United States. Her next position was president of the Inter-Networking Systems (INS) Access Group with the goal of positioning the company in the DSL market. As group president since May 2000, she has responsibility for the newly combined switching solutions and InterNetworking Systems, including development and sales of landline and optical products worldwide.

Davidson is known for her expertise in networking and technical areas as well as her knowledge of customers' needs. Her dynamic leadership is reflected in her three promotions in two years and increased responsibilities in supervision, from 4,000 to 20,000 employees. In 2001 she received a Women Elevating Science and Technology (W.E.S.T.) Award from *Working Woman*, one of six winners.

Further Reading
Howe, Peter J. "Executive Reflects on Painful Challenges to Recovery at Lucent."
"Lucent Technologies Names Frank D'Amelio Chief Financial Officer; Company Combines Switching and Data Networking Networks; Names Janet Davidson to Lead New Unit."

Davis, Alice Brown (1852–1935), Merchant

Alice Brown Davis and her husband ran a trading post and post office in the Seminole Nation in what is now Oklahoma. When he died in 1899, she took over and became a prosperous businesswoman, rancher, and for a brief time, chief of the Seminoles.

She was born in the Cherokee Nation, one of seven children of Lucy Redbird, a Seminole. Her father was Dr. John F. Brown, the contract physician for the government during the 1840s removal of the Seminoles from Florida to Oklahoma Territory. Davis was educated at home, in the Cherokee Nation schools, and the Presbyterian mission school. After her father died during a cholera epidemic in 1867 and her mother soon after, her brother John became head of the family. She met George Davis, a merchant's clerk, when he purchased materials from the tribe. In 1874 they married and had 11 children.

In 1882 Davis and her husband moved to the Seminole Nation, opened their trading post, and started a ranch. The following year he became a postmaster. She continued all three businesses—trading, ranching, and the post office—after his death in 1899. She also taught in the tribal boarding schools in the 1890s and early 1900s, serving as superintendent for the girls' school in 1905 and 1906. When the government questioned her finances, she turned the school over to them. Her businesses continued to be successful, and until Oklahoma became a state, she was very prosperous.

Davis was involved in tribal activities, serving as their interpreter on many occasions with the government and federal courts. She also acted as the disbursing agent of pensions due to Seminole Civil War veterans. One of her important, though fruitless, services was as a delegate to Mexico in 1903, 1905, and 1910 when the Seminole Nation attempted to persuade the Mexican government to honor land grants made to a Seminole chief in the 1850s. She was also in a 1909 missionary party to the Florida Seminoles who had refused to join the removal.

When Oklahoma became a state, life changed drastically for the Seminole Nation. They were given small allotments, lost their large communal grazing lands, and could no longer support their ranches. Because they also had no cash and relied heavily on credit, the Indian traders could not buy goods. After white traders moved in and provided heavy competition, most of the Indian traders failed. Davis moved into a modest house in Wewoka and became a tribal matriarch, helping her fellow Seminoles with advice and occasional financing as their lives deteriorated. It was said she kept a pot of chicken and rice on her stove at all times for the hungry.

In 1922 she was chief of the Seminoles. Because no one had succeeded her late brother as chief, President Harding appointed Davis when the government needed an official signature on the school's deed of sale. After she asked that the tribe be reimbursed for land the federal agents had lost because of mismanagement, she was removed from office almost before she had been appointed. It was yet another example of mistreatment of the Seminole Nation.

Alice Davis is remembered for her business acumen and contributions to her people. A bronze bust of her is in the American Indian Hall of Fame in Anadarko, Oklahoma, and a women's dorm at the University of Oklahoma is named for her.

See also: American Indian Businesswomen; Retailing Industry

Further Reading
Debo, Angie. "Davis, Alice Brown." In Garraty and Carnes, p. 163–164.
Sattler, Rich A. "Davis, Alice Brown." In Edward T. James, p. 438–439.

DeHaan, Christel (1942–), Travel Industry Entrepreneur

In 1974 Christel DeHaan and her husband revolutionized the travel industry with their concept of vacation condominium time-share swapping. The one problem of time-shares was that the owner was stuck in one place. Their company, Resort Condominiums International (RCI), offered a way for travelers to swap their week or two of time-share condos, freeing them to go all over the world for a modest price. It was an idea whose time had come.

DeHaan was born in Germany and came to the United States in 1962 as a nanny. She also worked as an interpreter and secretary before embarking on the travel business with her second husband, Jon. She is a naturalized citizen and has two sons and a daughter. She graduated from Indiana Central University in 1982.

In 1974 DeHaan and her husband started their business out of shoeboxes on a kitchen table, making it possible for time-share owners to swap their condominiums for a small fee. They would make swapping arrangements with other members of RCI using the software program it had developed. Their magazine, *Endless Vacation*, informed the members of swapping opportunities. At that time the company had twenty-four affiliated resorts. This concept contributed, in part, to the enormous growth of the time-share industry during the 1970s and 1980s. In the early 1970s time-sharing had a bad reputation because of false claims, bogus selling, and some sleazy companies. One of RCI's goals was to professionalize the industry, and DeHaan worked with the government to draft regulations and reform. By 1989 when she received (for $67.5 million) control of the company as part of her divorce agreement, RCI had 1.1 million members who made 664,000 exchanges that year, for sales of $100,000,000.

She began her tenure as president and CEO with a corporate restructuring, turning subsidiaries into divisions, prepaying the buyout, buying a large Michigan travel agency, and expanding the number of participating resorts in Europe, South America, and the Asian-Pacific basin. DeHaan's mission was to provide a full line of leisure travel services. She opened fourteen new offices in the United States, so that customers in the various regions would receive better service. In 1991 she was quoted in an *Indiana Business Magazine*: "In managing and advancing his or her own company, a successful entrepreneur must concentrate efforts on two critical elements—steadfast attention to customer needs and a commitment to the well-being of employees" ("Indiana's Entrepreneurs of the Year Awards 1991," p. 8). At that time the company employed 2,000 people in thirty-six branches worldwide, with 1,100 of those working in Indianapolis.

In 1996 on the basis of 1995 figures, RCI, with Christel DeHaan as sole owner, was number 27 on the *Working Woman* list of the top fifty woman-owned companies. Sales were $280,000,000 and employees numbered 2,178. That year it had 4,000 employees in sixty-eight offices in thirty-two countries. It was the world's largest time-share exchange with 2,983 participating resorts and 2,100,000 members. That October she sold it to HFS Inc., a hotel franchiser, for $625,000,000. The payment was in cash except for $75 million in HFS stock. There was also an agreement for a payment of $200,000,000 more if certain performance targets were met over the following five years. HFS agreed to keep the operations in Indianapolis with no layoffs or cutbacks; DeHaan sits on the board of directors. When the company was sold, she and her husband shared their wealth with the 4,300 employees, based on years of service.

DeHaan was named Entrepreneur of the Year in Indianapolis in 1991 and to the Central Indiana Business Hall of Fame in 1995 for success in building and maintaining her company. In 2000 she was named one of Indianapolis' most influential leaders. She founded ProjectE, a group created to improve Indiana's K-12 education and has donated to the Christel DeHaan Performing Arts Center at the University of Indianapolis, the Tourism and Travel Research Institute at the University of Nottingham Business School in England, and the Indianapolis Symphony Orchestra, underwriting a five-year guest soloist and chamber orchestra series. The Christel DeHaan Family Foundation funded an orphanage in Mexico and awards Indiana teachers monetary prizes for excellence. She has served on boards including the National Adoption Center, the Greater Indianapolis Progress Committee, the Indianapolis Symphony Society, The Indianapolis Museum of Art, and the Children's Museum. She is listed on the *Forbes* 400 list of wealthiest Americans.

See also: Immigrant Businesswomen; Travel Industry

Further Reading
Harton, Tom. "DeHaan has RCI on a Roll after 1st Year at the Helm."
"Indiana's Entrepreneurs of the Year Awards 1991."
Schmuckler, Eric and Harris Collingwood, p. 32, 37.

Deily, Linnet (1945–), Finance Industry Executive

Linnet Deily, vice chair of Charles Schwab, the online stockbroker, was number 41 on the October 2000 *Fortune* list of the most powerful corporate women in the United States. Before joining Schwab in 1996, she had risen to the position of chair, president, and CEO of the First Interstate Bank of Texas, and manager of retail operation of its parent company, First Interstate Bancorp. In 1992 she was one of *Business Week*'s fifty top women in business.

Born into a family of pioneer stock in McKinney, Texas, where her parents were both schoolteachers, Deily graduated from the University of Texas at Austin in 1968 with a BA in government. Because management training programs were not open to women in Texas then, she went into social work. In 1974 she changed careers, working for Republic Bank in Dallas until 1981, while earning an MS in international management from the University of Texas in 1976. She was one of two women in that program.

In 1981 Deily joined parent company First Interstate Bancorp as head of corporate banking, coordinated a merger, and was CFO of the wholesale banking division. Two years later she moved to First Interstate Bancorp of California where she held increasingly responsible positions and developed its teleservice operations. In November 1988 when she went back to Texas as president and COO of First Bancorp of Texas, she was the only woman to head a regional division in banking. Her responsibilities included supervising all the staff and line functions. She progressed and was elected chair, CEO, and president in December 1991. In November of 1995 she took on the added responsibility of overseeing First Interstate Bancorp's retail banking operations, including 1,514 branches in twenty-one states. After Wells Fargo & Company took over the next year, Deily left with a golden parachute of $5.5 million.

The following September Charles Schwab hired Deily as executive vice president and general manager for its investment management services, one of the fastest-growing segments. She inaugurated Advisorsource, which refers Schwab online customers to local investment advisors. In 1998 she was named president of the retail group, encompassing both the traditional and electronic brokerage businesses and launched SchwabLinkWeb, making Schwab's use of technology second to none. In 1999 she was included as one of the seventeen members of the planning committee. She became vice chair in the Office of the President and the president's right-hand person in October 2000, focusing on strategic initiatives and direction. In her time with Schwab, her annual compensation doubled.

Deily changed direction in December 2000, becoming the first non-bank executive appointed to the Federal Reserve Advisory Council, senior executives who advise the Federal Reserve Board of Governors. She had barely settled there when President Bush appointed her Deputy United States Trade Representative with the rank of ambassador extraordinary and plenipotentiary. She is based in Geneva, the U.S. Ambassador to the World Trade Organization.

Her management style is characterized by delegation, leading by example, and offering her employees a chance to make things happen. She is said to be an excellent listener, have extraordinary people skills, and is a wonderful leader. Deily says that she hit no glass ceiling at either the bank or Schwab; both corporations awarded promotions based on performance.

She has always been very involved in the community. While in Texas, she served on the boards of charitable entities and the University of Texas Board of Regents. She has chaired several United Way projects and is a member of the Committee of 200. She was also one of three Catalyst 2000 winners.

See also: Finance Industry

Further Reading

Mintz, Bill. "Bank Executive Deily Leaving After Buyout; First Interstate to Pay Her $5.5 Million."

"Schwab Announces Organizational Changes to Reflect Company's Growing Scale, Scope and Opportunity."

Demorest, Ellen Curtis (1824–1898), Fashion Designer

According to Drachman, Ellen Demorest "established an empire in the female-dominated fashion industry in New York City and became the arbiter of style for women" (*Enterprising Women*, p. 46).

She was born in Schuylerville, New York, the second of eight children and was educated at an all-female school. When she finished, her father, a farmer who owned a men's hat factory, helped her set up a millinery store in Saratoga Springs, then a fashionable resort. It was successful, and she moved to Troy, New York, then to New York City.

In 1858 she married William Demorest, a bankrupt widower with two small children and owner of Madame Demorest's, a fashion emporium catering to wealthy women. She ran the shop and he began *Mme Demorest's Quarterly Mirror of Fashions*, a national fashion magazine that included tissue-paper patterns of dresses found in the store. Some credit Demorest with the idea for these patterns, but Drachman credits her husband who "had gotten into the pattern business in the mid-1850s" (p. 49).

When the magazine debuted in 1858, most women had sewing machines and were copying high-fashion clothes for themselves. Demorest expanded into children's and men's patterns. She also designed a more comfortable corset, an easy-to-manage hoop, and the imperial dress-elevator, which allowed women to raise their skirts for gutters or puddles. By 1875 there were 300 shops and 1,500 national Demorest agents, who had distributed 3 million paper patterns. The following year they exhibited at the Centennial Exhibition in Philadelphia.

Demorest and her husband were social reformers. She promoted racial integration and equality by hiring African American women at an equal salary to white women. In 1868 she co-founded Sorosis, a woman's club committed to women's causes. She and realtor Susan A. King founded the modestly successful Women's Tea Company in 1872, which employed only women, to import tea from China and Japan and sell it in the emporium.

Demorest's empire peaked in the mid-1870s. During the 1880s Ebeneezer Butterick, who, unlike her, had patented paper patterns, became a force to be reckoned with. She and her husband had invented dress patterns, but Butterick became the name commonly associated with them because of his patent. She and her husband sold their pattern business in 1887, and she died in 1898.

See also: Fashion Industry

Further Reading

Bird, Caroline, p. 74–78.

Drachman, Virginia G. *Enterprising Women: 250 Years of American Business.*

O'Gorman, W. Farrell. "Demorest, Ellen Curtis." In Garraty and Carnes, p. 419–420.

Ross, Ishbel. *Crusades and Crinolines: The Life and Times of Ellen Curtis Demorest and William Jennings Demorest.*

Desmond-Hellman, Susan D. (1957–), Pharmaceutical Executive

As the executive vice president of development and product operations and the chief medical officer at Genentech, Susan Desmond-Hellman ranked number 38 on the 2001 *Fortune* list and number 30 on the 2003 list of the most powerful businesswomen in the United States. The company has been a major player in the battle against cancer, and Desmond-Hellman has steered three ground-breaking cancer drugs through the Federal Drug Administration process.

She was born in Napa, California, and raised in Reno, Nevada. After receiving her BA and medical degrees from the University of Nevada at Reno, she earned an MS in epidemiology and biostatistics at the School of Public Health at the University of California at Berkeley. She also trained for nine years at the University of California at San Francisco and joined their faculty. In 1989 to 1990 she went to Uganda with her physician husband to study AIDS and cancer. After two years in private practice, she joined Bristol-Myers Squibb Pharmaceutical Research Institute as the project team leader for the drug Taxol.

After joining Genentech in 1995 as a clinical scientist, Desmond-Hellman was promoted to senior director of clinical science, vice president of medical affairs, and vice president of development. In December 1997 she became executive vice president of development and product operations, continuing as chief medical officer; responsible for medical affairs, regulatory affairs, product development, pharmacological sciences, manufacturing, process sciences, quality, and engineering. She also serves on the Executive Committee.

Desmond-Hellman, winner of many awards for her work in oncology and AIDS research, has published over thirty-five journal articles and abstracts and is an adjunct Associate Professor of Epidemiology and Biostatistics at the University fo California, San Francisco. She has served on the board of directors at AeroGen and the Biotechnology Industry Organization.

Further Reading
"AeroGen Elects Susan Desmond-Hellmann, M.D., M.P.H. to Board of Directors."
"Fortune 50. . . ," p. 195–200.
"Physician First."

Dillman, Linda (1956–), Retail Executive

Linda Dillman is the senior vice president and chief information officer for Wal-Mart Stores, the company's first female CIO. She ranked number 28 in *Fortune*'s 2003 list of the most powerful women in corporate America.

She attended the University of Indianapolis. Following her first job at Hewlett-Packard, she joined The Wholesale Club's information systems team. After Wal-Mart bought The Wholesale Club in 1991, Dillman worked on applications development for in-store systems, Sam's Clubs, specialty divisions, Retail Link, and data warehousing. Later she helped develop Wal-Mart's data warehouse and supply-chain management systems. In 1997 she became director of applications development for pharmacy, inventory, and sales. Her system enabled all the price and item information to be accessed in real time. She was promoted to vice president of applications development in late 1998 and, later, to vice president of international systems development where she led the systems conversion effort of acquisition in the United Kingdom.

In August 2002 she began as senior vice pesident and CIO of the information systems department, responsible for overseeing all company information systems worldwide. Dillman implemented a change to Internet EDI from proprietary value-added networks and is currently working on radio frequency identification technology (RFID), a wireless technology for the company and all its suppliers. When this technology is applied, it will change the face of the retailing industry.

Dillman, one of the top females in the retailing industry, is known for her ability to combine technical and business acumen. She was named to *Business*

Week's e.biz 25 and *Supermarket News*'s "Power 50." *Network World*, in December 2002, named her to their list of the fifty most powerful people in networking.

See also: Retailing Industry

Further Reading
Garry, Michael. "Wal-Mart's CIO Dillman Details RFID Tag Plans."
Veiders, Christina, Stephanie Loughran, and Micheal Garry. "SB's Power 50 (Part Two) Wal-Mart."
"Web Smart."

Direct Sales, *see* Saleswomen

DiSesa, Nina (1946–), Advertising Executive

Nina DiSesa was on *Fortune*'s list of most powerful women in corporate America in 1999. She is the chair and chief creative officer at McCann Erickson New York, the largest advertising agency in the world, where she and her creative team effected a turnaround in 1996, adding billings of $1 billion. She was McCann's first woman creative head.

She was born and raised in Brooklyn in a second-generation Italian American family and received her BA in English literature from Brooklyn College. DiSesa feels her experience in college theater as a multi-tasking stage manager prepared her for an advertising career. She worked ten years at the now-defunct Richmond, Virginia, advertising agency Cargill Wilson and Acree.

In 1983 DiSesa returned to New York City to work with Young & Rubicam, whose clients included Frito-Lay, Jell-O, and Kentucky Fried Chicken. Three years later she became group creative director at McCann Erickson, responsible for several major accounts including L'Oreal, Alka Seltzer, and Nabisco crackers. In 1991 after she had been promoted to senior vice president and deputy creative director, J. Walter Thompson in Chicago recruited her to be their executive vice president and executive creative director, putting her in charge of more staff with larger billings. By then, with eighteen years of advertising experience, she attracted ten new clients and $100 million in billings to Chicago. She also met and married Brian Goodall, an advertising colleague.

In 1994 McCann Erickson lured DiSesa back to New York as its chair and first creative officer. Since then she has been responsible for a turnaround, changing the company's stodgy ads into colorful and humanistic successes. She also brought many large accounts including Lucent, Microsoft, Gateway, Sprint, Marriott, and Boeing.

DiSesa has a reputation for creativity, with a specialty of successful turn-arounds. With a strong belief in team building, she is extremely careful to give her teams the credit they deserve. She also pays attention to mentoring and promoting women because advertising has long been a male stronghold with a tough culture. She believes that her femininity has been an asset, particularly in dealing with the large egos and personalities that abound in this world. She says, "I'm really very competitive and find confrontation stimulating. But I keep these qualities in check. I use my feminine traits—empathy, collaboration" (*Fortune*, October 1999, p. 120).

After September 11, 2001, DiSesa co-chaired the creative review task force of a crisis-response team sponsored by the Advertising Council. Its purpose is to be ready to send messages about further terrorism acts.

See also: Advertising Industry

Further Reading
Sellers, Patricia. "These Women Rule," p. 106, 120.
Wells, Melanie. "Ad Exec in Business for Image."

Disney, Anthea (1947–), Publishing Executive

In 1998 Anthea Disney ranked number 46 on *Fortune*'s first list of the most powerful women in corporate America. At that time she was chair and CEO of News America Publishing Group, the American arm of Rupert Murdoch's worldwide empire. Since then, she has held two positions and is now executive vice president for content for the company, a position that was created for her.

She was born and raised in Dunstable, England, a small town near London. Her father was an engineer for a company that manufactured television sets; their family was one of the first to have a TV. She attended boarding school from age ten and later studied English at Queen's College, Oxford. After being a go-fer for several months in her first job at the tabloid, *Daily Sketch*, Disney was finally assigned to cover a murder in 800 words; she wrote 5,000. Several series that she wrote got the attention of the *London Daily Mail*, and she was tapped to be the foreign correspondent in New York. After two years she returned to London as features editor, but she went back to New York two years later as the New York City Bureau Chief. In 1980 she left the position, saying that the pace was too hectic. For four years she was a weekly columnist for the *London Daily Express*. In 1984 she met and married Peter Howe, a photo editor.

From 1984 to 1989 Disney moved into the magazine business, first as editor of *Us*, where she increased circulation by 16 percent; and then spent 1988 and 1989 redesigning *Self*, which became the country's best-selling woman's magazine in the United States. She has been with Rupert Murdoch's publishing empire since she became the magazine developer in 1989. Because she wanted television experience, Disney took a large pay cut in 1990 to be the executive producer for Fox TV's *A Current Affair*. The following year, she became editor in chief for *TV Guide* with the goal of halting its decline in circulation. She added more substance and strong opinion to the articles and increased advertising revenues. In 1995 her additional responsibilities included making I-Guide, the company's Internet service, competitive with the other more established Internet services.

One year later she was made president and CEO of HarperCollins, charged with putting the book publishing subsidiary back on its feet. It was then that she received the nickname "Angel of Death," for she completely restructured the company, cut overhead and inventory, and cancelled 106 book contracts with authors. These actions were very controversial, particularly in the book publishing world, but she did succeed in cutting the company's losses. In 1997 HarperCollins and *TV Guide* merged into NewsAmerica Publishing Group. In 1999 she was promoted to chair and CEO of TV Guide, Inc., but in November resigned to fill a newly created position, executive vice president for content of Murdoch's News Corporation. She launched the Health Channel and in 2003 added corporate marketing operations to her other responsibilities.

Disney's management style is said to be human but aggressive and effective. She is very ambitious but has a great deal of charm. Her talent for cleaning up a company's problems is well known, including at HarperCollins. Rupert Murdoch has called her a wonderful editor and businesswoman, not afraid to make hard decisions. She has served on the boards of CIT Group, Household International, Inc., and National Geographic Channels.

See also: Publishing Industry

Further Reading
Alioto, Maryann. "Anthea Disney."
"Disney, Anthea." In *Current Biography Yearbook 1998*, p. 152–155.
Machan, Dyan. "Death Angel's Endearing Side."

Diversity

The Human Resources Glossary defines diversity as "the ways in which people in organizations differ, including age, race, native language, gender, ethnic group, religion, personality, cognitive style, physical health, mental health, tenure, organizational function, and many others" (Tracey, p. 146). Other ways include economic background, sexual orientation, and physical disabilities.

Diversity became a buzzword in the 1990s due to growing realizations that affirmative action needed expanding, the population and thus the customer base was growing and changing, and diverse workforces stimulate innovation.

By 2003 companies were "embracing workforce diversity as a strategy to remain competitive in the face of changing demographics and the rapid globalization of business" (BSR Staff, "Diversity"). Several research studies showed that a diverse workforce increased productivity, financial performance, job satisfaction, innovation, and employee morale. It also reduced turnover and enhanced the company's public image. A good diversity program can also prevent legal problems. The Equal Employment Opportunity Commission received 84,000 complaints in 2002; 35 percent were related to race, 30 percent to gender, 20 percent to age, and 20 percent (some complainants are both, so the numbers exceed 100 percent) to disability.

In July 2003 *Working Mother* held a conference for women of color, both attendees and speakers, to share stories of the workplace. They concluded, "The multicultural workplace devoid of racial prejudice remains largely an elusive concept" (*Diversity Dialogues*, p. 65). On the plus side, many companies with diversity programs have remained committed to them, even during the economic downturn of 2000 to 2002. Of the *Fortune 500*, 75 percent had some kind of diversity program by 2002.

The aim is to create a corporate culture of inclusion, trust, and mutual respect. *Business: The Ultimate Resource* suggests eleven steps in implementing a program: gain support from management, commit financial and human resources, establish current levels of diversity management, conduct a gap analysis, identify areas that need change, write a diversity policy, compile a diversity action plan, set the program in motion, monitor and review, and establish an ongoing program (*Business: The Ultimate Resource*, p. 442–443).

Diversity policies focus on representation strategies concerning hiring, promotion, and retention; visible commitment by senior managers; career development and planning; mentoring and networking groups; and diversity education and training for the entire workforce. To be truly successful, a company must emphasize diversity as a core value and include it in performance evaluations.

See also: Affirmative Action; Minority Businesswomen

Further Reading
BSR Staff. "Diversity."
"Diversity Dialogues."
Finnigan, Annie. "Different Strokes."
Plummer, Deborah L. *Handbook of Diversity Management: Beyond Awareness to Competency Based Learning.*
Business: The Ultimate Resource, p. 442–443.

Donnelly, Nell Quinlan, *see* Reed, Nell Quinlan Donnelly

Dress Requirements

Dress for success was a mantra in the late 1960s and 1970s when women began vying for management positions and many books and articles offered advice, but appropriate business dress requirements are much older than that. Women copywriters and fashion editors wore hats to distinguish themselves from secretaries. Even now, many companies require uniforms or have dress codes.

Until the 1970s most companies required dresses, along with neatness and modesty. Men have always had suits and ties, while women have had a wider choice of dress. One of the more controversial styles of the 1970s, pantsuits for women, became completely accepted by the 1980s, and in the 1990s business casual was the trend.

There are some negative results from this trend. A 2001 survey by Jackson Lewis, an employment law firm, showed that 44 percent of 1,000 companies saw tardiness and absenteeism increase after implementing dress-down policies. An Incomm Center for Research and Sales Training poll in 2000 showed a decrease in trade show customers' favorable response to salespersons in casual clothes, from 86 percent to below 50 percent. Many employers feel that business attire is necessary for a professional image. On the other hand, as Claire Farley said, "Any company that puts too much emphasis on people's appearance is going to have some serious problems anyway" (Fisher, "Women Need at Least One Mentor. . . ," p. 208).

Further Reading
Araneta, Rana Lee. "Dressing Up for Success (Again)"
Fisher, Anne. "Women Need at Least One Mentor and One Pantsuit."
Schneider, Dorothy and Carl J. Schneider, p. 73.

Dubinsky, Donna (1957–), Computer Executive

Donna Dubinsky pioneered the Palm Pilot, one of the biggest hits in the high-tech industry. *Fortune* (October 16, 2000. p. 132) called her the "mother of the booming handheld computer market." It ranked her number 4 on its list of the most powerful women in corporate America in 2000. Her place dropped to number 32 in 2001, coinciding with the slip in the high tech industry.

She grew up in Benton Harbor, Michigan; her father was a scrap-metal broker, and her mother a homemaker. After earning a BA from Yale and an MBA at Harvard, in 1980 Dubinsky began work with Apple Computer's customer support. She held a variety of management positions, and in 1987 was a co-founder and vice president of Claris, the division of Apple that developed and marketed MacIntosh and Apple II applications software. When Apple decided not to make Claris a separate company, Dubinsky realized she really wanted to build her own company, so she left Apple and took a year off.

In 1991 she and Jeff Hawkins founded Palm Computing and pioneered its Palm Pilot. They had difficulty getting financing, however, so they sold it to U.S. Robotics in 1995 to obtain development money. In 1997, 3Com bought

U.S. Robotics, and Dubinsky became vice president of the Palm Computing Unit. By this time, Palm Pilots were the best-selling handheld computers, and a third version was being developed.

Neither she nor Hawkins liked working in a large company, so they left and co-founded Handspring. They paid 3Com to license the Palm Operating System, now holding 70 percent of the market, and focused on developing a less expensive handheld computer for children and families. In 1999 they launched Visor, a $150 product. By this time competition was rising, and Visor was not the success they had envisioned, although it had a 23 percent market share by April 2001. To raise more development money, they sold stock and in January 2002 launched Treo, a family of handheld devices, that combined a personal digital device with a cell phone. The product, Edge, got rave reviews but proved too expensive.

> Donna Dubinsky pioneered the Palm Pilot, one of the biggest hits in the high-tech industry.

Meanwhile, 3Com spun off Palm Computing, now its own entity. In June 2003 Palm bought Handspring for $192 million in stock. Dubinsky sits on the board of directors and Hawkins is the Chief Technology Officer.

Dubinsky, a natural entrepreneur, is a good match for Hawkins, the inventor. She thinks that, although the technology industry does not have a glass ceiling, it is important to be a role model. She is married with an adopted daughter from Russia.

She was inducted into the Industry Hall of Fame in 1999. That same year, the Handspring Visor received *PC Magazine*'s Technical Excellence Award, and Dubinsky and Hawkins were ranked number 39 in the *Business Week Digital 50*. In May 2000 they were named the most influential hardware designers by *The Industry Standard*, and in 2001 they were Ziff-Davis SMART BUSINESS "People of the Year" and won the Most Valuable Product Award.

See also: Information Technology Industry

Further Reading
Butter, Andrea and David Pogue. *Piloting Palm*.
Fortune (October 16, 2000), p. 132.
Frezza, Bill. "Champions of the New Economy Get Rich the Old-Fashioned Way."
"Palm Pioneers: The Palm Pilot's Parents Created One of the Greatest Hits in High Tech."

Dublon, Dina (1953–), Banker

Dina Dublon has been on *Fortune*'s lists of the most powerful women in corporate America since 1999. As the CFO and an executive vice president at Chase Manhattan bank, the second largest bank in the United States, she is one of the top women in the banking industry.

She was born in Brazil. When she was eleven, Dublon's family moved to Israel where she grew up with her two brothers. After receiving a BA in accounting and finance from Hebrew University in Jerusalem, Dublon made her first trip to the United States for a year of backpacking. Returning to Israel, she worked as a trader in the Tel Aviv stock market and for Bank Hapoalim.

She returned to the United States to earn a masters degree in economics and mathematics from the Graduate School of Industrial Administration at Carnegie Mellon. After working at Harvard Business School she joined Chemical Bank in 1981 in a management trainee program, starting in the capital markets group. In 1989 Dublon was promoted to senior vice president of corporate finance with responsibilities for debt and equity financing, as well as structuring and negotiating acquisitions. She was named corporate treasurer in 1994, and two years later, when Chemical Bank merged with Chase Manhattan, became the executive vice president of corporate planning and a member of the Chase Manhattan Policy Council.

Since December 1998 she has been the chief financial officer and an executive vice president. Dublon inaugurated a program of financial restraints across the company; each unit must show a profit or explain why it didn't. She is also responsible for strengthening the stock price and making acquisition decisions. Two of her acquisitions were Hambrecht & Quist and Flemings. Since Chase merged with J.P. Morgan in 2001, becoming the second-largest bank in the United States, her responsibilities have almost doubled.

Dublon, known for her expertise in strategy and finance, was named one of the smartest women in the money business by *Money* magazine in 2000. She credits her success to a willingness to be straightforward, courage to ask questions, and trust in her intuition. She is married with a family. Her philanthropic activities focus on refugees in Rwanda as part of the Women's Commission for Refugee Children. She has served on the board of directors of Hartford Financial Services Group, GovWorks.com, and Accenture.

See also: Banking

Further Reading
"Money Moms."
Sellers, Patricia. "Behind Every Woman. . . ."

Dunn, Patricia C. (1953–), Investment Banker

Patricia Dunn was the global CEO of Barclay's Global Investors from 1998 to July 2002, when she retired for health reasons. She was listed as one of *Fortune*'s most powerful American businesswomen from 1999 through 2001.

Born and raised in Las Vegas, Nevada, she was the daughter of a showgirl and a vaudevillian. Her father married in his fifties and was very involved in the lives of his three children. He brought many different show people home to dinner, including Walt Disney and Lena Horne. Her mother brought her up to know no limits. She graduated from the University of California at Berkeley in 1975 with a degree in journalism and economics.

Dunn was unable to find a job in journalism, so she took a temporary secretarial position at Wells Fargo Bank, feeling certain that she wouldn't stay in banking. For the next twenty-three years, however, she worked in every area of the company: portfolio management, marketing, consulting, and client services. During the 1980s all of its management left except for her. In 1987 she became executive vice president and in August of that year, president, COO, and co-chief investment officer.

In 1995 Barclays bought Wells Fargo, and two years later she was made co-chair of Barclay's Global Investors, responsible for enterprise services in the Americas, Australia, and Southeast Asia. Dunn was named global CEO in 1998 and chair in 1999, controlling $675 billion in assets as the overseer of the world's largest group of index funds. She was also a member of the management committee of the parent company. She held that position until retiring in July 2002, when she decided to focus on treatments for cancer.

Dunn has an intellectual mind and has written several articles on investment management. She has wonderful people skills and always sends thank-you notes and flowers for projects well done. She thinks a leader's job is to be the keeper of the corporate culture and avidly believes in building consensus. She credits her male colleagues for teaching her and being extremely open-minded and enlightened, considering this was during the mid-1970s.

Dunn has served on the Hewlett-Packard Board of Directors and the advisory board of the Haas Graduate School of Business at Berkeley. *Money Magazine* called her one of the fifty smartest women in the money business, and *Irish America Magazine* honored her with a Wall Street 50 Award in 2003. She is married with four grown stepchildren.

See also: Finance industry

Further Reading
Calvey, Mark. "ExecutiveProfile: Patricia Dunn."
Hopkins, Jim. "Vaudeville Daughter Now Star Player in Mutual Fund World."
Jurgens, Rick. "Making Your Mark Quietly."

Dwyer, Katherine M. (1949–), Cosmetics Executive

Kathy Dwyer was the president of U.S. consumer products for Revlon when she was ranked number 37 on *Fortune*'s 1998 list of most powerful women. The following year she resigned and in September 2001 opened her own company, Skinclinic, a chain of clinics offering anti-aging treatments.

She was born and raised in Boston in a second-generation Irish American family. She received a degree in psychology from the University of Massachusetts in Boston and an MBA in finance and organizational behavior from Boston University.

After Dwyer began her business career with Price Waterhouse, she held positions of increasing responsibility with Gillette from 1976 to 1985. After that she was director of L'Oreal Haircare from 1985 to 1987, vice president of U.S. Communications for Avon Products for two years, executive vice president of marketing and product development for Victoria Creations from 1989 to 1991, then vice president of marketing for two years for Clairol, Inc.

In 1993 she joined Revlon Inc. as an executive vice president and in 1995 became president of Revlon Cosmetics, USA. In the next five years she turned the company around through cosmetics lines that appealed to a wide audience. Dwyer, credited with bringing Revlon from number three to number one in the cosmetics field, became an executive vice president of Revlon Inc. in 1997, and was named president of Revlon Consumer Products, USA, in January 1998, with added responsibilities for the beauty care division. For the next two years she introduced many new cosmetics products.

In December 1999 she resigned and produced a foundation product with two purposes: skin protection and defect correction. In 2001 she opened Skinklinic, planning a national chain of anti-aging skin treatment clinics for a potential 67 million people who, wanting to look younger without plastic surgery, would make it, "the Starbucks of Skin." By November of that year, the customer counts were close to her vision, and one year later, Skinklinic was named a Gold Key Finalist-Spas and Resorts by *Hospitality Design*.

See also: Beauty Industry

Further Reading
"Kathy Dwyer, President of Revlon Cosmetics, USA Receives Achiever Award from Cosmetic Executive Women, Inc."
Neff, Jack. "No Downtime Face Time."

Dyson, Esther (1951–), Computer Industry Analyst

Esther Dyson was described by John Carlin in *The Independent* as "generally regarded not only as the most powerful and influential woman in the computer world, but as its brightest visionary and leading intellectual voice" (p. 3). A pioneer of the Internet, she is the CEO of her own company, EDventure Holdings, which publishes *Release 1.0*, one of the most influential newsletters on the industry. Because this is such an important publication, Dyson was ranked number 39 on the *Fortune* 1998 list of most powerful women in corporate America and number 31 in *Time*'s Digital 50 in 1999.

She was born in Zurich into a brilliant family; her father was a physicist and her mother a mathematician. The family moved to Princeton, New Jersey, when she was very young where her father worked in the Institute for Advanced Studies. Their neighbors were Nobel Prize winners, and Edward Teller (father of the hydrogen bomb) came to dinner regularly. When Dyson was five, her mother ran off with a fellow mathematician, and her father later remarried. A child prodigy, Dyson entered Harvard at age sixteen, spending most of her time at the *Harvard Crimson*, the campus newspaper.

After graduating in 1971 with an economics degree, she became a reporter for *Forbes*. In 1977 she decided to be a securities analyst concentrating on high technology stocks; and a few years later Edward Rosen persuaded her to write for his *Rosen Electronics Newsletter*, then known as the industry bible. After a year Rosen sold the newsletter and his prestigious seminars to Dyson who renamed it *Release 1.0* and called her company EDventure Holdings, Inc. One of her first articles was about a new company named Microsoft. The accompanying seminars were by invitation only to 500 people. They paid a high price to associate with their fellow high-tech denizens, to make deals and agreements to collaborate, to find out the latest innovations and inventions in the industry, and generally become up-to-date.

> Esther Dyson was described by John Carlin in *The Independent* as "generally regarded not only as the most powerful and influential woman in the computer world, but as its brightest visionary and leading intellectual voice."

Current Biography says of Dyson, "[her] reputation rests on her ability to predict industry trends with remarkable foresight and to help link 'idea people' with people who can put ideas into action" (p. 158).

In the late 1980s she became interested in the Eastern European countries. Since first visiting Russia during the Gorbachev years, she has focused on those emerging countries, helping them to access technology and training and to benefit from those industries. Dyson began EDventure Ventures, a venture capital fund focusing on investment in that part of the world.

Some say her influence in the United States is diminishing because of her strong focus on Eastern Europe. Others say her prestige is intact; people flock to her seminars. From 1999 to 2001 she was the chair of ICANN, the Internet Corporation for Assigned Names and Numbers and is still on ICANN's At-Large Advisory Committee. Dyson's company has invested in dozens of cutting-edge technologies and has considerable influence in Washington and in other countries. She has served on the boards of more than twenty companies as well as the nonprofit boards of Santa Fe Institute, Eurasia Foundation, the Electronic Frontier Foundation, and the Institute for East-West Studies. She is famous for her defense of the Internet as an ungoverned entity and freedom of speech. She does believe in standards, however, and fights hard for reasonable ones. In March 2003 she was appointed to the Task Force on National Security in the Information Age.

A 1999 photograph shows Dyson's casual style: barefoot and in blue jeans. She spends most of her time traveling or at her reportedly messy office, rarely in her New York apartment, but swims at least two hours daily wherever she is. She feels that being a woman has not made a difference in her career because the computer world allows for a broader range of acceptable character traits. As a woman she has the advantage over a man of not being compared to Bill Gates.

In February 2003 ThinkQuest New York City honored Dyson for her leadership in promoting the Internet as an effective tool for learning and for involving parents in the process.

See also: Consulting; Information Technology Industry

Further Reading

Carlin, John. "Queen of the Neterati; John Carlin on a Woman whose Intimidating Intelligence Dominates all Things Digital; PROFILE; Esther Dyson."

Current Biography Yearbook, 1997, p. 158–160.

Dyson, Esther. *Release 2.1: A Design for Living in the Digital Age.*

Gerstner, John. "The Civilization of Cyberspace; Interview with Cyberspace Specialist Esther Dyson."

E

Earnings Gap, *see* Compensation

Education

Education for a career in business can take place on many levels. Trade school courses offer practical knowledge. College and university courses lead to degrees: undergraduate (BA), Masters of Business Administration (MBA), and doctorate (PhD or DBA). They focus on core business concepts, providing a comprehensive understanding of accounting, finance, information systems, management, and marketing. The MBA is designed to prepare the student, a future CEO, for management in a corporation. The doctoral program prepares scholars who will teach at the university level and design original research into business topics. Many business schools incorporate entrepreneurship, international business, and ethics into their curriculum. Executive education programs or subject specialist programs are also available, as are professional development seminars through business associations.

Apprenticeships were the first form of business education. During the colonial period and until the industrial revolution, there was no need for anything else. The evolution of factories, however, necessitated education about management. In the 1820s the first private business schools appeared in New York and Boston. By 1893 there were more than 500 schools nationwide that taught bookkeeping, arithmetic, and penmanship. Stenography entered the curriculum in the 1860s and typing in the 1870s, followed by commercial geography and commercial law. The early schools had a poor reputation because the curriculum was very narrow, there were no admissions requirements, teachers were inexperienced and low paid, and graduates had trouble finding jobs. At the same time, colleges were under-enrolled and only taught students who wished to become ministers, doctors, lawyers, or engineers. They also, of course, taught the classics, but nothing leading to other practical work. Although people clamored for business education in the universities, they were opposed by those who thought commerce was low-class or undignified (Daniel, p. 27–28). Joseph Wharton established the first collegiate school of business in 1881. He gave a large donation for the Wharton School of Finance and Economy, "to provide for young men" an education in business (Daniel, p. 31). Harvard Business School, founded in 1908, was the first graduate business school, and that "conferred a dignity and legitimacy that broke down the last barriers of resistance" (Daniel, p. 39). By 1919 there were 36,456 business students nationwide; in 1926 they numbered 67,496.

The first women were admitted to the University of Georgia, which established a secretarial degree program in 1919. The University of Cincinnati enlarged a similar program in 1923 to include interior decoration, diet, office management, and industrial-chemical research fields. By 1927, 10 percent of the business students were women. Three years later Hunter College inaugurated a program to train women to be "leaders for the best places in business" (Daniel, p. 94).

During World War II, many colleges participated in the war effort by training women to be accountants and factory managers. When the men returned from military service, the women lost their places in the workforce. Business education returned to normal, which was an "almost entirely . . . masculine venue" (Daniel, p. 143). At the American Association of Collegiate Schools of Business convention in 1946, one of the speakers forecast an influx of women students. By 1950 course offerings included accounting, economics, banking and finance, marketing, statistics, business organization, and business law. The first PhDs were awarded as well as more than 4,000 MBAs. Business education, however, was still largely undergraduate and male-dominated.

In 1961 Harvard admitted the first women MBA students; in 1968 Dartmouth followed suit. Some universities established special MBA programs to encourage women, and during the 1970s, women entered in large numbers and formed networks in business schools. By 1975, 10 percent of MBA students were women. This number rose to nearly 35 percent in the late 1980s and peaked at 39.8 percent by 2000. Undergraduate enrollment in business programs reached 50 percent women by 2000, the same year that 31.9 percent of PhD business degrees were earned by women.

Catalyst, the University of Michigan Business School, and the Center for the Education of Women at the University of Michigan surveyed women with MBA degrees in 1998 and 1999 and found they were highly satisfied with the business school experience and the value of the MBA to their careers. Their most rewarding experiences were the interaction with fellow students and the teamwork required. They found a lack of diversity on the faculty and some felt the environment to be too aggressive and competitive. The majority of ethnic MBA students experienced discrimination.

There are three organizations that provide networking opportunities for women or minority-member MBA students: Graduate Women in Business (www.gwib.org), National Society of Hispanic MBAs (www.nshmba.org), and the National Black MBA Association (www.nbmbaa.org).

Further Reading
Daniel, Carter A. MBA: *The First Century.*
Morris, Betsy. "Tales of the Trailblazers: *Fortune* Revisits Harvard's Women MBAs of 1973."
Tyson, Laura D'Andrea. "Voices."
Women and the MBA: Gateway to Opportunity.

EEOC, *see* Equal Employment Opportunity Act

Ehmann, Freda (1839–1932), Olive Industry Developer

Freda Ehmann created the California ripe olive industry when she was fifty-six, an age when some contemporaries were dying. She not only perfected the processing formula but also packed and marketed her products nationally and built her company. In fact, she supervised the packing until age seventy-two. Born in Germany, she came to the United States in her teens with her widowed mother. She married Dr. Ernst Ehmann, and they had three children, Mathilde, Edwin, and Emma. Dr. Ehmann died in 1892, shortly after Mathilde's death from typhoid fever at age nineteen. Freda had always been a housewife and raised the children.

Her son Edwin, who lived in California and sold fine china, was very interested in growing olives. He persuaded his mother to sell her house and invest with him in Olive Hill Grove, a circa-1800 ranch in Oroville, California. Unfortunately, the next winter's heavy rainfall and floods washed out the ranch. Edwin's partner gave Ehmann twenty acres to make up for her loss. Edwin wished to declare bankruptcy but she said no; her family always paid their debts. As the Hubbards said in *An Appreciation*, "Mrs. Ehmann's capital stock was energy, a good brain, an undaunted will, and an Olive Grove" (p. 3).

Ehmann's trees bore their first olives two years later, but the price of olive oil, the chief product then, was dropping. Her caretaker suggested pickling the olives instead. High rates of spoilage nullified the quality of the product, and a pickling process was known, but seldom successful. Because olives have to be cured, they couldn't be sold right off the tree, so the process had to be stabilized to be successful.

Freda decided to experiment with a basic recipe from Professor Eugene Hilgard at the University of California at Berkeley and 280 gallons of olives. She had no equipment, so her son-in-law made vats out of old wine barrels and installed them on the back porch. Without water pipes to the porch, she had to carry over 200 gallons of water the first year.

Every morning Ehmann checked on the product and changed the recipe little by little until she had it right. Professor Hilgard tested her olives and pronounced them the best he had ever tasted. Better yet, one of the largest grocers in the area ordered all she had. The next year, deciding to move into the national market, she went to New York and Pennsylvania to sell her olives and returned with contracts totaling 10,000 gallons, many more than the 1,000 gallons she could produce. To handle this problem she bought another grower's entire crop and leased a pickling plant. After taking a nearby room, she was ready to go to work.

By 1898 the Ehmann Olive Company was incorporated and by 1904 distributed olives nationally. She was in charge of production and quality; no olive that was not cherry red in color escaped her eye. She also looked over every piece of equipment and every product that was to be shipped, supervising the packing operation into her seventies. Edwin was in charge of marketing and sales; her son-in-law, Charles, was in charge of the plant and any necessary construction.

She was known as a benevolent employer. Before World War I, Ehmann hired Asian immigrants, paying them the same wages as other employees and building a dining hall and barracks for them. This was very unusual for the time. Unfortunately, she received threatening, anonymous, anti-Japanese letters after World War I and so decided to stop. She also built a dining room for her women employees and joined them for lunch and tea every day.

Ehmann supported woman's suffrage but was principally busy as a very vocal advocate for the California olive industry. Known as the "Mother of the California Ripe Olive Industry" (Oppedisano, p. 94), she was writing letters about buying American, rather than foreign, products when she was in her nineties. Her grandson later wrote about her accomplishment: "Where science and chemical exactness had failed, the experience and care of a skillful and conscientious housewife succeeded" (www.calolive.org/foodoliveher.html). Her son Edwin was the mayor of Oroville from 1919 to 1923. Their house in Oroville is the headquarters for the Butte County Historical Society.

See also: Food Industry; Immigrant Businesswomen; Late Bloomers

Further Reading
"Freda Ehmann (1839–1932)." In Oppedisano, p. 94–97.
Hubbard, Elbert and Alice Hubbard. *An Appreciation.*
www.calolive.org/foodoliveher.html

Elder, Irma (1931–), Automobile Dealer

When Irma Elder was widowed in 1983, she knew little about the automobile dealership business. Out of necessity she took over Troy Motors, her husband's dealership, and built it into one of the *Working Woman*'s top fifty companies and one of the largest Hispanic-owned businesses in the United States.

She was born in Mexico, raised in Miami, attended the University of Miami in Florida, and moved to Detroit with her husband and three children. After she inherited her husband's Ford dealership, cars weren't selling well because of the recession. She could not afford to sell the company, so she had to learn to run it, and learn quickly. She had three children to put through college. When she took over, sales were $35 million.

The first year was the worst. In the first four months, all her sales staff and managers left, and Elder had to rebuild the sales force. She thought it was because of her, but later learned that changing jobs was common with car salespersons. Actually, some had left convinced she couldn't run the business. She had attended Ford conferences and meetings with her husband out of interest, however, and had learned a little.

One of the first things Elder did was to ask her nineteen-year old son to attend the automobile convention with her to show that she was serious about running the company. She then began to emphasize service and customer satisfaction, hiring people who would stay long enough to encourage repeat business. She included service as an important piece of the business, and her service manager pioneered a color-coded service team system. The company received customer satisfaction awards from Ford in 1991 and 1992.

In 1988 Elder bought a nearby absentee-owner dealership that was lagging in sales. She added a Jaguar dealership in 1993 and a year later, an Aston Martin dealership. She also has a huge fleet business that supplied Hertz and Budget. Then she started in the used car business by selling the rental cars when they were retired. With all her dealerships, service and repair are a primary concern. By 1997 sales were $381 million.

She credits her success to her attention to personnel management; she has cut the turnover rate to 20 percent of the sales force, phenomenal in this business. Elder carefully chooses staff, pays close attention to her hires, and knows each one by name. A gentle woman, she believes in management by consensus, has a knack for seeing possibilities, and has faith in her ability to build a strong management team. She empowers all her workers, emphasizing that sales staff are independent businesspeople who need to take good care of customers so that they return. She also believes strongly in training, staff development, and encouragement. Elder looks for integrity and respect for other people as well as an instinct for selling when hiring and can tell within three months if a person will work out.

As an "outsider owner," coming from outside the business to take it over, Elder has succeeded admirably. She has won several awards for entrepreneurship and has served on the board of directors of Lear Corporation, the Minority Business Roundtable, and the board of the Detroit branch of the Federal Reserve Bank of Chicago. Elder was inducted into the Automotive Hall of Fame in 2000. The following year, she won the Women's Automotive

Association International Professional Achievement Award and was inducted into the CATCH Hall of Fame for her charity work with the community.

See also: Automobile Industry; Latina Businesswomen

Further Reading

Bonk, Jenny. "Irma Elder: Strength of a Jaguar."

Guilford, Dave. "Rough Start Made Elder an Expert on Turnover."

Kaplan, James. "Amateur's Hour: Who Says it Takes Years of On-the-Job Experience to Run a Company?"

Eldridge, Elleanor (circa 1784–circa 1845), Entrepreneur, Real Estate Entrepreneur

Elleanor Eldridge, a free African American with Native American blood, began several businesses in Rhode Island and was active in real estate. There are several different accounts of her ancestry. Most agree that her father was a slave brought from Africa, and her maternal grandmother was an American Indian. Her father earned his freedom by fighting in the American Revolution. She was born circa 1784, the youngest of seven daughters. Her mother died when she was ten, and Eldridge went to work for Joseph Baker, where she learned numbers, how to spin and weave, and how to handle accounts. Later, she was placed in charge of Capt. Benjamin Greene's dairy farm. When Eldridge's father died when she was nineteen, she settled his estate.

In 1812 she and her older sister, Lettice, began businesses in weaving, soap-making, and nursing. Eldridge made enough money to buy a house, which she then rented out. Three years later she moved to Providence, Rhode Island, starting more businesses including painting, whitewashing, and wallpapering, and stayed for twenty years. Again, she bought a lot, on which she built a duplex. With borrowed money she purchased two more lots, promising to pay within a specified time, but was incapacitated for a year after she caught typhoid fever while on a visit. On her return, she learned that her death had been reported and her property had been auctioned off to pay the note. Since she had not been notified, she took the matter to court, and although she was supported by many of the townspeople, Eldridge lost the case. She did get her original property back, however, because the sale had not been legally advertised. The affair cost her $2,700 because the owner charged her for storing her furniture. It was an early and clear example of discrimination against a woman who was also an African American.

Although some question the authenticity of her 1838 memoirs, most historians agree that Eldridge really existed. Some parts may be fictitious, however, but it is one of the few accounts of a free African American woman of this period.

See also: African American Businesswomen; American Indian Businesswomen; Real Estate

Further Reading

Fisher, Vivian Njeri. "Eldridge, Elleanor (1784–c.1845)." In Hine, *Black Women in America*, p. 389–390.

Green, Frances W. *Memoirs of Elleanor Eldridge*.

Shannon, Sandra G. "Elleanor Eldridge." In Smith, Jessie, et al., Eds., *Notable Black American Women*, p. 319–321.

Electronics Industry, *see* Information Technology Industry

Employee Benefits

"Employee benefits are compensations given to employees in addition to regular salaries or wages . . . [usually] given at the entire or partial expense of the employer," (Satterwhite, p. 291). These benefits can be from 30 to 40 percent of the total compensation package, including those required by law: health insurance for job-related injuries, social security, unemployment insurance, and unpaid leave for family or medical emergencies. Other common benefits are used to attract and retain employees: health insurance, sick leave and vacation days, life insurance, and retirement options. Still others are incentives: end-of-the-year bonuses or on the employee's birthday, profit-sharing, and stock options. Other types of benefits were inaugurated in the 1980s because of the increasing number of women in the workplace, and the very healthy economy required aggressive recruitment of more workers.

From 1980 to 1990, working mothers with children under six-years-old increased almost 50 percent to 9 million women. In 2001 there were 25 million working moms, nearly 20 percent of the workforce. At the same time, workers also became scarce in the marketplace, so benefits became more important in order to recruit the best employees. These work/life or "family-friendly" benefits included on-site daycare, paid maternity leave, aid for adoption, flexible work hours, and paid family leave. While these were initially aimed at recruiting women, men were soon taking advantage of them. Additional benefits can include tuition reimbursement, extensive training and development opportunities, company credit unions, exercise facilities, subsidized cafeterias, on-site laundries, uniforms, discounts on company products, sports tickets, sabbaticals, paid time off for volunteer activities, parking privileges, massages, on-site jogging trails, company cars, career development counseling, membership in a country club or health club, home-purchasing insurance, financial counseling, group homeowner's or auto insurance, legal services, personal concierge services, transportation options, and one-stop shopping for personal needs. Many times, benefits can be the deciding factor when an employee chooses to work for a company.

In a booming economy with low unemployment, such as that of the 1990s, the cost of benefits seemed worth the high price; however, when corporations began to flounder, and the economy was not as healthy, cutbacks of both employees and benefits occurred. Managers lost many employees, but were urged to increase productivity, resulting in more hours of work. Although benefits are needed more during stressful times to make the employees feel valued and respected, many companies felt that they were extravagant and could be decreased. Some kept them, but asked employees to shoulder part of the cost. Also, when increased productivity is needed, many employees were reluctant to use the flexible work plans and leaves because their absence placed a burden on their fellow workers.

Some single and childless workers feel that the family-friendly benefits are discriminatory. Forty percent of the workforce is not married, and many of these workers feel that they pay for the leaves and flextime available to others because they feel overworked, particularly on holidays, weekends, evenings, or when a parent must leave because of an illness. Elinor Burkett, in the book, *The Baby Boom*, found that childless employees worked an average of seven hours per month more than employees with children (Briggs, p. 3F). One company dealt with this growing resentment by offering "unique opportunity leave." Another offered three levels of benefits, with salaries that differed according to each level.

Many surveys and studies have proved that benefits of all kinds ultimately save money for corporations through increased retention, decreased illness and injuries, less-stressed employees, and higher employee morale. During difficult economic times, managers and company executives must empower their employees to use their benefits.

See also: Childcare; Compensation; Flexible Work Arrangements

Further Reading

Briggs, Bill. "Pampered Parents? Childless Employees Beginning to Grumble about Inequalities."

Finnigan, Annie. "Benefits Under Fire."

Rosenbloom, Jerry S., Ed., *The Handbook of Employee Benefits: Design, Funding, and Administration.*

Satterwhite, Marcy. "Employee Benefits." In Burton S. Kaliski, ed., p. 291–295.

Energy Industry

The energy industry has been male-dominated since the discovery of oil and natural gas, but during the 1970s the number of woman-owned firms began to increase. As of 1983 more than 21,000 energy-related companies were owned by women, 9.8 percent of the energy companies in the United States. Most of these were oil and gas extraction companies. Some women, like Kathy Lehne, began as secretaries but saw possibilities in the field. Some are engineers, while others inherited the business.

Three organizations offering training, education, and networking opportunities are the Society of Professional Women in Petroleum (SPWP), Women in Energy (WE), and the Women's International Network of Utility Professionals (www.winup.org).

See also: Mining

Further Reading
Fraser, Edie, p. 91–92.

Entertainment Industry

The entertainment industry represents film, recording, and music. Although television provides entertainment, it is part of the broadcasting industry and is discussed in that entry.

The film industry, one of the world's largest, is very difficult to enter, and once inside, to stay in. At its beginning in the 1890s and early 1900s, the industry was open to anyone. Many women made films, mostly in New Jersey and New York. There were no large companies, and some women movie stars parlayed their popularity into power by producing, directing, and distributing. Mary Pickford and Alice Blache were active in the silent era of movies, from 1910 into the 1920s.

After the industry had moved to Hollywood in 1921, big production studios were established. With the exception of Pickford, women were squeezed out of power positions. By the 1940s film was a business first and then an art. Virginia Van Upp was an executive producer at Columbia Pictures, but she was the only woman in that position until 1975, when women became vice presidents of United Artists and Warner Brothers. In 1980 Sherry Lansing made history when she became president of Columbia Pictures. Dawn Steel was put in charge of both production and marketing at Columbia in 1998. By December 1990 there were twenty-two women presidents, but not one of them had the authority to green-light a project. It was not until 1992 when Sherry Lansing became the chair at Paramount that she had such power.

As of December 2002 women ran 45 percent of the studios in Hollywood. Three of the industry's top guilds had women presidents, but there were very few women on the boards of the entertainment corporations. Women held only 3 percent of the senior media positions, such as chair, CEO, or president. Although 25 percent of the producers were women, as were 15 percent of the executives, gains had been slow in these positions of real power.

The recording and music industry has long been known as dominated by fast-talking, aggressive white men in the top positions. In 1991 a landmark sexual harassment case at Geffen Records exposed sexism in the industry. Although the case was settled for $500,000, it and the other large recording companies realized that attitudes and practices needed to be changed. Women were hired, but they had to work harder than male employees, and still many were passed over for promotion. Sylvia Rhone was an exception, becoming the only woman recording company chair and CEO, although she had to endure many sexist and racist encounters along the way.

By 2002 progress had been made. *Hollywood Reporter*'s list of the most powerful women in Hollywood included Judy McGrath, head of MTV Networks; Michelle Anthony, executive vice president of Sony Music Entertainment; Hilary Rosen, chair of the Recording Association of America; Polly Anthony, president of Epic Records; and Sylvia Rhone.

Two associations seek to advance the professional development of women in film, video, and related media: Women in Film and Video (www.wifv.org) and Women in Film (www.wif.org).

See also: Broadcasting Industry

Further Reading

Acker, Ally. *Reel Women: Pioneers of the Cinema.*

Seger, Linda. *When Women Call the Shots: The Developing Power and Influence of Women in Television and Film.*

Seger, Linda and Mollie Gregory. "Femme Toppers Blaze Trails for New Generation of Women Exex."

Entrepreneurs

According to the 1977 Interagency Committee on Women's Business Enterprise, an entrepreneur is someone who takes a risk by investing capital, ability, time, and effort to start a business. *The Encyclopedia of Business and Finance* definition varies slightly: an entrepreneur is "an individual who owns, organizes and manages a business and, in so doing, assumes the risk of either making a profit or losing the investment" (Kaliski, p. 303). Others insist that real entrepreneurs begin with an idea they hope to build into a significant company that will build wealth and sustain itself; in other words, "create a company from scratch" (Brodsky, p. 33). No matter what the definition, women have become entrepreneurs in increasing numbers since 1980.

In the 1990s many researchers studied the phenomenon of women entrepreneurs, their personality traits, the obstacles they faced, and the rewards they gained. Many came from corporations, leaving after gaining business experience, often as a reaction to sex discrimination or after hitting the glass ceiling. The primary reason, however, was to gain flexibility in their lives and have time for their families. It was also a way to obtain pay equal to that of men in the same business and to gain freedom from corporate limitations.

Most entrepreneurs share traits that contribute to their success. They understand the value of a good idea, are comfortable with ambiguity, like change and risk, have high energy and self-confidence, appreciate complexity and process, and are decisive. They are also good at goal setting and problem solving and can use negative situations and attitudes as a challenge and advantage. For many years women entrepreneurs tended to be older than their male counterparts, but with the recent emphasis on entrepreneurship in universities, this has changed. Women entrepreneurs, according to the studies, have less ego involved in their businesses and tend to trust their intuition more than their male counterparts do. They focus on issues as well as profits, are strong at building relationships, have a high regard for social goals, and value cooperation and teamwork. They are also more likely to provide flexible work schedules and be proactive in helping solve problems of work/life balance. Integrating their personal values into their corporate culture, they tend to consider their employees as family.

The biggest obstacle for the woman entrepreneur continues to be finding financing. Historically, they used savings, mortgaged their houses, or borrowed from family and friends. Now the Small Business Administration (SBA) and banks offer loans, but these are not always granted. Venture capital is an option today but very difficult to obtain. Another obstacle is a lack of experience in financial planning. Many women entrepreneurs have to continually prove their capability to their suppliers and to male customers. Various studies list not being taken seriously as a major obstacle once women entrepreneurs begin doing business.

The rewards of entrepreneurship are high; these women have a sense of accomplishment and the satisfaction of building a business. They are independent and can shape their business culture using their own values. Many have also said they enjoy helping people, as well as having the potential for large profits and prestige.

The American Woman's Economic Development Corporation (www.awed. org) is dedicated to helping entrepreneurial women start and grow their own businesses. It provides course instruction, counseling, seminars, special events, and peer group support.

See also: Financing; Woman-Owned Businesses

Further Reading

Brodsky, Norm. "Who Are the Real Entrepreneurs?"

Buttner, E. Holly. "Examining Female Entrepreneurs' Man Style: An Application of a Religious Frame."

Drachman, Virginia G. *Enterprising Women: 250 Years of American Business.*

Fraser, Edie, Ed. *Risk to Riches: Women and Entrepreneurship in America.*

Hisrich, Robert. "Women Entrepreneurs: Problems and Prescriptions for Success in the Future." In Hagan, p. 3–32.

Kaminski, p. 303.
McDonald, Marci. "A Start-Up of Her Own."
Wells, Sandra J. *Women Entrepreneurs: Developing Leadership for Success.*
www.awed.org

Equal Credit Opportunity Act of 1974

This act prohibits discrimination against any credit applicant on the basis of sex, marital status, race, color, religion, national origin, or age. It covers all aspects of a credit transaction and all types of credit. It does not mean that anyone has a right to credit, but requires that the same standards apply to everyone who applies. It also requires the lending institution to explain why credit was denied.

See also: Financing

Further Reading
United States. Federal Trade Commission. *Equal Credit Opportunity Act.*

Equal Employment Opportunity Act of 1972, *see* Civil Rights Act of 1964

Equal Employment Opportunity Commission (EEOC)

The EEOC, established as a part of Title VII of the Civil Rights Act of 1964, is responsible for enforcing the laws against employment discrimination. Originally, the EEOC could only investigate complaints and try to remedy the situation through conciliation. The Equal Employment Opportunity Act of 1972 gave the EEOC enforcement powers to take cases through the courts. The Commission issues guidelines for employers and has attempted to bring state laws into compliance with federal laws. The Civil Rights Law of 1991 limited monetary awards for successful litigators. The Commission handles about 75,000 complaints per year.

See also: Sex Discrimination

Further Reading
Fuentes, Sonia Pressman. "The EEOC, NOW and Me: My Work in Women's Rights."
Schneider, Dorothy and Carl J. Schneider, p. 83–84.

Equal Pay, *see* Compensation

Equal Pay Act of 1963

The Equal Pay Act of 1963, mandating equal pay for equal work, resulted from a long struggle that began with demands from American feminists in the 1840s. While the National Labor Union worked on the issue in 1867, the legislation really grew out of experiences in the Great Depression and World War II. Michigan and Montana legislated equal pay laws in 1919, as did several other states between 1942 and 1945. Nothing much happened on the federal level until the 1960s. By then, twenty-six states and several cities had equal pay laws. Clearly there was a need; many workforce studies provided data proving pay disparity. The intent of the federal legislation was to provide equal pay for equal work; however, because women were segregated into low-paying occupations, some women advocated comparable worth. This controversial concept suggests that compensation be based on skills, effort, responsibility, and working conditions and evaluation be based on those criteria, ignoring position, title, and gender.

See also: Compensation

Further Reading
"Congress Passes The Equal Pay Act." In *Landmarks in Modern American Business,* p. 408–413.
Schneider, Dorothy and Carl J. Schneider, p. 59–60, 84–85.

Estaugh, Elizabeth Haddon (1680–1762), Land Manager

When Elizabeth Haddon Estaugh was twenty-one, she founded and developed the town of Haddonfield on 500 acres of land in New Jersey. She actively managed the Estaugh plantations during her marriage and long widowhood.

She was born to a Quaker family in the Southwark area of London, England. She was the eldest of two surviving children and was well educated in a Quaker school. Her father was a successful blacksmith who manufactured ship anchors. He had been fined many times for his religious beliefs, so he bought two large parcels of land in New Jersey and planned to emigrate but was prevented from doing so by failing health and a decline in business. Estaugh went in his stead. She had heard William Penn talk about the New World and felt a sense of mission to settle there.

She left England in 1701 with a power of attorney from her father for developing the land. Accompanied by a housekeeper and two male servants, she first landed in Philadelphia, then moved to New Jersey. In December 1702 she married John Estaugh, a Quaker minister she had met in England,

and together they developed the land into plantations. Because he was often absent for long periods of ministering travels, she was in essence the manager of the plantations. In 1713 they moved to one of their plantations, which would later become the village of Haddonfield.

Estaugh traveled to England three times to visit her parents. On the occasion of her last visit in 1723, she returned with her nephew Ebenezer Hopkins whom she adopted. Her father died the following year, leaving most of his New Jersey land to her. In 1742 her husband traveled to the British Virgin Islands to minister and died there the following year. She never remarried and continued managing her plantations until she died in 1762.

Estaugh had always adhered to the Quakers' plain and simple way of life. She was known as intelligent, gifted, and generous, always sharing with those in need. Her grave in Haddonfield Friends' Cemetery bears a tablet honoring her as founder and proprietor.

See also: Agriculture/Ranching; Colonial Businesswomen

Further Reading

"Estaugh, Elizabeth Haddon (1680–1762)." In Faragher, p. 132.

McDonald, Gerald D. "Estaugh, Elizabeth Haddon." In Edward T. James, p. 584–585.

Estrin, Judy (1955–), Entrepreneur, Technology Executive

Judy Estrin, because of her position at Cisco from 1998 to 2000, was named to the *Fortune* list of most powerful women in corporate America; however, she is really an entrepreneur extraordinaire. She and her husband have started four successful technology companies since 1981. Building a company is where she is most challenged and interested; she loves the process.

> Judy Estrin, because of her position at Cisco from 1998 to 2000, was named to the *Fortune* list of most powerful women in corporate America; however, she is really an entrepreneur extraordinaire.

She was born in Tel Aviv, Israel, the middle of three sisters, where her father was a computer scientist. Her mother, an electrical engineer, was the founder and leader of the Weitzmann Institute in Tel Aviv, a leading technology institute. Estrin's father was the head of the computer science department at the University of California in Los Angeles (UCLA). Her parents taught the sisters to think for themselves, and all were raised to know they could do anything they wanted.

Estrin graduated from UCLA with a BS in mathematics and computer science and later earned a masters degree from Stanford in 1976 in electrical and computer engineering. At Stanford she was one of three women in the engineering program.

Her first job was as an engineer for Zilog, a start-up company, with Bill Carrico as her boss. In 1981 she left Zilog and began Bridge Communications, a LAN and network router business. She was the vice president of engineering and later executive vice president of sales and marketing. Carrico was the CEO. In 1987 they sold the company to 3Com for $235 million, the same year they married. In 1988 they started another company, Network Computing Devices, which developed electronic-mail software and Xterminals. They took it public in 1992. Estrin was CEO and president her last year there. In 1994 sales reached $160 million. The next year the couple started yet another company, Precept, with her as president and CEO, producing software to stream audio and video over intranets. They sold it to Cisco in 1998, and Estrin became its senior vice president and chief technology officer, responsible for research and development strategy, mergers and acquisitions, joint ventures, and government and legal affairs. In 2000 she left Cisco to start another company, Packet Design, LLC, serving as president and CEO, with Carrico as board chair. Its purpose is to solve Internet infrastructure problems and improve performance and ease of use. Its first spin off was in March 2001, Vernier Networks, which offers wireless mobility to the Internet. In February 2003 they spun off two more: Packet Design, Inc. and Precision I/O. Estrin is the chairman of both companies.

Her management style combines problem solving with engineering skills and management expertise. She loves the challenge of building a company and the associated risks. She has the reputation of being highly effective at dealing with technology as well as sales. While her husband is more involved with the business details, she is people-oriented, creating a good balance. They waited until they had built the first two companies before having children, and now have one son. Estrin said that their life couldn't have worked having children first; now, they can afford a nanny.

She has served on the boards of Rockwell International, Federal Express, Sun Microsystems, and Walt Disney. Her awards include *Working Woman*'s list of the ten most important women in technology in 1997, the twenty-five most powerful people in networking from *Network World* in 1999, *PC Week*'s "15 Future Power Brokers," and *Money*'s "50 Smartest Women in the Money Business." In 2001 she was inducted into the Industry Hall of Fame.

See also: Entrepreneurs; Information Technology Industry

Further Reading

Ambrose, Susan, et al. "Judy Estrin." p. 150–153.
Bass, Evan. "Former Cisco CTO Now CEO of Fourth Start-Up: Packet Design, Inc."
Foremski, Tom. "Serial Entrepreneur Strikes Again."
Hiltzik, Michael. "A Veteran of the Fast Track Following Her Own Path."

Everleigh, Ada (1876–1960), Madam
Everleigh, Minna (1878–1948), Madam

The Everleigh sisters owned and operated the Everleigh Club in Chicago, the most opulent and expensive brothel in the United States. They were born either near Louisville, Kentucky, or in Virginia to a prominent attorney, attended private schools, and took lessons in elocution and dancing. They married brothers but were unhappy and eventually ran away to act in a touring company. In Omaha the troupe went bankrupt, but the sisters had meanwhile inherited a legacy of $35,000.

Budding entrepreneurs, they looked around for a business to open, and because choices were limited for female entrepreneurs, decided to open a high-class brothel. Their timing was perfect because the Trans-Mississippi Exposition was in Omaha that year, and there was a large supply of customers. With no real knowledge of any business or the particular business they were embarking upon, they remodeled a small building and hired beautiful women, some of them their actress friends. In two years of operation, they doubled their capital; however, the exposition ended and, with it, the supply of customers.

The Everleighs sold the business, moved to Chicago, and bought a flourishing brothel there for $55,000. After extensive redecorating which included gold cuspidors, a variety of elaborately named soundproof rooms, tapestries, oriental rugs, a music parlor with a $15,000 gold leaf piano, they opened in February 1900. Again, they chose well. Chicago was the home of the stockyards with its year-round conventions, captains of industry, and political aspirants, all providing plenty of clients. Their prices were high: $10 admission, $12 per bottle of wine, $25 for supper, or $50 for an evening with a "hostess." At this time the average price for a prostitute was $1.00 and sometimes as low as 25 cents. They employed thirty-five to forty girls with nightly receipts of $2,000 to $2,500. Minna handled the business while Ada interviewed and managed the girls. They were never personally involved with any of the clientele and were absolutely proper in speech and deportment.

The Chicago Tribune said that no house of courtesans in the world was so richly furnished, so well advertised, and so continuously patronized by men of wealth and slight morals (McHenry, p. 122). The establishment soon became known worldwide. When Prince Henry of Prussia was asked what he would like to see in the United States, he asked to go to the Everleigh Club. The sisters made hefty contributions to, and provided discounts for, important politicians, ran charge accounts for the more distinguished patrons, and promoted charge and expense account business. They advertised in the Republican Marching Club's Eighth Annual Reception souvenir booklet.

In 1910 a vice commission was appointed, and because the Everleigh Club was so visible, it was the first to be closed in October 1911. Minna and Ada auctioned off most of the furnishings and retired with an estimated $1 million in cash and $200,000 in jewelry. They then took an extended trip to Europe. On their return, they decided they were too notorious in Chicago, so they moved to New York City and took back their original name of Lester and lived as wealthy widows. After Minna died Ada moved to Virginia and lived there until she died in 1960.

See also: Prostitution

Further Reading

Kogan, Herman. "Everleigh, Minna." In Edward T. James, p. 589–591.

Wagner, R. Richard. "Everleigh, Minna and Ada." In *Dictionary of American Biography*, Supplement 4, p. 255–256.

Washburn, Charles. *Come into My Parlor: A Biography of the Aristocratic Everleigh Sisters of Chicago.*

Evinrude, Bess (1877–1933), Outboard Motor Manufacturer

Bess Evinrude and her inventor husband, Ole, were at the forefront of the modern marine industry. They founded two different companies based on his outboard motors; the second, Outboard Marine, is still thriving.

She was sixteen, a business student living with her family in Milwaukee, when she met Ole, who had rented a shed next door. He worked as a pattern maker for E.P. Allis Company during the day and on his inventions at night. She was intrigued by the inventions and offered to type letters for him. In 1906, when he was thirty and she was twenty-two, they married . He thought of inventing a motor for a rowboat while rowing across Pewaukee Lake to get ice cream for her.

By 1908 he had invented a motor that looked like a coffee grinder. Evinrude and her husband were partners. She insisted on reliability, so they tested it on a rowboat, and soon they had ten orders. She was the businessperson and put every penny into advertising: "Don't row! Throw the oars away! Use an Evinrude Motor!" (Carberry, p. A8). The campaign began in Milwaukee and later went nationwide. She had to hire six stenographers to handle all the inquiries. They raised $5,000 in capital from Chris Meyer, a partner, and formed the Evinrude Detachable Row Boat Motor Company. It began full production in 1910; by the next year it had sold 2,090 motors.

She contacted an export company who thought B. Evinrude was a man and ordered first 1,000 motors, then 3,000, and later 5,000. By 1913 they had 300 employees and sold 9,412 motors per year. Unfortunately, Evinrude's health had deteriorated since the birth of their son, and she had to quit work. Her husband sold the company in 1914 to his partner, and the couple traveled for a number of years.

By 1920 Evinrude was healthy again, and the non-compete clause had expired. Her husband invented a lightweight aluminum motor, the Evinrude Light

Twin Outboard, and showed it to his former partner who was uninterested; so the Evinrudes began another company, Elto Outboard Motor Company, selling 3,549 motors in 1922 and 7,600 in 1925, the year that their son, Ralph, joined the business. In 1929 Elto merged with Lockwood Motor Company and Evinrude Motors to become Outboard Motors Corporation, with Ole as president and Ralph as manager of exports. Evinrude's health had deteriorated again, and she retired in 1928. She died in 1933 at age forty-eight. When Ole died the following year, Ralph became president.

The company survived the depression and became Outboard Marine Corporation in 1956. Although it fell victim to the economic slowdown in 2000, the motors are still being made by Bombardier, Inc., who bought the engine assets.

See also: Manufacturing

Further Reading
Carberry, Sonja. "Innovators Ole and Bess Evinrude."
Rodengen, Jeffrey. *Evinrude, Johnson, and the Legend of OMC.*

Executive Order 13157—Increasing Opportunities for Woman-Owned Small Businesses

Signed by President Bill Clinton on May 23, 2000, this order was written to expand opportunities for women as suppliers to agencies and programs. It earmarked 5 percent of the approximately $200 billion in annually awarded government contracts for woman-owned businesses. Although 5 percent had previously been the goal, some federal agencies were not meeting it. Overall, government agencies were awarding only 2.4 percent of their contracts to woman-owned businesses in 1999 and, through August 2000, 1.9 percent. Executive Order 13157 restated the 5 percent goal and ordered agencies to work with the Small Business Administration to develop strategies and meet the goal.

See also: Woman-Owned Businesses

Executives

According to the 2002 Business Leadership Index of the Committee of 200, "Women business leaders continue to show slow, but steady and determined progress toward parity with men in major spheres of influence within the business world" ("Women Still A Long Way . . ."). The index also described persistent inequities in many areas, including wages, board directorships, corporate officer ranks, and attitudes toward job opportunities.

Only a few women had attained managerial positions in corporations prior to World War II, when women joined the workforce in large numbers. Although most left when the men returned, women had discovered their capabilities, and beginning in the early sixties, returned to work.

In 1965 the Civil Rights Act became law and its Title VII outlawed employment discrimination on the grounds of sex. The *Harvard Business Review* published an article that year describing the attitudes of 2,000 executives (half of them, men) toward "the role of women in the higher echelons of business management" (Bowman, p. 14). In that survey, 61 percent of the men and 47 percent of the women felt that the business community would never fully accept women executives. When describing their own basic attitude toward women in management, of the men surveyed, 9 percent were strongly in favor, 26 percent mildly in favor, 24 percent indifferent, 35 percent were mildly opposed, and 6 percent strongly opposed. One-third of the men saw women managers as being bad for employee morale, and 13 percent saw women managers as bad for efficiency. Also, 51 percent saw women as temperamentally unfit for management, while 74 percent of the women disagreed. Both men (90 percent) and women (88 percent) agreed that a woman had to be overqualified to succeed in management. The majority of men (86 percent) said they would feel uncomfortable working for a woman. Also, most of these executives felt that businesses had no responsibility to do anything to encourage women in management.

In 1980 an Arthur Young/Executive Resource consulting study concluded that the odds were better for a woman to be elected president of the United States than to become CEO of any top industrial company. Five years later Charlotte Sutton and Kris Moore reprised the *Harvard Business Review* survey, showing a large change in executive attitudes in particular. All executives' basic unfavorable attitude fell from 41 percent to 5 percent, and most realized that women do want positions of authority. While 90 percent felt that a woman had to be exceptional to succeed in business in 1965, only 58 percent agreed in 1985. By that time 82 percent of the men and 95 percent of the women executives saw women as being temperamentally fit for management; however, 33 percent of those surveyed thought that women would never be fully integrated into corporate life. One-third of all respondents still did not feel comfortable working for a woman boss.

In 2003 Catalyst reported six *Fortune* 500 companies with women CEOs, compared to three in 1987. However, 429 of these companies had one or more woman corporate officers. In sixty of the companies, women held 25 percent of the leadership positions, while seventy-one had no women officers at all, and 393 had no women among their top five officers. Progress has certainly been made since 1965, but it has been glacial.

Many barriers still exist, even a lingering attitude by some that women belong at home taking care of children. The old boys' network is also still very much alive, as are double standards on promotion and compensation. A

2000 *Catalyst* report, *Cracking the Glass Ceiling*, found most women managers were staff managers, rather than in decision-making line manager positions. Although 75 percent of the CEOs surveyed in that report believed that opportunities for senior leadership positions had improved greatly for women, less than 25 percent of the surveyed women agreed. The women (52 percent) felt that male stereotyping and preconceptions about businesswomen persisted, as did women's exclusion from corporate informal networks of communication (*Cracking the Glass Ceiling . . .*). All agreed that women had to work twice as hard to make an equal amount of headway up the corporate ladder.

Another Catalyst survey, published in 2001, *The Next Generation: Today's Professionals, Tomorrow's Leaders*, included recommendations for companies to follow for advancing women. Suggestions included: provide mentors, role models, and networks; provide work/life programs and support for them; and improve corporate culture and leadership commitment. It also recommended other organizational strategic programs, skill development and enhanced opportunities, and support for a meritocratic workplace. Only 4 percent of the women surveyed believed that companies were already doing a good job in this area. Of the men surveyed, 23 percent thought that nothing should be done specifically for women, and 8 percent thought that companies were already doing a good job (*The Next Generation*, p. 36).

Recommendations from women executives to those aspiring to executive positions include taking risks, accepting challenging assignments, networking to achieve highly visible positions, speaking up, developing a comfortable individual style, requesting desirable jobs or managers, and, most important, being confident and believing that reaching the top is possible.

The Committee of 200 (www.c200.org) and Executive Women International (www.executivewomen.org) are two organizations focusing on women business executives.

See also: Corporate Culture; Glass Ceiling; Power

Further Reading

Bowman, Garda W., et al. "Are Women Executives People?"

Cracking the Glass Ceiling: Catalyst's Research on Women in Corporate Management 1995–2000.

Driscoll, Dawn-Marie and Carol R. Goldberg. *Members of the Club: The Coming of the Age of Executive Women.*

Gallagher, Carol with Susan K. Golant. *Going to the Top: A Road Map for Success from America's Leading Women Executives.*

The Next Generation: Today's Professionals, Tomorrow's Leaders.

Sutton, Charlotte Decker and Kris K. Moore. "Executive Women—20 Years Later."

"Women Still a Long Way from Achieving Parity in the Workplace with Male Counterparts."

F

Family and Medical Leave Act of 1993 (FMLA)

The Family and Medical Leave Act, which became a law in February 1993, requires employers with more than fifty employees to provide twelve weeks of unpaid leave every year for the birth or adoption of a child or the serious illness of a family member, including a parent or the employee. The act guarantees no cessation of health benefits and the same or a comparable job when the employee returns.

Between 1993 and 1998, 35 million employees used this benefit; 42 percent were men. A survey in California showed that 76 percent of workers return to the same employer. Issues for the company include loss of productivity and the need to hire extra employees; however, various studies show that companies save money because recruiting, hiring, and training workers is so expensive. Through careful planning, it may not be necessary to replace an employee who is on leave.

See also: Employee Benefits

Further Reading
"Family and Medical Leave Act." In Schneider, Dorothy and Carl J. Schneider, p. 88–89.
Zachary, Mary-Kathryn. "FMLA Poses Many Issues for Companies."

Farley, Claire S. (1959–), Oil Industry Executive

Claire S. Farley, as the first woman president of Texaco's largest production division, was ranked number 27 on *Fortune*'s 1998 list of the most powerful women in corporate America. She is even more noteworthy for being in the male-dominated environment of the oil industry. In January 2001 after a brief foray as an entrepreneur, she became CEO of Trade-Ranger, an Internet oil marketplace funded by a consortium of large oil companies.

After graduating from Emory University in Atlanta with a BS in geology, she went to work for Texaco's New Orleans exploration and producing division. Farley gradually gained more responsibility, becoming area manager for exploration in 1989. She was appointed onshore exploitation manager in 1992 and assistant division manager of the onshore division in New Orleans in 1993. The next year she was asked to be assistant to management in the office of the chairman of the board and CEO of Texaco. Her initial reaction was to turn it down, but eventually she took the position, and in retrospect, felt that she gained valuable insights into how upper management and the board of directors made decisions. She later said that the view from the top was quite different.

Farley's next position was back in the field as general manager of strategic development for Hydro-Texaco Holdings, a position in the joint venture formed between Texaco and NorskHydro. She was responsible for developing entry strategies into Estonia, Latvia, and Lithuania and sat on the boards of the operating companies in Denmark, Norway, and Iceland, gaining her extensive international experience. Later that year she became managing director and CEO of Hydro-Texaco Holdings.

Beginning in January 1998 Texaco reorganized, and Farley was elected a vice president of Texaco Inc. and president of Texaco North America Production, a huge operation with a net income of $1.1 billion and a capital expenditure budget of $3 billion. Her experience in executive posts and U.S. and international production experience proved invaluable when she convinced Texaco's CEO and the board to buy Monterey Resources for $1.4 billion in August 1998.

In 1999 she left Texaco to become the CEO of AskRed.com (later Intelligent Diagnostics), a healthcare diagnostic software company, but when financing became a problem, she sold the company. Of the many offers, she accepted a job at Trade-Ranger, an opportunity to return to her first love, the oil industry, in a place where she could effect change. In September 2002 she was appointed CEO of Randal & Dewey, a provider of transaction and advisory services to the upstream oil and gas industry.

One of Farley's strong points is her expertise working with a team. She says she takes risks when necessary, screens out background noise, and picks her battles carefully. Determined not to let false protection for harsh situations (which she says often happens in a male environment) stop her career, she just pushed harder. From her own experience, she believes that mentors are an invaluable part of being successful in the business world but that it's best to pick your own.

Farley has two children. She won the 1998 Outstanding Proud Partner Award from Keep Houston Beautiful for her efforts to beautify the city. She has served on the boards of Boise Cascade, eNersection.com, and Newfield Exploration Company.

See also: Energy Industry

Further Reading

"Claire S. Farley Named General Manager of Strategic Development for Hydro-Texaco Holdings."

Fowler, Tom. "Barreling Back: Dot-Com CEO Back in Oil Industry She Loves."

Fashion Industry

The fashion industry is the "complex of enterprises concerned with the design, production, and marketing of men's, women's, and children's apparel and accessories" (Jarnow, p. vii). It comprises textiles, manufacturing, retailers, licenses, franchises, fashion communications, market consultants, and designers. In this tough industry, with its long learning curve, it is very expensive to enter and hard to succeed.

During the colonial era, obtaining clothing was more difficult than finding food or shelter. The well-to-do ordered textiles from Europe; everyone else raised flax or sheep and made their own cloth with rudimentary tools and no formal training. After the American Revolution new production methods for textiles emerged, and milliners, seamstresses, and tailors flourished. In the 1800s the first ready-to-wear garments appeared; clothing intended for male laborers, known as "slops." The first textile mill opened in New England in 1817. Brooks Brothers, the first men's clothing store, was founded the next year, and by the 1830s, the men's clothing industry was established. During the California gold rush in 1848, Levi Strauss designed his first pair of blue jeans. The sewing machine was introduced in 1846 by Elias Howe and modified with a treadle by Singer.

The garment industry flourished with factories in Boston, Baltimore, and New York City. Waves of women immigrants supplied the labor for the burgeoning ready-to-wear market, and children sewed in sweatshops under terrible conditions. By 1900, 55,000 people were employed in the industry. That year the International Ladies Garment Workers Union was formed and made efforts to improve working conditions. No real progress was made until the Triangle Shirtwaist Fires in 1911 that killed 143 workers, mostly young immigrant women. That tragedy triggered the establishment of workplace regulations.

The textile and clothing industry was well established by the 1920s, with the advent of faster production, a greater variety of fabrics, and wide distribution. One half of the country's output of manufacturing was due to this industry; output was valued at $1 billion. Upper-class women bought dresses from Paris designers, now the center of fashion. Everyone else wore ready-to-wear clothing, with better design and fit than the early garments. Store-bought was no longer a derogatory term.

In 1930 Fashion Group International (www.fgi.org) was founded to advance professionalism and develop the role of women in fashion. The founding members included Helena Rubenstein, Dorothy Shaver, Edith Head, Claire McCardle, and Eleanor Roosevelt. During the 1940s Shaver showcased American designers at Macy's and was largely responsible for the growth of fashion design in this country. There was increased spending during the 1950s, particularly on clothing. Giant factories mass-produced and distributed endless quantities of low-priced clothing, while Parisian and American designers made high-priced clothing to order. Men's clothing consisted of the dark suit with vest, white shirt, polished shoes, along with an overcoat and hat.

In the 1960s styles changed radically. Men's clothing became freer and more personal; women's hemlines went up to miniskirts, with styles ranging widely. Everyone searched for his or her own individual style, and almost anything seemed acceptable. Youthful fashions became common for all ages. During the 1970s more women began wearing pants, even to work, and everyone wore blue jeans. The 1980s and 1990s reflected the active and more casual life style. In 1990 the garment industry employed 100,000 persons, 90 percent women (among whom 40 percent Latina, 30 percent Asian American, and 20 percent African American). Outsourcing became common, and most manufacturing moved abroad, seeking lower-wage workers. The 1990s was also a decade of heightened celebrities; many of the stars were fashion designers such as Donna Karan and Josie Natori.

Women have always been a vital part of the fashion industry, from Elizabeth Boit and her textile factory to Donna Karan and her popular modern styles. Elizabeth Keckley designed and sewed for First Lady Mary Lincoln, Nell Reed designed and made pretty housedresses, while Lane Bryant first designed maternity clothes and then attractive clothing for larger women. Ida Rosenthal designed and popularized bras, and Josie Natori made underwear into high fashion. Gertrude Boyle turned a men's hat company into an attractive and popular sportswear manufacturer. The industry also includes African American and Asian American designers, although it has been very difficult for them to break through to mainstream success. Their businesses are usually small and independent.

Most fashion/clothing industry executives are men (84 percent), although 80 percent of the customers are women. Division presidents have a larger representation of women.

Further Reading
"Fashion Industry." In Juliet Walker, p. 405–410.
Gamber, Wendy. *The Female Economy: The Millinery and Dressmaking Trades, 1860–1930.*
Jarnow, Jeannette and Kitty G. Dickerson. *Inside the Fashion Business.*

Lockwood, Lisa. "Women CEOs: Arrival Time."
White, Nicola and Ian Griffiths, Eds., *The Fashion Business: Theory, Practice, Image.*

Fathers, *see* Husbands/Fathers

Fetterman, Annabelle Lundy (1921–), Packing Company Owner

Annabelle Fetterman's Lundy Packing, a pork processing company, was on every *Working Woman* list of top woman-owned companies, from the first in 1992 until 2001. The company slipped from number 10 in 1992 due to the slipping popularity of pork in the 1990s, but still ranked number 45 in 1999. She retired in 2000 and sold the company but is still known as one of the prominent businesswomen of North Carolina.

When Fetterman and her parents founded the company in 1950 in Clinton, it was one of the state's three pork processors and one of two slaughterhouses. Her son Lewis was the president, and daughter Mabel was a senior vice president. Its three brands are Lundy's, Tomahawk, and Tee Pee. As a commodity-based company, its financial health is strongly allied to the price of pork.

Even though pork products declined in unpopularity, the company remained profitable. It began breeding and processing its own leaner hogs to meet the demand for low-cholesterol products and to depend less on suppliers. After expanding the plant, in 1999 Lundy contracted to buy all the hogs bred by Jennings Humphrey, the last independent hog farmer in North Carolina.

The company had trouble during the 1990s after a brucellosis outbreak brought accompanying regulatory problems with OSHA, and later, a negotiated settlement. After a long-term attempt to unionize, the workers voted to join the United Food & Commercial Workers Union in 1994. The company appealed on the grounds that the union didn't really get enough votes to set up shop. The National Labor Relations Board (NLRB) initially upheld the union, but Lundy took the case to the fourth Circuit Court of Appeals and won. Then, after going back to the NLRB, which again ruled for the union, the company took its case to the Supreme Court, which upheld the Circuit Court ruling. In June 2000 Fetterman sold the company to Premium Standard, a Missouri pork processing company. Financial details were not disclosed.

See also: Food Industry

Further Reading
Feagans, Brian. "In the Swine Business, Little Guys Are Few."
Bamford Janet and Jennifer Pendleton, p. 46

Fields, Debbi (1956–), Food Industry Entrepreneur

In 1977 Debbi Fields, then age twenty, began her empire of warm chocolate cookie mall shops in California. Her husband had bet that she couldn't sell $50 worth of cookies her first day, and by noon she had not sold one. Putting all her cookies on a tray, she went around the mall giving away samples. By 5:00 that day, her sales totaled $75.00. Not only had she won the bet, she had launched a promising business.

Fields was born in East Oakland, California, the youngest of four daughters. She had a variety of jobs in her teens and was a cheerleader and prom queen in high school. With a passion for chocolate and chocolate chip cookies, she followed standard recipes but soon developed her own. After graduation she worked as a nanny, skied at Lake Tahoe, then attended college and worked to earn money for skiing. Snowed in at the Denver Airport, she met Randy Fields, an economist, and they married soon after. She began to bake her cookies for him to take to business meetings, and the clients loved them.

She thought that her cookies would make a good business, and even though friends and business acquaintances discouraged her, she borrowed $50,000 from a banker friend and her husband, rented a store in a mall, bought commercial equipment and supplies, and opened her business. In 1979 Fields added a store in San Francisco. On opening day customers were in line waiting for the door to open. By 1981 Fields had fourteen stores and headquarters in Park City, Utah. Fours years later there were over 200 stores, some in the Far East. In 1987 the company bought the La Petite Boulangerie franchise from Pepsico for $17.7 million.

> Debbi Fields's husband had bet that she couldn't sell $50 worth of cookies her first day, and by noon she had not sold one cookie.

By this time Fields' husband had joined the company as CFO, while she was president and CEO.

Debbi Fields was a micromanager: she needed complete control over the stores. Her belief in high quality demanded strict standards. Every cookie that was too flat or slightly overbaked was thrown out, and any cookie left unsold after two hours was given away to a food bank or community charity. She hired employees for their enthusiasm, outgoing personalities, and sense of fun, but they each had daily sales goals.

At the beginning of 1988 there were more than 500 stores in the United States, Japan, and Australia. When the business nearly failed during the economic downturn, she installed a middle management level, stopped trying to manage everything herself, and closed several stores. Fields later described this as a hard lesson. By 1989 sales were $118 million. The next year Randy Fields developed a computerized network and e-mail network that kept the managers in daily contact with all the stores and tracked sales statistics for each item (several kinds of cookies, brownies, soup and sandwiches, etc.), so the bakers could make informed decisions about what to make. This program, Retail Operations Intelligence (ROI), won the 1991 Optimas Award in the innovation category presented by *Personnel Journal*. By 1992, with stores in 34 states and six foreign countries, the company had 100 administrative staff, 4,000 employees in 466 cookie outlets, 97 La Petite Boulangeries, twenty-two Mrs. Fields Bakeries, and seven Mrs. Fields Marriott Cookie Stores.

Unfortunately, that was the last growth year under Fields' leadership. In 1993, due to another economic downturn, the overmalling of the country, fast overexpansion, and increased competition, she had to sell most of the company to her lenders. After selling La Petite Boulangerie, she stepped down as president and CEO of Mrs. Fields but remained on the board of directors. When the new owners franchised the business, she was active only as a spokesperson and consultant. In 1998 there were 1,342 company-owned, franchised, and licensed stores in the United States and ten countries, with sales of approximately $360 million.

Mrs. Fields Cookies is a good example of the perils of the retail food business: It was quickly established and just as quickly declined. During that time, however, she contributed a great deal to the communities where she did business, donating more than a million cookies to food banks and groups such as the Red Cross. She also funded Mrs. Fields Children's Health Foundation to find a cure for cystic fibrosis and for other research and education activities. In 1995 Fields was named the International Entrepreneur of the Year from the Council for Entrepreneurship at the University of Missouri at Kansas City. She has served on the board of directors of Shari's Berries, a gourmet chocolate-dipped strawberry retailer.

While operating her business, Fields also had five daughters. She said, when interviewed by the Montreal *Gazette* in February 1999, that her "family always came first. For me to do a good job, I had to know they were OK. And I'm teaching them that the moment you believe the glass ceiling exists, it becomes your barrier" ("How Mrs. Fields . . ." p. E6). She not only juggled motherhood and business, but also set a standard for delicious cookies. Her daughters helped by testing recipes, an enviable task. Fields felt that people didn't take her seriously because she was a woman, but she was a success due, she thinks, to her commitment to quality.

One year after divorcing Randy Fields in 1997, she married Michael Rose, a retired hotel executive, and changed her name to Debbi Fields-Rose. They live in Memphis where she has published a cookbook and has a successful new career as a motivational speaker. She has served on the board of Outback Steakhouse.

See also: Food Industry

Further Reading
Fields, Debbi and Alan Furst. *One Smart Cookie*.
"How Mrs. Fields Cooked Up Success."

Jeffrey, Laura, p. 92–100, 108–109.
LaTeef, Nelda. p. 61–65.
100 Greatest Entrepreneurs of the Last 25 Years, p. 199–201.

Fields, Mary (1832–1914), Frontier Entrepreneur

Mary Fields was a typical female entrepreneur of the early West. Like many she made a living in a variety of ways: as a teamster, restaurant and saloon operator, mail carrier, and laundry operator. She was not so typical, however, in her color and size: she was African American, over six feet tall, and weighed at least 200 pounds. Neighbors in Cascade, Montana, described her as a "cigar-smoking, whiskey drinking, two-fisted, gun-totin' pioneer" (Reasons, p. 28). She was a legend throughout the state of Montana.

Fields, a fugitive slave from Tennessee, was called both Black Mary and Stagecoach Mary after arriving in Montana by a circuitous route. After what she described as a very colorful life on the run (once she told of being at a famous steamboat race on the Mississippi), she settled with nuns at the Ursuline convent near Toledo, Ohio, in 1884, as their handyperson and became a devoted friend to Mother Amadeus, the head of the convent.

When Mother Amadeus moved to Montana to open a school for Indian girls and then contracted pneumonia, Fields followed her and nursed her back to health. She stayed to help build the mission, do all the handyman work, and bring supplies to the convent. Unfortunately, someone complained to the bishop about her personal habits (fist fighting, swearing, gun-toting, etc.), and he insisted that she leave the mission after working there for ten years. While the nuns and the children loved her, the townspeople were frightened of her.

With help from Mother Amadeus, Fields began a restaurant in town, but because she gave food for anyone in need, she soon went broke. Then, again with the help of Mother Amadeus, she was hired as the mail carrier between Cascade and St. Peter's. She became a legend, only the second female mail carrier in the United States, noted for always getting the mail through whether by stagecoach, horse, or snowshoes. In 1903 she retired and opened a laundry in Cascade where the townspeople had become used to her ways, and despite passing a law against women entering saloons, let Fields go in. She was also the official mascot for the town baseball team, and the school closed on her birthday when she gave a party for all the children.

A sketch of Mary Fields by the famous Montana artist Charles Russell is on display in the Charles Russell Museum in Great Falls. It is called "A Quiet Day in Cascade." Gary Cooper, a famous Montana actor, wrote a short piece about her for *Ebony* that concludes by saying, "Although born a slave, Mary lived to become one of the freest souls ever to draw a breath or a .38" (p. 100).

See also: African American Businesswomen; Western Businesswomen

Further Reading

Cooper, Gary. "Stage Coach Mary: Gun Toting Montanan Delivered U.S. Mail."
Franks, James A. *Mary Fields: The Story of Black Mary.*
King, Anita. "Black Mary: A Westerner with Style.
Reasons, George. *They Had a Dream*, p. 28

Fifty Most Powerful Women in Business, *see* Appendix I; Power

---

Fili-Krushel, Patricia (1953–), Television Executive

Patricia Fili-Krushel became the highest-ranking woman in the network television industry when she was appointed president of the ABC Television Network in August 1998. *Fortune* ranked her number 38 on that year's list of powerful women in corporate America. In May 2001 after leading a health web site, she joined AOL Time Warner as executive vice president of human resources and diversity.

She was born and educated in Queens, New York, receiving a BA in communications in 1975 from St. John's University. After obtaining her MBA in finance at Fordham University, Fili-Krushel joined ABC Television, eventually becoming the comptroller for ABC Sports. In 1979 she went to HBO as the director of sports administration, rising to director of production and then to vice president of business affairs and production.

In 1988 she joined Lifetime Television as a senior vice president and president of production, increasing its original programming by developing world premiere movies and more series. This helped solidify the company's niche as "the woman's channel." She later said the position at Lifetime helped her know female demographics and gain insight into their wishes. Her next position was as group vice president of Hearst/ABC-Viacom Entertainment Services. In 1993 she became president of ABC Daytime, responsible for all facets of daytime programming. Fili-Krushel stayed there until 1998, winning the Daytime Emmy Award for best drama and maintaining the network's top position with women viewers eighteen to forty-nine. Barbara Walters' daytime talk program, *The View*, was started under her supervision, as were a number of ancillary projects including coffee table books, video compilations, and Web sites.

In 1998 she was appointed president of the ABC TV Network with greater control over the programming than her predecessor had. Fili-Krushel was in charge of the its business operations, affiliate relations, and all the entertainment programming, news, and sports.

In March 2000 Fili-Krushel resigned rather than relocate to Los Angeles, and one month later, she was president and CEO of Healthon/WebMDs, the fast-growing consumer health network later renamed WEBMD Television.

She was lured by the new media and the opportunity to build a business while remaining in New York City. One year later, she joined AOL Time Warner, where she was the executive vice president of human resources and diversity, responsible for employee development, benefits, security, and improving diversity in the largely white male company.

Fili-Krushel, a child of divorced parents, is married, for the second time, to Kenneth Krushel, the vice president of strategic development at NBC. She has a son and a daughter and says that having children gave her the necessary negotiating skills. She has not found children to be a hindrance, and she leaves meetings to take their calls.

She is the past president of New York Women in Film and has served on the board of directors of Second Stage Theater. In 2000 she won the Matrix Award in Broadcasting from New York Women in Communications. In May 2003 she was honored with the Liberty Award from USO of Metropolitan New York.

See also: Broadcasting Industry

Further Reading
"AOL Invests in Diversity; Hires Female H.R. Chief."
Carter, Bill. "ABC TV Gets a New President with Wider Duties."
"Fili-Krushel, Patricia." *November 1999 Current Biography*, p. 17–18.
Machan, Dyan. "Executive Mom."

Film Industry, *see* Entertainment Industry

Finance Industry

"Corporate finance . . . is the acquisition and use of funds by business entities" (Oliverio, p. 370). The finance industry is inhabited by accountants, bankers, corporate financial officers (CFOs), security analysts, and stockbrokers. Accounting and banking are discussed under those headings; this entry will focus on security analysts and brokers.

Finance has evolved as businesses have become technologically advanced. Colonial finance was rudimentary with no regulations; most businesses were self-financed. During the 1800s there was great economic expansion with the development of large companies and railroads. Company executives began obtaining financing through the sale of stock in the company. Two years after the first stock exchange was established in Philadelphia in 1790, the New York Stock Exchange opened at 40 Wall Street, New York City. Financial journals and newspapers were introduced as investing in stocks became more and more popular in the late 1800s. On December 15, 1886, one million shares of stock were traded for the first time.

Without regulations, fraud and greed thrived. The post-World War I prosperity encouraged buyers of stock. When the stock market crashed in October 1929, many lost their fortunes. Out of the crash came regulation: the Securities Act of 1933 and the Securities Exchange Act of 1934, which established the Securities and Exchange Commission (SEC). The SEC enforces securities laws, requires financial disclosure from all companies selling stock, and promotes stability in the stock markets.

In 1999 Susan Caminiti called the Wall Street milieu "one of the last male bastions" (p. 57), and according to legend, the stock market was a "sexist, macho, cigar-loving world" (p. 58) that demanded aggressiveness, persistence, and a thick skin to survive. Sue Herera spoke of "pay differences, social slights, extended hours, solitary work, and preempted social lives" (p. xxiii) and the difficulty of maintaining an identity as a woman in a male milieu that judged "female traits as handicaps or exploitable weaknesses" (p. xxii).

A number of sex discrimination suits have been filed against brokerage houses. The first woman to buy a seat on the New York Stock Exchange, Muriel Siebert, faced many obstacles before achieving success in 1967. A second woman joined the exchange but not until 1977. There are no female CEOs in major securities firms, although women have been promoted to upper management positions in the past thirty years.

In 2003, 7.8 million people worked in the finance industry; 62.6 percent were women, but few were executives. In holding and investment companies, 56 percent were women, as were 44.3 percent of the securities and commodity brokers. Although half the general managers were women, very few were in the top management positions. Several women in finance are regularly among *Fortune*'s most powerful women in business, among them: Mary Meeker, Abby Cohen, Nancy Peretsman, and Sally Krawcheck. There are two associations actively representing women in finance: the National Association of Securities Professionals (www.nasphq.com) and Financial Women International (www.fwi.org).

See also: Accounting; Banking; Siebert, Muriel

Further Reading
Antilla, Susan. *Tales from the Boom-Boom Room: Women versus Wall Street.*
Caminiti, Susan. "What It Takes to Make It on Wall Street."
Herera, Sue. *Women of the Street: Making It on Wall Street—The World's Toughest Business.*
Oliverio, Mary Ellen. "Finance: Historical Perspectives." In Kaliski, p. 370–375.

Financial Women International (FWI)

200 N. Glebe Road, Suite 820, Arlington, VA 22203-3728
703-807-2007 http://www.fwi.org
info@fwi.org

In 1921 Financial Women International was founded as the Association of Bank Women by five banking pioneers: Virginia Furman, Nathalie Laimbeer, Kay Cammack, and Jean Arnot Rice. It was formed at a time when banks were beginning "women's departments," and these women were put in charge of them. Previously women had not done much banking , but the first trickle of women customers was appearing, and bankers recognized a great potential for clientele. The banks had hired women who had contacts, wealth, and social position, but no banking experience. The association was formed with the goal of establishing standards and providing members and their successors with educational opportunities in finance and banking. The first president was Virginia Furman, and Nathalie Laimbeer was vice president. By 1925 there were 110 members.

The association grew and organized divisions in each region of the country, established an award for outstanding accomplishments, and continued to provide opportunities for professional contacts and education as well as information on banking careers. The name was later changed to National Association of Bank Women, and in 1991 to Financial Women International to better reflect its membership. Today it provides a career center, a quarterly magazine, *Financial Women Today*, seminars and workshops, and awards and scholarships. In 2002 there were over 2,500 individual members in more than eighty chapters in the United States and 230 local groups worldwide.

See also: Banking; Finance Industry; Laimbeer, Nathalie

Further Reading
Gildersleeve, Genieve N. *Women in Banking: A History of the National Association of Bank Women.*

Financing

The ability to raise start-up and expansion money (capital) has always been a primary concern for woman-owned businesses. Before the 1974 Equal Credit Opportunity Act, it was almost impossible for women to obtain financing or credit of any kind without the signature of her husband or a man willing to be responsible. Because under-capitalization is the first cause of business failure, women have traditionally been at a disadvantage.

After 1974 obtaining bank loans became somewhat easier, but women owners still paid higher interest rates than men and needed more collateral. Two explanations are possible: women usually asked for less money than men and therefore had to pay higher interest, or they faced gender discrimination. As the number of woman-owned businesses ballooned from the 1970s to the end of the century, banks and other lending institutions became more accustomed to establishing credit with them.

Most aspiring women business owners have used a variety of ways to finance their businesses: savings, mortgaging their houses, credit cards, and bank loans. Most have used money from their immediate family and friends, some from local investors. Still others have persuaded suppliers to offer them a line of credit until the business begins making money.

The Small Business Administration (SBA) began a program in 1977 that provided seed money for woman-owned businesses or guaranteed bank loans up to $100,000. Today the SBA offers four different types of loan programs: Basic 7 (a) Loan Guaranty; Certified Development Company (CDC), a 504 Loan Program; and Loan Pre-Qualification. It also has a finance center that provides help in applying for loans and identifying the best loan for the business.

From 1987 to 1996 woman-owned businesses grew 78 percent while all businesses grew 48 percent. By 1999, 9.1 million businesses were owned by women, with $3.6 trillion in sales and 27.5 million employees. By 1998, 52 percent of these businesses had a line of bank credit. Initial financing was also more accessible, although not on a large scale. Although venture capital funding was popular in the late 1990s for start-up companies, most women did not use it. Out of 1,900 companies receiving venture capital in 1997, less than 2.5 percent were owned by women. Most woman-owned companies were a mismatch for venture capital interests that focused on high-growth manufacturing and communications products. Venture capitalists also want more control, high returns, and rapid growth, three factors many women owners find unattractive. Also, the venture capital industry is male-dominated, although that is slowly changing. By 2000 woman-owned firms received 7.9 percent of venture capital funding, although that was reduced to 5.4 percent in the lean markets of 2002. There are now many venture capital fairs or forums where women can network and find funding institutions for their businesses.

See also: Entrepreneurs; Small Business Administration; Woman-Owned Businesses

Further Reading

Coleman, Susan. "Access to Capital and Terms of Credit: A comparison of Men- and Women-Owned Businesses."

Green, Patricia G. et al. "Patterns of Venture Capital Funding: Is Gender a Factor?"

"A Network of Her Own."

www.sba.gov/financing/indexloans.html

Fiorina, Carleton S. (1954–), Computer Industry Executive

In 1998 *Fortune*'s first list of the most powerful woman in corporate America ranked Carleton (Carly) Fiorina as number 1, a position she held until

October 2004. She was recruited in July 1999 to be the new CEO of Hewlett-Packard (H-P), the only woman to head a Dow Jones Industrial 30 company and a *Fortune* 50 company, and the first outsider to become CEO of H-P.

She was born in Austin, Texas, the second of three children, and the ninth Carleton named after Civil War ancestors. Her father was a law professor, a former deputy attorney general under President Nixon, and later a judge in the Ninth Court of Appeals. Her mother painted portraits in oils and vibrant, colorful abstracts. Fiorina attended schools in Ghana, London, North Carolina, and Palo Alto, California, dreaming of becoming a concert pianist. She credits her success to the positive influence of her father's no-nonsense manner and her mother's positive outlook and zest for life. She says that her mother, with whom she was very close, worked hard to make her the best person she could be ("Fiorina," p. 40).

Fiorina graduated from Stanford with a BA in medieval history and a minor in philosophy. During the summer before her sophomore year, she worked at Hewlett-Packard as a secretary. After graduation, she entered law school but left during the first semester saying that she just couldn't stand the emphasis on precedents. She also said it was difficult to tell her father this, who predicted that she'd never amount to much. He has since changed his mind. For a while she drifted, married, divorced, and ended up in Bologna, Italy, teaching English. When she returned to the United States, she worked at a brokerage house in New York City and found the world of business an exciting one. She earned an MBA from the University of Maryland in 1980, later attending a one-year program at the Sloan School of Management at MIT.

At twenty-five she began her first business job as an AT&T long-distance representative selling services to the large federal agencies. Although she only planned to stay two years, she soon progressed through a number of sales and marketing positions, playing a key role in securing a contract with the U.S. government FTS 2000 program.

In 1989 Fiorina became the company's first female officer and by 1995 was president of the North American Region, responsible for telecommunications equipment market. When AT&T spun off Western Electric and Bell Laboratories into a new company, Lucent, in 1996, she planned and directed the strategy, not only developing Lucent's corporate image, but also leading the initial public offering. It was the most successful stock offering ever, worth $3 billion. Fiorina also became highly visible in the process and received many recruitment calls, including one from Hewlett-Packard. As one of one hundred candidates for its CEO position, she took the job in July 1999.

Fiorina won the job because in the crucial interviews she asked pertinent questions and offered some interesting suggestions, and had a reputation for fixing troubled situations. She spent the first month looking closely at the company, identifying both good and bad ideas, and talking of repositioning the brand. Then she began reorganizing the company, consolidating a number of divisions and groups into four, and encouraging communication between them.

In September 2001 her decision to merge Hewlett-Packard and Compaq Computer caused a bitter and acrimonious battle with both the Hewlett and Packard families. The proxy vote first seemed to favor the families, but the court ruled in favor of Fiorina, after she persuaded the board that the merger was in the best interests of the company. It was a nine-month struggle, but by 2003 the integration of the two companies was a success. Hewlett-Packard is one of the world's largest companies, with $70 billion in revenues. It is number one in at least six key technology markets, despite stiff competition.

Fiorina believes that power is the ability to change things. She is comfortable and adaptable in difficult situations. While having little patience with failure, she is quick to appreciate employee achievements. Her style is blunt, and she loves challenges. Her husband, a former vice president at AT&T, retired when he was forty-eight to support her career. She has two stepdaughters and a granddaughter.

> In 1998 *Fortune*'s first list of the most powerful women in corporate America ranked Carly Fiorina number 1, a position she held until October 2004. In July 1999 she was recruited to be CEO of Hewlett-Packard, the only woman to head a Dow Jones Industrial 30 company and a *Fortune* 50 company.

She has served on the boards of Merck, Kellogg, and Hewlett-Packard where she is the chair. In 1992 *Business Week* named her one of the fifty top women in business in the United States. In 1996 *Fortune* called her a woman to watch. *Time* ranked her *number* 17 on its Time Digital 50 in 1999, and CNET gave her its "Most Popular-Call of 1999 People Award." The next year *Money* called her one of the "50 Smartest Women In the Money Business," and *Computer Reseller News* said she was one of the "Top 25 Most Influential Executives." That November President Bill Clinton appointed her to the Digital Opportunity Task Force, which was charged with creating a strategy to bridge the global digital divide. She was listed in MacDirectory's list of "Top Ten Visionary Leaders," and *Forbes* named her one of its "Magnetic 40" in 2001. She was honored in November 2003 for her work on worldwide educational initiatives with the Seeds of Hope Humanitarian Award from Concern Worldwide U.S.

See also: Information Technology Industry

Further Reading

Anders, George. *Perfect Enough: Carly Fiorina and the Reinvention of Hewlett-Packard.*

Burrows, Peter. *Backfire: Carly Fiorina's High-Stakes Battle for the Soul of Hewlett-Packard.*

"Fiorina, Carleton." In *Current Biography*, January 2000, p. 39–44.

Hardy, Quinton. "Cover Story: All Carly, All the Time."

Fisher, Lucy (1949–), Film Industry Executive

One of the highest-ranking women in Hollywood, Lucy Fisher placed number 35 on the 1998 *Fortune* list of the most powerful women in the business world in the United States. As vice chairman of Columbia TriStar Motion Picture Companies, the film division of Sony Entertainment, she turned the company into the hottest place in town with movies such as *Jerry McGuire*, *Men in Black*, *My Best Friend's Wedding*, and *As Good as It Gets*.

Born in New York City, Fisher received a BA cum laude in English from Harvard University in 1971. After her first job in a newsroom at KFWB on the night shift, Fisher began her film career as a script reader for United Artists. During the 70s she held several positions as a story editor, first for Samuel Goldwyn Jr. Productions, then for MGM. In 1979 she became vice president of creative affairs, then production for 20th Century Fox. The following year, she was head of worldwide production for Francis Ford Coppola's company, American Zoetrope. Although the company only lasted two years, she claimed to have learned an enormous amount from him. In 1981 she joined Warner Brothers as senior production executive and gained increasingly responsible positions until 1996. While there she was involved in such blockbuster movies as *Chariots of Fire*, *The Color Purple*, *The Fugitive*, *Empire of the Sun*, *Malcolm X*, and *Bridges of Madison County* and worked with directors including Clint Eastwood, Spike Lee, and Steven Spielberg.

She met Douglas Wick during those years and married him in 1986. Because they have three daughters, Fisher negotiated a schedule to include working at home on Mondays and Fridays. She also proposed that Warner Brothers open a day care center and saw it through to completion. When it was ready, her youngest was in kindergarten, but she still feels it is one of her greatest accomplishments.

In 1996 Fisher became vice chairman of Columbia TriStar Motion Picture companies in a newly created position responsible for working with the president on the creative side and solidifying talent relationships within the industry. Because of her vast experience, she was expected to help Sony, the parent company, overcome the doldrums. She negotiated another four-day workweek so she was more available to her daughters. Six months later the president was fired, and Fisher took over, keeping her title as vice chairman because of her commitment to her family. In two years the company had the number one market share with its array of successful movies. In 1997 it had the highest gross in history, $1.27 billion, as well as the highest worldwide gross, $2.34 billion.

In December of 1999, Fisher announced that she was leaving to partner with her husband in his Red Wagon Productions, which produced *Stuart Little*, *The Hollow Man*, and *Memoirs of a Geisha*, the latter with Steven Spielberg.

It is based with Sony Pictures, so as she explained, she's just getting closer to the production end.

Lucy Fisher, a pioneer in the film industry, is known for mentoring and expanding opportunities for all women, particularly working mothers. She has a reputation for producing classy blockbusters. She received the Women in Film Crystal Award in 1998, *Premiere* magazine Icon Award, and was named to the *Hollywood Reporter* Women in Entertainment Power List and *Mirabella*'s smartest women in America list. She was also honored for her achievements as a producer at the Hollywood Film Festival in October 2002. She founded the Peter Ivers Artist in Residency Program at Harvard and has served on its board, as well as on the board of the Ivers Foundation, and as advisor to the Los Angeles chapter of the Juvenile Diabetes Foundation. Since one of her daughters is diabetic, she spends much time raising money for the foundation. She and Wick co-founded CuresNow, which encourages embryonic stem cell research.

See also: Entertainment Industry

Further Reading
Cox, Dan. "Sony Reels in Fisher."
Geitz, Christopher. "Fisher a Catch for Sony Pix."
"Lucy Fisher to Partner with Douglas Wick."

Fitt, Lawton W. (1953–), Investment Banker

Lawton W. Fitt, the managing director of Goldman Sachs & Co., is a genius at taking high-tech companies public. In 1999 *Fortune* ranked her number 33 on its list of most powerful corporate women in the United States, and *Business Week* named her as one of the E.Biz 25. That year she and her company managed more initial public offerings (IPOs) for technology firms than anyone else on Wall Street, twenty-two in all.

With over twenty years at Goldman Sachs, she is said to be the best-kept secret on Wall Street. After ten years in corporate finance, Fitt joined the Equity Capital Markets Group, beginning her focus on technology companies. The group brought Dell Computer and Microsoft to Wall Street in 1984. Her first initial public offering was UUNET in spring 1996; the next was Yahoo! She has guided IPOs for many successful launches: iVillage, Doubleclick, eToys, eBay, Red Hat, Juniper Networks, Starmedia, Insweb, and E-Loan. In 2000 she changed her focus to developing an online wealth management service for the company's private banking clients. In this role, she co-heads the European High Technology Investment Banking Group.

In interviews she has suggested what makes an Internet company "investible" is being there first and defining the space, but she also looks at the management, particularly its ability to deal with, and adapt to, change. Fitt feels that the best companies have the best people, and some of those need experience in managing. She has also said that her biggest challenge is pricing the IPO stock right, so that the investors and the owners are equally happy.

Fitt has served on the corporate boards of Wink Communications, CIENA, and e-Steel Corporation, as well as the board of trustees for the Darden School Foundation; P.S. 1, New York City; Jane Comfort Dance School; and Kunst Werke, Berlin. She has also chaired the Corporate Finance Committee of the National Association of Security Dealers.

See also: Finance Industry; Information Technology Industry

Further Reading

Aron, Laurie Joan. "Six Power Women: New York Women Who Are Emerging as Influential."

Flexible Work Arrangements

Flexible work arrangements are "individually negotiated conditions of employment involving adjustments in the timing, scope, and/or place of work" (Catalyst, 1998, p. 3). After the rigid eight-hour day and forty-hour week that developed in the mid 1800s, the first differential time schedule appeared in the 1930s at Kellogg, where eight-hour shifts were replaced with six-hour shifts, an attempt to save jobs for laid-off workers. This ended with the advent of World War II.

In the 1960s a German economist invented flextime to reduce absenteeism and lateness by permitting workers to design their own work schedules around a core time period when everyone was expected to be at work. Because of labor shortages, it became prevalent in Europe in the 1970s. In the United States an interest developed in telecommuting because of the energy crisis and the need to reduce oil consumption. In the mid-1980s women entered the workplace in droves, and family-friendly benefits helped to accommodate their needs. Flextime was heavily used as a recruitment tool in the competitive search for qualified employees. By 1990 companies saw that flextime also made economic sense and that men needed it just as much as women did. As a result, the movement shifted from accommodation to a business strategy, becoming one of the yardsticks for measuring the quality of life in a company. *Working Mother, Business Week,* and *Fortune* all consider flextime programs in their listings of the best companies to work for.

There are several basic types of flexible work arrangements. In flextime the worker chooses a schedule, but it includes core hours. In a compressed workweek the employee works more hours in fewer days. Job-sharing happens when two employees work halftime in the same position. Voluntary part-time work, usually permanent, is the most commonly used arrangement. Leaves and sabbaticals, either paid or unpaid, are an authorized period of time away from the job without loss of any employment rights; examples are parental and maternity leaves. In phased retirement an employee wishes to retire eventually and negotiates a part-time working arrangement, keeping all benefits until eventual retirement.

Telecommuting, a term coined in the early 1970s, involves periodic work at an office, but the majority of work is at home, in a client's office, or in a telework center. Technological improvements were driving factors in the rise of telecommuting. Home-based work is a paid position at home. Other options emerging in the early 2000s were paid time off, leave banks, and annual hours contracts.

The benefits of flexible work schedules are many. The employee may adjust the work schedule to her own biological clock, commute time and traffic logjams may be reduced, leisure time and time with family is increased, and last, but certainly most important, worker satisfaction and morale are improved. The company's productivity also benefits from increased employee satisfaction and morale. Because the availability of flextime is one of the most important criteria, especially for women, when assessing a company, recruitment is improved. It can also be a remuneration method for survivors of downsizing. Some companies can extend hours of service and thus increase customer satisfaction. According to Avery and Zabel, a 1998 study showed that "every $1 spent on family-friendly benefits yields a $2 savings in direct costs" (p. 12).

The largest barrier to flexible work programs is initial resistance by middle managers and supervisors. Others include resistance by top management and unions, and a corporate culture that may hinder a flex program, which tends to reward long hours of work. Some employees may have concerns about damaging their careers through negative evaluations or accusations of disloyalty if they take advantage of flex programs. Lingering issues needing to be addressed include equity, training opportunities in time management and supervision skills, promotion opportunities, and rigorous evaluation. Not all workers have access to flexible programs, particularly lower-paid or shift workers. Home-based workers and telecommuters may suffer from isolation and loneliness.

A company with a successful flexible work arrangement must consider all these issues before adopting a program. Suggested implementation includes gaining support for the program, particularly from top and middle management. After thoroughly analyzing staffing and workflow and assigning responsibility for the program administration, the company should develop resource materials for employees and supervisors, promote, and evaluate the program. After a trial period, it may need fine-tuning.

In 2000, 43 percent of American companies offered flexible work schedules, and 27 percent included a reduced workweek. A 2001 survey of 754 human resources professionals showed that 58 percent of them offered flextime, and 36 percent offered telecommuting, increasing from 51 percent and 26 percent, respectively, the year before. Of *Fortune*'s 100 best companies to work for in 2001, fifty-nine had flextime programs, forty had flextime on a case-by-case basis, thirty-seven used reduced-hour employment, twenty-five used a compressed workweek, eighteen had job sharing employees, and eighteen had telecommuters.

See also: Employee Benefits

Further Reading

Avery, Christine and Diane Zabel. *The Flexible Workplace: A Sourcebook of Information and Research.*

Catalyst, Inc. *A New Approach to Flexibility: Managing the Work/Time Equation.*

Nilles, Jack M. *Managing Telework: Strategies for Managing the Virtual Workforce.*

Reilly, Peter. *Flexibility at Work: Balancing the Interests of Employer and Employee.*

Floyd, Stacy Y., *see* Hubbard, Sonja Y.

Food Industry

In 1985 Edie Fraser said, "The cliché used to be that women belong in the kitchen. Today, women own the kitchen" (p. 107). There were more than 6,000 food product manufacturers, almost 50,000 woman-owned food stores, and almost 115,000 woman-owned eating and drinking places in 1997.

Women of all ethnicities have been making and selling food items since early colonial women sold baked goods and produce in the markets. They also owned taverns and inns that served food. Margaret Haughery baked bread and sold milk in New Orleans in the mid-1800s, and Freda Ehmann produced olives in California. Women catered parties in the large cities in the same era and continue to do so today. Rose Knox and her husband manufactured gelatin, developing the market through advertisements and recipes using their product. Catherine Clark and Margaret Rudkin experimented with more nutritious bread and parlayed their baked goods into large businesses. Debbie Fields founded a cookie chain, and Marian Ilitch did the same with pizza. Laura Balverde-Sanchez focused on Mexican food; Lisa Little Chief developed an Indian fry-bread mix. Joyce Chen complemented her Chinese restaurant with a cooking utensil business.

On the corporate front, Liz Minyard and Joyce Raley Teel preside over store chains inherited from their families. Both Kraft and Pepsico have a *Fortune* 50 powerful woman among their top officers: Betsy Holden is the co-chair of Kraft Foods, and Indra Nooyi is president and CFO of Pepsico. As in most industries, however, even those whose customers are mostly women, men predominate at the top levels. There are several women in middle management and upper middle management. Most grocery store managers and executives are men. The 14 percent (in 2000) of middle managers and executives who are women hold mainly marketing or sales positions.

Three organizations in the food industry focus on women: Roundtable for Women in Foodservice (RWF), Women Grocers of America (www.national-grocers.org), and Women Chefs and Restaurateurs (www.chefnet.com/wcr).

Further Reading
Coeyman, Marjorie. "No Man's Land: Women Are Emerging as a Force At All Levels of the Industry."
Copple, Brandon. "Shelf-Determination."
Walkup, Carolyn. "Women in Leadership: The Battle to Advance Continues."

Footwear Industry, *see* Fashion Industry

Francesconi, Louise L. (1953–), Aerospace Executive

Louise Francesconi, vice president and general manager of missile systems at Raytheon, has been listed as one of *Fortune's* most powerful women in corporate America since 2001. Her title was changed in August 2002 to vice president of Raytheon and president of missile systems. She is one of the highest ranking women in the international aerospace industry.

She was born in Santa Monica, California, where her father was an engineer at Hughes Aircraft. As a teenager, she formed and led a church folk-music group, attended an all-girls high school, and was president of her senior class. She received her BA in economics from Scripps College in 1975 and her MBA from UCLA in 1978.

Francesconi began her career with the Hughes Aircraft Company in 1974 while still in college, progressing through numerous key positions, including Hughes Missile Systems Leadership Council member, assistant group controller, a key member of the management team responsible for acquiring General Dynamics missile business, president of Hughes Missile Systems Company, and vice president of Hughes Aircraft Company. Under her leadership, the weapons systems segment received the Arizona Quality Alliance's Governor's Award for Quality.

In 1998 Hughes and Raytheon merged, and Francesconi became the senior vice president of the former Raytheon Systems Company and the deputy general manager of the defense systems segment. Francesconi was one of the key players in the merger. In 1999 she was promoted to her present position, responsible for the $3 billion missile system business, production and development, and over 10,000 employees. In July of 2001 her segment developed and built the Exoatmospheric Kill Vehicle, a missile that finds ICBMs and shoots them down. Raytheon's missiles were used in the Iraq War.

Francesconi has served on the board of trustees of Tucson Medical Center Healthcare, the board of directors of the Indra EWS, the Tucson Airport Authority, and the board of advisors of the University of Arizona Graduate School of Management. She is married to a former manager at Hughes and has three grown sons and two grandchildren. Because her work demanded at least ten days of travel per month, her husband stayed home when their sons were young.

Further Reading
Banchero, Paola. "Raytheon Workers in Tucson, Ariz., Cheered by Missile Test."
Fischer, Alan D. "Tucson Mom is also Raytheon Head, Takes Job in Stride."
http://www.hoovers.com/officers/bio/1/0.

Franklin, Ann Smith (1696–1763), Printer

Ann Franklin was probably the first woman printer in New England and the second, after Dinah Nuthead, in British North America. Born and raised in Boston, at twenty-seven she married James Franklin, Benjamin's older brother who was a printer and publisher of a Boston newspaper, the *New England Courant*. Because of his political anti-British diatribes, however, he had been forbidden to publish it without submitting each issue to censors. Instead, he made brother Benjamin the official publisher, until Benjamin went to Philadelphia a few years later.

At the suggestion of another brother, Franklin and her husband moved to Newport, Rhode Island in 1727. They began the first newspaper there, the ill-fated *Rhode-Island Gazette*, which lasted only eight months. The printing business was successful, however, producing Rhode Island currency in the basement shop. Of their five children, two daughters and a son survived.

After Franklin's husband died in 1735 at age thirty, and as was common for widows at that time, she took over the business. Her daughters learned to set type, proofread, copy edit, and occasionally report, while she did most of the reporting and ran the business. The first piece ascribed to her was a 1735 imprint, *A Brief Essay on the Number Seven: Often Occurring in the Holy Scripture; Or of Paradice, Lost and Found, By a Well Wisher of Truth*. Her name first appeared on the *Rhode-Island Almanack for the Year 1737*, a booklet of sixteen pages containing items of local interest, poetry, and astronomical calculations and predictions. She was one of the first women printers to compile her own almanac, continuing for three years under the name "Poor Robin."

In June 1736 Franklin became the colony printer, doing all official printing for the Rhode Island General Assembly. Her most impressive production was 500 copies of the 300-page *Acts and Laws of 1745*. She was also the first woman printer to have her imprint on the title page of a book, *The Charter Granted by His Majesty King Charles II to . . . Rhode Island and Providence Plantations.* There are about forty-seven pieces of printing ascribed to her, including religious tracts, almanacs, literary forays by Rhode Island would-be writers, and a variety of forms, that accounted for the major part of the business.

In 1757 her son, James, who had been apprenticed to Benjamin in Philadelphia, returned to run the business in Newport. He began publishing a newspaper, the *Newport Mercury*. After his death in 1762, Franklin took over again at age 65 before taking Samuel Hall, a son-in-law, as a business partner. They continued the newspaper and issued seven printings of statutes. She died the following year, having been a printer for twenty-three years. The site of her printing shop can still be seen in Newport.

See also: Colonial Businesswomen; Publishing Industry

Further Reading
Bird, Caroline, p. 28.
Chapin, Howard M. *Ann Franklin of Newport: Printer, 1736–1763.*
Swan, Bradford F. "Franklin, Ann Smith." In Edward T. James, p. 662–663.

Friedman, Rachelle (1950–), Retail Industry Executive

While on their honeymoon in 1971, Rachelle Friedman and her husband, Joe, decided to open a retail music store. Located near Wall Street in New York City, J&R Music evolved into a very successful electronics and music store. She has been among the *Working Woman* top women business owners since 1995.

Both Friedman and her husband emigrated from Israel to Brooklyn when they were children. In 1971 she was one of the first women to graduate from the Polytechnic Institute of New York. The store opened in a 500-square-foot space. She looked after the financial side and negotiations, while he took charge of retail operations. The business grew quickly and expanded into electronic products. The company began sponsoring an annual summer "J&R Downtown Jazzfest" in 1994 at City Hall Park. The company name changed in 1996 to J&R Music and Computer World.

The business grew to cover an entire city block, including ten superstores selling consumer electronics, computer hardware and software, music, and home office equipment. It also has a large mail-order business operating out of two warehouses in Queens. Although it is in a cutthroat industry, the business has survived due to a good location, very strong supplier relationships, discount prices, a conservative bottom-line approach, and an emphasis on customer service. With no plans for further stores, it has an extensive Web homepage and online catalog, allowing customers to hear and order CDs over the Internet. In 2002 J&R's sales were over $315 million, employing more than 600, and e-commerce and catalog sales were booming.

In March 2000 son Jason dropped out of law school to take charge of the online operation. One section of the site, Live@J&R, features interviews with music celebrities and a calendar of live entertainment. When the World Trade Center was destroyed in 2001, the store, only blocks away, served as an emergency command center. It had to close for six weeks but paid all employees in full during that time. The couple is very involved in rebuilding the devastated community.

The Friedmans feel their success as a couple managing a business is that they have different responsibilities and work schedules. She is an early bird, while he goes to work later. She has been called "The Empress of Park Row." *Success* named her one of the smartest women in business in 2000. In that article, she said her recipe for a successful business was "fiscal conservatism when it comes to expansion and never being afraid to spend on new technology."

See also: Immigrant Businesswomen; Retailing Industry

Further Reading

Bamford and Pendleton, p. 49.

Rigg, Cynthia. "Electronics Store Is a World Apart: J&R Grows in One Simple Location."

Traiman, Steve. "J&R Music World's 30th Anniversary: A New York City Mainstay." www.jandr.com

Fudge, Ann M. (1941–), Food Manufacturer, Advertising Executive

Ann Fudge was on *Fortune*'s lists of the most powerful women in corporate America in 1998 (number 30), 1999 (number 34), and 2003 (number 47). The earliest ranking was gained when she was an executive vice president for Kraft Foods, a member of the Operating Committee, and the president of the coffee and cereals division with sales of $16.8 billion. As chair and CEO of Young & Rubicam, she returned to the list in 2003.

She was born in Washington, DC, the elder of two children. Her father was an administrator with the U.S. Postal Service, and her mother was a manager at the National Security Agency. Fudge has said that she never worried about balancing a family and a career because her mother showed her how. She went to Catholic high schools and credits the nuns for insisting she always do her best. While at Simmons College in Boston, she married and had her first child but still graduated with her class. Often classmates would babysit in return for food.

Fudge worked in GE's human resources department before earning her MBA in 1977 at Harvard Graduate School of Business. After that she became a marketing assistant for General Mills, where her team developed and marketed brand items, most notably Honey Nut Cheerios, a huge success. She was promoted, becoming the company's first woman and first African American marketing director, before moving to General Foods in 1986 as director of strategic planning. In 1989 she became marketing director of the beverages division and, a year later, vice president of marketing and development.

By this time Fudge had a reputation as a resuscitator of older, tired brands, including Kool-Aid, for which her team began their "Wacky Warehouse" marketing campaign. She was an executive vice president and general manager of the dinners and enhancers division by 1991.

In 1994 General Foods merged with Kraft Foods, and Fudge became an executive vice president and the president of Maxwell House Coffee, whose earnings were $1.5 billion. Again, she inherited a tired brand and managed to double the sales in three years. The position included overseeing three coffee processing plants, which she visited immediately, and the 2,400 employees were delighted to see her. Another one of her first initiatives was to visit Seattle and all its specialty coffeehouses in an effort to solve the problem of their growing competition. In response, she launched a series of flavored coffees. After a 1997 corporate reorganization, she became the president of the coffee and cereals division, generating $2.7 billion of the total Kraft $16.8 billion sales.

In 1997 Fudge was one of three women considered for the top position at Kraft. Betsy Holden won the post, and in September 2000, after Kraft and Nabisco merged, Fudge became group vice president, Kraft Foods; president of beverages, desserts, and Post; and a member of the management committee. She resigned from Kraft the following February, but after two years away from the business world, in May 2003 she became CEO of Young & Rubicam, Inc., the first African American to lead a prominent advertising agency.

Ann Fudge's management style combines a forceful personality with sensitivity. She believes strongly in the team approach to problem solving and in seeking alternative ways to solve problems. She loves the creativity and innovation involved in marketing. According to her fellow workers and supervisors, her optimistic attitude has positively affected the divisions in which she has worked and made problem solution more effective. She follows the golden rule: treating people as she would wish to be treated. She also firmly believes in perseverance and patience, observing that the 1968 post-Martin Luther King assassination riots in Washington made her determined to succeed in ways that black people never had before.

Fudge didn't have the guilt problems many women have in balancing family and career because her mother always had a career. Balance she did, however, from the time she was a student at Simmons College throughout her corporate career until her two sons were independent. For many years she laid out their clothes for the days when she would be traveling, and she spent Sundays making meals for the rest of the week. Her husband also helped with many of the family chores.

Fudge has served on boards including Allied Signal, Liz Claiborne, Honeywell, General Electric, Marriott, the Federal Reserve Board of New York, Catalyst, Club Mom, and Simmons College. She has also been a trustee of the American Graduate School of International Management and a member of the Committee of 200 and the New York Women's Forum. She has served as president of the Executive Leadership Council and on the board of governors for Boys and Girls Clubs of America.

Her many honors include leadership awards from the Minneapolis and New York City YWCAs, an honorary doctorate from Adelphi University, the Candace Award from the National Coalition of 100 Black Women, woman of the year from *Glamour*, advertising woman of the year from the Advertising Women of New York City, and the 1997 Alumnae Achievement Award from the Harvard Business School Network of Women Alumnae. *Ebony* named Fudge one of fifty who changed America, and twice one of the one hundred most influential black Americans and organizational leaders, the last time in 1998. *Black Enterprise* in 1993 named her as one of the "Power 40" black executives and, in 1991, one of "21 Women of Power and Influence." In 1999 she won the Sara Lee Frontrunner Award, and the next year *Black Enterprise* named her one of the Top 50 Blacks in Corporate America. As one of the few African Americans and women in the top echelons of corporate power, she has not only bumped the glass ceiling several times but has also knocked against the concrete wall of minority discrimination.

See also: Advertising Industry; African American Businesswomen; Food Industry

Further Reading

Dobrzynski, Judith H. "Way Beyond the Glass Ceiling."
"Fudge, Ann." *Current Biography Yearbook 1998*, p. 212–213.
Fudge, Ann M. "The Boss; Nuns, Bicycles and Berries."
Schleier, Curt. "Kraft Foods' Ann Fudge."
Woolley, Jessie T. "An Interview with Ann Fudge."

Fuller, S. Marce (1960–), Electric Power Executive

In 2001 Marce Fuller was named to the *Fortune* list of most powerful women in corporate America for the first time. Her place, number 5 on the list, was due to her elevation to president and CEO of Mirant, a spin-off company from Southern Electric International. She has also served on the board of directors. She was one of six woman CEOs of *Fortune* 500 companies. After the company's sales dropped dramatically because of the bad U.S. economy, her rank dropped to number 37 in 2002.

She grew up in Wetumpka, Alabama. Her grandmother owned a small business and she wished to do the same. Fuller received her BS from the University of Alabama in 1983 and a masters degree in power system engineering from Union College in Schenectady, New York. Her first job was for Southern Company as a summer student engineer at Alabama Power.

After graduation, she joined General Electric in the power system and bulk power marketing department but returned to Alabama Power as an electric system planning engineer.

Several promotions gave her experience in strategic planning and international project development for Southern Utility International, and in 1994 Fuller became the vice president of domestic business development for Southern Utility International. She took that position with the goal of building a high-technology risk management and marketing organization with an expanding number of power plants. The unit grew to 600 employees, and in 2001 was spun off to become Mirant.

Fuller was, by that time, the company's highest-ranking woman, responsible for guiding it through its evolution as a separate company. She was in charge of Mirant's initial strategic direction, branding, and corporate positioning. In 2001 it was one of the top ten companies in Georgia. Economic problems in 2002 forced a reorganization of the company as well as reduced gas trading activities. In July 2003 Mirant filed for bankruptcy protection.

Fuller, known as a dynamic leader with both management and technical expertise, loves a challenge and acquiring new skills. She has said that women in management may be a little more sensitive to the needs of people and more focused on teamwork, but any challenges of being a leader at the top of a company are probably not much different than those for men.

She has served on the boards of the Curtiss-Wright Corporation and Earthlink as well as Mirant, on the board of trustees of the Atlanta International School, and on the University of Alabama Engineering Leadership Board. She has also chaired the Department of Energy's advisory board on electricity issues. In 2001 *Business to Business* magazine named Fuller one of Atlanta's most influential females. By the end of that year, *Time* and *Fortune* had named her one of the people to watch in international business. She was appointed to the Philippine Economic Advisory board in February 2002.

See also: Energy Industry

Further Reading
"Marce Fuller: CEO and President, Mirant."
Saporta, Maria. "'One of the Most Unknown Secrets' Blazing an Exciting Path at Mirant."
"Southern Company Names Fuller Executive Vice President."

G

Orit Gadiesh is the chair of Bain & Company, a Boston-based global strategy consulting firm. This position put her on *Fortune*'s lists of the most powerful women in corporate America from 1998 to 2000, when she was ranked number 47.

She was born and raised in Haifa, Israel. Her father was a general in the Israeli army, and she began two years in the army at seventeen. While on the personal staff of the head of the operations branch of the Israel Defense Forces, Gadiesh learned about forming strategy and living with the outcome. After earning a BA, summa cum laude, in psychology from the Hebrew University of Jerusalem, she went to the Harvard Business School and graduated in the top 5 percent of her class, even though she knew little English. Known as "Machine Gun Orit," she was a Baker's Scholar and won the Brown Award.

Her first job in 1977 was as a consultant in the steel business with Bain & Company, one of three women in an office of fifty-seven. By 1991 Gadiesh was managing director of the Boston office, with a staff of 220 consultants. After successfully restructuring the company with its fifteen offices worldwide that year, she became chair of the policy committee, the group responsible for setting business strategy and policy. Revenues in 1992 were up 40 percent, and that July she became vice chair of the board of directors; two years later she was elected chairman. By 1998 Bain was the eighteenth largest consulting company in the world, with 2,400 consultants in twenty-six international offices. The next year she created the Bain Labs, an incubator focusing on e-commerce, and revenues were $564 million.

Gadiesh's specialty is high-level strategic work with *Fortune* 500 CEOs and boards of directors. She is flamboyant, with magenta hair, flashy jewelry, and a charismatic personality. Known for her intuitive, straight-talking problem solving, she has a reputation for creative analysis and toughness. She credits her success to a love of learning and an ability to really listen. Her motto is: "Be good at the things you like to do, and if it's not fun, you're not going to do it well" ("50 Smartest Women" p. 76). Harvard Business School has a case about her and her leadership qualities. As a well known expert on management and corporate strategy, she is often quoted in the national newspapers.

She was named among the fifty smartest women by *Success*, by *Fortune* in 1996 as a woman to watch, and New Englander of the Year in 1997. In 2000 *Consulting Magazine* included her in the top twenty-five consultants in the country. Gadiesh is also one of twenty-five entrepreneurs and leaders honored by the NOW Legal Defense and Education Fund. She has been on the faculty of Hebrew University and the Jerusalem Institute of Management and has served on the board and council of the Harvard Business School, Wharton School, and Kellogg School, and the Harvard Business School Press Publications Review Board. Other boards include the Peres Institute for Peace, the Advisory Board Company, and Universal Stainless Alloy Products. She is married to an entrepreneur, Grenville Boyd.

See also: Consulting

Further Reading
Bernhut, Stephen. "Orit Gadiesh: Taking Charge in Uncertain Times."
Rifkin, Glenn. "Profile; Don't Ever Judge this Consultant by Her Cover."
Schuch, Beverly. "Bain & Co., CNNfn."
Sit, Mary. "The View from the Top: Orit Gadiesh Rises to Head Bain & Co. in Boston."

Gaines, Brenda J. (1950–), Banking Executive

Brenda Gaines, as president of Diners Club, North America, was ranked number 20 on the 2002 *Fortune* list of the most powerful black executives in the United States.

She received her undergraduate degree from the University of Illinois, Champaign–Urbana, and an MPA from Roosevelt University in Chicago. Her first positions were as head of the Chicago Housing Authority, a deputy general administrator in the U.S. Department of Housing and Urban Development, and, from 1985 to 1987, the deputy chief of staff for Mayor Harold Washington, the first African American mayor of Chicago. It was a time of turmoil, with large budget cuts and angry voters. After Washington had a heart attack, Gaines decided to tackle the challenges of business.

In February 1988 she began her corporate career as the vice president of external affairs for Citicorp Savings of Illinois, part of Citigroup, in charge of government and community relations. The following year she was promoted to senior vice president in charge of residential lending. In 1990 the bank changed its name to Citibank, and in 1992 she moved to its subsidiary, Diners Club. From 1994 to 1999, Gaines was the executive vice president of corporate card sales, and in 1999 was named the president of the North American Diners Club International, with responsibility for over 900 employees in what is now a $30 billion business.

When asked about opportunities for African American women in the corporate world, she said that they are given more responsibilities faster in government (Daniels, *The Most Powerful Black Executives*, p. 74). She manages through coaching, giving her staff opportunities to excel, and stressing the importance of recognizing and rewarding success.

Gaines has served on boards including Office Depot, the Dr. Martin Luther King Jr. Boys and Girls Clubs, Junior Achievement, and the Chicago Museum of Science and Industry. In 1998 *Travel Weekly* named her one of the influential women in travel, and in 2000 *Black Enterprise* listed her in the top fifty blacks in corporate America.

See also: African American businesswomen; Banking

Further Reading
Daniels, Cora. "The Most Powerful Black Executives in America."
"Office Depot Adds Two New Members to its Board of Directors."

Gallup, Patricia (1954–), Mail Order Executive

Patricia Gallup began PC Connection, a mail-order computer company, in 1982 with a partner, David Hall, and their joint savings of $8,000. Today it is one of the top woman-owned companies with sales over $1 billion. A pioneer in the direct-mail computer business, she is also famous for her ethical, customer-oriented approach.

She grew up in New Hampshire, the daughter of a carpenter and union organizer. To help the family finances, she baby-sat then worked three years to earn money for college. In 1979 she graduated with a BA in anthropology from the University of Connecticut while working on a public archaeology survey team. She met Randall Minard while dancing, married him in 1995, and they had twin daughters.

In 1980 she met David Hall while working on the support crew for endurance hikers along the Appalachian Trail. He hired her to help run his family's manufacturing audio business, Audio Accessories, in Marlow, New Hampshire. When IBM PCs were introduced, Gallup tried to buy one and discovered that the nearest store was in Connecticut. After deciding to begin a mail-order company to sell personal computers, she and Hall pooled their savings and launched PC Connection in 1982. She was president, in charge of marketing; he was vice president, responsible for technology and keeping current with computer industry. The company promised overnight delivery and was the first to offer free technical support through toll-free telephone lines. Sales were $233,000 in the first year. In 1984 it began selling Macs and, by the following year, had one hundred employees. In 1989 it began selling Lotus products and, later, introduced an educational public television show, PC-TV, showing reviews of software and demonstrations of new products. The company bought a distribution center in Ohio in 1992 because it was closer to Airborne Express, its shipper. The following year, it became a full systems supplier by adding peripherals and other computer brands.

In 1995 Wayne Wilson, a former Apple executive, became president and chief operating officer, and Gallup moved up to CEO and chair. By this time there were 800 employees and sales of $300 million. In 1996 headquarters moved to Milford, New Hampshire, to accommodate expanded needs. That year it was the state's largest private company, distributing 18.6 million catalogs and filling 1,252,000 orders. In 1998 Gallup and Hall, each with 40 percent of the stock, took the company public, sold stock on the NASDAQ Exchange, and raised $57.3 million. By April 2001 the company was number 894 on the *Fortune* 1000 list of the largest public companies. President/COO Wilson retired in December 2002, and Kenneth Koppel became president while Gallup remained CEO; the following March Koppel stepped down and she resumed as president and CEO.

The company is known for its environmentally friendly policies and generous benefits. Its salespeople all have college degrees, good communication skills, and a knowledge of geography. Each employee is trained for four to six months and receives free snow tires and windshield wiper blades. They are salaried, with incentives for converting phone calls to orders, for the length of a call, and for attracting new employees. Their benefits include twenty-six weeks for pregnancy leave and twelve for adoption, pay for childcare while at conferences, one month's leave for any reason, and free Thanksgiving turkeys. When the company went public, they also received stock options. The employee retention rate is 96 percent. When the company was in Marlow, Gallup and Hall focused on planned growth that would not strain the town of 655. It uses recycled newspapers and thick cardboard boxes in shipping packages instead of Styrofoam. The company has won many awards including *PC World's* "World Class Award for Best Online Computer Store" from 1989 through 2000.

Gallup is tenacious and determined, with a focus on the highest customer service. She nurtures her employees and cares for the environment. She won the Ernst & Young New England Entrepreneur of the Year Institute Award for Principle-Centered Leadership in 1998, which cited her "ability to parlay an $8,000 investment into an organization generating more than half a billion dollars in annual sales because she put the needs of her customers, employees, and community first" (*Business Wire*, November 16, 1998). In 2001 she won the New Hampshire Better Business Bureau Torch Award for Marketplace

Ethics. In addition to supporting the Girl Scouts and the Apple Hill Center for Chamber Music, she established an eye-care clinic in Guatemala.

See also: Information Technology Industry

Further Reading
Book, Esther Wachs. "Leadership for the Millennium."
Mamis, Robert A. "Real Service."
"PC Connection, Inc."
www.pcconnection.com

Gender Discrimination, *see* Sex Discrimination

George, Mari Hulman, *see* Hulman, Mary Fendrich

Gilbreth, Lillian Moller (1878–1972), Industrial Psychologist, Management Consultant, Industrial Engineer

The ideas of Lillian and Frank Gilbreth revolutionized the workplace and management practices in the twentieth century. When she was elected to the National Women's Hall of Fame in 1995, the web page inscription read: "An industrial engineer and expert in motion studies, Gilbreth was a pioneer in the relationship between engineering and human relations. She convinced managers that work-efficiency was the result of the quality of the work environment" (www.greatwomen.org).

She was born in Oakland, California, to one of the city's leading families. The eldest of three boys and five girls, Gilbreth was tutored at home until she went to public school at age nine. Because her mother was either ill or pregnant much of the time, she was in complete charge of her baby sister; however, she also frequently traveled with her father, so her education was broader than many of her peers. She led her class at Berkeley, earning a master's degree in English, and was the first female commencement speaker. She began studying for a doctorate, but took a leave for an extended trip to Europe. Just before departing, at age twenty-five, she met Frank Gilbreth, who was ten years older, in Boston. He met the boat when she returned, and a year later they were married.

For financial reasons, he had not gone to college, but when they married, he was one of the largest individual construction contractors in the United States. He began as a bricklayer, and because he always sought new and faster ways to

An industrial engineer and expert in motion studies, Lillian Moller Gilbreth was a pioneer in the relationship between engineering and human relations. She convinced managers that work-efficiency was the result of the quality of the work environment.

work, he quickly moved up in the ranks. He was also a liberal and had marched in a suffrage parade. His philosophy of marriage was one of partnership in everything: the home, work, and raising a family. Legend has it that on their honeymoon, he suggested twelve children, an even number of boys and girls. She agreed to all of his views, and in the next seventeen years, they did have twelve children, although one died when she was six.

Gilbreth's husband was developing a reputation for speed building, using techniques for completing a project quickly and accurately. This matured into motion study and she quickly became a full partner in his growing business, learning everything from him on visits to construction sites. He became more and more interested in motion study, closed the construction business, and became a management consultant. In the earlier years, because Gilbreth was frequently pregnant, she co-authored and edited his books and articles. In 1915 she received her doctorate from Brown; her thesis was published in book form, titled *The Psychology of Management*. She became a full member of the firm, Gilbreth, Inc. Her mother-in-law had lived with them, helping raise the children and run the household, until she died in 1920.

Together, the Gilbreths pioneered the application of motion study to industry. She influenced her husband a great deal with her focus on the human element, whereas he had studied the detailed job processes. The theory was that it was possible to find the one best way to do a task, or part of a task, that required the least exertion, stress and strain, and resulted in better health for the person and more productivity for the employer. This became the "Gilbreth One Best Way" system that became widely used, particularly during World War I. From 1910 to 1924, they both promoted their theories as a tool for management, installing a private teaching laboratory in their home, lecturing nationally, and publishing profusely.

In 1924 Gilbreth's husband died of a heart attack on his way to Prague to give a speech and receive an honorary membership in the Masaryk Academy. She went in his place and received the honor as well. On her return she found that businesses had cancelled their contracts, not wanting a woman to consult in their plants , but they did send people to the teaching laboratory. Rebuilding the business with Gilbreth at the helm took a while, but eventually succeeded. She was invited to take her husband's place as a visiting lecturer at Purdue, and in 1935 became a professor of management while continuing to run the consulting business.

Because businesses returned slowly, Gilbreth also began using her industrial management and motion analysis techniques for homemakers. Home economists and businesses catering to homemakers were changed completely through the use of her methods. She made further adaptations for handicapped people, developing a model kitchen designed for their special needs that became an internationally known training center.

Gilbreth was seemingly indefatigable. She and her husband raised eleven children, she obtained a doctoral degree, and they had a full business partnership. The household was run according to the "Gilbreth One Best Way" method, and the children helped according to their age. A family council decided all weighty matters, including the purchase of a dog. The best place to get the full flavor of their household is in the movies, *Cheaper by the Dozen* and *Belles on Their Toes*, based on books written by Frank and Ernestine, two of the older children. As a widow, Gilbreth carried on, even though she initially had considerably less money. Eventually all eleven children attended college.

She consulted and worked well into her eighties, receiving many honors along the way. She was named an honorary member of the Society of Industrial Engineers in 1921 at a time when it didn't admit women, and in 1931 was the first recipient of the Society's Gilbreth Medal, created and named for her husband. In 1944 she and her husband were awarded the Gantt Medal by the American Society of Mechanical Engineers and the American Management Association, and in 1948 she was named Woman of the Year by the American Women's Association. In 1954 she received the Gold Medal of the International Committee of Scientific Management (CIOS), its highest award, chosen by the management leaders of twenty-two nations. In 1996 she was the first woman to win the Hoover Medal for distinguished public service. She had received more than twenty honorary degrees and special commendations from a variety of associations. She died at age ninety-three, leaving eight books, numerous articles, eleven children, twenty-eight grandchildren, and one great-grandson. As one of the first consulting industrial management engineers and the first woman in that profession, she revolutionized work, the home, and life for handicapped people.

See also: Consulting

Further Reading
"Frank and Lillian Gilbreth." In *Business: The Ultimate Resource*, p. 994–995.
Gilbreth, Frank Bunker and Ernestine Gilbreth Carey. *Belles on Their Toes*.
Gilbreth, Lillian Moller. *As I Remember: An Autobiography*.
Yost, Edna. *Frank and Lillian Gilbreth, Partners for Life*.

Glass Ceiling

The term "glass ceiling" was first used by Carol Hymowitz and Timothy Schellhardt in their 1986 *Wall Street Journal* article to describe the invisible barriers that exclude women from upper management in American corporations. The concept was studied extensively during the 1990s and, although

Carly Fiorina denied its existence when she was appointed CEO of Hewlett Packard in 1999, many believe it persisted into the twenty-first century. There are now many more women in upper management and executive positions, but parity has certainly not been reached.

Exclusion of women in businesses has a long history. The problem of entry-level positions was solved with the Civil Rights Act of 1964, Title VIII, and later, the Equal Opportunity Act of 1972. Moving up the corporate ladder, however, was still a problem. In 1968 women could not even get into management training programs and only began to enter business and graduate schools in significant numbers in the 1980s. By 1990 however, there were still only three female CEOs in *Fortune* 1000 companies: Katherine Graham, Linda Wachner, and Marion Sandler. Very few other women were even near that level. That year a UCLA survey found that 3 percent of all upper management positions were filled by women.

In 1991 President George H. W. Bush appointed the Glass Ceiling Commission, chaired by Robert Reich, Harvard professor and future Secretary of Labor, to study and prepare recommendations for eliminating the glass ceiling. The twenty-one-member commission consisted of sixteen women, three of whom were senators, and five men. Many members were minorities. They defined the glass ceiling as "the unseen, yet unbreachable barrier that keeps minorities from rising to the upper rungs of the corporate ladder, regardless of their qualifications or achievements" (United States Commission, *Good for Business*, p. 4). It issued two reports in 1995, one showing its findings (*Good for Business*) and the other with recommendations (*A Solid Investment*). After summarizing research from a number of organizations, the findings showed that the glass ceiling did indeed exist and that it excluded women and minorities from leadership positions. The commission was also convinced that it was not good for business and that there was a need to address the issues. The first report identified the barriers as prejudice, stereotyping, and bias leading to a lack of training, development, and experience.

The commission made eight recommendations to business: CEO commitment; inclusion of diversity in strategic business plans; manager accountability; use of affirmative action; selection, promotion, and retention of qualified individuals; mentoring; training of all the managers on merit-based practices; and initiation of work/life and family friendly policies. It also recommended that the federal government lead by example, strengthen enforcement of anti-discrimination laws, improve data collection, and increase disclosure of diversity data.

In 1997 the glass ceiling made the cover of *Business Week*. In a more difficult economy and a year of financial cutbacks, many of the corporate initiatives addressing the problems of the glass ceiling eroded. The comfort zone surrounding promotion still prevailed for the highest positions: Who do we know that could do this job? However, some progress was made. In 1998 Catalyst noted that 11 percent of the senior executives in *Fortune* 500 companies were women.

Also sixty-three of the 2,257 top earners were women. On a more positive note, 49 percent in the professional management and administrative positions were women. That year *Fortune* began its annual list of the most powerful women in American business. Eight of the women owned, or had founded, their own companies (Winfrey, Nelson, Ingram, Sandler, Stewart, Laybourne, Dyson, and Bartz) and four held the position of chairman or president (Barad, Scardino, Moore, and Gadiesh). By 2003 the list included two who owned or founded their companies (Winfrey and Nelson), nine who were CEO or chairman, and one (Holden) who was co-chairman. Many of the women on the original list were succeeded by women who are upper executives over large divisions or groups within *Fortune* 1000 companies.

In 2001 among *Fortune* 500 companies, 12.5 percent of the executive positions were held by women and two were CEO or president (Andrea Jung and Carly Fiorina). Ninety of the 500 companies had no women in executive positions. By 2003 nine held the positions of CEO, chairman, or president of the company in the *Fortune* 1000 list. Many others were presidents or chairmen of large divisions. Progress has been made from 1998 to 2003, as many more women were well positioned to be considered for future top positions.

See also: Executives; Power

Further Reading

Barriers to Women's Upward Mobility: Corporate Managers Speak Out: A Position Paper.
Cracking the Class Ceiling: Catalysts' Research on Women in Corporate Management, 1995–2000.
Gutner, Toddi. "The Rose-Colored Glass Ceiling."
Hymowitz, Carol and Timothy D. Schellhardt. "The Corporate Woman (A Special Report): The Glass Ceiling: Why Women Can't Seem to Break the Invisible Barrier that Blocks Them from the Top Jobs."
United States. Federal Glass Ceiling Commission. *Good for Business: Making Full Use of the Nation's Capital: the Environmental Scan: A Fact-Finding Report of the Federal Glass Ceiling Commission.*
United States. Federal Glass Ceiling Commission. *A Solid Investment: Making Full Use of the Nation's Capital: Recommendations of the Federal Glass Ceiling Commission.*

Gleason, Kate (1865–1933), Construction Innovator

Kate Gleason was the first to build low-cost housing in the United States using mass-production methods. These projects, the precursor of real estate developments, were built of concrete.

She was born in Rochester, New York, to a small-machine toolmaker and his suffragist wife. She was encouraged to learn about the wonders of machine tools by her father and to think about a career by her mother. Gleason graduated from high school, and from age fourteen, was assistant bookkeeper in her father's factory. Her ambition was to be the first woman graduate in engineering at Cornell, but she interrupted her education twice to return to the factory, once because of the depression of 1893. Her father worked for twenty years developing a machine to manufacture beveled gear planers. In 1874 he began using it. At this time, only bicycles needed beveled gears, but soon the automakers did also. His firm became the country's leading gear-planer manufacturer with the inspired help of Gleason as its secretary, treasurer and, most importantly, traveling saleswoman extraordinaire.

Ironically, she was not only credited with inventing the machine, but was invited to join the Verein Deutscher Ingenieure and the American Society of Mechanical Engineers on the strength of it, the first woman in both organizations. She did not claim to be the inventor but many, including Henry Ford, believed she was because of her success in promoting it.

In 1913 she resigned from the firm because of family differences. She rehabilitated a debt-ridden machine tool company, making a profit of $1 million in three years. In 1914 she became acting president of a bank in East Rochester where she constructed several small factories. While there she conceived of low-cost, mass-produced housing using concrete. Called Concrest, this was the first housing development in the United States. She built one hundred houses using the mass-production methods she had seen in the Cadillac factory, her own system of mixing and pouring concrete from a telescoping tower, and cheap, unskilled labor. Each house had six rooms, included kitchen appliances, bookcases, and other amenities, and sold for a low down payment and $40 per month. Workers were then paying $65 rent for four rooms. This experiment showed that housing could be mass produced and sold on affordable payment plans to the working class. As a result of this work, Gleason became the only woman elected to membership in the American Concrete Institute.

She also began other developments. In Septmonts, a tiny village in France, she bought and restored many old houses and two historic towers. In 1927 she began a home building project in Sausalito that was stopped short by California Public Works projects. In Beaufort, South Carolina, she bought land and built a beach, golf course and clubhouse, and a few concrete houses for what she envisioned as a writers' and artists' colony. Her sister finished the project after her death.

Kate Gleason is described as energetic and enthusiastic, so successful as a saleswoman and promoter that she was the primary reason her father's business became a national force. Her accomplishments in the field of real estate development foreshadowed the mass-housing tracts and the accompanying financial arrangements that were prevalent after World War II. She was one of the first to use mass-production methods and easy payment plans in building low-cost housing. The housing development still stands in East Rochester, New York.

See also: Construction Industry; Inventors

Further Reading
Bird, Caroline. p. 171–175.
Lindley, Christopher. "Gleason, Kate." In Edward T. James, ed., p. 51–52.
Vare, Ethlie Ann and Greg Ptacek, "Mothers of Invention." p. 163–164.

Go Public, *see* Public Company

Goddard, Mary Katharine (1736–1816), Colonial Printer
Goddard, Sarah Updike (1700–1770), Colonial Printer

The Goddards are particularly famous for two accomplishments: Sarah was the first woman to publish a book in America, and Mary Katharine printed the first signed copy of the Declaration of Independence.

Sarah, born in Rhode Island, was uncommonly well educated, tutored in French, Greek, mathematics, history, literature, and Latin. She married Dr. Giles Goddard in 1735 and bore four children; two lived to adulthood, Mary Katharine and William. When her husband died, Sarah inherited £780, 300 of which she lent to William to start Providence's first printing shop and newspaper, the *Providence Gazette*, in 1762. Because the number of subscribers did not meet William's expectations, he ceased publication in 1765 and moved to New York City. Sarah and Mary Katharine continued to run the printing shop, however, issuing *West's Almanac* and pamphlets under Sarah's imprint. In 1766 she revived the *Gazette* and continued to print it, running the bindery and a bookstore until 1768 when William, the legal owner of the paper, sold it and persuaded them both to come to Philadelphia to help him run the *Pennsylvania Chronical*, a newspaper he had started there.

Before moving, William had written numerous diatribes against the infamous Stamp Act. Sarah continued the patriotic articles, but in a more balanced way. She also included humorous essays, readers' views, local and foreign news, poetry, and entertaining articles. She was the first woman in America to publish a book, the first American edition of the *Letters of Lady Mary Wortley Montagu*, a British feminist.

In December 1768 Sarah deeded William the remaining interest in Giles's property, wiping out a debt of 109 pounds, in return for support for the rest of her life. She and Mary Katharine continued to run the *Pennsylvania Chronical* during William's many New England trips the following year. She died in 1770, soon after making the financial arrangement with William.

After Sarah's death, Mary Katharine took on the role of running the shop, one of the largest in the colonies, while William was off with his various projects. In 1773 he opened a new print shop in Baltimore and began its first newspaper, the *Maryland Journal*. He closed the Philadelphia paper in 1774, and Mary Katharine moved to Baltimore, once more supervising the shop while William set up the Constitutional Post Office, an intercolonial postal system. The May 10, 1775, issue of the paper contained the new colophon, "Published by M.K. Goddard." In January 1777 she printed the first signed copy of the Declaration of Independence. One of the copies resides in the Library of Congress today.

During the Revolutionary War, inflation was rampant, and there was a paper shortage. With newsprint from William's paper mill and a willingness to raise rates, the *Maryland Journal* was one of the few newspapers printed throughout the war. It continued under Mary Katharine's imprint until 1784, when a bitter and very public quarrel with William ended her career as a printer. In 1775 she became the first woman postmaster and continued until 1789, when the fledgling nation appointed a postmaster general who thought a man should have the position. Although she had a reputation as an exceptional postmaster and hundreds of Baltimore citizens signed a petition on her behalf, she was relieved of her duties. She continued to operate a bookstore and stationery store until 1810.

> The Goddards are particularly famous for two accomplishments: Sarah was the first woman to publish a book in America, and Mary Katharine printed the first signed copy of the Declaration of Independence.

Both Sarah and Mary Katharine were victims of their times and of William who, because he was the legal owner of his various printing establishments, had the right to sell what the women had so diligently turned into successful ventures. He was a quarrelsome, hot-tempered, erratic, and restless man, always off to a new project while his mother and sister were left holding the fort. They were examples of ingenuity, fortitude, and determination, but unfortunately, neither reaped the rewards. Mary Katharine in particular suffered. In fact she was probably one of the nation's earliest public examples of gender discrimination. Her quarrel with William was never resolved, even after his marriage and retirement from newspapers. She died alone except for her slave and companion, whom she freed in her will, as beneficiary of all her worldly goods.

See also: Colonial Businesswomen; Publishing Industry

Further Reading

Bird, Caroline, p. 20–29.
Demeter, Richard L., p. 64–83.
Dexter, Elisabeth. *Colonial Women of Affairs*, p. 170–173.
Drachman, Virginia G., p. 14–18.

Gold, Christina A. (1947–), Financial Services Executive

In her first year as president of Western Union Financial Services, a division of First Data, Christina Gold expanded the business by 17 percent with sales of $2.6 billion and ranked number 49 on *Fortune*'s list of the most powerful businesswomen in America in 2003.

She was born in the Netherlands to a Dutch father and Canadian mother, the middle child of three. The family moved to Canada when she was four. Her father was a hard-working, reserved former military officer and Olympic gymnast; her mother was an extroverted painter and nurse. Gold was shy and introverted as a teenager. Her first job was at a coupon-center clearinghouse. She graduated from Carleton University in Ottawa in 1969 with a degree in geography.

After joining Avon Canada in 1970 as an inventory control clerk for $100 per week, she progressed through more responsible positions in every phase of the business during the next nineteen years. In 1989 Gold became president and CEO of Avon Canada, responsible for the Avon operating business unit for Canada and the north-central United States. When she was promoted in 1993 to senior vice president of Avon and president of the United States, Canadian, and Puerto Rican operations, she was the first woman to be named to this division that represented 40 percent of sales. With a priority to build up sales force morale while also cutting costs, she resumed sending birthday cards and added items such as lingerie and Barbie dolls to the reinstated sales incentives. By 1995 sales had grown 20 percent. When the president of Avon retired in 1996, Gold was one of three women considered for his job, but the board hired a man instead. By that that time, she was executive vice president in charge of global direct selling development.

In 1998 Gold left Avon and formed a consulting group specializing in global direct selling and marketing and distribution strategies. The following September, she became vice chairman and CEO of Excel Communications, responsible for leading a turnaround of the Teleglobe unit. In May 2002 First Data recruited her to be senior vice president and president of Western Union Financial Data Services. She has been very successful, focusing on building both the domestic and international business and the Western Union brand. She also has served on the First Data executive committee.

Gold's management style is characterized by directness and modesty. She is a people person, a loyal insider with simple tastes and charm who understands consumer needs and how to deliver them. She loves the challenge of turnarounds but is also a chronic worrier with terrible stage fright. She has served on the boards of ITT Industries, Torstar Corporation, New York Life, and the Direct Selling Education Foundation. She is a director of the Conference Board of Canada and a member of the executive committee of the Conference Board in

New York. In 1997 Birmingham Southern University gave her its Woman of Distinction Award, and *Business Week* included her in the top twenty-five managers of the year. She co-chaired The Domestic Strategy Group at the Aspen Institute in 2002. She is married to lawyer Peter Gold, who she met in college.

See also: Finance industry

Further Reading

Deutsch, Claudia H. "Profile; Relighting Fires at Avon Products."

Dwyer, Kelly Pate. "Fortune Smiles on Colorado Woman. Magazine Puts Exec in Top 50."

Silcoff, Sean and Andrew Wahl. "Save Teleglobe?"

Golf

Golf, now a $25 billion business, was introduced in this country during the colonial period. Although the first private golf course was built in 1786 in Charleston, South Carolina, the game didn't really grow as a pastime until after the Civil War. The 1898 invention of the wound golf ball improved the game, and the 1913 U.S. Open made the front pages of many newspapers.

"Through the first decades of the twentieth century, golf continued to grow in America, both as a business and as a business tool" (Dobrian, "Golf," p. 7). Because it was an expensive game, most of the players were upper class, wealthy, and powerful. Businessmen believed, and still do believe, that they can assess people by their golf game: how they handle pressure, how they show temperament, or whether they invent their own rules. Golf is seen as a bonding event, often a chance to talk business.

Women have always been at a disadvantage because golf was traditionally played on private courses that either excluded women or offered them limited tee times. This improved in the late 1970s when women golfers mounted pressure to open up private courses. Although there had been early women golfers, the well-publicized Dinah Shore Professional Women's event helped the wider acceptance of women players.

The Executive Women's Golf League, established in 1991, teaches beginners not only how to play, but also how to conduct themselves in a golf environment. In 2001 it had 14,500 members. Ernst & Young, Deloitte & Touche, and the National Coalition of 100 Black Women have sponsored golf events, teaching the rudiments of the game and also how to do business on the golf course.

Women have long realized that deals are often consummated on the golf course and that they miss out on information, contacts, negotiations, and social bonding if they don't play. As of 1998 there were 5.2 million women golfers, 21 percent of all players. With women making up 32 percent of new golfers, many courses are now adding amenities such as child care, and manufacturers are designing golf clubs tailored to a woman's swing.

From the time of J.P. Morgan and Andrew Carnegie, the golf course has been a place of important business moments. During the 2002 Masters Tournament, the National Council of Women pressured the Augusta National Golf Club (the tournament's long-time host) to admit women members. Although the club manager refused, some corporate leaders resigned because the men-only policy contradicted their corporate diversity policies.

Further Reading

Dobrian, Joseph. "Golf Grows Up." In *Playing Through: The Rise of American Golf*, p. 7.

"Golf & Business."

Smith, Dena. "Black Women Get a Shot at the Corporate Game: Golf."

Woo, Suzanne. *On Course for Business: Women and Golf*.

Goon, Toy Len (1892–1993), Laundry Businesswoman

Toy Len Goon, named Mother of the Year in 1952, single-handedly managed the family's hand laundry in Portland, Maine, after her husband died. At the same time, although speaking little English, she raised eight children to be outstanding citizens.

She was born in Canton, China; her name means brilliant lotus. She never attended school, which was common for a girl in the China of that day. When she was nineteen, Dogan Goon came from Portland, Maine, to find a wife. After a three-day wedding, they boarded a steamer to San Francisco and then traveled on to Portland where he owned a business, the Chinese-American Laundry.

When he left to serve in World War I, Goon was responsible for the business. He returned an amputee, remaining in very poor health until his death in 1940, leaving eight children, the youngest, only three. She put them to work in the laundry, but made sure they graduated from high school and attended college. The youngest child checked through pockets, while the oldest made deliveries and ironed. With the business growing, she purchased machinery that cut the work by a third. Through her prudent financial management, she was eventually able to buy the three-story building that housed the laundry and their living quarters.

Goon was a hard worker, dedicated to the business and her family. She had no vacations, taking off only one week of work to accept her honor in 1952. After being named State of Maine Mother of the Year, she became the first Chinese American woman to receive the national Mother of the Year award from the Golden Rule Foundation. Goon was invited to visit President Truman in Washington and to visit Chang Kai-Shek in the Republic of China. When asked how she managed to run the laundry, feed, clothe, and discipline eight children, she answered, "If there is harmony in the family, there is food in the larder and peace in the country" (Davis, *Mothers of America*, p. 107).

Goon died in Swampscott, Massachusetts, at the age of 101, leaving five sons, three daughters, twenty-four grandchildren, and twenty-one great-grand-children. Most of her children graduated from college; three, from graduate school.

See also: Asian American Businesswomen; Immigrant Businesswomen

Further Reading

Davis, Elizabeth Logan. *Mothers of America*, p. 105–110.

"Toy Len Goon, 101; Won '52 Mother of the Year Honor."

"Toy Len Goon: Portland." In American Mother's Committee, p. 244–245.

Gordon, Ellen Rubin (1932–), Food Industry Executive

Ellen Gordon and her husband own and run Tootsie Roll Industries, a public company in which the family owns the majority of stock. She is president and COO, he is chairman of the board and CEO. More than 100 years old, it is a very successful business specializing in such niche candies as Tootsie Rolls, Tootsie Roll Pops, Charms, Junior Mints, and other lollipops. It has been on the *Working Woman* list of top woman-owned companies since the list began in 1992. Gordon has also been on *Working Woman*'s list of top paid women executives.

Leo Hirschfield invented the Tootsie Roll in 1896 and named it for his daughter. In 1917 he formed his company, Sweets Company of America, and began selling stock in 1922. The Rubin family bought stock then, and in 1930 during the Great Depression, took over the company in payment for bad debts. In 1938 they moved the company to Hoboken, New Jersey, and began mass producing candy using conveyor belt systems. Gordon's father William became the president in 1948.

She was born and raised in New England, daughter of a successful manufac-turer who took her to visit the candy factory frequently. Although fascinated by her father's business, she grew up thinking of getting married and hav-ing babies, a common destiny for women in the late 1940s. Gordon was well educated in private schools, before attending Vassar in 1948. During a Florida vacation in her sophomore year, she met Melvin Gordon, who was eleven years older. He had served in World War II, had an MBA from Harvard, and was employed in his family textile firm. After they married seven weeks later, she transferred to Wellesley; however, she became pregnant with the first of four daughters and had to leave school, another commonplace occur-rence for women at that time. When the third daughter attended nursery school, she went to Brandeis, graduating in 1965. After she started graduate work at Harvard in Indo-European linguistics, her husband issued a call for help.

In 1952 he had joined the board of the Sweets Company of America, succeeding the ailing William Rubin ten years later. In 1966 he changed the name to Tootsie Roll Industries, and in 1968 Gordon joined the board. She taught herself the financial and investment side, and recommended that the family obtain a majority of the stock, thus heading off any takeover attempts. By then the company had leased a large plant in Chicago that became the headquarters. The couple commuted every week from New Hampshire, accompanied by their youngest daughter, who attended two schools each week, a New England private school and a Chicago school with 50 percent minority students. Gordon served as corporate secretary, then as vice president of product development and quality assurance, increasing factory automation. Later she became senior vice president and director of the family investment company, and in 1978 was elected president and COO.

The two Gordons run a conservative company; it has very little debt, only makes acquisitions when profits can finance them, and pays for upgrading automation in the same way. It has bought several other candy brands: Mason and Bonomo hard candies and taffy; Cella's Confections, famous for chocolate-covered cherries; Charms, which gave it 50 percent of the lollipop market; some Warner-Lambert brands, including Junior Mints; and Andes Candies, Inc. Interested only in leading brands with niche markets, it only acquires companies that fit its philosophy of candy-making and marketing. Once bought, the candy gets upgraded packaging to add to its allure. The company is self-sufficient, having its own sugar refinery, own art department, own advertising agency, print shop, machinery shop, and trucking subsidiary; it even makes its own lollipop sticks. By the 100-year anniversary, its candy was marketed in over thirty countries, 45 million Tootsie Rolls were made daily in the completely automated factory, sales had increased from $1.3 million in 1922 to $313 million, and profits from $6,000 to $40 million. Tootsie Roll candies were on the menu during World War II, the Korean War, and the Gulf War. Celebrities such as Frank Sinatra, Telly Savalas, and Jackie Onassis relied on them. Tootsie Rolls are available in many sizes, including one that still costs a penny.

Gordon and her husband have a slow but steady management philosophy and make decisions by consensus. She knows most employees and considers their experience, ideas, and input when solving problems. She is known as a tough but friendly negotiator, particularly when she persuaded the city of Chicago and the state to extend the enterprise zone to include the Tootsie Roll factory, resulting in several tax breaks and other benefits for the company. The company's success is credited to her insistence on constant upgrading and her management style. In combining a high-powered career and raising her family, she acknowledges her husband as her mentor, always nurturing.

Gordon has served on the board of directors of Bestfoods, the Dean's Council for the J.L. Graduate School of Management at Northwestern University, the Advisory Council of Stanford University Graduate School of Business, the Board of Fellows of the Medical School of Harvard, the President's Export Council, and the University Resources and Overseers Committee at Harvard. She has been a trustee and member of the Committee for Economic Development at Northwestern and a member of the Radcliffe College Partners. She has also served on Women Inc.'s board of advisors and the board of directors of the National Confectioners Association. Gordon was a founder of the Committee of 200, president from 1987 to 1989. She won the Kettle Award in 1985 and the company ranked number 96 on the 1988 *Forbes* list of the 200 best small companies. In 1992 *Business Week* listed her as one of the top fifty women in business in the United States.

See also: Food Industry

Further Reading

Burns, Greg. "She's on a Roll; Decades of Waiting Makes Success Even Sweeter for Tootsie President."

Toops, Diane. "On a Roll: Candymakers Ellen and Melvin Gordon, Tootsie Roll's Leaders Keep Brand on Track in its 100th Year."

Wilkinson, Stephan. "The Practical Genius of Penny Candy."

Gorelick, Jamie (1950–), Fannie Mae Executive

Jamie Gorelick was the vice chairman of Fannie Mae, the entity that sets credit policy for the United States. She was one of a three-person chairman office, from 1997 until July 2003, before stepping down to devote more time to her duties on President Bush's National Commission on Terrorist Acts.

She was born in 1950 to Russian Jewish immigrants who instilled liberal intellectual values in their children. She grew up attending civil rights marches and anti-war protests in the 1960s and later recruited young supporters for Robert F. Kennedy. Gorelick won a Fulbright Scholarship after graduating magna cum laude in 1972 from Radcliffe, but chose to go to Harvard Law School, graduating cum laude in 1975. She married that same year, and her husband became chief of pulmonary medicine at Georgetown University Hospital. They have a son and a daughter.

Upon graduation she joined a Washington law firm, but in 1979 became assistant to the U.S. Department of Energy Secretary and counselor to the deputy secretary. In 1982 and 1984 Gorelick taught trial advocacy workshops at Harvard Law School, and served on the editorial board of the *Corporate Criminal Liability Reporter* from 1986 to 1993. She has also been a member of the chairman's advisory council of the U.S. Senate Judiciary Committee. She was a teaching fellow in government at the Kennedy School for Government and a member of the Harvard Board of Overseers from 1989 to 1993.

In 1993 she became general counsel for the Department of Defense and was promoted in 1994 to deputy attorney general of the Department of

Justice. At the right hand of Janet Reno, she was responsible for managing the organization and budget of the department. She was appointed to help lead Fannie Mae in 1997. After the September 11, 2001, attack on the World Trade Center, Gorelick was appointed to the bipartisan national commission to investigate the attacks. She resigned from Fannie Mae in 2003, stating that she could not do a quality job on both the new commission and Fannie Mae.

Her management skills are based on problem solving and diplomacy. Janet Reno credits her with a "marvelous ability to analyze an issue, size it up, and give extraordinary judgment" (Schmitt, "Washington at Work," p. 13). Gorelick has a very active social conscience and is a list maker who is able to anticipate and respond to critical issues. One of her priorities at Fannie Mae was to build flexibility into the workplace.

She has served on the boards of Fannie Mae, United Technologies, Schlumberger Ltd, Fannie Mae Foundation, National Park Foundation, Carnegie Endowment, National Women's Law Center, Bazelon Center of Mental Health Law, Washington Legal Clinic for the Homeless, Local Initiatives Support Corporation, and National Legal Center for the Public Interest. Gorelick has been a council member of the American Law Institute, president of the D.C. Bar Association from 1992 to 1993, and on its board of governors.

Gorelick has written many articles and is widely quoted. Her many awards include the Secretary of Defense Distinguished Service Medal, the Director of Central Intelligence Award, the Margaret Brent Award from the American Bar Association, the Woman Lawyer of the Year Award from the Women's Bar Association, the Judge Learned Hand Award from the American Jewish Committee, and the Department of Justice's Edmund J. Randolph Award. *Working Mother* included her on its list of the twenty-five most influential working mothers in America. In 2002, she was honored by the NOW Legal Defense and Education Fund.

See also: Finance industry

Further Reading
"Fannie Mae's Vice Chair Jamie Gorelick to Step Down in July."
"Jamie Gorelick Named Vice Chair of Fannie Mae."
Schmitt, Eric. "Washington at Work; Pentagon Lawyer Quietly Gets Notice as a Rising Star in the Administration."

Graham, Bette Nesmith (1924–1980), Office Products Executive, Inventor

Bette Graham's invention, Liquid Paper, was the basis for the cottage industry that she began in 1956. She developed and manufactured the corrective substance in her kitchen, packaging and distributing it from her garage. By 1979 it had grown into an international corporation when she sold it to Gillette for $47 million. She also pioneered a more humanistic management approach than the hierarchical style in vogue at the time.

She was one of two daughters born to an automobile wholesaler in Dallas. Graham dropped out of high school, preferring to work, and became a legal secretary without being able to type. The firm sent her to secretarial school, and she earned her high school diploma at night school. In 1942 she married her high school sweetheart, Warren Nesmith, and had a son the next year at nineteen. Her husband immediately went off to World War II, and they divorced when he returned.

She kept her job, and by 1951 had worked her way up to executive secretary. These were the days of non-erasable carbon paper and the need for multiple copies; but not being a perfect typist, Graham sometimes had to type documents over and over. One day while painting the local bank's windows for Christmas, she realized that a painter just covered over any mistake. Realizing that this would also work with paper, thereafter she kept a little bottle of white tempura paint in her desk. When the other secretaries saw what she was doing, they wanted some "Mistake Out" too. Graham soon realized that this might be a marketable idea.

After obtaining a trademark, she improved the mixture to make it thicker and quicker drying. She found the formula for tempura paint at the library, a chemistry teacher helped her modify the formula, a paint manufacturer taught her how to grind and mix paint, and she got samples of wetting agents and resins. She mixed everything in her kitchen until she got it right before sending a sample to IBM, hoping that the company would be interested, but she was turned down.

At this point she had three options: drop the idea, go to another large company, or market it herself. She decided on the last, first changing the name to Liquid Paper, then testing different types of packaging. After flirting with tubes and applicators, she decided on a bottle and brush combination, marketing it through product sheets sent to businesses and office supply dealers. By the end of 1957, she was selling one hundred bottles each month that she mixed in the kitchen and her son Michael and his friends packaged in the garage: a typical cottage industry.

In 1958 she widened her market by sending press releases and product sheets to office supply magazines, hoping for a free article about her correcting fluid. That October's *The Office* had an article about Liquid Paper under "New Products of the Month." Five hundred people wrote to the magazine, and more wrote to the company to order the product. In December *The Secretary* also ran a short item. Graham was still working, but was fired after signing her company's name to a document rather than that of the law firm.

Liquid Paper couldn't support the family yet, so Graham got a part-time job. She improved the drying time of the product, and began traveling around Texas with her son, visiting office supply dealers. Her largest offer was one gross from a San Antonio dealer, then another gross, and another. By 1962 she was in business, had two part-time employees, and obtained a $500 loan for a portable building in her backyard. That year she also met and married Bob Graham who became part of the company. They traveled outside Texas, and the next year, the company bought a booth at the National Office Products Association convention. In 1964 it hired an office manager, the first full-time employee. As more and more orders poured in, more employees were hired. By the end of the decade, sales were more than $1 million in the United States.

In 1968 the company, with new headquarters and automated equipment, sold one million bottles. Two years later, it was five million. The little cottage industry had become a large corporation. Graham was chairman of the board and developed a unique management structure for the time. She was determined that everyone had a voice in all operations, including new product development, marketing strategy, manufacturing techniques, and office operations. Each employee sat on a committee that brainstormed ideas, refined them into workable strategies, and then made proposals to the executive committee. This worked well then, but as the company grew bigger and more unwieldy, it had to be abandoned.

She was still dedicated to her employees' well being and established an on-site childcare center as well as an employee library. In 1972 Liquid Paper started international sales. By 1975 more than 200 employees produced 25 million bottles for distribution to thirty-one countries. Also that year, the headquarters were totally remodeled, one of Graham's last projects before resigning in 1976. Gillette Corporation bought the company in 1979 for $47.5 million, plus royalties on every bottle sold until 2000.

In retirement, she set up two foundations: the Bette Clair McMurry Foundation and the Gihon Foundation, among the first private philanthropic foundations devoted to helping women in the work force. She was named one of Texas's most influential women of the century. When she died, her son Michael and her foundations equally divided her multi-million dollar estate. Michael, who was a member of the Monkees rock group of the sixties, established and headed the Council on Ideas, a think tank based on his mother's ideas. Because of her management style, the company is used as one of the Harvard Business School's case studies.

See also: Inventors

Further Reading
"Bette Graham (1924–1980)." In Altman, Linda Jacobs. *Women Inventors*, p. 88–99.
"Bette Nesmith Graham." In Vare, Ethlie Ann and Greg Ptacek, *Mothers of Invention*, p. 38–42.

Graham, Katharine (1917–2001), Newspaper Publisher

From 1963 through the early 1970s, Katharine Graham was the only woman CEO in the *Fortune* 500 companies as well as the most powerful and influential woman in the American newspaper business. As publisher and CEO of the *Washington Post*, she was responsible for influencing the course of history through her courageous publication of the *Pentagon Papers*, as well as the ongoing investigation of the Watergate scandal that led to the resignation of President Richard Nixon. Although attacked and excoriated, she stood firm on her principles and the freedom of the press.

She was born into a wealthy New York City family that was active politically and philanthropically. Her father was an internationally known financier who held many government appointments before he bought the *Washington Post* in 1933. She was the fourth of five children who were raised by nannies and governesses before going to boarding school. Graham attended Madeira School where she was editor of the newspaper and excelled academically, athletically, and in extracurricular activities. She attended Vassar College for two years before transferring to the University of Chicago, then known for political radicalism and stimulating intellectual debate, where she earned an AB in journalism in 1938. Her first job was as a reporter for the *San Francisco Daily News*, but she was resented and ridiculed both for the fact that her father arranged the job and that she was a woman. Her pay was $25 per week. By the time she left a year later, she had managed to earn a better beat through her reporting.

In 1939 her father asked her to help with the *Post*, wanting her to learn about the paper because she would eventually be responsible for it. This did not mean he expected her to run it, but as his only heir interested in the paper, she would be at least a part owner. She wrote articles, edited the letters to the editor, sat in on editorial policy conferences, worked in both the advertising and circulation departments, did page layout, and wrote headlines. In 1940 she married Philip, who worked for Supreme Court Justice Felix Frankfurter. Shortly after their marriage, he went off to World War II. She followed him until he was shipped to the Pacific then she returned to her work at the newspaper. On his return in 1945, Graham's father made him associate publisher of the *Post*. The following year he became publisher. She stayed home and raised one daughter and three sons.

In 1948 Graham and her husband bought the newspaper for $1. He expanded the paper, bought the *Washington Times-Herald* in 1954 and *Newsweek Magazine* in 1961, and founded an international news service with the *Los Angeles Times* in 1962. Their marriage became an unhappy one; he was charming and witty, one of John F. Kennedy's elite reporters, but also a philanderer who had been diagnosed as a manic depressive many years earlier. In 1963 she refused a divorce in which he wanted to have sole ownership of the paper. In the midst of a reconciliation, he committed suicide. She was devastated, but decided to keep and run the family business.

The *Post*, in disarray from poor leadership, had a demoralized staff that wanted no part of a woman owner and publisher. Graham was very shy and insecure, but decided that she would make the paper work and work well; her goal was to "pursue truth for the public good" (*Current Biography*, 1971, p. 171). Although she had learned the workings of the paper as a girl, publishing had changed, and she now needed to learn how to run the business side. Loyal staff members became her mentors, and she learned all that she could from them. Her second year she hired Ben Bradlee, one of the best in the business, to be managing editor. She cut costs while improving editorial quality, increased advertising, and hired the best investigative reporters. By 1966 the paper ranked third in the nation for advertising lineage. Graham modernized the equipment, increased the editorial budget, and beefed-up salaries to attract the best journalists she could find.

In 1971 she made the first decision that catapulted her into the national limelight: she agreed to publish the Pentagon papers, secret military documents that proved the war in Vietnam was not going as well as the military claimed in press releases. Although the *New York Times* had been restrained from publishing the documents by a court order, Graham felt that the public had a right to know the truth, so she stood behind Ben Bradlee and the reporters, and the *Post* published the papers.

Soon after that, the *Washington Post* followed up on a break-in at Democratic headquarters at the Watergate apartments in Washington. At first, no other newspapers were interested in the story. As the *Post* continued to investigate and publish, the story became an important part of history. The facts as they emerged eventually led to the resignation of President Richard Nixon in 1974. Graham withstood an enormous amount of political pressure and a variety of threats, but kept publishing the facts, a very courageous act. *All the President's Men*, by *Post* investigative reporters Carl Bernstein and Bob Woodward, is a fascinating account of the events of that time. The paper received a Pulitzer Prize for its coverage of the story.

> As publisher and CEO of the *Washington Post*, Katharine Graham was responsible for influencing the course of history through her courageous publication of the *Pentagon Papers* as well as the ongoing investigation of the Watergate scandal that led to the resignation of President Richard Nixon.

The third crisis during the 1970s was a bitter pressmen's union strike that led to vandalism of the presses. Graham broke the strike, but not until all nine of the presses had been damaged. She and the other managers learned all about the mechanics of producing a newspaper. One of her roles as publisher was to keep costs down, but the union wished to keep all their jobs, even the unnecessary ones, and she would not give in to their demands. Again, she was vilified for her part in breaking the strike, but she held firm and was tough, quite a feat for the shy woman who had taken over the paper only ten years before.

In 1979 her son Donald became publisher after apprenticing for eight years, learning every area of the publishing business. Graham stayed as CEO and chairman of the board, but in 1991 he succeeded her in both positions, and she continued to chair the board's executive committee. She wrote her autobiography in 1997, receiving rave reviews and the 1998 Pulitzer Prize for Biography.

Her management style included hiring the best people, paying them well, and then encouraging them to do the best job they could. She backed them up all the way, even during disagreements. She was logical, methodical, and had the highest principles about publishing, taking very seriously the newspaper's role in publishing the truth. She brought performance reviews and rigorous cash management to the newspaper, building it into one of the most prestigious papers in the country, as well as a successful and highly professional billion-dollar enterprise. When she took over she made mistakes, but learned from them as well as from her mentors. The *Washington Post* and Katharine Graham have become synonymous with courage, grace, and the highest journalistic quality.

Her awards and honors are legion. In 1968 she received an honorary degree from Dartmouth College; the following year the American Newspaperwoman's Club honored her for outstanding personal achievement in professional journalism. In 1970 she was awarded a gold medal from the National Institute of Social Science for her distinguished services to humanity and, in 1974 was the first woman elected to the traditionally male Associated Press board of directors. She received the John Peter Zenger Award for Distinguished Service on Behalf of Freedom of the Press and the People's Right to Know in 1973 and was named by *U.S. News and World Report* as the top leader and shaper of national life among women in a 1977 poll of business and political leaders. In 1983 Graham received the Isaiah Thomas Award from the Rochester Institute of Technology that is given to a newspaper leader who has made a significant contribution to the profession. In 1991 she was named to the National Sales Hall of Fame, and two years later to the National Business Hall of Fame. She also received the "Four Freedoms" award that honors an American whose contributions have helped fulfill one of the four freedoms as outlined by Franklin Delano Roosevelt. In 1999 she was named one of the twenty-five most influential newspaper people of the twentieth century by *Editor & Publisher*. The next year she received the Matrix Award from New York Women in Communications and was the first woman to receive the Robie Award for Achievement in Industry.

She has also served on many committees and boards over the years, including the New York Publishers Association, the University of Chicago, George Washington University, the National Gallery of Art, the American Assembly of Columbia University, the Foreign Relations and Overseas Development Council, and the First Lady's Commission for a More Beautiful Capital.

Graham died in 2001 at eighty-four from injuries sustained in a fall in Sun Valley, Idaho. At the time of her death, she was working on an anthology of her favorite writings about Washington. Her posthumous awards include the W.H. Kiplinger Distinguished Contributions to Journalism Award from the

National Press Foundation and inductions into the National Women's Hall of Fame and the American Advertising Federation's Advertising Hall of Fame.

See also: Publishing Industry

Further Reading

Bernstein, Carl and Bob Woodward. *All the President's Men.*

Graham, Katharine. *Personal History.* "Graham, Katharine (Meyer)." *Current Biography Yearbook 1971,* p. 170–172.

Platt, Adam. "Special Kay; *Washington Post* Publisher Katharine Graham."

Rowland, Mary. "The Mastermind of a Media Empire."

"Special Report: Katharine Graham, 1917–2001."

Green, Henrietta (1834–1916), Financier

Hetty Green's wealth began with one black cow, purchased by Henry Howland in Plymouth, Massachusetts, in 1624. By the time the inheritance reached Green, it had grown to $1 million and she, through shrewd financial management and a reluctance to spend, accumulated over $100,000,000. At her death, she was the richest woman in America.

Known as the "Witch of Wall Street," Green was born a Quaker, the only daughter and surviving child of wealthy parents. Her inherited fortune came from the Howland family's New England whaling empire and trade with China, as well as her father's tough business practices. She opened her first bank account at age eight, read stock quotes to her grandfather, and learned respect for the value of a dollar from her father. Business was the focus of her life. Her investment strategies were conservative; she aimed to make and keep 6 percent profit per year; however, it was said she could smell a bear market. In both the Panic of 1890 and the Panic of 1907, she converted assets into cash and lent to those caught short.

She began making money on her honeymoon by investing in the U.S. government savings bonds that flooded the country after the Civil War and later in Rock Island Railroad bonds, other railroad stocks, and real estate in Chicago and New York City. She also owned a considerable amount of stock in Chemical National Bank of New York; in fact, she had an "office" in one of their vaults.

Stories of her miserliness abound, many exaggerated by the newspapers. Her eccentricities in dress and habits were legend: she wore outdated, long black dresses until they were green with age and dirt, carrying certificates in their voluminous pockets rather than buying a purse. She lived in a variety of cold-water apartments to avoid taxes and the cost of electricity, eating her porridge cold. She used free health clinics to avoid the cost of a doctor. This resulted in the amputation of her son's gangrenous leg because she waited too long to see the doctor. Green was not alone in her opinions, however, doctors were seen by many people as little better than butchers at this time. She didn't like to spend money unnecessarily; she said it went against her thrifty Quaker upbringing. Her family and close friends said she was misjudged, that she was a kind woman with a sweet smile. Her son claimed that many of the stories were untrue. She paid her free-spending husband's debts many times until she finally lost patience and kicked him out. Green taught her son business by sending him to Chicago to manage their real estate holdings and to Texas, where he bought and managed the Texas and Midland Railroad.

Hetty Green was the first female operator on the New York Stock Exchange. In amassing her fortune, she competed with the best businessmen anywhere. Her financial acumen, coupled with an exaggerated thriftiness, built her fortune into the largest in America. Unfortunately, she is remembered more for the stories of parsimony than her very real business abilities.

See also: Finance Industry

Further Reading
Coryell, Janet L. "Green, Hetty." In Garraty and Carnes, p. 491–493.
Drachman, Virginia G., p. 70–75.
Lewis, Arthur H. *The Day They Shook the Plum Tree.*
Sparkes, Boyden and Samuel Taylor Moore. *Hetty Green: The Witch of Wall Street.*
Wyckoff, Peter. "Queen Midas: Hetty Robinson Green."

Greene, Catherine Littlefield (1753–1814), Agriculture Industry Pioneer

Catherine Greene suggested the idea for Eli Whitney's cotton gin, the invention that revolutionized southern agriculture. She also promoted it and financed the lengthy patent litigation. She has been called his patron; some sources give her credit for improving the design by using wire brushes instead of Whitney's original wooden pegs. This may just be a legend, but she absolutely did describe the plantation owners' problems with separating the seed from the cotton boll, told him what had already been tried, supported him while he tinkered with the idea in her basement, and promoted the prototype to her neighbors.

Greene was born in Rhode Island to a prominent family, the third child of five. She attended town schools and later met her future husband, Nathaniel Greene, through her uncle the governor. They married when she was eighteen and he was thirty-one. He was one of the first to join the Revolutionary War and quickly became George Washington's second in command. She traveled with him from camp to camp, including Valley Forge, bearing three children during the course of the war. She is credited with raising the morale of the troops with her spontaneous, warm, generous, and charming nature. All the officers respected her courage and gallantry of spirit.

After the war ended in 1783, the Georgia legislature awarded her husband a plantation, Mulberry Grove. The family moved there, but he died nine months later, leaving her with five small children and an estate in debt. Unfazed, Greene still went to Newport, Rhode Island, every summer to partake in society life. Returning in 1792, she shared the trip with Eli Whitney, who was on his way to a tutoring job at a neighboring plantation. His tutoring job, obtained for him by his fraternity brother, Elias Miller, Greene's tutor and estate manager, fell through, so she invited him to stay as a houseguest.

Knowing Whitney was a tinkerer and inventor, she encouraged him to solve the problem of separating the seeds from the cotton fiber. She described the manual process and the previously unsuccessful devices. For the next six months, he worked in her basement, finally building a prototype that seemed to work. Greene then showed all the neighbors the invention. Perhaps this was a mistake, for it was a simple machine, and soon everyone else had made one. Elias Miller and Whitney set up a company and applied for a patent. By 1794 a patent was granted, but there were so many bootleg copies that they only sold six machines. They sued the copiers, but the litigation costs were enormous. In fact, Greene, who had pledged her entire estate to the invention, went bankrupt because of the court battles.

She married Elias Miller in 1796, and they moved to another plantation near by. He died in 1803 at the age of thirty-nine, and she died of a fever in 1814 at fifty-nine.

See also: Agriculture/Ranching; Colonial Businesswomen; Inventors

Further Reading
Andrews, Edmund L. "Patents: New Exhibit Shows History of Women Inventors."
"Catherine Littlefield Greene." In Vare, Ethlie Ann and Greg Ptacek, *Mothers of Invention*, p. 204–206.
Green, Constance. "Greene, Catherine Littlefield." In Edward T. James, p. 85–86.

Greene, Mary Becker (1869–1949), Steamship Line Owner

Mary Greene, one of seven women in the National Rivers Hall of Fame, owned the Greene Line Steamship Company with her husband Gordon. Later she and her sons operated the Line until her death in 1949. She died on the river in the spring, "probably the best-known personality on the Ohio and Mississippi Rivers in the first half of the 20th century" (Cantwell, "Hall of Fame," p. 1A).

The company began in 1890 when her husband bought the *H.K. Bedford* steamboat, their first steamboat home. From the beginning they were partners. He taught her how to pilot, and she received both her pilot's license and her master's license before the first of their three sons was born in 1898. She was in charge of the bookkeeping duties and did maintenance as well. The company concentrated on freight although it did carry passengers occasionally. The cost for a round trip ticket (five days plus three meals per day and a berth) from Cincinnati to Charleston, West Virginia, was $8 per person.

Her husband built four more steamers: the *Greenland*, the *Cricket*, the *Argand*, and the *Chris Greene* with its three boilers. The *Cricket* towed a tent circus with the first calliope on its barges. It also acquired the up-river boats belonging to the White Collar Line, but in 1922 a fire destroyed four steamers, and the company was back to one, the *Greenwood*. The *Tom Greene* and the *Chris Greene*, with steel hulls to withstand the heat of fire, were quickly built. At the time of her husband's death in 1927, the company had owned and operated 28 steamers.

Greene and her sons continued, initiating steamboat races in 1928, 1929, and 1930. They expanded in the passenger business in 1930 as well as the transportation of automobiles. The company was famous for its cruises to New Orleans, St. Paul, Knoxville, Charleston, and Nashville. Chris Greene, who served in World War II, returned only to die of a heart attack in 1944. One other son also died young, but Captain Mary, as she was called up and down the river, and Tom, her last son, operated the company. His dream was to operate the finest passenger steamboat in the world, and he bought the *Delta Queen* in 1946 for $46,250, bringing her home from Sacramento, California, up the Mississippi and Ohio rivers. It was their most famous ship and is still in operation today. Captain Mary moved aboard and died there in the spring of 1949.

Further Reading

Cantwell, Alice. "Hall of Fame Pays Tribute to the Heroines of Maritime." National Rivers Hall of Fame, www.mississippirivermuseum.com/fame/greene.htm.

Simcox, Betty Blake. *Greene Line Steamers, Inc. Celebrates its 75th Anniversary.* 1965.

Greenfield, Marguerite (1883–1968), Ice Cutter

Marguerite Greenfield not only founded and ran her own ice business in Montana from 1912 to 1934, but she also fought and exposed graft and dishonesty in the Great Northern Railway.

She was born in 1883, the eldest of four children, in Helena, Montana, to the city editor of the *Helena Daily Independent* and the *Helena Herald*. She grew up in a happy, sheltered environment, graduated from Helena High School, spent summers traveling to California with a schoolteacher aunt, wrote stories and historical sketches, and did household chores so her mother and sister could do the social round.

In 1912 in her late twenties, Greenfield decided to go into business after rejecting a prospective suitor. The ice business was not only an essential service, but would give her the opportunity to work outdoors. She thought it would be fun, as well as cause a fuss because it was traditionally a man's business.

She persuaded a family friend to show her how to prepare the ice for cutting, make accurate markings, cut and move the blocks, split the blocks, and store them in sawdust-insulated sheds. Greenfield began her small wholesale business, the Independent Ice Company, relying on Helena ponds. It quickly evolved into retail as well, despite competition from one Meyer Fish who may have resorted to some dirty tricks to force her out of business. After a 1915 advertisement in which he implied that she sold "duck pond ice" (meaning dirty ice), she sued him for slander and malice. Although she lost the suit, he accepted that she was in the business to stay.

From 1913 to 1917 her profits increased from $2,000 to $9,000, due both to a number of cold winters with two to three cuttings per season, and her hard work. The winter of 1919 was mild, however, with little snow. Greenfield rented a higher, and therefore colder, pond in Elk Park, Montana, for $1,000 per year, including the two-acre pond at 6,732 feet altitude and a ninety-foot by seventy-nine-foot ice-house. She moved to a two-room cabin and hired a crew of seventeen men. She also had a field saw named Maud and eight expert ice handlers who loaded five to eight freight cars for $6.50 per day.

In 1920 her dispute with the Great Northern Railway began when a superintendent wanted a payoff to contract with her ice business. After she refused, he retaliated, thinking of new ways to harass her when she complained and tried to work around his barriers. Because she had to use the railway for her ice shipments, these actions caused real privation for her company. She complained to men higher and higher in the company who ignored her.

Meanwhile in 1921, her father became the agricultural agent for the Railway, and one of his friends was Ralph Budd, the president. In 1924 Greenfield decided to write directly to him, and at his instigation, the company investigated. Unfortunately however, all the men involved lied, including the former owner of her pond, and they found nothing concrete.

Inspired by Ida Tarbell's fight against Standard Oil Company, she continued the fight from 1925 to 1928 and, in that year, again wrote to the president. with specific details and was prepared to sue. For two years Greenfield wrote dozens of letters, and in October 1929, she met with Ralph Budd for three hours. He was finally convinced and fired the perpetrators.

It was, unfortunately, too late. By 1930 the company was almost out of money. Besides the fight with the railway, the stock market crashed, and in 1931 there was a drought. In addition, advances in electric home refrigeration and railway-refrigerated cars negated the need for natural ice. In September of 1933 she had sold only $100 worth of ice, and she was broke. In 1934 she sold the pond, closed the company, left Elk Park, and moved back to Helena. Greenfield died in 1968.

See also: Western Businesswomen

Further Reading

Bishop, Joan. "Game of Freeze-Out: Marguerite Greenfield and Her Battle with the Great Northern Railway, 1920–1929."

Dishon, Betty. "A Woman in the Ice Business."

Grogan, Barbara B. (1947–), Construction Contractor

Barbara Grogan was the founder of Western Industrial Contractors, Inc. in Denver, the first woman chair of the Denver Chamber of Commerce, and the first woman to chair the board of the Denver Branch of the Federal Reserve Bank of Kansas City.

She began Western Industrial Contractors, Inc. (WIC) in 1982 with a 1969 orange pickup truck, a small rented office across from a junkyard, and three employees. At that time she was in the midst of a divorce, had her husband's debts to pay, and two children to support; but she used a degree in psychology and one year of experience in her husband's crane and truck rental business to create a highly successful millwrighting company through bidding on large national jobs, renting equipment, and hiring union contract labor.

Grogan's company moves, erects, and installs heavy industrial equipment, relocating entire plants for clients such as Ralston Purina, Ball Corporation, and IBM. Her first contract was with Johns Manville to move a manufacturing plant from Florida to Malaysia. Other projects included installing the underground baggage-handling system at O'Hare Airport in Chicago, providing project management services during the Denver International Airport's construction, and relocating fifty-five medical research laboratories. In 1988 the company grossed $5 million; by November of 1997 that figure had doubled. It has made a profit every year except one, even during an economic recession in Colorado.

Since 1993 she has also started three sister businesses with various partners: Black Mountain Construction, which builds log homes in Winter Park, Colorado; Grogan & Strickland, based in Phoenix, which serves a variety of corporate relocation needs; and Western GBS, which offers consulting to firms involved in new building construction.

Grogan has given back to the community through her service on the Denver Chamber of Commerce, beginning a Small Business Profit Center and developing a mentoring program between small and large businesses. She was the chamber's first woman president. In December 1995 she represented small businesses at President Clinton's economic forum in Little Rock. She has also served on several corporate boards of directors, the U.S. Chamber of Commerce, the Committee for Economic Development in New York City, and Volunteers of America in Denver, and as chair of the Denver Branch of the Federal Reserve Bank. She is a member of the Committee of 200.

Caudron states that Barbara Grogan is an example of a woman thriving in a male-dominated industry ("Constructive Criticism," p. 12). Grogan herself has said that being a woman got her in the door during cold calls (the curiosity factor), but then she had to work twice as hard to sell her services. By focusing on customer service and hiring the best employees possible, she has succeeded. The Denver Metro Chamber of Commerce awarded her the Vanguard Award in April 1999 for her long-time advocacy of small business.

See also: Construction Industry

Further Reading
Caudron, Shari. "Constructive Criticism."
Harrell, Wilson. "Female of the Species: Entrepreneurship: Do Men and Women Do it Differently?"
Wymard, Ellie, p. 218–221.

Grossinger, Jennie (1892–1972), Hotel/Resort Owner

Jennie Grossinger, owner of Grossinger's in New York's Catskill Mountains, parlayed her family's ramshackle farm into a seven-acre resort catering to over 150,000 visitors annually before she died in 1972.

Born in Austria, she moved to New York City with her mother and sister, following her father who had immigrated to the Lower East Side two years earlier. She worked as a buttonholer for $1.50 per week when she was thirteen and attending night school. In 1912 she married her cousin Harry, also a Grossinger, and the family opened a dairy restaurant where she was a cashier and waitress. Because of stress and overwork, her father suffered a nervous and physical breakdown in 1914, so the family bought an old farm, planning to grow crops. Grossinger moved with them while her husband stayed in the city. It soon became clear that farming was poor, so they took in nine summer boarders for a total of $81. The next spring they expanded and took in twenty guests recruited in the city. By 1916 the hotel was established despite having no heat, electricity, or indoor plumbing. That year Grossinger's husband moved to the Catskills.

The first guests were fellow Jewish immigrants who liked the good kosher food and modest rates. It was a family affair: Grossinger was in charge of bookkeeping and managing, her husband was responsible for buildings and expansion, her mother took care of the kitchen, and her father did the farming, marketing, and met guests at the railroad.

In 1919 Grossinger bought a nearby hotel, a lake, and sixty-three acres of woodland. The resort expanded until by 1972 it consisted of 1,200 acres, a number of cottages, a training center for prize fighters, an Olympic-size swimming pool, a children's day camp, tennis courts, dancing studio, two nightclubs, its own post office and airport, and accommodations for 600 guests. The dining room seated 1,300, with two kitchens adhering to strict Kosher dietary rules. Grossinger's was called the apotheosis of resorts, and Jennie the hostess extraordinaire.

With the addition of sports activities and effective advertising, the resort flowered in the 1920s and hung on during the Depression. The first prize-fighter to train there was Barney Ross in 1934, followed by seven world champions, including Joe Louis and Rocky Marciano. By the forties and fifties, Grossinger's was internationally renowned for the charm and family atmosphere that she furnished, the excellent and bounteous kosher kitchens, the variety of activities, and the celebrities. Many entertainers got their start there, including Milton Berle, Sid Caesar, Danny Kaye, and Eddie Fisher. Sports greats Babe Zaharias and Florence Chadwick were on the staff. The guest list included kings, scientists, politicians, Dr. Jonas Salk, Eleanor Roosevelt, New York Governors Dewey and Rockefeller, Ralphe Bunche, Jackie Robinson, Lucille Ball, Cardinal Spellman, and Robert and Ted Kennedy.

Reports differ on Grossinger's business ability, but all agree that the resort's success was largely due to her friendliness and personal concern about the satisfaction of her guests. The resort always had a family enterprise aura; she was a genius at hostessing and loved what she did. The *New York Times* wrote when she died: "Jennie epitomized the tone of the place—an atmosphere that combined urgent family solicitude for guests with an elegance that gave to many an opulent feeling they never enjoyed at home." (Shepard, "Jennie Grossinger," p. 1,965).

The story of Grossinger's ends sadly. Some said the sparkle left when she died. Certainly, times and tastes changed with the advent of air conditioning, the acceptance of Jews into the social mainstream, changing eating habits, and the arrival of gambling in Atlantic City. The Grossinger heirs, Paul and Elaine Grossinger, tried to introduce gambling as did their rival Catskills hotel owners, but the New York State Legislature would not give permission. They finally sold the resort to a corporation for $9,000,000 that planned on renovating and reopening with a different focus, but it went bankrupt. Grossinger's closed its doors in 1986 after seventy-one years in business. Thousands worldwide remember their experiences there with fondness. The Jewish Federation/Valley Alliance put on a play on June 2000 called "Grossinger's . . . the Last Resort" starring many of the entertainers who began their careers there.

See also: Immigrant Businesswomen; Travel Industry

Further Reading
Drachman, Virginia G., p. 124–130.
Grossinger, Tania. *Growing Up at Grossinger's.*
Pomerantz, Joel. *Jennie and the Story of Grossinger's.*
Shepard, Richard F. "Jennie Grossinger Dies at 80 in Her Resort Home in Catskills."
Taub, Harold Jaediker. *Waldorf-in-the-Catskills; The Grossinger Legend.*

H

Haben, Mary Kay (1956–), Food Industry Executive

Mary Kay Haben is group vice president of Kraft Foods, North America and the president of the Kraft cheese, enhancers, and meals group that controls and is responsible for all of the activities of one of Kraft's largest groups. This level of power garnered her the number 33 spot on *Fortune*'s 2002 list of the most powerful women in corporate America.

After graduating from the University of Michigan with a degree in marketing in 1979, Haben joined Kraft Foods as an assistant product manager on Cracker Barrel Cheese. During the next few years, she worked on almost all the cheese products. In 1984 she became a category manager, focusing on business development and strategy. Five years later she was promoted to vice president of marketing and strategy for the refrigerated products group. She moved to the specialty products division and in 1992 became president of the Churny Cheese division. Four years later Haben was president of the pizza division, where she was involved with Tombstone and DiGiorno Pizza. During her tenure, sales increased 8 percent. She became an executive vice president in 1997, first of the enhancers division, then of Kraft Foods. In September 1998 she took on the additional responsibilities of the Kraft Cheese division and, in November 2000 joined the senior management committee. In February 2001, she attained her present position.

Haben, a self-confessed cheese fanatic, is said to be evangelical about her products and works on every one from developing the presentation through sales and placement. She is noted for her ability to mobilize a team quickly. She empowers front-line employees through support and encouragement, but then lets them do the job.

In 1988 *Advertising Age* called her one of the one hundred best and brightest women in advertising and marketing. Two years later *Savvy* listed her as one of forty women to watch. In 1992 she won the Kraft President's Award for Excellence, and in 1997 she was named *Brandweek*'s Marketer of the Year. She has chaired the University of Michigan Business School Board of Governors and has served on the board of directors of Junior Achievement. In November 2002 she was elected vice chair of the National Cheese Institute.

See also: Food Industry

Further Reading
Fusaro, Dave. "For the Love of Cheese."
Haben, Mary Kay. "Shattering the Glass Ceiling."
Thompson, Stephanie. "Mary Kay Haben."

Haircare Industry, *see* Beauty Industry

Hancock, Ellen (1943–), Electronics Industry Executive

In 2000 Ellen Hancock was ranked number 5 on the *Fortune* list of the most powerful women in business in the United States. She was then the president and CEO of Exodus Communications, the largest Web hosting company, with clients such as Yahoo, eBay, Priceline.com, Merrill Lynch, GeoCities, Lycos, and Hewlett-Packard. She has had a long and illustrious career, and at one time was the highest-ranking woman at IBM.

She was born in the Bronx, raised in Westchester County, New York, and attended Catholic schools before graduating from the College of New Rochelle with a BS in mathematics. She earned a doctorate in mathematics at Fordham and then joined IBM as a programmer. After a number of increasingly responsible positions, including vice president of communication programming, assistant group executive of systems development, president of the communications products division and, in 1992, senior vice president, a member of the corporate executive committee and of the IBM Worldwide Management Council, Hancock was caught in a management restructuring which significantly reduced her responsibilities. The press announcement said that she had decided to retire; in reality, she was fired after twenty-nine years at IBM.

In September of 1995 she was appointed one of three chief operating officers at National Semiconductor Corporation, responsible for the technological arena. The following year after a management reorganization, she followed her boss, Gil Amelio, to Apple Computer. This proved to be a challenge, for Apple was having major problems both in developing and then delivering their new systems. In July 1997 Amelio resigned after the board showed their dissatisfaction with the declining sales, and Steve Jobs took over again. He fired Hancock, the second very public firing she had had to endure. She almost decided to retire in earnest, but friends and colleagues talked her out of it, and she began job-hunting again.

In March 1998 she was hired as president of Exodus Communications, nine days before they went public. Six months later she was appointed CEO, while the former CEO and co-founder of the company became chairman of the board. It was a vote of confidence for her achievements, including huge growth in revenues quarter after quarter. By the end of 2000, there was still no profit, but revenues had increased by over 20 percent for seventeen straight quarters. Their clients included both dotcom companies such as Lycos and enterprise companies such as Sun Microsystems, Microsoft, and British Airways.

In 2001 the dotcom companies started dying. Exodus, which had built sales to $188 million, began to falter also because they sold to these companies. Orders were cancelled and profits plummeted, top officers resigned. By August Hancock tried to sell the company and failed. On September 5 she resigned, and the company later filed for bankruptcy. In April 2002 she agreed to serve as a special advisor to P-COM, a wireless telecommunications company. She is also a member of the company's board of advisors.

Hancock is known for the depth of her technological expertise and her no-nonsense approach. Fiercely ambitious, she has always stated her career goal is to be a CEO. She is also said to be generous with praise for her employees, which generates a great deal of loyalty. In 1992 she was listed in *Business Week's* top fifty women in business; in 1999 she was named one of the e.biz 25 by the same magazine. In November 2000 she was number 33 on *Upside Magazine's* Upside's Elite 100. She and her husband, a retired IBM executive, live in Connecticut and have no children. She has served on the board of directors of Aetna Life & Casualty, ROLM Co., and Colgate-Palmolive and as a trustee of Marist College and Santa Clara University. She is a member of the Committee of 200. A devout Catholic, one of her prized possessions is a photograph of herself with the Pope when she gave him an IBM ThinkPad laptop. She and her husband recently gave $5 million to the College of New Rochelle for a college center to be named for her parents.

See also: Information Technology Industry

Further Reading

Hua, Vanessa. "CEO Quits Santa Clara's Exodus Communications."

Kaplan, Karen. "Female CEO Describes View from the Top; Internet: Ellen Hancock of Exodus Says West Coast Entrepreneurial Culture Takes Some Getting Used to."

Leibovich, Mark. "Apple's Chief Technology Officer Faces Challenge of Her Life."

Lynch, Karen. "The Start Up and the Grown Up—a 30-Year IBM Veteran Ellen Hancock Gets Exodus Down to Business."

Handler, Ruth (1916–2002), Toy Executive, Prostheses Manufacturer

Ruth Handler, who co-founded Mattel with her husband, not only revolutionized the doll industry with her Barbie doll but also changed forever the way all toys are sold. After a radical mastectomy and legal problems with Mattel ending in her resignation, she invented an artificial breast that was a vast improvement on the available prostheses. Her new company was called Ruthan and the breast "Nearly Me."

She was born in Denver, the tenth child of Jewish Polish immigrants. Her father was a blacksmith, and her mother became ill shortly after her birth. She was raised by her eldest sister and her husband, owners of a drugstore where she worked from age ten, loving every minute. When she was sixteen, she met Elliot Handler, a poor art student, and they fell in love. She graduated from high school in 1934, went to the University of Denver to study pre-law, but left after two years to go to Los Angeles. She got a job working in the stenographer pool at Paramount Studios. Elliot followed six months later, and in 1938 they were married.

The following year they began their first business creating household items and jewelry from Lucite, then a new acrylic plastic. Her husband made the items, and she sold them during her lunch hour. In 1941 she had a daughter, Barbara, and in 1944, a son, Kenneth. Handler was a stay-at-home mother during those few years. The business was successful, but World War II rationing slowed the availability of Lucite. The three other partners refused to change the direction of the company, so in 1944 her husband left it. He and his friend, Harold Matson, formed a new company, Mattel, named after a combination of their names, and began by selling imported Japanese toys and making picture frames, doll furniture, toy pianos, and music boxes from the huge stocks of wartime scrap.

The men produced, she sold the items. After a year, Matson left because of ill health and sold his interest to them. Handler then took over marketing and managing, and Elliot was in charge of product design. By 1951 they employed 600 persons working in a 60,000 square foot building. In 1955 they branched into toy burp guns, and she suggested that they advertise on television. They sponsored the *Mickey Mouse Club* for an entire year, the first time a toy manufacturer had bought ads for that long. Most advertised only during the Christmas season. It was wildly successful; sales were $6 million that year.

Meanwhile, she had noticed how Barbara and her friends always played with adult women paper dolls and fantasized themselves as grown-ups with glamorous sophisticated clothes and interesting lives. During a visit to Switzerland in 1956, Handler saw a German doll, "Lilli," who was intended as an adult doll for men. She bought two, gave one to her daughter, who loved the ski outfit, and used one as a possible model for the doll she envisioned. Her doll was much more wholesome and softer, but the same size with breasts and a blonde ponytail. She named the doll Barbie in honor of her daughter, had a fashion designer create the clothes, and went off to the New York City Toy Show. The other toy manufacturers were unimpressed because they all knew that little girls only played with baby dolls.

She received very few orders from toy stores, but the public loved Barbie; the demand was much more than Mattel's production could fill. The following year, Ken made his debut in response to letters from little girls who thought Barbie needed a boyfriend. A sister, cousin, friends, and their boyfriends followed. By 1965 sales were $100 million; doubling by 1969 . Also in 1965 the company was listed on the New York Stock Exchange. With Handler as president and her husband still in charge of product design, the company continued to expand into different toys. It introduced Hot Wheels in 1968 with its own television show. The FCC eventually banned this type of show, but only for ten years.

> Ruth Handler, who co-founded Mattel with her husband Elliot, not only revolutionized the doll industry with her doll, Barbie, but also changed forever the way toys of all kinds are sold.

In the early 1970s, the company encountered fiscal problems due to its Mexican plant burning, a shipping strike that cut supplies from the Far East, and too rapid growth. It bought Ringling Brothers-Barnum and Bailey Combination Circus in 1971, a move Handler later called ill advised. In early 1973 the company posted a $32 million loss, and the Securities and Exchange Commission launched an investigation, later citing Ruth Handler and Seymour Rosenberg, her executive vice president and chief financial officer, for conspiracy, mail fraud, and making false financial statements in 1971, 1972, and 1973 in order to influence the stock price. She maintained her innocence, saying her attention was on a 1970 bout with breast cancer and a subsequent mastectomy. She also believed that the wrong people were indicted, but she pleaded no contest to the charges.

In 1978 the court fined her $57,000, gave her a suspended prison sentence of forty-one years plus 500 hours of charitable work annually for five years. They also ordered that the company be completely restructured with outside directors. She chose to work with diabetic children and took underprivileged children to their beach house for summer weekends. She resigned from Mattel in 1975; Elliot followed six months later. In 1980 they sold almost all their stock, around 12 percent of the company, for $18.5 million. She did help celebrate Barbie's thirty-fifth birthday in 1994, however, by touring toy stores all over the country. At that time, Barbie was available in 150 countries, and sales reached $1 billion. On Barbie's fortieth birthday, Handler rang the opening bell at the New York Stock Exchange.

After her mastectomy, she found that the available prostheses were horrible. She made an appointment with Peyton Massey, a craftsman who specialized in making artificial body parts, to see if he could devise a better fit. She was depressed after leaving Mattel, so she decided to go into the artificial breast business. She worked with Massey, developing a lightweight, naturally shaped prosthesis that could be mass produced in regular bra sizes for both right and left breasts. Known as the "Cadillac" of breast prostheses, it was made of liquid silicone enclosed in polyurethane with a rigid foam backing. Handler was a genius at promotion, appearing on talk shows and television interviews, sometimes opening her blouse and asking reporters to see if they could tell the difference. She only hired women, and the artificial breasts were sold only by trained fitters at $116 to $154 per piece. She toured the country, sending invitations to breast cancer patients in an area, held seminars in the stores, and gave fitting instructions to the clerks. By 1980 sales had passed $1 million. In 1991 after heart surgery, she sold the company to Kimberley Clark.

Handler and her husband revolutionized the toy business by changing the relationship between toy makers, retailers, and consumers. They were the first to market directly to their customers through the medium of television. Their genius was to realize the potential of television advertising and tie-ins, as well as the need for little girls to play grown-up. She in particular had an uncanny sense of potential trends and was known as a genius in business. She also had a reputation for being ambitious, aggressive, persistent, and blunt. She strongly believed in the potential of women in business, saying many times that the glass ceiling in her day was made of cement (Jeffrey, *Great American Businesswomen*, p. 45). She managed to balance her family and the company by always leaving work at 5:30 and, when the children were young, never talking about business until they were in bed.

Ruth Handler was named Woman of the Year by the *Los Angeles Times* in 1967, and both she and her husband were honored by the Toy Manufacturers Association for their contributions to the toy industry. She was named to the Inventors Hall of Fame in 1996 and the National Business Hall of Fame in 1997, was the first United Jewish Appeal Woman of Distinction, was the first female board member and vice president of the Toy Manufacturers Association, and first woman to serve on the Federal Reserve Board. She died in 2002 from complications from surgery.

See also: Inventors

Further Reading
Altman, p. 100–111.
Handler, Elliot. *The Impossible Really is Possible: The Story of Mattel.*
Handler, Ruth with Jacqueline Shannon. *Dream Doll: The Ruth Handler Story.*
Jeffrey, Laura. *Great American Businesswomen.*
Mesdag, Lisa Miller. "From Barbie Dolls to Real Life."

Harris, Carla A. (1961–), Financial Services Executive

Carla Harris, as head of private equity placement at Morgan Stanley Dean Witter, ranked number 48 on *Fortune*'s 2002 list of the most powerful black executives.

After graduating from Bishop Kenny High School in Jacksonville, Florida, Harris earned a magna cum laude undergraduate degree in economics from Harvard. During the summer of her sophomore year, she received a Sponsors for Educational Opportunity internship on Wall Street, discovering an interest in finance and later earning an MBA from Harvard. In 1987 she began working at Morgan Stanley Dean Witter in the mergers and acquisitions department, and four years later she was promoted to operations officer and syndicate deal captain in the equity markets division. In October 2000 Harris became managing director for equity transactions, responsible for the marketing and execution of new issue equity financing. She was the second African American woman to become a managing director at the company. Her areas of expertise are technology, media, telecommunications, transportation, industry, and healthcare. She has handled some of the company's biggest initial public offerings including UPS, Donna Karan, Martha Stewart Omnimedia, and Immunix Corporation. She is also chair of the private equity committee.

Harris says that she wants people to think of her as tough, smart, and hardworking. She is goal-oriented, writing down her goals at the beginning of each year. Because of her internship and an early supervisor who didn't know how to teach her, an important part of her work is mentoring and coaching younger colleagues.

Harris is dedicated to giving back to the community. She founded scholarships at Harvard and at Bishop Kenny High School and financially sponsors the Student/Sponsor Partnership program in New York City. She has served on the executive boards of Food for Survival of the New York Food Bank, the Manhattan Council of the Boy Scouts, and the Brooklyn Alumnae Chapter of the Delta Sigma Theta Sorority. She also has a successful second career as a gospel singer. She is the vice president and a member of the St. Charles Gospelite Choir in Harlem and recorded a CD, "Carla's First Christmas," the proceeds of which are slated for scholarships for Bishop Kenny High School and the St. Charles Borromeo Catholic School in the Bronx.

See also: African American Businesswomen; Finance Industry

Further Reading

Clarke, Caroline V. "Carla Harris Uses Her Prowess to Make Billion-Dollar Deals and Uplift Youth."

"Investment Banker/Singer's Debut Music CD 'Carla's First Christmas.'"

Scott, Matthew S. et al. "B.E. Wall St. All-Stars: From Investment Banking to Asset Management, These 50 MVPs Score Bit in the Financial Markets."

Hart, Patti S. (1956–), Telecommunications Executive

Under her maiden name of Patti S. Manuel, Patti S. Hart was on the 1998 *Fortune* list of the most powerful women in corporate America. At that time she was the president and CEO of Sprint's long distance division. Since then she married Milledge A. Hart and served as the CEO for two different information technology companies, Telocity and Excite@Home. The latter went bankrupt in September 2001.

One of five children, she was born in Chicago, where her father worked at the Ford manufacturing plant. She was partially raised by her grandmother, who passed down a strong work ethic to the children. Hart worked at odd jobs from an early age, earning money for luxuries. She graduated from Illinois State University with a degree in business administration, marketing, and economics.

Hart's career in the telecommunications industry began in 1979 with a sales job at GTE Corporation. In 1986 she moved to Sprint as the national account manager and was promoted several times until, in 1997, she became president of the Sprint business division. One year later she was named president and chief operating officer of the long distance division, the first woman at Sprint to run a division. In this position she was the number 3 executive at the company, responsible for all the operational functions of the division, which employed 17,000 people.

In June 1999 she joined Telocity as president and CEO with the goal of launching national broadband high-speed access to the Internet. She took the company public at $12 per share the following March, but by August the dotcom bubble had burst, and the stock had plummeted to $3.25. She did negotiate the sale of the company to Hughes Electronics Corporation, but at a greatly reduced price. In April 2001 she became the chairman and CEO of Excite@ Home, a company going through enormous losses with no cash and slowing online advertising revenues. She cut 380 jobs and tried to save the company or find another company willing to buy it. She asked At&T for backing, but they refused. In September 2001 the company filed for bankruptcy. She stated that she didn't have a true picture of just how deep the financial problems were when she was recruited to the position (Richtel, "Private Sector," p. 2).

Hart's management style is characterized by loving to solve problems. She was excited by the challenges of the Internet companies and saw the experience as a chance to learn. Her expertise is in telecommunications; finance is not her forte. She has a very strong work ethic and pays meticulous attention to detail. She is also skilled at building relationships with her employees.

She has served on the boards of Vantive Corporation, Earthlink, Mariner Networks, Premisys Communication, Plantronics, and Korn Ferry International. She is a member of the Committee of 200. She is married with a daughter.

See also: Information Technology Industry

Further Reading
Kopytoff, Verne. "Patti Hart; Hart at Home."
Richtel, Matt. "Private Sector; Crisis Control at Warp Speed."
"Telocity Names Former Sprint Executive Patti Manuel as CEO and President."

Haubegger, Christy (1968–), Magazine Publisher

In 1996 Christy Haubegger launched *Latina*, the first magazine aimed at bilingual and bicultural Hispanic women. She has been honored for that achievement many times, including by *Newsweek* in 2001, which called her one of the "Women of the New Century."

She was a Mexican American baby, adopted by white parents who always stressed the importance of her heritage and promoted a bilingual and bicultural life for her. When she was ten, she looked at the magazines in the grocery store and noticed none addressed who she was and what she looked like. Haubegger began to dream then of a magazine that reflected her. She graduated from the University of Texas at Austin with a degree in philosophy in 1989 and received a law degree from Stanford University in 1992, where she was president of the class and senior editor of the *Stanford Law Review*.

That year, with a Stanford classmate, she instigated her plan to publish a magazine aimed at Latinas. She took a part-time job doing legal research while she wrote a comprehensive 200-page business plan. They formed their own company, Allegre Enterprises, Inc., and raised $250,000. Haubegger walked one potential investor through the Mission District and pointed out which magazines the women were carrying. In 1996 it launched *Latina Magazine* in a joint venture with *Essence*. By August 1997 circulation was 200,000 through subscribers and newsstand sales; advertising sales were also good. The focus was on Hispanic culture, self-esteem, fashion, and inspirational articles about role models. *Latina* became a monthly magazine that summer.

In December 2000 Solera Capital bought the majority share of Latina Publications and changed the name to Latina Media Ventures, with plans to enter the integrated media market through television and music festivals. Total readership had soared to 1 million. Haubegger and Essence Communications stayed on as president and shareholders. In June 2001 she resigned as CEO and president but remained on the board as the founder, focusing on strategic initiatives, advertising, and brand development.

In February 2003 she joined Creative Artists Agency, a talent and literary agency, to advise on marketing to Hispanics. She remains active on *Latina*, however. Haubegger has been honored for her accomplishment. *Library Journal* called *Latina* one of the best new titles launched in 1996. Tom Brokaw profiled her on "NBC Nightly News" in 1997, as one of the most inspirational women of the year, and the New York State Federation of the Hispanic

Chamber of Commerce named her Business Woman of the Year. The following year, she was honored by the Hispanic Public Relations Association and the National Association of Sunday and Features Editors. In 1999 she was named to the American Advertising Federation's Hall of Achievement and the next year was the New York City Business Owner of the Year. The *New York Daily News* called *Latina* one of five magazines to watch in 2001, and *Adweek Magazine* listed it third in their list of hottest magazines. That January *Newsweek* named Haubegger one of their "Women of the New Century."

See also: Latina Businesswomen; Publishing Industry

Further Reading

"Creative Artists Agency Hires *Latina Magazine* Founder Christy Haubegger."

Quintanilla, Michael. "With *Latina,* Christy Haubegger Aims for Women Like Her—Bilingual, Bicultural and Underrated."

Ubinas, Helen. "Bringing Up Her Baby; Publisher Finds Growing Niche for *Latina Magazine.*"

Haughery, Margaret Gaffney (1814–1882), Baker, Philanthropist

When Margaret Haughery died, offices closed in New Orleans, stores were draped in black, and people lined the street to mourn the "Bread Lady of New Orleans." On July 9, 1884, a statue and a park on the corner of Camp and Prytania Streets were dedicated in her honor. In 1958 the mayor established a Margaret Haughery Day.

She was born in Ireland in 1814 and immigrated to Baltimore with her parents and two other siblings in 1818. After her parents died of yellow fever, neighbors took care of her. Later she began work as a domestic. In 1835 she married Charles Haughery. After moving to New Orleans because of his poor health, he decided that Ireland might be a healthier environment; however, he died shortly after arrival there, as did their baby daughter who stayed behind in New Orleans with Haughery, barely twenty years old.

She worked as a laundress in the new St. Charles Hotel across the street from the Sisters of Charity Poydras Orphan Asylum where she lived. With her savings, she bought two cows and began to peddle the milk on the city streets. By 1840 she had a dairy of over forty cows. Even at the beginning, she gave away more milk than she sold and was known to the people of New Orleans for her generosity. With her proceeds, she helped the Sisters of Charity finance a new orphanage, the New Orleans Female Orphanage Asylum, which opened that year, the first of eleven orphanages she founded. In June 1858 Haughery established a special asylum for infants and acquired the D'Aquim Bakery in payment of a debt. She gave up the dairy and turned the bakery into the first steam bakery in the south. It was very successful and soon she employed forty men, giving them hot lunches every day. She invented packaged crackers and had the city's largest export business.

Her philanthropy continued; she still sat outside the bakery, offering sympathy, counsel, or largesse to those who asked for help. During the Civil War she founded knitting groups, assisted with the free market for food and clothing, and aided soldiers from both sides. In the 1870s she established a Home for the Aged, giving $9,000 for repairs. Because she kept no records, being unable to read or write, no one knows how much money she made or gave away, but she left an estate of half a million dollars, most of which was left to ten charitable institutions of differing denominations. She is remembered as one of New Orleans' shrewdest businesspeople, and one of the most humble of human beings, disliking public acknowledgement of her many charities. Unlike Hetty Green, Margaret Haughery was not an accumulator of wealth; in fact, as soon as she made it she gave it away to her beloved orphanages and other worthy causes.

See also: Food Industry; Immigrant Businesswomen

Further Reading
Bird, Caroline, p. 83–85.
Strousse, Flora. *Margaret Haughery; Bread Woman of New Orleans.*
Widmer, Mary Lou. *Margaret, Friend of Orphans.*

Helmsley, Leona (1920–), Hotel Executive

Leona Helmsley, called "the Queen of Mean" by New York City newspapers in the 1980s, was the owner of vast real estate holdings in the city as well as a chain of luxury hotels. She inherited the estate from her husband Harry, a real estate mogul, after ten years marked by a flurry of lawsuits and, finally, a prison term for income tax evasion for her. Her company was the eighteenth-largest company on the 2000 *Working Woman* list of woman-owned companies.

She was born in Coney Island, New York, to a family plagued with financial problems that had moved five times by the time she was thirteen. She married in 1938, and one son was born in 1943. She divorced, married again, and was divorced after ten years of marriage. After working as a Chesterfield cigarette girl, she began selling residential real estate in the 1960s. In the early 1970s she met Harry Helmsley, who was already extremely successful in New York real estate and development, with holdings including the Empire State Building and many hotels. He had been married for over thirty years, but their romance blossomed and, after he obtained a divorce, they were married in 1972. He made her a partner in his real estate empire, giving her the hotels to manage. Together they embarked on a life of ostentation and extravagance that was accompanied by trying to wrest the maximum amount of profit from their holdings, even to the detriment of the properties and their employees.

Stories of their peccadilloes abound. In late 1984 they bought and renovated an estate in Greenwich but failed to pay the bills and illegally charged much of the work to their commercial properties. Many lawsuits followed, and then the state attorney general and the U.S. Attorney General's office launched investigations. The Helmsleys were indicted for extortion and income tax evasion. When her husband suffered a stroke, Leona took over the business. In July 1989 he was declared unfit to stand trial and she was acquitted of extortion but was convicted on thirty-three counts of tax evasion, sentenced to four years in jail, and fined $7.1 million for tax evasion and $2 million for restitution. She appealed, lost, and finally went to prison on April 16, 1992, at age seventy-one. The day she entered prison, her husband ordered the lights dimmed on the Empire State Building. Even while in prison, she was sued by a disgruntled employee.

At a later date, her husband died. When Leona was released, having served eighteen months of her sentence, she began selling off her real estate empire, piece by piece. Since then, she has been sued several times. By October 2003 she still owned six hotels. They have a lower occupancy rate than the city average, however, and have been dropped from ratings lists. These hotels are all that remain of her husband's real estate empire.

Helmsley was in charge of the hotels and insisted they be as luxurious as possible. As day-to-day manager, she cut costs, usually at the expense of her employees, and paid close attention to marketing and quality control. She had lunch in a different hotel every day to evaluate food quality. She was rude and abrasive to her employees, firing them at a whim. She was disliked by everyone, even her lawyer.

See also: Real Estate; Travel Industry

Further Reading
Hammer, Richard. *The Helmsleys: The Rise and Fall of Harry and Leona.*
Klemsrud, Judy. "Leona Helmsley: Power Becomes Her."
Sommerfield, Frank. "The Inevitable Fall."
Sontag, Deborah. "A 'Queen' in Seclusion Is Now a Lonely Widow."

Henretta, Deb (1961–), Baby Care Industry Executive

Deb Henretta is the president of global baby care at Procter & Gamble, a position that placed her in both the 2002 and 2003 *Fortune* lists of the most powerful women in corporate America. She has been mentioned as being on the track for CEO at the company.

She began working at P&G in 1984, marketing detergents Tide and Cheer. After working in several departments, she joined the baby care division in late 1999, with the responsibility of reviving the lagging sales of Pampers. She began using focus groups of mothers to find out their needs and was successful in improving sales. Her job expanded to include all aspects of baby care, and in 2000 she became the vice president of North American Baby-Care at the company. She introduced new Pampers that featured the Sesame Street Muppets and began a licensing program for diaper bags. In August 2001 she was promoted to president of global baby care and inaugurated a Web site, www.pampers.com, that gave advice on parenting. She also introduced Bibsters disposable bibs and Pampers Baby Stages of Development, a line based on the baby's development. The Pampers Perks program, which gave points for earning Fisher-Price toys on Pampers packages, was another marketing program. By 2003 she was running a $5.5 billion business.

Henretta is married with three children.

Further Reading
Nelson, Emily. "Bottom Line: Diaper Sales Sagging, P&G Thinks Young to Reposition Pampers—How to Sell Premium Brand in Penny-Pinching Times: Casting it as a Lifestyle—'Actually a Piece of Clothing.'"

High Tech Industry, *see* Information Technology Industry

Hinojosa de Balli, Rosa Maria (1752–1803), Rancher

Rosa Maria Hinojosa de Balli, also known as "La Patrona", was the first cattle queen of Texas. From 1790 to 1803, she turned a 55,000-acre, debt-ridden estate into a huge cattle ranch with double the land it had spanned previously. At the time of her death in 1803, her ranch encompassed land in several lower Rio Grande Valley counties, present-day Hidalgo, Cameron, Willacy, Starr, and Kenedy counties.

She was born in what is now Tamaulipas, Mexico, to Spanish aristocrats who were the first European settlers. Her father received an official appointment in Reynosa, so the family moved there and became one of the wealthy controlling families. She was educated in Reynosa, most probably by the parish priest. She married Jose Maria Balli, a captain of the militia and had three sons.

In 1776 her father and husband jointly applied for a large land grant in the La Feria tract. By the time it was approved in 1790, they had both died, and she inherited her husband's share, 55,000 acres, which came with a large debt. Over the next thirteen years, Hinojosa de Balli not only rid the estate of debt but also doubled the acreage through applying for grants in the name of her sons and herself. She also made extensive improvements to the land and bought large herds of cattle, horses, sheep, and goats. Her various ranches were territorial landmarks.

Rosa Maria Hinojosa de Balli, also known as "La Patrona," was the first cattle queen of Texas.

Hinojosa de Balli was a devout Catholic who built a chapel on the ranch and also endowed churches in Reynosa, Camargo, and Matamoros. One of her sons, also her business partner, was Padre Nicolas, for whom Padre Island was named. Another of her tracts is now Harlingen, Texas. The headquarters of her ranch was La Feria, which is now Florida County.

Today many of her descendents still live on land that was originally part of the ranch. She was the Spanish matriarch and was in complete control of her kingdom, keeping meticulous records. She was also known for her warmth and generosity. She was godmother to a number of the ranch children, lent money and tools to neighboring ranchers, kept money for them in her strongbox, and lent animals to her ranch hands to begin their own holdings. In her will, she cancelled all outstanding debts owed to her by her majordomo and several foremen. Two of her three sons died shortly after she did. She had one grandchild in whose name she had reregistered one of the tracts of land.

See also: Agriculture/Ranching; Latina Businesswomen

Further Reading
American Mother's Committee, p. 513.
Handbook of Texas Online.
Roots by the River.

Hispanic Businesswomen, *see* Latina Businesswomen

Hoffman, Ebba C. (1911–1999), Office Supplies Manufacturer

When Ebba Hoffman's husband died in 1955, she took over his company, Smead Manufacturing, and turned it into what is now one of the top fifty woman-owned companies in the United States. She was forty-five with two children, and she ran the company for forty-four years.

In 1955 Smead Manufacturing, an office supplies manufacturer, was a struggling, debt-ridden company that made specialized file folders for courtrooms. Hoffman's husband had not been president long when he died of a heart attack. Rather than sell the company, she took it over and expanded into more conventional filing folders as well as envelopes and other office supplies. She also changed the boxes from brown to plaid, now a trademark of the company. After two years in college, her daughter began working full-time in the credit department. Her son worked in manufacturing until he died in 1986.

Hoffman had an eighth-grade education but a wealth of both common and people sense. Customer relations was of great importance to her, and in fact when the large superstores, Office Max and Office Depot, began to buy out the small stores, these satisfied customers recommended Smead as a supplier.

The advent of the superstores did cut into profits because they demanded large discounts. Hoffman streamlined operations, increased efficiency, laid off some part-time workers, stopped new hires, and invested in the latest technology in the plants.

She and her daughter, Sharon Avent, who had become the executive vice president and shared management, created a new product, Smeadlink, an integrated software package that kept track of a variety of kinds of files. By 1996 when the company celebrated its ninetieth anniversary, sales were $295,000,000, and it had 2,000 employees with six manufacturing plants.

From the beginning, Hoffman's management style was focused on the prevention and/or correction of customer complaints. She also kept the door open to her employees. She was a firm believer in giving back more than she received both at work and in the community.

In July 1998 Avent was named to succeed her mother as president and CEO. Her mother was at the board meeting, and the succession took place with her blessing. On February 8, 1999, Hoffman died from pneumonia. In her forty-three-year tenure as president of Smead Manufacturing, she focused on customer satisfaction, taking the company from $4 million in sales with 350 employees to $315 million in sales with 2,500 employees. She was named "Boss of the Year" by the U.S. Chamber of Commerce and, in 1977, was the first woman inducted into the Minnesota Business Hall of Fame.

See also: Avent, Sharon Hoffman; Late Bloomers

Further Reading

"Betting on Farm-Girl Grit; Smead's Ebba Hoffman."

Palmer, Rosemary. *Mrs. Ebba C. Hoffman: Celebrating 40 Years of Leadership and Dedication to the Smead Manufacturing Company.*

Wascoe, Dan Jr. "Ebba C. Hoffman, Company Dies."

Holden, Betsy D. (1957–), Food Industry Executive

As co-CEO of Kraft Foods, Betsy Holden is one of the most prominent executives in the food industry and is responsible for Kraft's reputation as a woman-friendly company. She has been on *Fortune*'s list of the most powerful businesswomen in the United States since 2000. When she assumed her position, she was one of three women heading Fortune 500 companies.

She was born in Texas and has one brother. Her father was a surgeon. During high school she was a cheerleader and student council member. She received a BA in education from Duke University, graduating summa cum laude. After a brief stint as a fourth grade teacher, she earned an MA in education from Northwestern and then an MBA from their Kellogg School of Management in 1982. She concentrated in marketing and finance and was valedictorian of her class. She met her scientist husband Arthur during her MBA studies. They have a son and a daughter.

Holden joined General Foods in 1982 as an associate product manager of the desserts division. In 1985 General Foods merged with Kraft, and she took over the pizza and cheese division. In 1990 she was promoted to vice president of new product development and strategy, responsible for one of the most successful new brand launches in Kraft's history, Di Giorno Pizza. She managed a direct-delivery sales force, the only one at the company. From 1995 to 1997 she was executive vice president of Kraft Foods North America and general manager of the Kraft Cheese Division. Cheese sales grew 18.5 percent during her tenure; she became known as the "cheese whiz."

From 1998 to 2000 she was the executive vice president of operations for Kraft Foods North America, responsible for technology, procurement, e-commerce, and marketing. She cut costs, focused on quality, and developed one hundred new products. In May she was named director and co-CEO of Kraft Foods, Inc. and president and CEO of Kraft Foods North America. In this position, she runs Kraft's domestic food industry and chairs the management committee. She oversaw the buyout of Nabisco with its $7 billion in sales and was responsible for its smooth integration. Since then she has looked for growth in health food products as well as in snacks and drinks. She also wishes to sell more products to the growing ethnic population in the country. In 2003 the company started to place a new emphasis on fighting obesity.

Holden is known for her teamwork, strong leadership abilities, and her talent in revitalizing old products. She has a passion for the food business and insight into the consumer. She has been responsible for marketing a variety of products but is also known for the breadth of her management experience. One of her management goals is to make Kraft more welcoming to women and ethnic minorities. In 2002 eight of the top managers were women; four were African American.

Holden was number 5 on *Working Mother's* 2001 list of *Working Mother* champions. She has served on the boards of Tupperware, the *Tribune*, the Grocery Manufacturers Association, Evanston Northwestern Hospital, and the Ravinia Music Festival. She is president of Off the Street Club and on the advisory board of the Kellogg Graduate School of Management at Northwestern. To commemorate Kraft's centennial year, the company gave $1 million in annual support to fund innovative library and parks services for high-need neighborhoods in Chicago, a public-private partnership between Kraft Great Kids and Mayor Daley's KidStart.

See also: Food Industry

Further Reading

Barboza, David. "Private Sector; Teacher Cheerleader and CEO."
Cohen, Deborah L. "Kraft CEO is Ready to Enter Food Fray."
Edgecliffe-Johnson, Andrew. "Two Brains May be Better than One Big Cheese."

Homeworkers, *see* Flexible Work Arrangements

Hopkins, Deborah C. (1955–), Banking Executive

Deborah Hopkins is head of corporate strategy at Citigroup; however, she earned her places on *Fortune*'s 1999 and 2000 lists of the most powerful women in corporate America while CFO and senior vice president of Boeing and CFO and executive vice president of Lucent.

She was born in Milwaukee, went to high school in Detroit, and attended college at Michigan State, planning to go into advertising. After her family asked her to return to help in the family business, she finished at Walsh College in Troy, Michigan, in 1977 with a BA in accounting and finance. Her mother wrote the weekly social column for the *Birmingham-Bloomfield Eccentric* newspaper, and Hopkins accompanied her as photographer, meeting many of the automobile executives. She credits her mother for her self-confidence and belief that she can succeed at any job.

She began her career at First National Bank of Detroit, then worked five years at Ford as the only woman in finance. In 1982 she joined Unisys as the vice president of corporate business analysis. Her restructuring plan helped save Unisys when it had financial trouble. She also founded its diversity council and executive woman's group. In 1995 Hopkins joined General Motors as the chief financial officer of GM Europe, becoming vice president and CFO in 1997. In December 1998 she joined Boeing as CFO and senior vice president, cleaning up the balance sheet and its reputation with investors, after the first loss in fifty years. She was the top woman executive and developed an extensive business education program for the executives and employees. One year after she reorganized the financial operations, the stock was up 40 percent.

In April 2000 Lucent enticed her away to be CFO and executive vice president. Hopkins accepted because she preferred the technology industry and liked the challenge of Lucent's need for a turnaround. She was responsible for the executive management and oversight of all financial operations as well as, later, developing the information systems infrastructure. The company did not respond well to her treatment, however, and the CEO was forced to resign. In May 2001 she was fired after only one year. She joined Marakon Associates, an international consulting firm, as senior partner and in January, 2003 took her present position at Citigroup, where she will take part in restructuring the company's research and investment banking business.

Hopkins is known as "Hurricane Debby" because of her high energy and take-charge style. She has been described as a fearless straight-talker with a backbone of steel. Her ability to analyze complex financial problems and offer successful solutions has earned her a reputation as a change maker. She also has masterful, if blunt, communication skills and a pleasant personality. She married while at Ford, had two children, then divorced, and remarried a man with three adult children in Great Britain. Her second husband, David, is retired from General Motors and is a stay-at-home dad.

Hopkins has served on the board of directors of DuPont and the board of trustees of Walsh College. She won the Pinnacle of Excellence Award from Unisys and the Distinguished Alumni Award from the Walsh College Alumni association. *Money* named her one of the fifty smartest women in the money business in 2000, and *Business Week* called her a person to watch in international business in 2001. She is a trustee for the Committee for Economic Development.

See also: Accounting; Banking

Further Reading
"Getting Boeing to Fly Right."
Green, Leslie. "Hopkins Credits Walsh College for Her Success."
Sellers, Patricia. "The 50 Most Powerful Women in Business," 2000, p. 130–134, 147–148, 156.

Hospitality Industry, *see* Travel Industry

Hotel Industry, *see* Travel Industry

House, Pat (1954–), Software Executive

Pat House is the vice chairman of Siebel Systems which she co-founded with Tom Siebel. She ranked number 26 on the 2000 *Fortune* list of the most powerful women in corporate America.

She graduated from Western Michigan University with a BA in education. After holding a variety of managerial and executive positions in Verbatim Corporation, Frame Technology Corporation, and Oracle Corporation, House and fellow employee Tom Seibel decided to found their own application-software company. She is the executive vice president of marketing, handling 647 alliances with IBM, Compaq, and other companies. She was offered the chief operating officer position but decided not to accept because she loves marketing. The company is now the leading provider of e-business applications software, which enables multi-channel sales, marketing, and customer service systems to be deployed over the Web, call centers, field, reseller channels, and a variety of networks.

In 2000 House and Seibel wrote a book detailing how to decide if the Internet fits into a business. Reviews of the book lauded their clear observations. She has served on the board of Levi Strauss.

See also: Information Technology Industry

Further Reading
"Levi Strauss & Co. Names Pat House to Board of Directors."
Siebel, Thomas M. and Pat House. *Cyber Rules: Strategies for Excelling at E-Business.*

Howard, Agnes Hodgkinson (1912–), Rancher

Agnes Howard, a Sioux Indian, parlayed 160 acres of land on the South Dakota Standing Rock Indian Reservation into the largest individually run ranch on the reservation.

Born to a British father and an American Indian-German mother, she was legally a Sioux Indian and, as such, received 160 acres of land near the Grand River in South Dakota, a gift of the U.S. government. As part of the Homesteading Act, every child registered with the tribe did so at that time. Her father was a sign painter by trade but ranched, then tried farming but returned to ranching when the farm failed. She was the seventh of nine children, six girls and three boys. Howard attended the girls' Indian school in Bismarck but came back to South Dakota to go to high school. After graduating from Ponca City Business College in Oklahoma, where she lived with a sister, she held a variety of jobs in Oklahoma.

In 1940 she married J. Dan Howard who joined the navy the next year. During World War II Howard and her youngest sister lived and worked together in Oklahoma and then Wichita, Kansas. Eventually, she got a job with the Bureau of Indian Affairs in North Dakota. When her husband returned, they began to consider cattle ranching. She had kept her land although her brothers and sisters sold theirs for around $2 per acre. After much discussion, they sold his land and bought a car.

In 1952 they began their ranch on her land with a loan from the tribe, leasing four sections of unimproved range, purchasing twenty-eight head of Hereford heifers and one bull from the reservation cattle pool, and building a two-room house. The first year there were twenty-seven calves. Howard continued working, commuting one hundred miles every weekend and living on $20 per week, while her husband ran the ranch. By 1955 they had paid off all their loans, bought more cattle, and added more land. After five years, they owned one hundred cattle. In 1964 they finally installed indoor plumbing. Her husband, who was more interested in Indian political affairs than ranching, eventually became tribal chairman, so Howard decided to quit her job and run the ranch. He died in the late 1960s.

She hired a foreman and continued to improve the ranch, building a barn, corrals, a new bunkhouse, and three new stock wells. Howard also planted 158 acres of alfalfa. As of 1976 she owned 800 acres of land and leased 11,490 more. This supported 250 commercial cow/calf pairs and fourteen bulls. It was the largest ranch on the reservation.

See also: Agriculture/Ranching; American Indian Businesswomen

Further Reading

Adams, David J. "Agnes Howard—A Woman Meeting the Challenges of Today's Ranching."

"Indian Ingenuity: Agnes Howard." In Rich-McCoy, Lois, p. 189–206.

Hubbard, Sonja Y. (1961–), Convenience Store Executive

Sonja Hubbard is the CEO of E-Z Mart Convenience Stores, Inc. In 2001 the company was number 27 on the *Working Woman* list of the top 500 woman-owned companies. After her father's death in a 1998 airplane crash, Hubbard, her mother, and her sister became the three owners of the company. Her mother, FaEllen Yates, is the chairman of the board while her sister, Stacy Floyd, is the CFO.

She was born in Oklahoma City and graduated from the University of Arkansas in 1985. Her father had founded E-Z Mart in 1970 with the first convenience store in Nashville, Arkansas. By 1992 there were 297 stores in Arkansas, Louisiana, Texas, Kansas, and Oklahoma. On his death, the three women inherited about 400 stores with sales of $475 million.

After Hubbard took over as president and CEO, the company acquired the Stax convenience stores in Arkansas and Oklahoma as well as many others. It also installed video-at-the-pump and partnered with Orion in branded fast foods and with TeleCheckServices for electronic-check services. By May 2000 E-Z Mart was the nation's largest independently owned convenience store chain. It is also the sixth largest privately held company in Arkansas. On *Forbes's* list of the top 500 private companies, E-Z Mart is number 465.

The Hubbard family is one of Arkansas' wealthiest families with an estimated fortune of $135 million in 2000. Hubbard has served on the boards of Fowler Equipment Company and Tie Way Transport and as president and CEO of Young Oil Company and Yates Vending Company. She won the Arkansas Society of Certified Public Accountants Outstanding CPA in Business and Industry Award in 1999 and 2000. In December 2001 she was elected to the board of the National Association of Convenience Stores.

See also: Food Industry

Further Reading
"Arkansas Business Rankings: Wealthiest Arkansas Families."
www.e-zmart.com

Hudson, Dawn (1958–), Beverage Industry Executive

Dawn Hudson is the president of Pepsi-Cola North America, a $3.4 billion division of the company. *Fortune* ranked her number 50 on its 2003 list of the most powerful businesswomen in the United States.

She grew up in Winchester, Massachusetts, the eldest of three daughters to parents who were in law and banking. After earning a degree in English and economics from Dartmouth College, she took a job in their fund-raising office. In 1979 Hudson began her career in advertising as the product manager for Clairol at Compton Advertising. In 1983 she joined Tatham-Laird & Kudner, becoming a partner in 1986. That September she was recruited to DDB Needham Worldwide as the management representative heading the Kraft account. She became the managing partner at DDB Chicago, with accounts of Helene Curtis, Dial, and Frito-Lay, and moved to New York City as an executive managing partner in 1994. Two years later she was recruited to DMB&B as the managing director of the agency's flagship office. That October, however, Hudson was persuaded to join Frito-Lay in the new position of executive vice president of sales and marketing.

In May 1998 she went to Pepsi to head new ventures and partnerships, such as one with Starbucks. In a re-organization later that year, she became the senior vice president of marketing, one of the top five executives in the company, responsible for brand strategy, advertising, product innovation, consumer research, and in-channel and cross-marketing activities. In January 1999 her department created a new slogan after months of brainstorming, formal research, and consumer testing: "the joy of cola," tying in with the *Star Wars—Episode I* release. The next year she began a new campaign, "the joy of Pepsi," with advertising featuring Britney Spears and the launch of two new products, Mountain Dew Red and Pepsi Twist. In June 2002 she was named to her present position.

Hudson's greatest strength is her ability to focus advertising campaigns based on industry research. A strategic thinker, she is adept at working with clients as well as the creative team. Being absolutely attuned to the marketplace, she has developed an effective program designed to produce sales growth.

She has served on the board of Lowe's Companies, Inc. and has chaired the Association of National Advertisers. She has been named to *Advertising Age*'s "Power 50" list twice. Hudson and her husband, Bruce Beach, president of an executive search firm have two daughters.

See also: Food Industry

Further Reading
Hays, Constance L. "Private Sector; Bridging a 'Generation Next' Gap."
"PepsiCo Inc. Announces Executive Appointments for New Division."
"Pepsi's Dawn Hudson: Concentrating on What Consumers Want."

Hughes, Catherine L. (1948–), Radio Executive

Cathy Hughes is founder and owner of Radio One, the largest African American radio broadcasting company in the United States. Beginning with one station in 1980, it is now the tenth-largest radio broadcasting company, growing to forty-nine stations in nineteen major African American markets with approximately 9 million listeners. In 1999 she took the company public, becoming the first African American woman to own a publicly traded company. Radio One reached number 29 on the *Black Enterprise* list of African American-owned companies in the United States. By 2003 Radio One was the country's seventh-largest radio broadcasting company, and was 140 on the 2001 *Working Woman* list of the country's top woman-owned companies.

She was born in Omaha, Nebraska, the oldest of four children. Her father, the first African American to earn an accounting degree from Creighton University, founded an African American boarding school that still operates. Her mother was a nurse who had played trombone in an all-girl orchestra. The family lived in an Omaha public housing project. Hughes adored radio and received her first transistor when she was nine. She was the first African American girl to attend the Duchesne Academy of the Sacred Heart, a Catholic girls school. However, at sixteen she became pregnant, dropped out of school, married Alfred Liggins, and had their son. They soon divorced, and she finished high school and studied business administration at Creighton University.

Hughes began her radio career in college at the campus radio station. In 1969 she transferred to the University of Nebraska at Omaha. At KHOW, the African American owned radio station, she did every job and learned about the profession. In 1971 Howard University in Washington D.C. asked her to lecture in its communication department. Although she had not yet graduated, she felt compelled to seize the opportunity. Two years later she was hired as sales manager at SHUR-FM, the Howard campus radio station. In 1975 she became its general manager and vice president, the first woman at that level in Washington

> In 1999, Catherine Hughes took Radio One public, making her the first African American woman to own a publicly traded company.

D.C. There she created her now-famous late-night format, *Quiet Storm*, that was soon copied nationwide. With five uninterrupted hours of love ballads, it is recognized as the main reason the station's advertising revenue increased from $300,000 to $3.5 million.

In 1979 she married Dewey Hughes, and they bought WOL, a small dying AM radio station, with $1 million from a minority investment group and $500,000 from Chemical Bank. After thirty-two bankers had turned her down, the thirty-third, a Puerto Rican woman with one week on the job, agreed to the loan. Shortly after the sale was completed in 1980, Hughes's husband decided to move to California, and they divorced. She bought out his share, $950,000, by giving up everything she owned, and named her company Radio One. For a while she and her son lived in the station, an old run-down trailer attached to a sidewalk glass booth in an African American neighborhood.

Here she began her famous talk show, *The Cathy Hughes Show*, with the goal of informing and empowering African Americans. Again, she pioneered the format: It was the first radio program that addressed the concerns of the African American community. She was expressive and passionate about her community, covering all the city's controversial events. In 1986 she led a protest against the *Washington Post* for printing a picture of a murder suspect who was an African American rap artist. In 1990 she raised money to pay Mayor Marion Barry's lawyers.

For the first five years Hughes built up her listener pool but lost money, finally showing a profit in 1986. Her son, Alfred Liggins, who was helping with the business, thought they needed an FM signal, so in 1987 she obtained $4 million from a minority venture capital fund and $5 million from a bank to buy WMMJ-FM. After the bankers insisted the station appeal to white audiences, ratings took a nosedive. Eighteen months later she instituted black urban formats, and ratings went up.

In 1989 she handed over the president and CEO positions to her son; he runs the day-to-day operations while she sets company policy, oversees accountability, and recruits and hires people. She also kept *The Cathy Hughes Show* running until 1995. In 1997 she began Music One, a gospel recording company. She and her son both worked at expanding the company, buying more stations in Washington, Baltimore, Detroit, and other cities with large African American populations.

Their strategy is to buy underperforming stations then attract African American listeners by using formats of rap, hip-hop, and talk programs. By the end of 1999 the company owned twenty-five stations. That May they took it public, raising $172 million in the IPO, which was used to pay off debts and buy additional stations. At that time the company had revenues of $46.1 million, earnings of $841,000, and 454 employees. Its next three stock offerings freed them of debt. Hughes and her son now own 54 percent of the stock in the country's tenth-largest radio company. It has evolved from an intensely community-oriented organization into a national company. Some of the local appeal has been lost in the expansion, although it does continue to serve the African American community; however, the days of the glass booth on the sidewalk are over.

Hughes' mission has always been to "stand up for those who don't have a voice" (www.radio-one.com). Over the years she has passionately championed

African American causes as well as equal pay for women. Her company has always been community-oriented, raising money for many worthy causes. She is known for being idiosyncratic, charming, powerful, and combative. Her natural empathy toward those suffering from injustice empowered her as the voice of the African American community. Many of her opinions have been controversial, but she has always been willing to take risks and speak out.

Hughes has earned many awards, including an honorary doctorate from Sojourner-Douglass College, the Trumpet Award from Turner Broadcasting, the 1997 Dow Jones/*Our World News* Award for Entrepreneurial Achievement, the 1998 People's Champion Award from the National Black Media Coalition, Entrepreneur of the Year in 1998 from the National Black Chamber of Commerce, an award in 1999 from One Hundred Black Men, Inc., and the Seventh Congressional Humanitarian Award. She was inducted into the Maryland Business Hall of Fame in 2000, the same year that Radio One was the *Black Enterprise* Company of the Year. She was the winner of the 1998 Lifetime Achievement Award from the Washington radio community area broadcasters. In 2000 she was honored at a party, "Divas Without Attitude," that celebrated her successful IPO. One hundred African American women and one hundred white women attended; the only men were the servers. In 2001 she was named one of the 50 greatest women in radio and television by American Women in Radio and Television, won the Jesse Louis Jackson Economic Empowerment Award, and was appointed to the Florida A&M College Board by Governor Jeb Bush. After September 11, Radio One sponsored a nationwide blood drive and featured an original composition, "Psalm 23." In March 200, she received the Lifetime Achievement Award from the National Association of Black Owned Broadcasters.

See also: African American Businesswomen; Broadcasting Industry

Further Reading
Clarke, Robyn D. "High-Frequency Profits."
"Hughes, Cathy." *Current Biography* (February 2000): 33–38.
Noguchi, Yuki. "The Money of Color: Built on High-Wattage Black Advocacy, Radio One Is Turning Its Dial to the Bottom Line."
www.radio-one.com

Hulman, Mary Fendrich (1905–1998), Car Racing Executive
George, Mari Hulman (1956–), Car Racing Executive

Mary Fendrich Hulman owned the Indianapolis Motor Speedway Corporation from 1977, when her husband died, until her death in 1998 when her daughter, Mari Hulman George, took over. The company was on *Working Woman's* list of the top woman-owned companies in 1999 and 2000. Hulman's husband, Tony, purchased the derelict race speedway in 1945 from the World

War I flying hero, Eddie Rickenbacker, for $750,000. He turned it into the home of one of the most famous and prestigious car races and largest spectator event in the world, the Indianapolis 500, held every Memorial Day.

Hulman was born in Evansville, Indiana, to a cigar company heir and his wife. She married in 1926. Her husband came from a wealthy family who had made their money in baking powder. He embarked on a many-sided career: the wholesale grocery business, bottling plants, breweries, television and radio, cable television, and real estate. Together they created the Hulman Foundation. He died in 1977 from emphysema.

Hulman opposed his purchase of the speedway at first, thinking it a poor investment and a noisy dirty sport, but grew to love it. When he died, she became chairman of the board and, for twenty years, issued the famous command, "Gentlemen, start your engines." In 1978, 1979, and since 1992, it changed to "Lady and gentlemen, start your engines." In 1997 she was inducted into the Speedway Hall of Fame.

She was a generous philanthropist, giving $3.5 million to the Indianapolis Museum of Art, $2 million to Indiana State University, $1.1 million to St. Mary-of-the-Woods College to establish the Mari Hulman George School of Equine Studies, and $500,000 for the Mary Fendrich Hulman Hall of the Arts and Sciences. She was the first woman on the boards of the Rose-Hulman Institute of Technology and the Terre Haute First National Bank. She received an honorary doctorate from the Rose-Hulman Institute in 1994.

Her daughter, Mari Hulman George, was born in 1956 and became a widow with four children. She was chairman of the board in 1988 and named her son, Anton George, as president of the company in 1990. He was a professional race-car driver. She stayed as executive vice president. In 1995 she took over as owner from her ailing mother and, in 1997, began starting the race. She has been on the *Forbes* 400 list of the richest people in the United States since 1997. Like her mother, she is a philanthropist. In 1980 she inaugurated Arnold Day, named after the family pet pig, an annual benefit for the Indianapolis Special Olympics attended by over 4,000. She gave $2.7 million to Purdue and Indiana University in 2000 for their joint paralysis research.

Further Reading
Herman, Steve. "Woman Who Issued Command 'Gentlemen, Start Your Engines,' Dies."
Newcomb, Peter. "High-Octane Octogenarian."
www.mybrickyard.com

Human Resources Management

Human resources management is responsible for the people in an organization. The human resources department has seven major functions: staffing, performance appraisal, compensation and benefits, training and development, employee and labor relations, safety and health, and human resource research. Research includes record keeping, maintaining the history of the organization, tracking a variety of personnel and workplace issues, and gathering statistics on the demographic characteristics of employees.

As businesses became more complex in the late nineteenth century, the new field of employment management emerged. After World War I, it became known as personnel management. It seemed a natural fit for women because of their reputation for sensitivity and tact and experience in social work. Many women were promoted into personnel from clerical work. However, by the 1920s, most large departments were headed by men, with women subordinates specializing in one or more functions.

During the 1980s the name changed again, to human resources management. Women were still attracted to it because of the opportunities for service. However, jobs in human resources are staff jobs with no real responsibility for the profit and loss. Therefore, these jobs rarely lead to top management positions.

Further Reading

"Human Resources Managers." In Dorothy Schneider and Carl J. Schneider, p. 125–126.

Jahn, Christine. "Human Resource Management." In Kaliski, p. 445–449.

Husbands/Fathers

As the possibilities for women in business and the workplace are changing, so too are the roles of husbands and fathers. For women executives, the traditional role of the corporate wife has been lost. In the 1950s and, in the majority of cases today, the male executive "got the title, the boardroom battles, the ulcer, while the corporate wife planned the dinner parties, kept house in fitting style, dropped old friends to keep pace with his rising social requirements, traveled at the drop of a hat . . . humanized his image . . . listened, privately advised and supported [him] (Walsh, Mary Williams, "For Women at the Top" p. 3.1).

In the international business world or at a conference, the corporate wife's role is to talk to the other wives, gather intelligence, listen to problems and sort out their importance, and make the husband look caring. She often helps her husband with names and relatives of the people he will meet and can devote herself to making things comfortable for him. Executive women, although many have retired husbands who travel with them, do most of these chores themselves. The husbands share, probably give advice, and act as sounding boards, but the domestic and feminine side of the corporate wife is still the female role. Husbands of these high-powered women have taken to calling themselves "accompanying spouses."

Another trend is the stay-at-home dad or househusband, or domestic engineer. The Bureau of Census, in 2003, estimated 105,000 stay-at-home dads in the United States, based on its definition of primary care provider: a married father with children under fifteen who is not in the labor force and whose wife works. It excludes men who are entrepreneurs or who work part-time or at home, or who are divorced with children, so the total is probably considerably understated. Others estimate the true number as between 2 and 2.5 million fathers who take care of the children. This has happened for several reasons: the wife earns more, the couple has decided that one should stay home, the husband has lost his job or been laid off.

See also: Childcare; Work/Life Balance

Further Reading

Frank, Robert. *Parenting Partners: How to Encourage Dads to Participate in the Daily Lives of Their Children.*

Gill, Libby. *Stay-at-Home Dads: The Essential Guide to Creating the New Family.*

Kissell, Margo Rutledge. "Mr. Mom . . ."

Morris, Betsy. "Trophy Husbands."

Walsh, Mary Williams. "For Women at the Top, Something Is Missing: Social, Wifely Support."

I

Marian and Michael Ilitch built their one-store pizza takeout business into an empire that rivaled Domino's for the number 2 spot in pizza franchises. With 4,700 stores, 20 percent company owned and the rest franchises, Little Caesar's has been at or near the top of the *Working Woman* list of woman-owned businesses since the list's inception in 1992. Ilitch takes care of the financial side, and her husband is responsible for marketing and products in the co-owned company. It has grown into a sports empire as well, owning the Detroit Red Wings hockey team, the Detroit Tigers baseball team, the Detroit Rockers soccer team, as well as the arenas where they play. In March 1999 all their interests were under Ilitch Ventures, Inc., which has also invested millions in downtown Detroit by renovating the Detroit Fox Theatre and other buildings.

Ilitch grew up in Michigan and attended Dearborn Junior College. She met her future husband on a blind date in 1954 when she was an airline reservation clerk for Delta Airlines and he was playing baseball for the Detroit Tigers farm team. Both children of Macedonian immigrants, they married in 1955. His baseball career was plagued by injuries; during one episode with a broken ankle, he made pizzas for a living. After a brief, unsuccessful stint in the majors, he gave up baseball. After he tried the cement and awning businesses, the couple opened their first Little Caesar's restaurant in a strip mall in Garden City, Michigan, in 1959. It was takeout only: pizza, fried shrimp, fish & chips, and roasted chicken. One large pizza with pepperoni and cheese cost $2.39. Their timing was perfect. It was the beginning of the strip-mall boom, and the Ilitch emphasis on takeout and discounted prices was as popular as pizza. Their first franchise (and fourth store) opened in 1962 in Warren, Michigan.

From the beginning, Ilitch oversaw the finances, although she had taken only one high-school accounting class. Her husband made pizza and did the marketing. For the first ten years, the business expanded slowly. From 1971 to 1984, however, the number of stores jumped from 100 to 500. By 1986 that number doubled, and since then 3,400 stores have been added. It was in 1974 that Michael Ilitch conceived of his now famous Pizza! Pizza! television ads, in which he starred, offering two-for-one pizzas. At this time women were entering the workforce in droves and needed a fast and easy dinner option. Little Caesar's low prices and eye-catching ads made pizza seem the perfect choice, especially for a large family.

The couple also expanded into other ventures, in 1982 buying the financially troubled Detroit Red Wings. The resulting turnaround culminated in Stanley Cup victories in 1997 and 2002. At the same time they bought its management company, Olympia Entertainment, and embarked on a crusade to revive downtown Detroit. The acquisition and restoration of the historic 5,000-seat Fox Theatre eventually adding shops and restaurants, and the 1993 purchase of the Detroit Tigers and the Detroit Rockers, an indoor soccer team, added to the plan. They moved their headquarters into the Olympia Entertainment office building. As usual, while he conceived entrepreneurial ideas, she watched the bottom line and was responsible for financial planning. Since their investment into Detroit's rebirth, the downtown theater district is thriving.

The company management style is down-to-earth, still mom-and-pop. He tests new recipes; she looks at each store's income statements. The corporate culture is that of a small family business. Ilitch feels that the employees are her family. Staff turnover is low, and advancement from within is important. In 1996 she began a subsidized daycare center for employees' children. In 2000 the couple turned the day-to-day management over to their daughter Denise and son Chris. They now focus their efforts on long-term projects.

In 1987 Little Caesar's was named "the best pizza value in America" by *Restaurant & Institutions* magazine, the first of ten such awards. Ilitch was given the Pacesetter Award and named the 1988 Michiganian of the Year. In 1990 she won the Preservation Award from the National Trust for Historic Preservation. The company's advertising campaign was named the most popular television ad in America in 1992. In 1995 President Clinton invited her to a special CEO luncheon at the White House. The company donated $7 million to build the Sam and Mitra Bayoff Hospice Home, which was named for her parents. In 2003 according to *Women's Money Magazine*, Marian Ilitch was the second richest woman with a self-made fortune in the United States.

See also: Food Industry

Further Reading

Hallett, Anthony and Diane Hallett. *Entrepreneur Magazine Encyclopedia of Entrepreneurs*, p. 277–278.

Kapner, Suzanne. "Marian and Michael Ilitch: Secretary-Treasurer and Chairman, Respectively, Little Caesar Enterprises, Detroit."

Immigrant Businesswomen

The United States was settled by immigrants. From colonial times to the present, people have come to this country because they saw opportunities for independence and freedom. The colonists with their agrarian culture were the first European immigrants. Of those that lived in towns, some women were merchants or owned shops, while others became seamstresses or cooks. Some ran boardinghouses or taverns, and some became prostitutes. In the South, women ran plantations.

The first wave of immigrants following the colonial period and the Revolutionary War came in 1845, when the Irish arrived in droves. Germans added to the influx in the 1850s, and by 1865, 250,000 immigrants were arriving every year. Many settled in urban areas, and the women worked in factories or as domestic servants. Middle class women did not work at all. The latter part of the nineteenth century saw increasing numbers of women working, some in white collar professional jobs such as librarians, secretaries, teachers, and nurses, professions that were eventually dominated by women. It was the social norm to stop working once married, but many women remained single and continued working.

Between 1880 and 1920, 7 million women immigrated to the United States, either as single women or to join their husbands. Most were from eastern European countries or were Jews fleeing from restrictive laws. Most of the land had been claimed and farmed, so they settled in industrial cities and lived in tenements. A few were entrepreneurs, turning traditional women's activities into businesses. For example, Jennie Grossinger began her resort, and others started restaurants, catering to their immigrant group. Most of the wives had to work so their families could survive. Many sewed at home, finishing clothing with fine needlework, or took in boarders. Single women worked in factories for lower pay than the men who were paid poorly to begin with. They were very badly treated and worked under unsafe and unhealthy conditions, particularly if they did not speak English. Fifty percent worked in the clothing industry.

There were fewer immigrants from 1920 until after World War II when they came from Latin America and Puerto Rico to New York City, and from Mexico and Asia to California. They settled in ethnic neighborhoods, the Chinatowns and Germantowns. Those that became businesswomen catered to, for the most part, their own neighborhoods. They baked and sold Irish soda bread and German strudel. Other immigrants opened Vietnamese restaurants and grocery stores. Cubans settled in Florida and opened Cuban restaurants. Germans published German newspapers, and other ethnic groups followed suit. The Hmong women sold their needlework. Ethnic contributions varied according to their cultural, ethnic, and social background. Their educational level and ability to speak English also had an impact on their success.

In the early days, a few women managed to start businesses with their families and husbands or by themselves. As the immigrant women became acclimated, they also became more entrepreneurial.

See also: Colonial Businesswomen; Minority Businesswomen

Further Reading
"In the Business World." In Neidle, Cecyle. *America's Immigrant Women*, p. 268–285.
Opdycke, Sandra. *The Routledge Historical Atlas of Women in America.*
Schneider, Dorothy and Carl J. Schneider, p. 129–130.

Information Technology Industry

According to the *Encyclopedia of Business and Finance*, information technology is "the study, design, development, implementation, support or management of computer-based information systems, particularly software applications and computer hardware" (Austin in Kaliski, p. 468–472). Known as high tech, this industry has ballooned into a multifaceted arena that now includes not only hardware and software, but also services, importing, computer peripherals, distribution, the Internet, and e-commerce. It has been volatile, with the dot-com boom of the mid and late 1990s and the subsequent demise of many of those companies beginning in 2000. From 1995 to 2000, 12,000 companies were founded, many by women.

The computer industry has long been known for its male-dominated atmosphere. Although there have been notable women—the six women who programmed ENIAC, the first computer produced in the United States during the early 1940s Manhattan Project, and Grace Hopper who developed the first computer code—women have always been a distinct minority in the industry.

It was not until the 1970s that women began entering the field. The most significant barrier has been a lack of education; very few women majored in computer science or engineering until the 1980s. In 1976, 5 percent of the engineering graduates were women. Sandra Kurtzig was the first woman to develop software and found her own company in 1973. Other software developers followed her, most notably Ann Winblad, who began her accounting software company in 1976, and Margaret Hamilton and Saydean Zeldin whose software was used on the Apollo space flights. Carol Bartz was the first woman CEO of a large technology company in Silicon Valley, but not until 1993. She said in an interview, "to survive and succeed in the hi-tech world of Silicon Valley requires a great deal of stamina, particularly for a female CEO" (Marquardt, p. 93).

During the late 1980s and 1990s, several women began companies based on newer and better ways to use technology: Donna Dubinsky, Judy Estrin, Pam Lopker, and Kim Polese. Others migrated from traditional companies to the high-tech world: Ellen Hancock, Heidi Miller, and Meg Whitman. In

April 1999 Carly Fiorina was appointed CEO of Hewlett-Packard. She was then, and still is, the highest-ranking businesswoman in the United States and one of the very few women CEOs in the information technology industry. In *Fortune 500* technology companies in 1999, 1 percent of the CEOs were women, and 3.8 percent of senior management were women.

The Internet and its phenomenal growth from 1995 to 2000 spawned thousands of companies funded by venture capital. In 1999, 6 percent of these companies had woman CEOs, but in 45 percent women held top management positions. As Marci McDonald pointed out in 2000, "commercialization of the Internet brought a demand for marketing savvy and consumer service—fields in which women have long flourished" (McDonald, "A Start-Up," p. 37). There was a labor shortage, and women were welcomed, perhaps not at the top but in middle and senior management. Esther Dyson became "Queen of the Internet." Springboard was founded, a venture capital fair that focused on woman-owned companies. Between 1995 and 2000, almost 12,000 companies were founded. Stock of these companies zoomed to unrealistic highs, and many of the companies failed to reach their expected profits or any profit at all. Around 2000 many began to take bankruptcy, and by 2002 the stock market bubble had burst.

There are many organizations dedicated to educating, supporting, and advancing women in information technology. These include African American Women in Technology (www.aawit.org), Association for Women in Computing (www.awc-hq.org), GirlGeeks (www.girlgeeks.org), The Institute for Women and Technology (www.iwt.org), WebGrrls (www.webgrrls.com), and Women in Technology International (www.witi.org).

Further Reading

Austin, Linda J. and Debbie Hughes. "Information Technology." In Kaliski, p. 34–42.

Carlassare, Elizabeth. *DotCom Divas: E-Business Insights from the Visionary Women Founders of 20 Net Ventures.*

McDonald, Marci. "A Start-Up of Her Own."

McGee, Marianne Kolbausk. "Leaders Among Leaders."

"Women Lag in Technology & Engineering: New Report Challenges Educators, Policy Makers and Industry Executives to Advance Women and Girls."

Ingram, Martha (1935–), Distributor Conglomerate Executive

When Bronson Ingram died in 1995, his widow, Martha Ingram, inherited and took over the management of his billion-dollar distribution empire, Ingram Industries. This catapulted her into the number 1 spot on the *Working Woman* top 500 list of woman-owned companies and earned her a number 33 ranking on the 1998 *Fortune* list of most powerful women in corporate America. She was not new to the company as some widows are, but had been a partner in decision-making and involved with the company since 1979.

She was born in Charleston, South Carolina, the eldest child. Her father owned a broadcasting company and prepared his children to take over if anything happened to him. She went to a private high school in Charleston and then graduated from Vassar. She met Bronson Ingram, then at Princeton, on a blind date. They had four children. After they were first married until 1979, she was very active in philanthropic activities in Nashville. She is described as a genius at raising money, and, after an eight-year crusade that funded the Tennessee Performing Arts Center, her husband asked her to join the company.

Ingram's approach was typical for her, learning everything about the business from the ground up. Her title was director of public relations, but she also became a partner in decision-making and eventually a member of the board of directors. At the time of Bronson's death, Ingram Industries was a huge ($2.4 billion) wholesaler of computer components, books, and videocassettes, as well as a shipping company and seller of high-risk insurance. When she took over, there were several challenges. Her husband had intended to take the company public; she and her sons decided to do this with only one part, Ingram Micro. They spun this off in 1996 in a very successful public offering and hired a non-family CEO. Ingram still sits on the board, however, and the family controls 80 percent of the voting power.

In 1997 son David became president of Ingram Entertainment, the videocassette part of the company. The other two sons are co-presidents of Ingram Industries; John manages the book group, and Orrin the shipping component. Ingram still presides over all the companies as chairman of the board and is very active in the company management. She has been called "the quintessential steel magnolia" (Faircloth, "Minding Martha's Business," p. 173) and "the country's most anonymous and under-appreciated businesswoman" (ibid.). She also believes that fun in the workplace increases productivity. A 1999 attempt to merge with Barnes & Noble was scuttled by the Federal Communication Commission because of antitrust implications.

Martha Ingram has served on the board of directors of Baxter International, Weyerhauser, and First American Corporation. With a strong interest in philanthropy, she has served on several boards including the Tennessee Performing Arts Center and several other Nashville cultural groups. She chaired the Tennessee Bicentennial Committee and founded the Tennessee Repertory Theater in 1972. She has also served on the boards of Ashley Hall, Vassar, Harpeth Hall School, and the advisory board of the Kennedy Center for the Performing Arts. In 1987 she was named the *Advantage* (the monthly business magazine of Nashville) Woman of the Year and, in May 1999, was inducted into the South Carolina Business Hall of Fame. In 1998 she put 20 million shares of Ingram Micro into a trust for Vanderbilt University and other beneficiaries that was valued at $300 million, the largest private education gift. Also, the company regularly gives 2 percent of its pretax income to charity. She was, in 1999, the country's wealthiest active businesswoman. That year she was elected to the Junior Achievement National Business Hall of Fame.

Further Reading
Bianco, Anthony. "Inside a $15 Billion Dynasty."
Faircloth, Anne. "Minding Martha's Business."
Gaw, Jonathan. "The Spine Behind the Ingram Empire."

Initial Public Offering (IPO), *see* Public Company

Institute for Women's Policy Research (IWPR)

1400 20th Street, NW, Suite 104
Washington, D.C. 20036
www.iwpr.org

The IWPR, a nonprofit, scientific organization, was established in 1987 with the goal of conducting original research and publishing reports on women's issues. It involves policy makers, scholars, and public interest groups in focusing on employment and earnings, family and work, and issues.

Insurance Industry

Insurance companies sell two different types of insurance: life/health and property/casualty. In 1997, 909,000 people were employed selling life/health insurance and 635,000 selling property/casualty.

The concept of the industry is very old, as evidenced in the Bible story of Joseph telling the pharaoh to store grain for the coming Egyptian famine. British ships sailing from London to the New World were insured. Benjamin Franklin helped establish the first colonial life insurance company in 1759. The first U.S. automobile liability policy was sold in 1887 (Keller, "Insurance," p. 475).

African American secret mutual aid savings and insurance societies also started concurrently, initially to provide for burial expenses. They were secret because slave owners were afraid of slaves organizing for any purpose. From 1880 to 1910 about 500 African American fraternal insurance organizations were founded. Maggie Walker was the most famous, and her order of St. Luke evolved into a savings bank. Because white insurance companies saw African Americans as high risk, African American companies flourished until the 1960s. In 1993 only twenty-three remained from 204 that existed in 1946.

In 1977 women owned 25.2 percent of American insurance agencies. By 1983 39.5 percent of the agents or brokers were women, but there were no women in the top echelons of the large insurance companies. Women held 66 percent of all insurance positions by June 2000 and had made progress into middle and upper management positions. Since the mid-1990s, many journal articles commented on the progress. Sally Roberts stated in 2000 that women in insurance have "literally moved from being primarily secretaries to being active participants of middle and upper management" (Roberts, "Women Making Strides," p. 11). A 1999 Catalyst study found that 14 percent, 184 out of the 1,318 corporate officers of the *Fortune* 500 insurance companies, were women. Women board members numbered 11 percent of the total board members. Ten of these companies had no women on their boards while State Farm had six. There were a few women CEOs of company subsidiaries.

Women are seen by many as ideal insurance agents for their strong communication skills, particularly in dealing with personal issues. Because of an increasing number of female customers, more women have become agents despite a lingering male culture that rewards achievement with hunting, fishing, or golf outings. There are two organizations for women in insurance: National Association of Insurance Women International (www.naiw.org) and Women in Insurance and Financial Services (www.w-wifs.org).

Further Reading
Fleming, Jane Hill. "Women Evolve to Survive in Competitive Work Force."
Keller, Edward J. Jr. "Insurance." In Kaliski, p. 475–479
Roberts, Sally. "Women Making Strides In Industry Leadership, But Obstacles Remain."

International Federation of Business and Professional Women's Clubs, *see* National Federation of Business and Professional Women's Clubs

Inventors

"Inventors are people who develop new devices or processes" (Zierdt-Warshaw, Winkler, and Bernstein, *American Women*, p. 151). These can range from a dishwasher, to a new kind of cereal, to a new method of weaving. Women have been inventing since history began. They were not recognized in colonial America because anything women did belonged to their husbands by law. Sybilla Masters's husband patented her invention in England in 1715 under his name, but she is remembered because he credited her in the text.

Congress passed the first patent act in 1790, but even then, many states prohibited women from owning property. The first woman to receive a U.S.

patent was Mary Kies for her process of weaving silk into straw. Even after women could own property, many female inventors did not apply for a patent for fear of drawing attention to themselves. The patent process intimidated others.

Most early female inventors focused on devices and processes that eased the burden of domesticity. During the Civil War, their arena widened to include farm machines. One notable exception was Mary Jane Montgomery, who improved the planking on war ships to discourage barnacles. Many African American women were also inventors, although they had to deal with racial, as well as gender, barriers. Ellen Elgin, who invented a clothes-wringer, sold her 1880s invention to an agent for $18, rather than apply for a patent. She was sure her color would prevent her patent from being registered. Early inventions by other African American women include a folding cabinet bed (precursor to today's sofa bed), a permanent wave machine, and an improvised ironing board.

The Woman's Building in the 1893 Columbian Exposition in Chicago included a number of inventions. Josephine Cochran's dishwasher was not only an exhibit, it was also used in restaurants throughout the fairgrounds. Also on exhibit was an iceless milk cooler, a heat-conserving dinner pail, a gravity elevator with safety features, and signal flares. New food items included Cracker Jacks, Cream of Wheat, and the hamburger.

As women's worlds widened and more became educated, so did their spheres of inventions, including the material used in bulletproof vests, windshield wipers, submarine periscopes, stovetop stuffing, the bra, a device for removing cataracts, and home security systems. During the twentieth century many women inventors worked for companies who owned the patents. Others began companies with their inventions, most notably, Bette Graham with Liquid Paper, Ruth Handler with Barbie, and Ann Moore with Snugli.

In 1976 women held 2 percent of all patents. Ten years later 8 percent of the patents issued were to women, half of which were in technology fields.

See also: Entrepreneurs

Further Reading
"Invention/Inventors." In Zierdt-Warshaw, Linda, Alan Winkler, and Leonard Bernstein, *American Women in Technology*, p. 151–152.
Macdonald, Anne L. *Feminine Ingenuity: How Women Inventors Changed America.*
Vare, Ethlie Ann and Greg Ptacek. *Patently Female: From AZT to TV Dinners: Stories of Women Inventors and Their Breakthrough Ideas.*

IPO, *see* Public Company

J

Jackson, Jeanne (1951–), Retail Clothing Executive

As president of Banana Republic, Jeanne Jackson changed this division of Gap from stores selling a stagnating inventory of safari clothes to purveyors of clothing for middle- to upper-class men and women wanting fashionable chic. She introduced new products, completely reformatted the stores, and boosted revenues to $825 million. This feat earned her spots on the 1998 to 2000 *Fortune* lists of the most powerful women in corporate America. In 2000 she became the CEO of Wal-Mart.com but resigned in November 2001.

She was born and educated in Denver, the daughter of a Colorado pilot. She earned a BS in finance from the University of Colorado in 1974 and an MBA from Harvard in 1978. While at Harvard, an instructor noticed that she was working at two jobs, and he suggested that anyone who worked so very hard should look at retail as a career. Jackson began as a buyer and quickly was promoted to assistant manager with Bullock's Department Stores. After a stint as a merchandising manager, she became senior vice president at Saks Fifth Avenue. In 1989 she was senior vice president of merchandising for Walt Disney Attractions in Orlando, and in 1992 an executive vice president for Victoria's Secret in Ohio.

In 1995 she joined Gap, Inc. as president of the Banana Republic division, responsible for revitalizing and differentiating the chain from Gap clothing stores. One of her first steps was to change the dressing room lighting from florescent to gentle white and to paint the walls a soft off-white. That first year Jackson opened twenty-six new stores; in 1996, eighteen more. She also remodeled most of the remaining stores and added new products such as footwear, hosiery, accessories, home goods, and beauty and personal care products. Larger stores were needed to accommodate the new lines and, later, separate stores for men's and women's products.

These changes were more than just successful; because of strong growth in the Banana Republic division, Gap reorganized the management structure and made Jackson the CEO, a new position, as well as president of Banana Republic with an added management layer and responsibility for merchandising. The number of stores had grown to 232 from 184 in 1994. In 1998 she became CEO of Gap Inc. Direct, the catalog and web division.

> As president of Banana Republic, Jeanne Jackson changed this division of Gap from a stagnating safari clothing chain to stores for middle- to upperclass men and women wanting fashionable chic.

In March 2000 she joined Wal-Mart as the CEO of Wal-Mart.com. Jackson saw the move as an opportunity to create a new organization from the beginning; however, the site had a slow start and needed tweaking until the end of that year. By November of 2001 Wal-Mart decided not to launch Wal-Mart.com as a separate company, reduced its funding, and Jackson resigned.

In the January 12, 1998, issue, *Business Week* named her a "marketing star" and one of the world's top managers. That year *Vanity Fair* called her one of America's 200 influential women, and she won the Woman of Achievement Award from the National Foundation of Woman Legislators. In 2000 the *Los Angeles Times* included Jackson in its list of twenty-two movers and shakers likely to reshape business and the economy (Goldman, "1999/2000 Review" p. 4). She has served on the boards of MacDonald's, Nike, and the Harvard Business School. In late 2001 she was appointed trustee of the U.S. Ski and Snowboard Team Foundation.

She is married to a retired pilot, and they have a son and a daughter.

See also: Retailing Industry

Further Reading

Goldman, Abigail. "1999/2000 Review & Outlook; People to Watch in 2000."
Hammond, Teena. "Banana Republic Eyes New Formats and Revived Catalog."
Lazarus, David. "Wal-Mart Names Web Chief; Jackson Headed Gap's Internet Wing."
Sperling, Nicole. "Jeanne Jackson Says Walmart.com Is Not Damaged Goods."

Johnson, Abigail Pierrepont (1962–), Investment Manager

Abby Johnson is the president of Fidelity Management and Research Company, the mutual fund company founded by her grandfather and run by her father. She has been on *Fortune*'s list of the most powerful businesswomen in the United States since the list began in 1998. In 2002 she was ranked number 9.

She was born in Boston, the eldest of three children. Her father periodically took her to the office as a child, where she was captivated by the trading room. During high-school summers, she worked as a waitress and t-shirt vendor.

The summer before college, she answered customer calls at Fidelity. She graduated from Hobart and William Smith College in 1984, majoring in art history with a minor in economics. After working two years at Booz-Allen and Hamilton, she went to Harvard for an MBA. In 1998 she married Christopher McKown. They have two daughters.

In 1988 she began her career at Fidelity. She and her father planned for her to work her way up in the company in the same way he did, by managing a few funds and then larger and larger ones. From 1988 to 1991 she concentrated on industrial equipment before focusing on telecommunications for two years and all communications the following year. In 1994 she was promoted to portfolio manager of Fidelity OTC. The next year she was appointed to the board of directors and received 25 percent of the stock. In May 1997 she became the senior vice-president of the equity division and one of the three vice presidents of the core management team.

In 2000 her father created a management team made up of the chair and three vice chairmen, of which she was one. In June 2001 she was appointed president of the Fidelity Management Research Company, the number three spot in the Fidelity hierarchy. She is responsible for more than 1,000 people, including all of the portfolio managers, analysts, and traders in Boston. She is also on the operating committee. As of October 2002 she managed over 300 mutual funds for 18.4 million individual and institutional clients. Fidelity is the world's largest mutual fund company.

Johnson rarely gives interviews; she is low key, soft spoken, and avoids publicity. She loves investing, and her priority is to increase the value of the funds, thus serving her customers well. Her leadership style is one of gentle pressure. Since working out the conflicts between motherhood and career, she is now taking hold of the role of heir apparent and is one of the most powerful women in finance in the United States.

In 1996 *Business Week* called Johnson a manager to watch, and *Success* listed her as one of the fifty smartest businesswomen. In 2001 *Business Week* called her a person to watch in international business. She is also active in Planned Parenthood.

See also: Finance Industry

Further Reading
Gabriel, Frederick P. Jr. "Fast Track: Abby Johnson: Promotion Goes Beyond Dad's Fidelity."
Smith, Geoffrey. "Here Comes Abby."
Wyatt, Edward. "Mutual Funds; Making Way for Fidelity's Heir Apparent."

Johnson, Antonia Ax:son (1943–), Telecommunications and Shipping Executive

Antonia Ax:son Johnson is one of the world's leading industrialists. Her U.S. operations of Axel Johnson Group alone rates it as one of the country's largest woman-owned firms. In fact she was on the *Working Woman* list from its inception, leading the companies in 1992, and in the top fifteen through 2001, the last year of the list.

She was born in New York City but is Swedish and lives in Sweden with her husband and four children. Her great-grandfather founded the multinational shipping company in 1873, and a family member has operated it ever since. Johnson, an only child, was brought up to run the company. She attended Radcliffe and received a master's degree in psychology and economics at the University of Stockholm.

She joined the company in 1975 as a member of group management, progressing through a variety of more responsible positions. When Johnson was thirty-nine, her father had a stroke, and she was named CEO, president, and chair. The company is a multinational conglomerate and now reflects her interests in the environment, energy, and telecommunications equipment. When she took over, there was a shipping glut so she diversified into retail operations as well as metals and telecommunications, a move that eventually saved the company. Later she began to reduce the diversity in products to just those that made sense to her. The products now are wastewater treatment and environmental services, telecommunications equipment, and other new technologies. One of the subsidiaries is a pioneer in the use of sand filtration to be used in reclaiming wastewater. She has been the chairman of the company since 1982.

Johnson is committed to furthering women in employment; 60 percent of her Swedish employees are women. She began a training program there, the in-house Antonia Johnson Institute for Women in Management. In 1995 she established the Institute for Women at Stanford University. She is married with two daughters and twins, one of each.

Johnson has served on the board of directors of Xerox and several international boards and Swedish commissions, as a trustee of the Carnegie Institute and the University of Lund, and a member of the advisory counsel of the Graduate School of Business at Stanford. She was a member of *Working Woman*'s Billion Dollar Club in June 2001, one of ten women.

Further Reading

Bamford, Janet and Jennifer Pendleton. "The Top 50 Women-Owned Businesses," p. 37–38.

The Complete Marquis Who's Who Biographies. (Retrieved from *LEXIS-NEXIS Academic Universe*, April 29, 1999.)

Schmuckler, Eric and Harris Collingwood. "The Top 50 Women Business Owners," p. 33.

Johnson, Claudia Alta (Lady Bird) (1912–), Broadcasting Executive

Claudia Alta (Lady Bird) Johnson was the only First Lady of the United States to own and run a business. She bought KTBC, an almost-bankrupt

Texas radio station in 1943 and turned it into a multimillion-dollar radio and television broadcasting company.

She was born in the small town of Karnack, Texas, the youngest of three children and the only daughter. She got her nickname when she was two, and it stuck. Her father was a landowner and merchant, her mother was an advocate of women's suffrage and of integration, but died when Lady Bird was two. An aunt raised her. She graduated third in her high school class, attended the University of Texas, and received a degree in journalism in 1934. That year she met Lyndon Baines Johnson and married him after a brief courtship. They had two daughters, Lynda Bird and Luci Baines.

She financed her husband's first congressional campaign and was very active throughout his political career, even though she was very shy. While he was in the navy during World War II, she managed his congressional office and learned business skills. She liked business and looked around for something to buy. First she tried two newspapers. Then KTBC, a small radio station in Austin, Texas, caught her eye. The station was losing money and had liabilities of $19,000, as well as operational problems, but she bought the license.

It was approved by the FCC in February 1943, and she worked there full-time for seven months, commuting between Austin and Washington, DC. She learned everything she could about the finances and personnel during that time and literally cleaned it up. When she found that it was losing $600 per month, she hired a station manager and new staff and moved the headquarters. She also asked the FCC to increase the station's power and frequency and grant unlimited broadcasting hours. Her request was granted and, that August, the station showed an $18 profit. In September she affiliated with CBS. By 1945 the profit was $40,000, with an audience of 2.5 million. That year she formed her company, Texas Broadcasting Corporation.

Johnson was in Washington during her husband's years as congressman, vice president, and president, but she managed to keep a close eye on her business through monthly management and financial reports. In 1951 she expanded into television with her first program, a University of Texas–Texas A&M football game. She had a monopoly in Austin and in 1959, bought stations in Waco, Bryan, and Weslaco, Texas. By the mid-1960s, Johnson also owned a cable television company and a bank. In 1963 she changed the name to LBJ Holding Company. Ten years later she named the radio station KLBJ. She retired as chairman of the board in 1996, and her daughter Luci bought her sister's share for $80 million. Her small radio station had become a million dollar radio and television broadcasting corporation. In March 2003, the family sold its interest in the broadcasting company.

Lady Bird Johnson was known as a careful, shrewd, and successful business-woman. Although she was away from the business in Texas for much of the time, she was an excellent judge of character and succeeded in choosing good managers. She kept a very close eye on the bottom line and always knew the financials. At the same time, she was a significant factor in her husband's political career, a celebrated hostess, and lover of wild flowers.

She was honored many times, mostly for her beautification efforts. She holds honorary doctorates from Texas Women's University, Radcliffe College, and George Washington University. She has served on the Board of Regents of the University of Texas at Austin and as an honorary trustee of the Women of the West Museum. She served on the National Park Service Advisory Council and won the Congressional Gold Medal in 1988. In 1997 she won the International Award of Excellence from the Botanical Research Institute of Texas. The following year, the greater San Antonio Chamber of Commerce awarded her the Freeman Award for Agribusiness Achievement. The Women's Chamber of Commerce of Texas named her among Texas's 100 Most Influential Women Of This Century. She also received a 2002 Gold Medal Award from the U.S. National Arboretum. A park in Austin is named for her.

See also: Broadcasting Industry

Further Reading

"Johnson, Claudia Alta (Taylor)." In *Current Biography 1964*, p. 212–215.
Russell, Jan Jarboe. *Lady Bird: A Biography of Mrs. Johnson.*

Juliber, Lois D. (1949–), Soap/Cosmetics Manufacturer

Lois Juliber, named one of corporate America's most powerful women in four consecutive years by *Fortune*, is often referred to as the next CEO of Colgate-Palmolive. Many times during her career she has been the highest-ranking female executive at different companies. At Colgate-Palmolive she was the person most responsible for turning around the company's U.S. sales. In October 2001 she was promoted to chief operating officer and executive vice president.

The younger of two sisters, she was born in Brooklyn to a Revlon executive and his teacher wife. The family moved to Long Island when Juliber was nine, and she became enchanted by the competitiveness of sports. She says now that she was always career-oriented, even at a very young age. After graduating from Wellesley, she found that the available jobs were not very interesting, so she applied and was accepted to Harvard Business School. Her class contained an unprecedented number of women, 4.4 percent. She admits to being frightened most of the time there; because she had no real job experience, she was at a disadvantage in the rough and tumble of the case study method. After graduating with an interest in marketing, she worked for General Foods where she stayed for fifteen years, helping to re-energize Kool-Aid, Shake 'n Bake, Post cereals and other brands. About this time she also met and married her husband.

In 1988, realizing that she had hit the glass ceiling several times at General Foods, Juliber decided that she needed to change companies and also that she needed international experience. She joined Colgate–Palmolive as head of the Far Eastern and Canada Division, later introducing dental floss and shampoo to consumers in the Pacific Rim countries and supervising Colgate's entry into China. This involved enormous amounts of traveling. During this time she and her husband decided not to have children. She had been advised by a colleague to make that a conscious choice rather that letting it creep up on her.

In April of 1994 Juliber became the first woman president of Colgate-Palmolive North America, charged with improving their market share in the United States. She did it in record time through a variety of initiatives: she closed inefficient factories, overhauled contracts with suppliers, gave managers a bigger role in decision-making, invested heavily in training, and built morale. In addition she successfully launched new products, particularly Colgate Total, the first toothpaste that was approved by the Food and Drug Administration to fight gingivitis. In just three years, sales increased 23 percent and profits were up 86 percent. She was responsible for one of the most dramatic overhauls in packaged goods history. In 1997 she was promoted to executive vice president of operations for developed products, responsible for one half of Colgate's $9.1 billion revenue. She is, as stated above, widely recognized as perhaps the next CEO of the company.

In a 1998 speech in Louisville, Kentucky, Juliber advised women to find what they love to do and to go for it: don't look back, be fully committed, be persistent, and set milestones for themselves (Haukebo, "Revamped Chamber Gets First Pep Talk," p. 1). She believes that one must persevere and put up with both the good and the bad. For example, she found that she had to prove herself over and over because she was a woman. She says that much of her success is due to a gender-blind upbringing; her parents encouraged her as both ambitious scholar and competitive athlete. She also feels that she is adaptable to new business philosophies as times change; that and her leadership skills have stood her in good stead.

Lois Juliber serves on the board of directors at DuPont and State Street Boston. She has also served on the boards of the Brookdale Foundation Group and Wellesley College and is a member of the Committee of 200. In 1992 she was listed in *Business Week*'s top fifty women of business in the United States. In 2002 she received the Luminary Award in the Corporate Innovator category from the Committee of 200. Her hobbies are tennis, gardening, and cooking.

See also: Beauty Industry

Further Reading

Caminiti, Susan. "Turnaround Titan."

Hartman, Mary S., Ed., *Talking Leadership: Conversations with Powerful Women,* p. 117–133.

Haukebo, Kirsten. "Revamped Chamber Gets First Pep Talk."

Morris, Betsy. "Tales of the Trailblazers: *Fortune* Revisits Harvard's Women MBAs of 1973."

Jung, Andrea (1958–), Cosmetics Executive

In November 1999 Andrea Jung joined the three other female CEOs of Fortune 500 companies. After being passed over fifteen months before, she was asked to take the top position at Avon Products. This placed her as the highest ranking Asian American woman, the highest-ranking woman of color in corporate America, and the first woman to lead Avon.

She was born in Toronto where her father was an architect. Her mother had emigrated to the United States from Shanghai to obtain a chemical engineering degree. She had in some ways a traditional Asian American family with values centered on achievement and education. Both she and her younger brother were brought up to have careers, and against Chinese tradition, she was told that she could do anything her brother could. When she was ten, the family moved to Wellesley, Massachusetts. After graduating magna cum laude from Princeton with a BA in English literature, Jung was recruited for Bloomingdale's department store training program in New York City in 1979, where she rose steadily into the executive ranks.

She moved to I. Magnin as a senior vice president and general merchandise manager and later to Neiman Marcus in Dallas as the executive vice president of merchandising. While she was with Neiman-Marcus, she decided to change her focus. A single mother of a little girl and traveling extensively, Jung decided that her priority was to be with her daughter. She moved to New York City and began consulting with Avon on their line of intimate apparel. In 1993 she joined Avon as president of U.S. marketing, moving from "class to mass" as *Fortune* put it. (Sellers, "The 50 Most Powerful Women," p. 80).

When Jung came to Avon, her goal was to modernize the company and its image. She launched new products, including Perfect Wear, a transfer-resistant lipstick, and several fragrances partnered with designer names, such as Josie Natori and Diane von Furstenberg. Based on her brief foray as her own neighborhood's Avon lady, she had the advantage of knowing what the Avon customer was looking for: low price and high value. During her first few years, sales rose by 32 percent. In 1996 she secured a $20 million Olympic sponsorship with an accompanying advertising campaign and licensed products. She designed new packaging and added housewares and upscale fragrances at mass prices.

During a highly publicized search for a new CEO in 1997, Jung and two other qualified women were passed over. The Avon board explained, after a flurry of negative publicity, that the women weren't quite ready, and that she in particular lacked global experience. Jung was appointed president and COO and designated the next in line for the top job. She took that opportunity to obtain the required international experience, and in 1999, when the CEO unexpectedly retired, she succeeded him.

Since then Jung has masterminded a strategic change at Avon, including modernizing the Avon lady image and recruitment; overhauling advertising, product positioning, manufacturing and packaging; cutting costs; selling on the Internet; developing new products such as Retroactive, an anti-aging skin cream as well as nutritional and aromatherapy line; beefing up the research and development budget; and venturing into a retailing partnership of more expensive products with J.C. Penney. She also changed Avon's slogan to "the company for women" and introduced the first retirement savings plan in the direct selling industry. After her promotion, sales increased, as did the stock value. In September 2001 she was appointed chairman, a position contingent on her performance as CEO.

> Andrea Jung is the highest ranking Asian American woman as well as the highest-ranking woman of color in corporate America.

Her management style has been described as personable and energetic. She has a wonderful sense of style and a very strong ability to focus, never getting flustered or angry. Wall Street analysts respect her strong marketing and managerial skills and her ability to motivate, shown by her employees' strong loyalty of. Although she is very smart, she accomplishes her aims in an understated way, leading by example but always raising the standards and pointing toward her vision. She feels that being a woman helped her because she has a passion for the customer.

Andrea Jung has been on the *Fortune* list of most powerful corporate women since 1998. That year she said that she views her power "with a great deal of awe . . . [that] power is the power to influence . . . it's an unbelievable responsibility to influence decisions, shareholder value, and most important to me, people's careers and livelihood" (Sellers, p. 80). She has served on the boards of Avon, General Electric, the Fragrance Foundation, Cosmetic Executive Women, and Princeton University. She was also the first woman to be invited onto the International Advisory Board of Salomon Smith Barney. In 1996 she was named *Brandweek*'s Marketer of the Year in the health and beauty category and was elected into the 1998 Advertising Hall of Achievement. The Skin Cancer Foundation awarded her the 1999 Skin Sense Award for her exceptional achievements in the fields of skin care and sun protection. In 2000 *Success* listed her as one of the fifty smartest women in business; *World Journal* named her to their list of one hundred Chinese Americans/Canadians who have significantly impacted and contributed to mainstream society. She received the 2002 Best Boss Award from Cosmetic Executive Women. That year the company was named number one of the top twenty-five companies for executive women by the National Association of Female Executives, one of the top ten best corporate citizens by *Business Ethics Magazine*, and the fourth most admired company and the second most socially responsible company by *Fortune*.

One of Jung's most memorable accomplishments resulted from her focus on Avon's support for breast cancer research, partly because her grandmother died from the disease. As of December 2002 the company had raised a record $250 million and sponsored a variety of projects.

Jung is very devoted to her second husband, Bloomingdale CEO Michael Gould, her daughter and son.

See also: Asian American Businesswomen; Beauty Industry

Further Reading

Brooker, Katrina. "It Took a Lady to Save Avon: Elegant and Poised, with a Will of Iron, Andrea Jung Knows How to Win."

Canedy, Dana. "Passed Over Before, A Woman is Named Chief Executive."

Jones, Del. "Avon Takes Breast Cancer Personally; CEO Andrea Jung Leads Company's Fundraising Efforts."

Larson, Soren. "Jung's Focus: Avon Product Line."

Mehegan, Sean. "Andrea Jung."

Sellers, Patricia. "The 50 Most Powerful Women in American Business."

www.avon.com

Junior Achievement's Global Business Hall of Fame

The Junior Achievement Global Business Hall of Fame started in 1975, a joint effort of Junior Achievement and *Fortune* magazine, intending to honor living business leaders but not those still in CEO positions. *Fortune*'s editors chose fifteen men the first year, including several historical business leaders, four still living. Leadership was defined as "outstanding and enduring contributions to improving the products, the processes, the efficiencies or the human relations of business" (Ways, "A Hall of Fame," p. 68). The first woman was not added until 1980, when Lila Wallace was inducted with her husband.

As of 2002 there were thirteen women and over 180 men. *Fortune* editors chose inductees until 1998, when sponsorship shifted, and anyone could nominate a businessperson. Inductees are selected first by a past laureates committee that reduces the list from fifty to twenty, and then by the final selection committee that is comprised of past laureates, national Junior Achievement board members, and representatives from CNBC.

The nomination form is available from the Junior Achievement Web page. Having changed somewhat over the years, the criteria now read, "an individual's record of business achievement must demonstrate: a) business excellence, b) courageous thinking and acting, c) vision and innovation, d) inspiring leadership, e) and community mindedness. In addition, nominees must serve as a role model for those who follow" (www.ja.org/gbhf). The Business Hall of

Fame Laureates are part of a permanent exhibit, Enterprise, a hands-on entre-preneurial learning laboratory for children and adults, in Chicago's Museum of Science and Industry.

Further Reading
Guzzardi, Walter. "Wisdom from the Giants of Business."
Ways, Max. "A Hall of Fame for Business Leadership."
www.ja.org/gbhf/index.shtml

K

Rosabeth Moss Kanter, one of the top managerial theorists in the United States, is the author of more than 100 journal articles and several books. Some of her ideas have become general management wisdom. She owns her own management consulting company, Goodmeasure, Inc. and is a professor at Harvard University.

She was born in Cleveland, Ohio, to a lawyer/small business owner and a schoolteacher. After graduating from Cleveland Heights High School in 1960, she majored in sociology and minored in English literature at Bryn Mawr College. She spent her junior year as a special student at the University of Chicago and then returned to graduate from Bryn Mawr magna cum laude in 1964. The previous year she had married Stuart A. Kanter who died in 1969. She continued school at the University of Michigan, earning a master's in 1965 and a PhD in 1967 in social organizations, while working as a research assistant, a teaching fellow, and a sociology instructor.

From 1967 to 1973 Kanter was an assistant professor of sociology at Brandeis University and began consulting. In 1972 she published her first book, *Commitment and Community: Communes and Utopias in Sociological Perspective*, combining her dissertation, experiences with communal living, and further research, to explain why communes succeed or fail. That year she married consultant Barry Stein. They have one son.

In 1973 Kanter took a leave of absence to teach at Harvard. She returned to teach at Brandeis, continuing as a visiting scholar at Harvard. Her groundbreaking book, *Men and Women of the Corporation*, was published in 1977. It used sociological research techniques to analyze the corporate environment and employee and management behavior patterns of a fictional midwestern company. It won the C. Wright Mills Award and is now seen as a classic.

From 1977 to 1986 she was an associate professor and then full professor of sociology and organization management at Yale University. In 1977 Kanter and her husband founded their consulting firm, Goodmeasure, Inc., with her as chair. Its specialty is organizational effectiveness and change. She wrote *The Change Masters* in 1983, case studies of one hundred U.S. corporations, a classic text.

In 1986 Kanter joined the Harvard Business School as a tenured professor of business administration, only the second tenured woman in its history. She was the first to be appointed as a Class of 1960 Professor, a professorship dedicated to innovation and entrepreneurship in established companies. In 1989 she was the first woman editor of the *Harvard Business Review*. When the journal hired a full-time professional editor in 1992, she became vice chairman of the newly created Harvard Business School Publishing Group.

Kanter's consulting company is one of the most sought-after in the management field. Clients include General Electric, Honeywell, Xerox, IBM, and Apple Computer. She is an intelligent, highly articulate overachiever. She describes herself as task-oriented, organized, and obsessed with things that go wrong. Her "success is due to a combination of rigorous research, practical experience, and her ability to write in a clear and concrete way, using many illustrative examples" (*Business, the Ultimate Resource*, p. 1008).

She has seventeen honorary doctorates and has served on several boards. Kanter was a founding member of the Committee of 200 and is active on the NOW Legal Defense and Education Fund, the American Center for the Quality of Work Life, and the Educational Fund for Individual Rights. She was elected to the Working Woman Hall of Fame, the Ohio Women's Hall of Fame, and named Ms Magazine's 1975 "Woman of the Year." In 2000 the London *Times* listed her among their "50 Most Powerful Women in the World."

See also: Consulting

Further Reading
Business: The Ultimate Resource.
Bisoux, Tricia. "A New E-Attitude."
Kanter, Rosabeth Moss. *Men and Women of the Corporation.*
Kanter, Rosabeth Moss. *The Change Masters.*
Merriden, Trevor. "Rosabeth Moss Kanter."
"Rosabeth Moss Kanter. Pioneer of Empowerment and Change Management."
"Rosabeth Moss Kanter: The Professor As Business Leader."

Karan, Donna (1948–), Fashion Designer

Donna Karan is known as the "Queen of Seventh Avenue" in the fashion press, and her designs for professional woman are world-famous for sophisticated layers of comfort and understated sexiness. Donna Karan International was on the *Working Woman* list of top woman-owned companies from the first list in 1992 until its last in 2001. In June 2004 she received a lifetime achievement award from the Council of Fashion Designers of America.

She was born in Forest Hills, the younger of two sisters, to a New York garment district family. Her father, who died when she was three, ran a custom tailoring shop, and her mother was a model and a showroom saleswoman. After attending Parsons School of Design for two years, Karan dropped out to work for Anne Klein, then famous for developing designer sportswear. She had met Mark Karan at Parsons and married him. After being fired from Anne Klein, she later returned and stayed for sixteen years, as co-designer from 1971 to 1974. After Klein's death in 1974, Karan became head designer, showing her first complete collection that year. In 1983 she divorced Karan and married Stephen Weiss, who died from lung cancer in 2001.

In 1984 after months of agonizing, Karan started her own company with the backing of Tomio Taki and Frank Mori of Takihyo Inc. in Japan, also part-owner of Anne Klein. She created her own look: swaths of fabric enhancing the natural curves of a woman's body—comfortable, sophisticated, and sexy. Her emphasis is on functionality, comfort, and femininity. She is inspired by the fabric and designs her clothes by wrapping, draping, and manipulating it on the model in front of her. She initially designed the upscale Donna Karan collection, followed by the more moderately priced DKNY collection, which was popular from the beginning. She expanded DKNY to include menswear, and by 1986 she was the newest fashion darling. She was involved in all aspects of the company.

A problem endemic to the fashion industry, and particularly rampant in her company, is that expenses are higher than sales, even though sales climbed every year. In the early 1990s the company was plagued by late shipments, low-quality workmanship and production, and soaring expenses. In 1994 Karan considered selling stock in the company but decided against it. Instead she obtained financing from Citicorp, paid off some of the debt, and rewarded the backers, herself, and her husband. She also launched a new advertising campaign, became very popular with the media such as Oprah Winfrey, who devoted an entire hour to her, and appeared in *Women's Wear Daily*, *Harper's Bazaar*, *Vogue*, and *Elle*. She had many shops in Europe, including a flagship store in London.

By 1996 the company had turned around and it went public in July, receiving $58 million for stock at $24 per share. Unfortunately, the company did not show a profit until 1999 when shares sold for $8. In 1997 she hired John Idol as CEO, stepping down to focus on design and fashion while still chair and chief designer. Idol's mission

> Known as the Queen of Seventh Avenue in the fashion press, Donna Karan and her designs aimed at the professional woman are world-famous for sophisticated layers of comfort and understated sexiness.

was to turn the company around and make it a financial success. He began a corporate restructure, launched several stores countrywide, including a flagship in New York City, and licensed the Donna Karan name to Liz Claiborne and Estee Lauder, always a money making move. In November 2001, LVMH Moet-Hennessy Louis Vuitton bought the company for $243 million.

Karan has an honorary degree from the Parsons School of Design and won the 1977 and 1984 Coty Award; the Awards Council of Fashion Designers of America in 1985, 1986, and 1992; the 1992 Frontrunner Award from the Sara Lee Corporation; and the Raymond Loewy Foundation Designer Award. She was the co-recipient with Louis Dell'Olio of the Coty Return Award and named to the Coty Hall of Fame in 1982. She also was named the Best Menswear Designer in 1992, the Best American Designer to Emerge in 20 Years, and the Best Woman Designer in the World. The Council of Fashion Designers of America designated her the 1997 Woman's Wear Designer of the Year. In 2002 she was awarded the first Liz Tilberis Humanitarian Award.

See also: Fashion Industry

Further Reading

Donovan, Carrie. "Designer Donna Karan: How a Fashion Star Is Born."
"Donna Karan." In Logan, Mary Simmerson, p. 222–225.
Sieder, Jill Jordan. "Donna Karan's Chic Design for Success; the Fashion Entrepreneur Tailors her Business Plan and Stretches a Global Empire Together."

Katen, Karen L. (1949–), Pharmaceuticals Executive

Karen Katen, president of Pfizer's Worldwide Pharmaceutical Organization and executive vice president of Pfizer, Inc., has been on *Fortune*'s list of the most powerful women in American business since 1998, ranking number 6 in 2003. She is also on the Pfizer leadership team.

Born and raised in Kansas City, she received a BA in economics and political science from the University of Chicago, and in 1974 an MBA in marketing and finance. After graduation Katen joined Pfizer as a marketing associate and remained, earning positions of more and more responsibility. In 1993 she was appointed vice president of the U.S. Pharmaceuticals Group, responsible for all sales and marketing divisions of Roerig, Pfizer Laboratories, Pratt Pharmaceuticals, and National Healthcare Operations. She was promoted to president of this 4,500-employee group in 1997, the first woman in this position, responsible for Pfizer's drug manufacturing operations in the United States. She is also vice president of Global Pfizer Pharmaceutical Group, overseeing medical and regulatory activities and new product development on a global scale.

Katen's accomplishments include the launches of Viagra, the antibiotic Trovan, the allergy medication Zyrtec, the anti-depressant Zoloft, cholesterol-lowering Lipitor, and an arthritis medication, Celeba. Under her leadership,

Pfizer vies with Merck for top pharmaceutical company honors. She has also engineered lucrative partnerships with other drug companies, most notably Warner-Lambert and its cholesterol-lowering drug, Lipitor. She is known for her aggressive marketing, ability to build and lead teams, and leadership in managing change. In April 2001 she was promoted to her present position. The following March, under her direction, Pfizer launched a Share Card program to enroll eligible Medicare recipients in a prescription drug coverage program.

Katen has served on the boards of General Motors, J.P. Morgan & Company, Harris Corporation, and the American Cancer Society. She is vice chairman of the National Pharmaceutical Council, a member of Pharmaceutical Research and Manufacturers of America and of its Public Policy Analysis Section, the National Coalition of Hispanic Health and Human Services Organization, the American Bureau for Medical Advancement in China, Inc., and the Women's Forum, Inc. She is also a council member of the Graduate School of Business at the University of Chicago. Katen was named one of the "50 Smartest Women" by *Success* and a top executive by *Business Week* in 1999. In March 2002 she was selected to serve on the U.S.–Japan Private Sector/Government Commission. She lives in New York City.

Further Reading
Gross, Daniel. M. "The Next CEOs."
"Pfizer's Pep Pill."
Sellers, Patricia. "These Women Rule."

Katz, Lillian Vernon, *see* Vernon, Lillian

Keckley, Elizabeth Hobbs (1818–1907), Dressmaker, Entrepreneur

Elizabeth Keckley started her dressmaking business in St. Louis during the 1850s and moved it to Washington, D.C. in 1860. She became so well known through her prominent clients that Mary Todd Lincoln asked her to come to the White House as her dressmaker, fashion designer, and personal maid.

She was born to slaves in Dinwiddie Courthouse, Virginia. Her father and birth date are not certain. Her master, Colonel A. Burwell (perhaps her father), loaned her to poor relations where she endured several beatings, but learned self-reliance. One of the relations, Alexander Kirkland, was the father of her son, George.

After she was loaned to Anne Garland, one of Burwell's daughters, she started dressmaking and invented a system for cutting and fitting dresses. In 1852 she married James Keckley, who masqueraded as a freeman. He was lazy and refused to work, so she supported him until they separated in 1860.

Meanwhile she developed a clientele among the St. Louis society women, supporting the seventeen-member Garland family with her earnings. She persuaded the Garlands to grant freedom to her and her son for $1,200. By 1855 she had raised the money and was free.

In 1860 Keckley moved to Baltimore then back to Washington, DC, running her dressmaking business out of her rooms. At her peak, when she was one of the most popular dressmakers in the city, she employed twenty young women, teaching them sewing, elegance, and charm. Her clients were the wives of such prominent Washingtonians as Stephen Douglas and E.M. Stanton, who recommended her to Mary Todd Lincoln.

Her first visit to the White House was on March 3, 1861. Mary Lincoln loved Keckley's dresses and also grew close to Keckley. A further bond developed when they both lost their sons that year. Keckley's son, a Union soldier, was killed at the Battle of Wilson's Creek in Missouri in August. She soon became Mrs. Lincoln's dressmaker, fashion designer, confidante, personal maid, nurse, and traveling companion. She designed the inaugural ball gown, which is now in the Smithsonian. After President Lincoln was assassinated in 1865, she accompanied the grieving widow to Chicago.

Later in 1865 she returned to Washington and reopened her business. Mary Lincoln stayed in touch through letters and asked for Keckley's help with selling Lincoln's old clothes and jewelry in New York City. So in 1867 she went to New York. She also tried to raise money by writing her autobiography. Unfortunately she published some of Mary Lincoln's letters in the appendix, and Robert Lincoln became angry at what he saw as an invasion of privacy. He subsequently cut the ties between the two women. Keckley's wealthy women clients were also outraged, and her dressmaking business suffered. In addition she lost the respect of many African Americans who thought the book was disloyal to the Lincolns.

In 1892 she taught dressmaking in the domestic arts department at Wilberforce University, but ill health forced her to leave after one year. She moved to Philadelphia, then back to Washington DC. Her only income was a pension of $12 per month for her son's Civil War service. She died in an institution she helped found, the Home for Destitute Women and Children.

Keckley was a tall, intelligent woman, with impeccable manners and pleasant conversational ability. Her success in St. Louis and Washington was due as much to her personality as to her sewing and teaching skills. During the Civil War she founded the Contraband Relief Association that raised money and collected clothes for African American refugees in Washington, DC.

See also: African American Businesswomen; Fashion Industry

Further Reading

Garrett, Marie. "Elizabeth Keckley." In Smith, *Epic Lives*, p. 313–318.

Keckley, Elizabeth. *Behind the Scenes; or, Thirty Years a Slave and Four Years in the White House.*

Marlowe, Gertrude Woodruff. "Keckley, Elizabeth Hobbs." In Garraty and Carnes, p. 432–433.

Keeth, Fran (Martha Frances) (1946–), Chemical Industry Executive

Fran Keeth is president and CEO of Shell Chemical LP, executive vice president of customer fulfillment and product business units, and deputy CEO of Shell Chemical Ltd., the parent company. As the first woman to head a major U.S. chemical business, she was ranked number 49 in *Fortune's* 2002 list of the most powerful women in corporate America.

She grew up in Texas, one of three children, and earned a BA in accounting in 1967, an MBA in 1980, and a law degree in 1998, all from the University of Houston. Keeth's first job was for Shell Oil Company in the tax department, where she was the only woman. After the death of her boss, she became the group leader and later rose to director of tax compliance in 1986. She held many domestic and international finance positions between 1989 and 1996, when she was made head of the finance department for worldwide oil products for the then parent company Royal Dutch Shell.

In August 1996 Keeth was elected controller of Mobil Corporation and Mobil Oil Corporation, responsible for worldwide accounting, auditing, external reporting, and financial analysis. In September 1997 she returned to Shell Chemicals as the executive vice president of finance and business systems. Shell embarked that year on what became a five-year major reorganization, and Keeth was an integral part of developing its goals and strategies. In 1999 she became the CFO of Shell's chemical operations. The next year she was appointed to the supervisory board for ventures. By June 2001 she achieved her present position.

Keeth, believing strongly that diversity is a critical issue for the chemicals industry, sits on the Shell Global Diversity and Inclusiveness Council. She is also very concerned about environmental issues and chaired a task force that explored the relationship between responsible care and sustainable development. It sponsored an initiative on security, quality standards, and regulation. In 1986 *Oil Daily* named her one of the top women in the U.S. oil industry.

See also: Energy Industry

Further Reading
Keeth, Fran with Eve Tahminicioglu. "In Shock, and In Charge."
"Martha Frances (Fran) Keeth Joins Mobil as Controller."
"Rising from the Ranks: Fran Keeth."

King, Henrietta Chamberlain (1832–1925), Rancher

When Henrietta King died in 1925, she owned the largest ranch in the world, the King Ranch in Texas. She left an estate of $54 million, almost 95,000 head of cattle, and more than 1 million acres of land, an area larger than Rhode Island.

She was born in Boonville, Missouri, grew up in Tennessee, the oldest daughter of a preacher, and was educated at the Holy Springs Female Institute in Mississippi in 1847 and 1848. Her father built the first Presbyterian church in Brownsville, Texas, on a houseboat. She met her future husband, steamboat master Richard King, when he almost rammed their houseboat. In 1854 after a four-year courtship, they married and moved to his new ranch, then called Rancho Santa Gertrudis. They had five children, and she managed the ranch while he was away on business trips and during the Civil War.

When Richard King died in 1885, she inherited more than 600,000 acres and a debt of $500,000 and made Robert Kleberg manager. He had been handling the legal affairs of the ranch and married her daughter Alice the following year. King sold land to pay the debts and changed to shipping the cattle by train rather than the long cattle drives. After taking ten years to pay the debt, she began to buy land. She planned and contributed the land for the town of Kingsville. She owned the lumber company, the ice plant, the newspaper, and the cotton gin, donated land for churches, and built the first school. There were no saloons; she believed strongly in temperance.

In 1885 she gave Kleberg the power of attorney. The ranch prospered, and she concentrated on improving the breeding and care of cattle, producing the Santa Gertrudis breed which was fatter, thrived in the Texas environment, and was less prone to diseases. King was the first to dip cattle to protect them from tick fever. She also tried scientific ways to find water and developed the King Ranch quarter horses, three of which won the Kentucky Derby. Her greatest achievement was her pioneering method of producing beef through scientific, assembly-line methods.

King was widely known for her generosity and hospitality. She did, however, insist that her guests dress for dinner. She was a strict Presbyterian, a community builder, and a pioneer in beef cattle-breeding techniques. When she died, the 200 King Ranch cowboys dressed as vaqueros and escorted her coffin in the funeral procession. Her twenty-two-page will forbade breaking up the ranch, which thrives to this day.

See also: Agriculture/Ranching

Further Reading

Fox, Mary Virginia. *A Queen Named King: Henrietta of the King Ranch.*

"La Patrona." In Crawford, p. 89–101.

Linderman, Kathryn. "Ranching Entrepreneur Henrietta King: Determination Helped Build a Million-Acre-Plus Cattle Empire in Texas."

Sizer, Mona D. *The King Ranch Story: Truth and Myth.*

Kipper, Barbara Levy (1942–), Book/Magazine Distributor

In 1986 Barbara Levy Kipper inherited Charles Levy Co, a wholesale book and magazine distributor, from her father, who had inherited it from his father.

Founded in 1893, it has been on *Working Woman*'s list of top woman-owned companies since the first installment in 1992.

Kipper was born in Chicago, worked in the family business as a girl, graduated from Evanston High School, and received her BA from the University of Michigan. After graduation she worked as a reporter for the *Chicago Sun-Times*, where she says she earned renown from the copy desk as the most creative speller. She was a photo editor for *Cosmopolitan Magazine* in New York City from 1969 to 1971. After she married David Kipper in 1974, they lived in Israel where he was a clinical psychology professor at Israel's Bar Ilan University. They have two daughters who have worked in the business.

In 1984 she came back to Chicago to become vice chair of Charles Levy Company and in 1986 took over as chair and owner. She says that her worst time was when she brought in her own management team and board; it was difficult dealing with people's loyalties and feelings. Kipper sold the music and video distribution business in 1994, deciding to focus on the core businesses and upgrade customer service.

She believes in acquisitions as a way to grow and has purchased the Philadelphia News Agency, the Brauninger News Service in New Jersey, and Badger News, a Wisconsin competitor. She also merged the magazine operation with North Shore Distributors, a company owned by her grandfather's brother's grandson. Now the company runs book departments for stores including Kmart, Target, Office Depot, and Stop & Shop as well as magazine distribution. It takes pride in fast inventory return. When she leased the L'eggs plant in Chicago, she rehired their employees at a higher wage. In December 1998 she bought a Dublin wholesale magazine company, Unimag.

Kipper's management style is collegial. She firmly believes that all employees must be involved in making business decisions and have current knowledge of the clients and their needs. She encourages employees to follow literary trends and watch for anything that would help in selecting materials. She has also formed "solution teams" of management and staff who brainstorm to solve problems. In 1991 she appointed the company's first woman CEO, Carol Kloster.

Kipper believes in community service. She is a chair of the Spertus Institute of Jewish Studies, a trustee of the Chicago Historical Society and of Roosevelt University, and a member of the Chicago Workforce Board. She has served on the boards of the Chicago Foundation for Women, the Shoah Foundation, and the Joffrey Ballet. In 1992 she won the Deborah Award from the Committee on Women's Equality of the American Jewish Congress, the Shap Shapiro Human Relations Award from the Anti-Defamation League of B'nai B'rith, and was named a Distinguished Philanthropist by the National Society of Fund Raising Executives. She belongs to the Committee of 200, the Women's Issues Network, and the Chicago Network.

See also: Publishing Industry

Further Reading
Bamford, Janet and Jennifer Pendleton, p. 44.
Lea, p. 109.
McFarland, Lynne Joy, Larry E. Senn, and John R. Childress. *21st Century Leadership.*
Schmuckler, Eric and Harris Collingwood, p. 40.

Kitchen, Louise (1969–), Energy Industry Executive

Louise Kitchen was the chief operating officer of Enron Americas before the company's demise. In 2001 she ranked number 17 on *Fortune*'s list of the most powerful women in U.S. corporations. According to Steiner, she "made her name with the audacious manner in which she set up the . . . company's online trading arm." She was promoted at Enron seven times in five years. Her story is used as a case study in business schools.

Kitchen was born in 1969 and is the mother of two children. She calls herself a loudmouth and has a reputation for being blunt and pushy as well as inspiring. Her first job was for PowerGen where she worked in electricity trading and then directed gas trading. In 1994 she joined Enron, began building their gas-trading activities in Europe, and served on several industrial panels while developing that market. During 1997 and 1998 she concentrated on introducing Enron's electricity sales in the United Kingdom and in 1999 became co-president and COO of Enron Online, LLC. This project was her idea, and she developed it, launched it, and operated it for five months before telling the board. By that time it was highly successful and had revolutionized the energy-trading industry.

In 2001 she was named COO of Enron Americas, a division responsible for wholesale services in North America, South America, and Canada. Later that year the company took a highly publicized nosedive due to allegations of monetary and fiscal fraud by the highest officials and their accountants.

See also: Energy Industry

Further Reading
http://www.hoovers.com/officers/bio/1/0.3353.10521_12902156.html
Saito-Chung, David. "Enron's Ken Lay Focus on Finding the Best People Helps Keep His Energy Company at the Top."
Steiner, Rupert. "Briton Who Took Trading Online."

Knight, Margaret (1838–1914), Paper Bag Manufacturer/Inventor

Margaret Knight invented the square-bottomed paper bag, the basis of today's grocery bag. When her paper-bag machine invention was stolen by someone who had seen it, she fought him in the patent courts and won. She established the Eastern Paper Bag Company of Hartford to make the bags, receiving $2,500 for the patent rights and royalties for every bag made until the sum reached $25,000.

She was born in York, Maine, and was always interested in making things. Her sleds, in particular, were the best in town. At age twelve Knight visited a cotton mill and saw a weaving accident, so she developed a device, her first invention, for preventing similar accidents. Although she had no formal post-secondary education, she was a prolific inventor all her life. During her early years she had many jobs, including an upholstery business, and learned home repairs, photography, and silver engraving.

She received her first patent at thirty-two while working for the Columbia Paper Bag Company in Springfield, Massachusetts. It was an improved paper-feeding machine that could fold square-bottomed paper bags. The following year, 1871, she invented the paper-bag machine, which she improved throughout her life. Knight partnered with a businessman in Newton, Massachusetts, who financed her first machines. Then she established her company but sold the patent agreements in return for cash, royalties, and 214 shares of company stock to support herself.

In the 1880s she invented a dress and coat shield, a clasp for holding robes, and a spit. In the early 1900s she had a workshop in Boston and concentrated on engines for the Knight-Davidson Motor Company of New York. She eventually held twenty-seven patents, selling most of them to the companies who employed her. Although she was independent and self-supporting, she was not in good health through much of her life. When she died from pneumonia and gallstones, her personal estate was $275.05.

In 1871 Queen Victoria decorated her for her paper-bag invention.

See also: Inventors

Further Reading

Allen, Stacey L. "Knight, Margaret E." In Garraty and Carnes, p. 815–816.

Lovett, Robert W. "Knight, Margaret E." In Edward T. James, p. 339–340.

MacDonald, Anne L. *Feminine Intuition: How Women Inventors Changed America,* p. 50–56.

Knopf, Blanche Wolf (1894–1966), Book Publisher

Blanche Knopf, one of the most prominent female book publishers, was a full partner in the Knopf Publishing Company since it began in 1915. Robert Nathan, a Knopf author, once called her "the soul of the firm" (Whitman, p. 68). Knopf was a two-person firm in every sense, although her title was vice president and director of the corporation. Later she became president and her husband was chair of the board. Until her death, she was active in finding

Once Blanche Wolf Knopf was asked to talk to a group about the future of women in publishing; she refused, stating that there was no future worth talking about.

European and Latin American authors and was responsible for publishing many of their finest works.

She was born in New York City to a wealthy jeweler, tutored by French and German governesses, and attended a private school. She met Alfred Knopf when he was still at Columbia University in 1911. In 1915 he borrowed $5,000 from his father to begin a publishing company, and they married the next year. They had one son who was raised primarily by a nurse.

From the beginning their goal was to publish fine literature and to establish a reputation for the best quality of book publishing. They took their first annual trip to Europe in 1920 with the objective of signing European authors. Knopf, with her command of languages, was instrumental in this quest, eventually signing Andre Gide, Jean-Paul Sartre, and Albert Camus. In 1930 she obtained the first Sigmund Freud manuscript to be published in the United States. She and her husband also published American writers including Dashiell Hammett, James Cain, Willa Cather, and Raymond Chandler. Clarence Day's *Life with Father* was also published during the 1930s. During World War II when travel to Europe was impossible, Knopf went to Latin America to find authors.

The company's first publications included Barrett Clark's translation of four French plays by Emile Augier, Gogol's *Taras Bulba*, and short stories by Guy de Maupassant. The first Knopf best seller was W. H. Hudson's *Green Mansions* that established its reputation as a prominent publishing house, followed by works by British authors A.A. Milne and E.M. Forster, and German author Thomas Mann. Its perennial best sellers were Kahlil Gibran's books, particularly *The Prophet*, with over two million copies sold.

Knopf books have won eighteen Pulitzer prizes, six National Book Awards, and eleven Nobel prizes for their authors. When Camus won the Nobel Prize in 1957, Knopf and her husband went to Stockholm. Their goal of fine publishing had been fulfilled, and they were particularly known for their impeccable translations. Their son Alfred joined the company for a while but left to begin Atheneum in 1959. That year Knopf's sales were $4 million before it merged with Random House, but remained autonomous, in 1960.

Although the publishing industry was a man's world then, Blanche Knopf succeeded admirably. Once she was asked to lecture about the future of women in publishing; she refused, stating that there was no future worth talking about. She made room for herself however, and subsequent events have proved her wrong. She tried to establish a woman's publishing group, since women were excluded from the Publishers Lunch Club, but felt that it failed because there weren't enough of them.

Knopf and her husband each had their own authors that they befriended and encouraged in their writing. She won many awards, including the Chevalier of the Legion of Honor in 1948 for her support of French literature and the Cavaleiro of the Brazilian National Order of the Southern Cross in 1950. In 1964 she was promoted to the rank of officer in the Legion of Honor. She received an honorary Litt.D. from Franklin and Marshall University and also honorary doctorates from Adelphi University and Western College for Women. She received the Constance Lindsay Skinner Award posthumously from the Women's National Book Association that honored meritorious service by a woman to the book industry.

See also: Publishing Industry

Further Reading
Hellman, Geoffrey. "Profiles: Publisher."
"Knopf, Blanche." In *Current Biography 1957*, p. 308–310.
Marchino, Lois. "Knopf, Blanch Wolf." In Garraty and Carnes, p. 821–823.

Knox, Rose Markward (1857–1950), Gelatin Manufacturer

When Rose Markward married glove salesman Charles Knox in 1883, he had $11 in his pocket after he paid the minister. By 1890 they had saved $5,000 and invested it in manufacturing prepared gelatin. They moved to Johnstown, New York, to begin production near the tanneries that provided the calf parts that produced gelatin.

Because gelatin was seen mainly as food for invalids, they had to expand the market. Knox wrote a booklet of recipes called *Dainty Desserts* and learned the details of the business. With a passion for flamboyant advertising, her husband used balloon ascensions and horse races to make his point. When he died in 1908, she was fifty-one and quite able to manage the business herself, although against the advice of friends and relatives. She explained that she was continuing it for her son Charles, and then when he died, for her son James.

In reality she ran Knox Gelatin as president for the next forty years, immediately changing the focus of advertising to concentrate on women. She emphasized nutrition, economy, sanitary production, and recipes through her newspaper column, Mrs. Knox Says. She also produced another cookbook, gave cooking demonstrations, and established a kitchen to experiment with new uses for gelatin.

Knox emphasized managing the business in a woman's way. Her first change was to make everyone enter through the front door. She cleaned up the plant, added attractive flowers and shrubs, and in 1913 began a five-day work-week, with the proviso that it would produce the same amount of work as had the previous five-and-a-half-day week. She also instituted paid vacations, time off for illness, and pensions. Her management style was described as benign but brisk. Her son James joined the firm that year, but she remained president.

In 1911 the company moved into a larger building. In 1915 sales had tripled, and the company incorporated at $300,000. By 1925 its value had increased to $1 million. The company continued to expand, including a 50 percent interest in Kind & Landesmann, importer of calf pates. In 1930 Knox became a vice president of Kind and Knox Gelatin Company. It expanded, building a plant in Camden, New Jersey, for flavored gelatins, spurred by competition from Jell-O. Her employees loved and respected her; in that year 85 percent of them had been with the company for at least twenty-five years. There was never labor trouble, and she ruled with a benevolent hand.

On her ninetieth birthday, Knox named her son president of the company. Two years later *Collier's* named her America's foremost woman industrialist. Her abundant philanthropy, particularly in Johnstown, included an athletic field, stadium, clubhouse, swimming pool for the YMCA, the establishment of the Willing Helpers Home for Women, and the start of a student loan fund for the Business & Professional Woman's Club. She was the first woman to attend meetings of the American Grocery Manufacturers Association and the first woman to be elected to its board.

See also: Food Industry

Further reading
Asbury, E. "Grand Old Lady of Johnstown."
"Knox, Rose." In *Current Biography Yearbook*, 1949, p. 330–332.
Lovett, Robert W. "Knox, Rose." In Edward T. James, p. 343–344.

Koplovitz, Kay (1945–), Cable Television Executive

Kay Koplovitz, one of cable television's pioneers, was the first female CEO of a television network. She founded and was the driving force behind USA Network, the first network in cable television, and was the first to produce original movies and series for cable. In addition, she was the first to negotiate cable rights with the National Hockey League, the National Basketball League, and major league baseball. Currently she is CEO of her own consulting company, Koplovitz & Co., and managing director of the media and entertainment division of Prima Consulting Group.

She was born in Milwaukee and, at age three, persuaded her mother to let her attend kindergarten. Her first serious responsibility as publisher of the class newspaper in fifth grade was selling enough copies to pay for the class trip. Koplovitz also cites two high school activities that taught her business skills: as assembly announcer, she learned the power of communication, and as cheerleader, the importance of encouraging people to do their best (Wheeler, "She Thinks Like a CEO," p. 32). She graduated Phi Beta Kappa from the University of Wisconsin in 1967 where she started in pre-medicine but fell in love with the new field of communications, earning a master's degree in communications at Michigan State in 1968.

Her first job was in Milwaukee producing a talk show about sports for WTMJ-TV. In 1971 she married William Koplovitz, and they were both salespeople for Comsat, signing up seventy-five communities in two years. She ran her own communications management and public relations business for a few years but went back to the cable business with United Artists Columbia Satellite Services. It was a new business then, and she was the only woman, which she saw as an advantage.

While there she created the Madison Square Garden Network, an all-sports channel and the first to distribute live events via satellite to cable stations. In 1980 it was renamed USA Network with Koplovitz as chair and CEO, the most powerful woman in the cable industry. During the next ten years, programming expanded to other kinds of programs, original movies, and series. In 1992 she developed and launched the Sci-Fi Channel that had 46 million subscribers by 1988. That year USA Network counted 73 million subscribers and revenues of over $500 million. Together the channels were worth $4 billion.

In April 1998 Barry Diller bought the parent company of USA Network. Koplovitz resigned and began her own consulting company. In November 1999 she was elected chair of the board of directors of Working Woman Network, Inc., an online adjunct of *Working Woman*, becoming CEO in January. Her goal was to transform the network into a business community for women by offering all the resources needed to develop a business, to rise in the corporate world, or to find financing and/or venture capital. An added offering was software enabling business applications such as calendaring, bookkeeping, bill paying, and payroll. The network was launched in April 2000, but she left one year later when the owners decided to sell the journal. She continues to consult and published her book in 2002.

Koplovitz thinks of herself as a builder; she loves new ideas and looks for those that interest and excite her. Her theory of management is threefold: have a vision and express it clearly, understand the business, and hire the best people and motivate them. When cable was a new industry, she joined on the ground floor. Now she is involved in a variety of projects designed to enable businesswomen's access to venture capital and other resources.

A vital part of several professional organizations, Koplovitz has served on the boards of the National Cable Television Association, the Advertising Council, the Cable Advertising Bureau, the Tennis Hall of Fame, National Junior Achievement, Nabisco Holdings Corporation, Liz Claiborne Inc., Instinct Group, and General Re Corporation. She has been the vice president, president, and chair of the International Council of the National Academy of Television Arts and Sciences. She has also served on the board of trustees of the Museum of Television and Radio, and the board of overseers for the NYU Graduate School of Business.

In 1998 President Clinton appointed Koplovitz chair of the National Women's Business Council. As part of her mission she developed an investor fund for woman-owned high-tech companies and helped organize Springboard

2000, one of the first venture capital fairs for women. Its successful January forum grew into eight forums in six cities. By July 2002, 85 percent of the funded companies were still in business. Boldcap Ventures, a New York City all-woman investor group, grew out of Springboard.

Koplovitz has won many awards. In 1985 she was named a "Corporate Climber" by *Industry Week* and received the Outstanding Alumnus Award from the Michigan State Graduate School of Business. Over the next few years she received the Women Who Run the World Award from Sara Lee Corporation, the Muse Award from New York Women in Film and Television, the Ellis Island Medal of Honor, and the Crystal Award from Women in Film. In 1992 she was on *Business Week*'s list of the fifty top women in business, and the following year they named her one of the five best managers. In 1994 she began "Erase the Hate," a USA Network public affairs initiative for fighting hate and racism for which she received the 1998 Champion of Liberty Award from the Anti-Defamation League. Two years later she was the first woman to win the NATPE Chairman's Award. In 1999 she was included in *Broadcasting and Cable*'s list of the one hundred most influential figures in twentieth century journalism. She entered the Cable Television Hall of Fame in 2001 and named one of American Women in Radio and Television's "50 Greatest Women in Radio and TV."

See also: Broadcasting Industry

Further Reading

Block, Valerie. "Multimedia Effort Aims to Empower Business Women: *Working Woman* Network Debuts Web Site."

Cooper, Jim. "The USA According to Kay."

Koplovitz, Kay. *Bold Women, Big Ideas: Learning to Play the High-Risk Game.*

Wheeler, Carol. "She Thinks Like a CEO (Because She Is One)."

Krawcheck, Sallie L. (1965–), Financial Analyst

Sallie Krawcheck first appeared on the *Fortune* list of the most powerful women in business in the United States in 2002, ranked at number 42. She was then CEO of Sanford C. Bernstein, a stock market research analysis company. In the uneasy stock market of 2001 to 2002, it stood out as an analysis company that did not monetarily back the businesses it analyzed, thus avoiding conflict of interest. When she joined Citigroup in 2003 as the head of their Smith Barney division, she rose to number 14 in the 2003 *Fortune* list.

She was raised in Charleston, South Carolina. Her father is a lawyer as are her siblings. In high school she was an outstanding student, cheerleader, and a high-jump star. She received a degree in journalism from the University of North Carolina at Chapel Hill, where she was a Morehead scholar. She also earned an MBA from Columbia in 1992.

Krawcheck worked at Salomon Brothers and Donaldson, Lufkin, and Jenrette investment firms as an investment banker. In 1995 now the mother of a baby boy, she joined Sanford C. Bernstein as a research analyst. She wrote an impressive report on bank annuities, and in 1996 was asked to be in charge of brokerage stocks.. In late 1998 she was promoted to director of research, when most institutional investors were uninterested in research, and she tripled the size of the staff. In June 2001 she was named chairman and CEO of the company.

In October 2002 she was recruited to lead Smith Barney, Citigroup's new, independent division of stock research and brokerage businesses, responsible for restoring Citibank's image as a brokerage house, one that can give unbiased investment advice. She reports directly to Citibank's CEO and serves on the executive committee.

Krawcheck has been called one of the most insightful voices covering the banking industry. She is said to be funny, personable, fearless, and clever. She hires experts in the field and firmly believes in teamwork. When she was named chairman of Sanford C. Bernstein, she was one of the youngest women in that position.

Her awards include being number 1 on the 1997 *Institutional Investor* rankings of U.S. brokers and asset managers, on the first team in the area of written reports noted by *Institutional Investor* in 1998; "The Straight Shooter" in the *Money's* 2001 Ultimate Investment Club, and one of ten "all-star analysts" by *Fortune* in June 2002. *Time* named her one of fifteen global business influentials in December 2002, *Fortune* called her a leader of 2002, and *Crain's New York Business* listed her in their annual "40 Under 40" the next year. *Fortune* ranked her number 1 on its 2003 list of the top ten most influential businesspersons under forty.

See also: Finance Industry

Further Reading
Berenson, Alex. "From Low-Key Boutique to Pressure-Cooker Firm."
Herera, Sue and Ron Insana. "Sallie Krawcheck of Sanford Bernstein on Independence of Research Analysts."
Kadlec, Daniel. "Sallie Krawcheck: CEO of Citigroup's New Smith Barney Unit."
Rynecki, David. "The Bernstein Way: There is a Firm that Does Research Right. Inside the Best Little Shop on Wall Street."

L

Margaret LaForge is known as America's first woman boss of a sizeable retail enterprise and one of the earliest woman business executives in the United States. In the 1860s, the early days of Macy's Department Store in New York City, she supervised over 200 employees and was responsible for running the store.

She was born in Nantucket, Massachusetts, and had a brother who died as an infant. After graduation, she taught in various positions for three years. At some point she had one eye removed and decided a different job would be less demanding of her vision. One of her distant Nantucket relatives was Rowland H. Macy who had opened a fancy dry goods store in New York in 1858. He hired her as a cashier at a time when Macy's was selling ribbons, fabric, laces, hosiery, gloves, feathers, etc.

She was a natural at business. Because of her flair for numbers, she was promoted to bookkeeper and soon was keeping all of the accounts. In 1866 she was promoted again to superintendent of the store, responsible for the now 200 employees. The store had an annual business of $1 million and much of it was due to LaForge's acumen and sense of what women customers would buy. As supervisor, she was responsible for routine matters such as hiring, firing, training employees, and handling complaints. She was a talented marketer, promoting several new lines of merchandise, including flowers, potted plants, housewares, jewelry, gifts, clocks, and home furnishings. She also suggested that Macy put his logo on all his price tags and letterhead. When soda fountains became popular, she put one in the middle of the store, so that customers had to pass the merchandise to reach it for their refreshing drink. When she noticed the new interest in country excursions, she stocked picnic baskets.

Much of Macy's success as a retailer can be attributed to LaForge's flair for marketing, awareness of new fads, ability to relate merchandise to them, and her careful supervision and training. She was known as firm, smart, fair, and tactful. Her motto was "Be everywhere, do everything, and never fail to astonish the customer" (Moskowitz, Milton, et al. *Everybody's Business*, p. 329).

In 1869 she married Abiel La Forge, who had befriended and helped Macy's son during the Civil War, and was given a job as a lace buyer. Between 1869 and 1877 they had six children, including twin daughters. They lived in an apartment over the store, and she still worked at night on inventory and accounts. Her husband was made a partner in 1871. La Forge was not paid after that, although she was in complete charge when the two men were on buying trips. When one trip occurred during the panic of 1873, she took this opportunity to open a grocery department that became very successful. Although her husband suggested that she be paid for this time, Macy gave her a gift of furniture instead, completely in keeping with the times when married women just did not work.

In 1878 LaForge's husband contracted tuberculosis and died, two years before she did. She was the first of many woman retailers and one of the most influential, demonstrating that a woman's understanding of potential customers was an important part of the business.

See also: Retailing Industry

Further Reading

Bird, Caroline. *Enterprising Women*, p. 78–81.
Goodman, Paul. "LaForge, Margaret Getchell." In Edward T. James, p. 358.
Johnson, Curtiss. *America's First Lady Boss*.
Moskowitz, Milton, et al. *Everybody's Business*, p. 329

Lagomasino, Maria Elena (1950–), Investment Banker

Because of her position and accomplishments as chair and CEO of the J.P. Morgan Private Bank, Maria Elena Lagomasino has been on the *Fortune* list of the most powerful women in corporate America since 2001; in 2003 she ranked number 39. J.P. Morgan is the largest private bank in the United States with assets of $300 billion.

She was born in Cuba to a wealthy family; her grandfather founded a cigar factory that the government took over after the Cuban revolution. The family was left with nothing and escaped to the United States. Lagomasino earned a degree in French literature from Columbia University, an MBA from Fordham University, and a master's degree in librarianship from Columbia University. Her first job was as a librarian at the United Nations.

Her banking career began in 1976 at Citibank as a specialist in Latin American private banking. In 1983 Lagomasino joined Chase Manhattan Bank as the manager and division executive for Chase Private Banking International.

She was appointed vice president of Western Hemisphere Private Banking in 1990, and in 1994, manager of the private Bank for the Americas. In December 1997 she became the senior managing director in charge of the Global Private Banking Group and was named to the policy council, its policy-making body. After Chase Manhattan merged with J.P. Morgan in 2000, she was named the managing director and co-head of the J.P. Morgan Private Bank, responsible for developing the client base, attracting new clients and deepening relationships with existing clients. She focused on formulating client strategies and strengthening service standards. She was promoted to her present position in June 2001. Her forte is keeping in close contact with her clients who have an average net worth of $100 million.

Lagomasino travels 50 percent of the time and is wedded to her beeper full-time; she has said that she paid for her career with a lack of private life, but she loves it. Her responsibility is huge because, with her wealthy clients, trust and integrity are key. After September 11, she immediately called to reassure her clients and discuss what to do in case of problems in the economy.

She is a former director of Asia Global Crossing Ltd and Phillips-Van Heusen and sits on the boards of Coca Cola and Avon, who noted in its announcement of her appointment her global perspective and expertise in international marketing. The YWCA of New York named her to its Class of 1992 Woman Achievers. She is also a member of the Committee of 200.

See also: Banking; Latina Businesswomen

Further Reading
Fabrikant, Geraldine. "Making Sure the Rich Stay Rich, Even in Crisis."
Gold, Jacqueline S. "Chase's Private Bank Chief Applies Life Lessons, Has a 'Blast.'"
Habal, Hala. "Expert: Don't Get Emotional with Investments."

Laimbeer, Nathalie Schenck (1882–1929), Banker, Financial Writer

Nathalie Laimbeer was the first woman to hold an executive title in the National City Bank of New York, the most conservative and largest bank on Wall Street. She was also the first woman financial writer and one of the founders of the Association of Bank Women, now National Association of Bank Women.

She was born to a socially prominent family in New York City. Her interest in finance showed itself at an early age when she accompanied her grandmother to the bank and became fascinated with the bright orange coupons of the clipped bonds. As a young woman, she concentrated on social and charitable activities. She married twice; the first ended in divorce with one son; and the second, to William Laimbeer, in disaster. He was killed in a 1913 automobile accident, and she took two years to recover from her injuries. She volunteered for the United States Food Administration during World War I, working to preserve food. In 1918 she managed the Bureau of Home Economics for New York Edison, giving demonstrations to students at colleges and high schools.

In 1919 she began her banking career in a clerical position. Laimbeer was hired to manage the women's department at the U.S. Mortgage and Trust Company. This department was formed to take care of the very few female clients by walking them through their banking business and personally serving their needs. Many banks had such departments at this time, seeing it as a way to gain more customers. The following year Laimbeer was appointed assistant secretary of the organization that oversaw the establishment of women's departments at all the U.S. Mortgage and Trust branches.

When she was hired by National City Bank in 1925, she was the bank's first woman to be appointed with a title: assistant cashier in charge of the women's department. It may not sound impressive now, but until then, women were thought not fit to handle money or to be in charge of important matters like banking. Laimbeer prepared the way for women to become an integral part of the banking profession. In 1921 she and four other women formed the Association of Bank Women to establish standards and an educational program for women without training or experience in banking. She was the first vice president and second president, serving from 1923 to 1926. This activity as well as her banking position made her nationally known for her ability and judgement.

Unfortunately, with deteriorating health, she was in the bank position for only one year. She did talk her way into a job as editor of the finance department for the *Delineator* and was the first woman to write a financial column. She also wrote articles on financial matters for the New York newspapers before she died suddenly in 1929.

See also: Banking; Late Bloomers

Further Reading
Fisher, Kenneth L. *100 Minds that Made the Market*, p. 210–212.
Ingham, John N. *Biographical Dictionary of American Business Leaders*, p. 749–750.

Lansing, Sherry (1944–), Film Producer, Executive

Sherry Lansing, chairman of the Paramount Motion Pictures Group and one of the most powerful women in Hollywood, is credited for the turnaround of Paramount from a company in financial trouble to number one in the industry. She has been on *Fortune*'s lists of the most powerful women in corporate America since 1998. In 2003 she ranked number 20. Several of her colleagues have also called her the nicest person in Hollywood, a town not known for niceness.

She was born and raised in Chicago. Her mother came to the United States as a seventeen-year-old refugee from Nazi Germany. Her father died when

Lansing was nine, and her mother took over his real estate business, teaching herself everything she needed to know. She quit when she remarried, however, sending a mixed message to her daughter. Lansing graduated from the Chicago Laboratory School, a high school for gifted children. After receiving a BA in theatre, summa cum laude, from Northwestern, she married and moved to Los Angeles. Lansing taught high-school math in the inner city for three years before deciding it was not the career she wanted. By then she was divorced and modeled in television commercials for Max Factor and Alberto Culver. In 1970 she appeared in two movies, *Loving* and *Rio Lobo*; and in *Banyon*, a 1972 to 1973 television series.

In 1972 she launched her third career as a story editor with Wagner International Production Company. After a two-year stint at MGM, she moved to Columbia Pictures in 1977 as the vice president of production, responsible for two pictures that won four Oscars, *China Syndrome* and *Kramer vs Kramer*. In 1980 she became the president of 20th Century Fox Productions, the first woman president in the industry. Two of her movies were successes, *Taps* and *The Verdict*, but she also produced four expensive flops. She and Stanley Jaffee formed their own studio in 1982, Jaffee-Lansing Productions, which was responsible for *Racing with the Moon*, *Fatal Attraction*, *The Accused*, and *Indecent Proposal*. After Jaffee left in 1991 she continued under Sherry Lansing Productions.

The next year she took over as chair and CEO of Paramount Motion Pictures Group, then a struggling production studio reeling from a long takeover battle in which Viacom bought the company. In this position she was the highest-ranking woman in Hollywood. One of her biggest accomplishments was stabilizing the company with such films as *Forrest Gump*, *Titanic*, *Saving Private Ryan*, *Mission Impossible 2*, *Tomb Raider*, and *The Hours*. The studio has won numerous Oscars since she started there.

> Sherry Lansing, chairman of Paramount and one of the most powerful women in Hollywood, is credited for the turnaround of Paramount to number one in the industry.

Lansing is known for her hands-on approach: She appears on the set every day and pays close attention to every detail. She has a reputation for creating big movies on a sensible budget. She says her success is due to the strong work ethic she learned from her mother. She is enthusiastic and emotionally involved with her films, preferring those that have a message dealing with important and timely issues.

Lansing has served on the board of trustees of the American Film Institute, University of California at Los Angeles, Scripps College, and the Times Mirror Company. She is a regent of the University of California. In 1995 she received a star on the Hollywood Walk of Fame. *Biography Magazine* named her as a top achiever of the century, and in 2001, *Hollywood Reporter* named her to the Power 100 of Women in Entertainment, ranking number 1 on that list in 2002. That March she won the Dr. Donald A. Reed Award from the Academy of Sci-Fi, Fantasy and Horror Films, its highest honor. She married William Friedkin in 1991 and has a stepson.

See also: Entertainment Industry

Further Reading
Conant, Jennet. "Sherry Lansing."
Johnson, K. "Making Movie Magic."
Mansfield, Stephanie. "Hollywood's Leading Lady."
"Sherry Lansing." In Acker, p. 140–142.

Largest Female-Owned Firms, *see* Top Women Business Owners

Late Bloomers

Late bloomers are those who achieve success later in life or who change careers completely and take a new path for many different reasons. Women in particular have often been late bloomers due to early obstacles such as widowhood, postponing a career, or beginning a business after raising children. There are many famous female late bloomers, including Harriet Ayer, Mary Kay Ash, Katherine Graham, Pleasant Rowland, and Irene Elder. Their stories are inspiring because they usually overcame great challenges on their way to success.

Further Reading
Snodgrass, Mary Ellen. *Late Achievers: Famous People Who Succeeded Late In Life.*

Latina Businesswomen

In Florida and in the Southwest, Spanish people were the settlers. Along the Rio Grande River, Latinas were well settled long before the area became a state. Their culture allowed these women to retain control of their property, own their own businesses, and enter into contracts. Many owned ranches; a few were very wealthy, with large tracts of land.

When statehood came, they lost these rights and in some cases, their property. In the late 1800s mutual aid societies were formed in the Hispanic communities of the Southwest to provide community support by offering low-interest loans, medical and life insurance, and burial services; encouraging education; and providing legal services. One of the earliest was Alienza Hispano Americano, organized in Tucson in 1894, that continued into the

1960s. Some of these societies were founded by groups, including women; those that had women members and included social activities were the strongest.

In 1900 a wave of Puerto Ricans immigrated to the United States seeking work. The United States annexed Puerto Rico in 1917, making these immigrants citizens. During the Great Depression, many returned home.

Before World War II there were few opportunities for employment, and non-citizens were not hired. During the war thousands emigrated, particularly from Mexico, to work in the factories and defense industry. The garment industry plants along the Mexican border doubled, and many Mexican women worked away from home, a big break from their traditional culture. These women gained a sense of pride in their accomplishment, but it was coupled with tension in their family lives. Most did not stay employed after the war, and many of the newer immigrant women obtained only low-paying or transient jobs. After Fidel Castro came to power, many Cubans immigrated to Florida.

By 1976 44.4 percent of the Latinas were in the workforce as opposed to 84.1 percent of the Latinos. That year there were more than 3 million Latinas in the United States, the majority from Mexico. They were mainly employed in clerical and service jobs. During the 1980s huge waves of immigrants came from Mexico, Cuba, and Latin American countries; more than any other ethnic group. Most were adults in their early twenties. By 1999 there were almost 22 million women, the majority working as cashiers, secretaries, sales persons, retailers, cleaners, maids, cooks, and receptionists; 18.1 percent were managers and professionals, less than other ethnic groups. Their educational level was low; many had not even graduated from high school.

The Hispanic culture has always valued a traditional family, with women staying at home and raising the children. This still prevails in many homes. Latinas did not benefit from feminism as much as some other groups, and as they become educated, they become increasingly alienated from their culture. More are attending college now, providing role models for the younger generation.

In 2001 Catalyst published a study of women of color executives, their voices, and their journeys in which Latina executives spoke of barriers in the corporate world. They felt stereotyped as too emotional and were only marginally included in corporate activities. There are few mentors or sponsors, and the company seemed to have unspoken rules on how to speak, act, and dress. They were not given visible or high-risk assignments, and consequently many Latinas became entrepreneurs. Between 1987 and 1996 Latina woman-owned businesses increased 206 percent overall, with employment increasing 487 percent and sales up to 534 percent. Because there is little ethnic solidarity among the various Hispanic cultures, however, Latinas have more difficulty raising capital and running successful businesses. Individual businesses tend to be small, with low sales and slow growth. Latina business owners are also more likely to be younger and unmarried than Hispanic male business owners. A large number are in service industries, rather than manufacturing.

The United States Hispanic Chamber of Commerce (www.ushcc.com) offers support and educational opportunities for Hispanic business owners. They communicate through a network of nearly 200 state and local Hispanic chambers of commerce and Hispanic business organizations.

Further Reading

Giscombe, Katherine and Mary C. Mattis. "Leveling the Playing Field For Women of Color in Corporate Management: Is the Business Case Enough?"

"Patterns of Latina Entrepreneurship." In Sally Ann Davies-Netzley, p. 97–122

Shim, Soyeon and Mary Ann Eastlick, "Characteristics of Hispanic Female Business Owners: An Exploratory Study"

Lau, Joanna (1958–), Electronics Manufacturer

Inc. magazine named Joanna Lau the 1995 Turnaround Entrepreneur of the Year for her success with an unprofitable electronics defense company that she had acquired in 1990. She learned about the company through an MBA case study and leveraged a buyout, changed the name to LAU Technologies, and made it profitable.

She was born in Hong Kong. Her widowed mother emigrated to the United States in 1976 with Lau and her six brothers and sisters. Her first job was in the garment district of New York City, but she found that she couldn't sew, so she decided to go to school. She learned English and earned a BA in computer science and math at the State University of New York in Stony Brook, a masters in computer engineering from Old Dominion University, and an MBA from Boston University. During this time she worked at GE and Digital Equipment, attending night school for the MBA.

Lau became intrigued with a case study about an ailing defense electronics company called Bowmar/ALI and began thinking about how she would get it back on its feet. After calling the company and finding that it was almost bankrupt, she decided to buy it. She talked to the employees and executives, offering shares of ownership if they would invest in the company; twenty-four of the sixty-four did. Then she secured a $750,000 loan from the Small Business Administration, re-mortgaged her house, cashed in her pension, persuaded Bowmar/ALI's parent company to give her a $300,000 note, and received a bank loan for $1.2 million. The entire financing package totaled $3.1 million. On February 28, 1990, she bought the company and renamed it LAU Technologies. She is president, chair, and owns 56 percent, the remainder owned by the employees.

Lau replaced the entire information system, met with suppliers to reassure them of the company's ability to pay bills, and identified new customers. Every day she checked the cash flow to ensure that the company remained solvent. In August 1990 the Gulf War started. The Army equipment used in Operation

Desert Shield and Desert Storm was flawed, and to fix it the circuit system needed to be redesigned. After LAU was awarded the contract, the company worked around the clock to deliver. Because of their commitment to time and quality, the company won the U.S. Army Contractor Excellence Award that year for its exceptional efforts. Lau hired a public relations person to capitalize on the award and to make their products known, and in 1991 the company landed a Lockheed Martin contract.

In 1992 she decided to diversify into the civilian market and develop digital imaging products. By 1995 the company had contracts for drivers' license and welfare systems in Massachusetts, Ohio, Arizona, Connecticut, and New York and also a contract with the U.S. Immigration and Naturalization Service. There was a problem at first with fading photographs, but Lau replaced all the faulty IDs at company expense.

The growth of the digital imaging business justified creating an independent public company named Viisage. Another subsidiary, LAU Defense Systems, was bought by Curtiss-Wright for more than $40 million. LAU Technology was left with two divisions and Viisage. In November 2001 Lau's testimony to the Senate Subcommittee on Technology, Terrorism, and Government Information explained how face-recognition technology could help prevent terrorists from entering into the country.

Rosabeth Moss Kanter called Joanna Lau "a role model for entrepreneurs" (Ericksen, *What's Luck...*, p. 64). In her book, *World Class*, Kanter commented, "she shows up, speaks up, and always contributes" (Jones, Sarah, p. 27). Lau is known for her people skills, particularly her persuasive and motivating skills. She is an excellent entrepreneur, willing to take risks, persevering, creative, and inventive. She sometimes micromanages, feeling that it is a necessity in a small company, and attends team meetings at least twice a month. She knows all the employees by their first names. Quality is a mantra for her.

Lau has served on the board of directors of INSO, Harrison & Troxell, BostonFed Bancorp, and the John F. Kennedy Library Foundation. She's a trustee of Bryant College and an overseer of Northeastern University. She holds honorary doctorates from Bryant College, Bentley College and Suffolk University. Her awards include the Young Engineering Award in 1987, the SBA Minority Small Business Person of the Year, the *Inc.* Turnaround Entrepreneur of the Year in 1995, and the Management Excellence Award from the World Young Business Achievers in 1997. She was recently honored at the Academy of Women Achievers Awards Luncheon by the YWCA in Boston. Her husband is the general manager and executive vice president of the company, and they have one daughter.

See also: Asian American Businesswomen; Information Technology Industry

Further Reading
Brokaw, Leslie. "Case in Point."
"Joanna Lau: LAU Technologies." In Ericksen, *What's Luck Got to Do with It?*, p. 61–80.
Jones, Sarah P. "*Herald* Business Profile: Crises Create Opportunity & Challenge."

Lauder, Estee (1908–), Cosmetics Manufacturer

Josephine Esther Mentzer dreamed of beauty in a bottle. As Estee Lauder, she transformed herself into a sophisticated society woman, and her dream into a billion-dollar cosmetics corporation. Without a formal education past eighth grade or experience in merchandising, skin care, beauty chemistry, or business, she created a cosmetics empire. She pioneered the giveaway sample as a marketing technique and is now one of the richest women in the world.

She was born to Slavic immigrant parents in Corona, Queens, New York, in a largely Italian immigrant neighborhood. Her father owned a hardware store where she sometimes worked. When she was six, her uncle, John Schotz, came to visit and stayed to live with the family. A chemist, he had his own formula skin creams and became her mentor. Lauder sold his creams from then through her teenage years. She said later that there wasn't a girl in her school who remained unslathered. In 1930, at age twenty-two, she married Joe Lauter (he changed his name later), an accountant. Three years later their first son, Leonard, was born.

She continued to sell the creams and received permission from her uncle to put her name on the bottles and sell them in New York. She began selling though beauty salons and giving free demonstrations anywhere, in the subway, in the salon, and on the streets. Lauder called one product "Super-Rich Creme." She concentrated so fiercely on getting started in the beauty business that her marriage suffered, and she and Joe divorced in 1939. Meanwhile, she began making herself over to fit the image she wished to project. She introduced herself to the most prominent hostesses and never missed a chance to go the best parties, hoping to sell her skin cream. For a long time, she told a completely fictitious story of her origins and childhood.

She and her son moved to Miami Beach, which was at its height in the social world and spent three years there, cultivating people, making contacts, and learning about the perfume business. When her son became ill, she and Joe Lauder were reunited during visits to the hospital. They decided that together they would make her business a success. He would be in charge of finance, manufacturing, and administration, and she would concentrate on what she did best: selling, marketing, and developing new products. In 1942 they remarried.

They opened their first store in New York in 1944, the same year that their second son, Ronald, was born. They bought an old restaurant to use for the factory and cooked their four products on the stoves: "Creme Pack" for skin, face powder, eye shadow, and red lipstick. She decided that she wanted to limit sales to department stores, such as Saks Fifth Avenue where she convinced them to order $800 worth of face creams. The order sold out in two days and started the company's success.

She spent the next years traveling all over the country, selling to only the best: I. Magnin, Bloomingdale's, Marshall Field, Neiman-Marcus, and Bonwit Teller. She hired only pretty, confident, and committed young women as salespeople and personally trained them. She constantly fought for store floor space and made sure her products were positioned in the best places. The company's first fragrance, Youth Dew, made its debut in 1953; bath oil and perfume sold at the low price of $8.95. It was a success and, thirty years later, was still a best seller with $100 million in revenues

Son Leonard joined the company in 1958 at age twenty-four. Two years later the company expanded internationally into Harrods in London and the Galleries Lafayette in Paris. It also made its first million dollars in sales. Aramis, a men's fragrance, made its debut in 1964. In 1968 the company launched Clinique, a hypogenic skin care line aimed at teenagers with troubled complexions. Lauder asked her saleswomen to wear white lab coats to underline the care part of the cream and hired the editor of *Vogue* to be the head of the division. The line lost money for four years, but by 1985 was a major product with $200 million in revenue. There was an initial problem with the name. The company discovered, after the products had been packaged, that someone else had registered the name, and Lauder had to pay $100,000 for the rights.

By the middle of the 1970s, Estee Lauder products were sold in more than seventy countries. In 1973 total company sales had reached $85 million, and there were 1,000 employees. This was also the year that she made her son president of the company, her husband became chairman of the board, and she remained as CEO. In 1983, her husband died.

Estee Lauder sold more than half of all beauty aids and one quarter of all men's cosmetics by 1989. It had grown from hawking skin cream on the streets of New York to ranking as the country's third-largest cosmetics company, with 10,000 employees and sales of $2 billion. This was due mainly to the panache, style, marketing genius, and energy of its founder. Her vision of "beauty in a jar" made her a billionaire, one of the richest women in America, the only self-made woman to be on the *Forbes* list of wealthy Americans. Today the company is still more than 90 percent private, owned and run by family. Her marketing strategy of providing education as well as cosmetics has been called brilliant.

Lauder is an indefatigable woman, more interested in quality than quantity, extremely focused, and a superb saleswoman. Energy and perseverance are her middle names. Her charitable endeavors focused on funding the Museum of Modern Art, the Wharton School of Business, many Jewish charities, and children's parks in New York City. She was named one of *Harper's Bazaar's* "100 Women of Accomplishment" in 1967 and received the Spirit of Achievement Award from the Albert Einstein College of Medicine in 1968. *Forbes* named her one of the "Outstanding Women of Business" in 1970, and she was named to the National Business Hall of Fame in 1988. The Boy Scouts and Girl Scouts honored her, as did many of her department stores including

Bamberger's, Neiman-Marcus, and Gimbel's. She also received the French Legion of Honor for her contributions and fund-raising efforts in the restoration at Versailles. *Biography Magazine,* in December 1999, called her one of the fifty most famous people of the century (Cawley, "The 50 Most Famous People," p. 108) while *Time* put her on its "Builders and Titans of the 20th Century" list (Mirabella, p. 183).

See also: Beauty Industry

Further Reading

Cawley, Janet. "The 50 Most Famous People," p. 108.

Israel, Lee. *Estee Lauder: Beyond the Magic.*

Landrum, Gene N. *Profiles of Female Genius,* p. 254–259.

Lauder, Estee. *Estee: A Success Story.*

Mirabella, p. 183.

Lavin, Bernice Elizabeth (1925–), Toiletries Executive

Bernice Lavin is the co-owner of the Alberto-Culver Company in the top ten on *Working Woman*'s list of woman-owned companies in the United States. In 2001 it had sales of $2,247 million and employed 15,300 persons.

She grew up in Chicago; her father was a printer. She studied business at Northwestern University for three years, and in 1947, she married Leonard Lavin. Her first job was as the assistant to the controller of an auto-parts company. In 1955 she and her husband bought Alberto-Culver for $400,000 and brought it to Chicago. Its main product was Alberto VO5 Conditioning Hairdressing, developed by a chemist named Alberto to be used by Hollywood actresses whose hair had been damaged by the studio lights. It was a small company when the Lavins bought it, and they built it into a global business.

She was the secretary-treasurer at first and, after the children were born, did everything but sales before becoming secretary-treasurer, vice chairman of the board, and a director. Their daughter, Carol Bernick, is president. The company went public in 1961, with the family retaining 46 percent of the stock. Their acquisitions included Sally Beauty Supply, Cederroth International AB, a health and hygiene goods company, and St. Ives Laboratories. In 2002 they sold more stock, lowering the family voting power to 27 percent, saying it was for investment diversification and estate planning purposes.

Racing horses is an important recreational activity for the Lavins. They own a breeding and racing farm in Florida, and after a training rider was injured, funded a Rehabilitation Institute of Chicago study of the kinds of injuries sustained by jockeys and training riders. Bernice Lavin also founded the Bernice E. Lavin Jumpstart Fund to aid worthy programs that need additional support to aid in visibility and impact. It focuses on health care, rehabilitation, education, and women's workplace issues.

See also: Beauty Industry; Bernick, Carol Lavin

Further Reading
"Alberto-Culver Company."
Robertson, W. "Ten Highest-Ranking Women in Big Business."

Lawrence, Mary Wells (1928–), Advertising Executive

Mary Wells Lawrence founded and ran one of the most successful advertising agencies in the United States in the 1970s and 1980s. She was the country's highest paid woman executive for several of those years and certainly the most famous woman advertising executive. Her firm, Wells, Rich and Greene, was responsible for some of the most memorable advertising campaigns of those years. In 1968 she became the first woman to list her company on a stock exchange.

She was born in Youngstown, Ohio, the only child of a furniture salesman. Her parents gave her every opportunity, raised her to succeed at whatever she decided to do, and expected her to achieve. She went to elocution class, dancing class, drama class, and music lessons. After graduating from high school, she went to New York and enrolled at the Neighborhood Playhouse. A year there was enough to convince her she didn't like acting, so she attended Carnegie Tech in Pittsburgh and met and married Burt Wells. They moved back to Youngstown where she got her first job writing advertising for the bargain basement sales in McKelvey's Department Store.

In 1950 they moved to New York City, and she became fashion advertising manager at Macy's Department Store. In 1952 she moved to McCann-Erickson, the advertising agency, as copy group head and, in 1957, to Doyle, Dane, Bernbach, one of the most prestigious agencies in the city, noted for its highly successful Volkswagen and Avis Rent-A-Car campaigns. She rose quickly, becoming copy chief and vice president in 1963 with what was then a handsome salary, $40,000. In 1964 she was asked to join John Tinker and Partners, a fledgling agency and then a think tank, for a salary of $60,000 and a promise of becoming president of the agency. Her highly imaginative campaigns for Alka Seltzer and Braniff Airlines put the agency on the map. The more notable one was the latter, which included a complete remake of the airplanes' appearance by painting the exteriors vibrant colors and completely remodeling the interiors, even including the attendants' uniforms. The campaign was called "The End of the Plain Plane," and it not only brought attention but also many more sales for the airlines.

In 1965 she divorced Burt Wells for the second time. They had earlier remarried and adopted two daughters. By 1966 she was earning $80,000 per year. When the presidency of John Tinker did not seem to be forthcoming, she decided to begin her own agency with Richard Rich and Stewart Greene, also from John Tinker. Wells, Rich and Greene Inc, was an immediate success. One of their first clients was Braniff. Others were Benson & Hedges 100s, Personna Razor Blades and the Burma Line of men's toiletries from Philip Morris, Utica Club Beer, and La Rosa Spaghetti. Within six months their billings totaled $30 million and employees numbered forty-five. She was president, then chairman of the board, CEO, chief administrator, and chief presenter.

In 1967 she married Harding Lawrence, the president of Braniff. In order to avoid problems, she resigned from the Braniff account and took on TWA instead, saying, "I lost an account but gained a husband" (McDowell and Umlauf, p. 210). The next year she sold shares in the company, making a tidy profit of several million dollars. By 1974 she was the highest paid executive in the industry with a gross income of over $440,595. Billings in 1973 were over $183 million, thirteenth out of 689 in the yearly ranking by *Advertising Age*. By 1975 gross billings were $187 million with a net income of $1 million. Two of their more memorable slogans were "Try it, you'll like it" and "I can't believe I ate the whole thing." The company was an incredible success, particularly in this cutthroat industry. In 1978 she took the company private again.

The agency continued to be successful until Lawrence began her long trek toward retirement. She said later that her retirement plan had evolved over five years. She began cutting back in 1987, spending more and more time at her villa in southern France, but keeping in touch through daily phone calls with Ken Olshan, who was now in charge. The agency lost some accounts but picked up others. She was no longer responsible for the creative side but returned to work until the transition from her management was complete.

In 1990 she sold 40 percent of the agency to BBDP, a French advertising network, and also stepped down as chair and CEO. The following year, she sold another 30 percent. At this time Wells, Rich and Greene's billings were $860 million. Her receipt from these transactions was rumored to be $50 to $60 million. Although there were still major clients, the management she left behind was accustomed to following her. By 1993 Lawrence held no shares in the company. Unfortunately, the agency's demise had begun. In 1997 Mike Greenlees took over BDDP; by this time Wells Rich and Greene had lost more clients and had been through a succession of executives. In 1998 Omnicron bought Greenlees' empire and closed Lawrence's agency. The loss of her presence, creativity, and the emotional link to her long-time clients seemed to be irreplaceable.

Mary Wells Lawrence is described as brilliant, charming, tough, shrewd, very creative, and physically stunning. She wasn't particularly interested in the women's movement or even providing women with jobs. She felt that being a woman made things easier rather than harder for her. She changed advertising forever and also left a legacy of clever ads and slogans, some of which have entered American slang.

She has won many awards. In 1969 she was the youngest person to be named to the Copywriters Hall of Fame. The next year she won Marketing

Stateswoman of the Year from the American Advertising Federation, and in 1971 she was named Advertising's Woman of the Year by the American Advertising Foundation. In 1988 *Adweek* took a poll asking which women in advertising women admired most: Mary Wells Lawrence was number 1. She also served on the Ralston Purina board of directors from 1975 to 1987. An *Advertising Age* poll in 1999 of the top one hundred advertising people in history listed her at number 19. That year she was inducted into the American Advertising Hall of Fame.

See also: Advertising Industry

Further Reading
Bird, Caroline, p. 217–220.
Current Biography Yearbook, 1967, p. 450–453.
Lawrence, Mary Wells. *A Big Life (in Advertising)*.
McDowell and Umlauf, p. 210.

Laybourne, Geraldine B. (1947–), Television Executive

In 1995 Geraldine Laybourne was the youngest person inducted into the Broadcasting and Cable Hall of Fame. She was honored for building the Nickelodeon channel for children into a successful basic television network. She was included on *Fortune*'s list of most powerful women in corporate America in 1998 and 1999.

She was born in Plainfield, New Jersey, the middle of three daughters. Her father was a stockbroker, and her mother was a former actress, producer, and writer for radio soap operas before retiring to become a full-time mother. Her mother encouraged the children's creativity by turning off the television in the middle of the program, telling them to write their own endings. During Laybourne's high school summers, she worked at her father's office, writing to foreign embassies and filing their brochures. She received a BA in art history from Vassar College in 1969 and a master's degree in elementary education from the University of Pennsylvania in 1971. She married Kit Laybourne in 1970, and they had a son and a daughter. Before embarking on her production career, she taught media classes at Concord Academy in New England, founded the Media Center for Children, a school resource, and became the assistant to the director of the EPIE Institute, a consumer group that evaluated educational materials.

Laybourne's first television production experience was as a partner in Early Bird Special Company. In 1980 she joined one of her their clients, Nickelodeon, a new channel, as a program manager. Through focus groups she thoroughly researched what children wanted to watch and built the channel by launching original programming and bringing in carefully chosen advertising. In 1985 she began Nick-at-Nite, with reruns of the best situation comedies including

The Mary Tyler Moore Show and *Dick Van Dyke*. By 1989 she was promoted to president of Nickelodeon/Nick-at-Nite and, two years later, began to originate new animated series such as *Rugrats* and *Ren & Stimpy*. The network reached 66 million households by 1993 when she became vice chairman of MTV Networks, serving on Viacom's operating and executive committees. In 1996 she left to become the president of Disney/ABC Cable Networks.

In May 1998 Laybourne resigned to form Oxygen Media with her husband. It bought three Web sites that targeted women: Electra, Thrive, and Moms Online. In a partnership with AOL, Carsey-Werner-Mandabach, and Harpo Entertainment (Oprah Winfrey) it launched a new cable channel for women, Oxygen with lofty goals, but had problems getting channel carriage. The February 2000 launch could be reached in only 10 million cable homes, and it had only eleven hours of original weekday programs, including two talk shows with Oprah and Candice Bergen. Even after comedies and movies were added, by the second anniversary ratings were low, with a small reach, only up to 30 million homes. By May 2003 it reached 50 million and half the programming was original. Unfortunately, the Nielsen ratings were very low.

Laybourne's management style has been compared to that of a teacher: she individualizes jobs and tries to find the person's strengths and build on them. She is creative, energetic, and inspirational and feels that employee involvement in projects is mandatory for quality programming. She emphasizes brainstorming and focus groups for decision making and believes strongly in a win-win work environment. She also has advanced the careers of many women. She says that she's managed to "combine career and family and that her children have influenced her work" (Forgrieve, Janet. "Pioneering Cable Exec," p. 2B).

Her many awards include the American Women in Radio & Television Genii Award and Women in Cable Award in 1992, the Matrix Award from New York Women in Communications in 1996, the Sara Lee Frontrunner Award, and being named one of *Time Magazine's* America's 25 Most Influential People. In 1995 she became the youngest person inducted into the Broadcasting and Cable Hall of Fame. Laybourne was named one of the fifty most influential women in radio and television by the American Women in Radio and Television in 2001 and won the "Corporate America Award," one of the 2003 Office Depot Visionary Awards given to women who are pioneers and role models for other women striving to succeed in business and the community. She has served on the National Council for Families and Television and Children Affected by AIDS Foundation.

See also: Broadcasting Industry

Further Reading
Carey, Robert. "Geraldine Laybourne—a.k.a. the Velvet Hammer—Uses Her Teaching Background and a Culture of Fun to Keep Children's Television Nickelodeon Creative, Productive and Profitable."

Forgrieve, Janet. "Pioneering Cable Exec Gets Help from Kids; Keynote Seaker for
   Athena Awards Lunch Began at Nickelodeon."
Hofmeister, Sallie. "Kids' TV—She Walks the Walk."
Stanley, Allessandra. "The Oxygen Channel is Bowing to Tastes."

Lazarus, Rochelle P. (1947–), Advertising Executive

In 1998 when Shelly Lazarus was promoted to CEO of Ogilvy & Mather, it was the first time that one woman succeeded another as CEO of an advertising agency. Her promotion also earned her the number 4 spot on *Fortune*'s list of most powerful women in corporate America that year, maintaining a high ranking on every subsequent list.

She was born in Oceanside, New York, to a homemaker mother and a father who ran an accounting firm. She was the editor of her high school newspaper. While at Smith College, she went to a career conference sponsored by Advertising Women of New York and decided that was the career for her. She graduated with a BA in psychology in 1968. While studying for an MBA at Columbia University, one of four women in the program, she worked as an intern and assistant to a product manager at General Foods. In 1970 she married George Lazarus, a medical student.

Her first job was as an assistant product manager at Clairol. Lazarus really wanted to work at an advertising agency, however, and finally landed a job at Ogilvy & Mather, handling the Lever Brothers account. By 1974 she was account supervisor, the highest-ranking woman at the agency. She was also pregnant, but her boss said there was no reason she should quit, as was the custom at that time.

From 1974 to 1976, she and her husband had to go to Ohio for his military service, but Lazarus later returned to Ogilvy as account supervisor for Avon, Ralston-Purina, and Campbell's Soup. Each succeeding position carried more responsibility. In 1977 she became the general manager of the Direct Marketing Branch. Two years later she was appointed president of Ogilvy & Mather Direct and in 1991 headed the New York office, which was in a slump. She turned the business around by winning all of IBM's advertising business, which had previously been split between several agencies. She also acquired the American Express Credit Card account. In 1995 she became president of Ogilvy & Mather Worldwide and on January 1, 1997 succeeded Charlotte Beers as CEO of the agency. Since then she has continually won new accounts; in 2001, TIAA-CREF and AT&T Wireless.

In a 1991 interview, Lazarus said: "I believe very strongly the only way to create a great organization is to develop people and nurture them. Challenge them. Make sure they are working up to full capacity. And get them to participate fully in the agency's life and management" (Much, Marilyn and

Toni Apgar, "Direct from O&M," p. 16). Her theory of advertising is called 360-degree branding, where everything ties together: packaging, brochures, and all media advertising. An unpretentious natural leader who builds strong relationships with both employees and clients, she believes that motherhood has made her a better leader and that she seldom neglected her family for her career, sometimes attending her children's activities rather than a client meeting.

As well as having served on the boards of GE, Ann Taylor, and Ogilvy & Mather, Lazarus has chaired the American Association of Advertising Agencies and Smith College's Board of Trustees. She is also a director of the Advertising Educational Foundation, the National Women's Law Center, and the World Wildlife Fund. She is a member of the Committee of 200. In 1995 she won the Matrix Award from Women in Communication, Inc., New York.

See also: Advertising Industry

Further Reading

Kanner, Bernice. "Trumpet of the Swan."

Marshall, Caroline. "Shelly Lazarus—After 28 Years, O&M's Leader Is Steeped in Its Culture."

McDonough, John. "Creating an Environment 'Where People Can do Great Work': Shelly Lazarus Talks about the Challenges and Satisfactions of Her Role as CEO of Ogilvy & Mather."

Much, Marilyn and Toni Apgar. "Direct from O&M New York: Shelly Lazarus."

Leadership

According to the *Encyclopedia of Business and Finance*, leadership "is a process in which a leader attempts to influence his or her followers to establish a goal or goals" (Lee in Kaliski, p. 542). A leader inspires and motivates; the process is continuous. A corporate leader has a deep impact on a company in that he or she defines or approves the mission and provides the vision for its successful accomplishment. The leader is also the voice of the company, both internally and to the external world. Throughout history, leaders have been important. From Moses to King Arthur to Alexander the Great to Henry Ford to Margaret Thatcher, leaders have had an impact on the world in which they lived.

Leadership literature describes three distinct styles: autocratic or command-driven, democratic or participative, and laissez-faire where the group takes actions. Rene Likert (in Kalisky p. 543) describes business leadership styles as either job-centered or employee-centered. Appropriate styles may vary according to the particular situation, and, of course, cultural values can also come into play.

A good leader's characteristics include self-confidence, communication skills, determination, creativity, and personal integrity. Many research studies have examined women's leadership styles in an effort to determine if they differ from those of men. Traditionally, male leadership traits have been characterized as aggressive, assertive, decisive, competitive, and autocratic. Women are seen as less hierarchical and slower to make decisions, due to a desire to consider more information and input from a variety of sources. When women first entered the business world, many adopted a masculine style. As they became more comfortable and the numbers of businesswomen grew, they developed their own leadership styles, which encouraged more participation and sharing of power and information. The focus, for many, was to motivate using credit and praise, along with symbols of recognition. Many women leaders also use inclusion and an enthusiasm for the project or job to mobilize and inspire their co-workers and employees.

Women tend to lead through collaboration and teamwork. According to a *Business Week* article, their strengths are motivating others, fostering communication, producing high quality work, and listening to others ("As Leaders, Women Rule," p. 74). They themselves are, as a rule, more motivated by what they can do for the company, not by power or glory.

See also: Management

Further Reading
"As Leaders, Women Rule."
Book, Esther Wachs. *Why the Best Man for the Job Is a Woman: The Unique Female Qualities of Leadership.*
Helgeson, Sally. *The Female Advantage: Women's Ways of Leadership.*
Lee, Lee W. "Leadership." In Kaliski, p. 542–545.
Rosener, Judy B. "Ways Women Lead."

Leave, *see* Employee Benefits

Lee, Thai (1958–), Software Distributor

Thai Lee's Software House International was number 21 on *Working Woman*'s 2000 list of the top woman-owned companies in the United States and number 15 in 2001. It describes itself as a "global procurement outsourcing company and leading business to business solution provider . . . that fulfills orders for over 100,000 hardware and software products and offers a full menu of services, comprehensive consulting, licensing, configuration and support services" (www.shi.com). The company has also been listed on the VAR 500 since 1995, beginning at number 114 and moving up to number 40 in October 2002.

Lee graduated from Amherst College in 1980 and Harvard University in 1985. She began the business in 1989 in Somerset, New Jersey. In 1998 it was called one of the country's largest and fastest-growing software providers. She is president and CEO and, in 1998, also became a director. The company, which she built through partnerships, sells software such as Adobe, Citrix, IBM Lotus, Macromedia, Microsoft, NQL Technology, Novell, and Veritas. Its customers include Boeing, Bank of America, Hewlett Packard, IBM Technologies, MCI, Merrill Lynch, and the states of Florida and Minnesota. Expected sales for 2003 were estimated at over 2 billion dollars. It employs 1,000 people.

The company encourages employees' community service and matches their charitable gifts; holds an annual hardware sale for United Way; and partners with Salvation Army, Little League, Red Cross, and ASPCA. In 2002 *Forbes* ranked the company number 115 in its list of the largest private companies in the country.

See also: Asian American Businesswomen; Information Technology Industry

Further Reading
"Software House International Signs On as Unicenter TNG Channel Partners." www.shi.com

Leeds, Lilo (1928–), Magazine Publisher

Lilo Leeds was a pioneer in on-site corporate day care as well as other socially responsible benefits, particularly for women employees. CMP Media, founded by Leeds and her husband Gerard in 1971, was the first on Long Island to offer subsidized day care on the company premises. The company was named six times to *Working Mother*'s list of "100 Best Companies for Working Mothers".

She was born in Germany and escaped the Nazis in 1939 at age eleven when she came to the United States. She became a mathematician and worked at Bell Laboratories. In 1950 she met Gerard Leeds on a holiday skiing trip to the Adirondacks, married him the next year, and eventually had five children. He was an entrepreneur who worked for several electronics companies before starting his own company, Lumatron Electronics, in 1957. She was his partner and the accountant/bookkeeper. They sold it in 1962 and immediately began another electronics company that eventually merged with another.

In 1971 they decided to stay in electronics but focus on publishing. They launched the *Electronic Buyers' Guide* from their living room with the help of their eldest son Michael who was home for the summer from the University of Colorado. Their company, CMP Publishing, soon expanded to include a second magazine, *Electronic Engineering Times*. In 1984 Michael joined the company and began a group of travel magazines. Four years later he became the CEO while his parents stayed as co-chairmen. By 1991 the company published ten business newspapers and magazines. When the company went public in 1997, the elder Leeds, in an unusual gesture, gave stock to almost all of the employees, based on longevity. In 1999 Miller Freeman bought the company for $920 million. Again, every employee received a cash bonus based on longevity. This was also funded by Lilo Leeds and her husband.

Their goal was to run an ethically driven business noted for its progressive employee policies. Leeds, in charge of the management side of the business, began an on-site day care center that evolved into a licensed full-time infant program with a staff of four CMP employees plus a visiting nurse. Subsidized by the company, it later included after-school care, holiday programs, and summer programs. She firmly believed that this contributed to the health of the company and retention of the best employees. She was also an early believer in diversity. As a victim of gender discrimination in the form of unequal pay at Bell Labs (which she was instrumental in alleviating) she passionately believed in feminism and women's rights. Other benefits she initiated included adoption and infertility assistance, spousal leave and spousal equivalent benefits, vision care, dependent care reimbursement, tuition assistance, college scholarships for full-time employees' children, on-site fitness classes, annual bonuses based on years of service, and paid sabbaticals in the eighth and fifteenth years of service.

Both Leeds and her husband are also committed to giving back to the community in the form of philanthropy and instilled that value in their children, who started with donating some of their allowances to charity. In 1990 they formed a nonprofit organization, the Institute for Community Development (now called the Institute for Student Achievement) to fund programs for high school dropouts and at risk students who would otherwise not receive an education. They run two programs, believing that education is the key to stopping the circle of poverty: STAR for disadvantaged high school students and COMET for junior high students. In 1990 Leeds was named Woman of the Year by the Action Committee of Long Island and in 1993 received the "Women's Equality Award by the Long Island Chapter of NOW." She and her husband were honored by the Alumni Association of State College at Old Westbury for excellence in community service and in 2000 received a "Fulfilling the Dream" award for their positive impact on the quality of life of others. The company was featured in an NBC special on how businesses share their success with their communities and make a difference. In 1997 it was named the Mass Mutual Family Business of the Year and was one of *Fortune*'s 100 Best Companies to Work For. In 2001 the Leeds family gave $35 million to the University of Colorado College of Business to fund a curriculum incorporating social responsibility and diversity. They said at the time that it was a chance to shape the ethics and values of the business leaders of the country. The school's name was changed to the Leeds School of Business.

See also: Childcare; Immigrant Businesswomen; Publishing Industry

Further Reading
Fischler, Elizabeth. "Making a Difference: Another in a Series of Articles about Men and Women Who have Changed Life on Long Island."

Rostky, George. "A 25-Year Love Affair."
Sanger, Elizabeth. "L.I. Stocks/CMP Media Shares the Wealth."

Lehne, Kathy Prasnicki (1961–), Petroleum Industry Entrepreneur

Kathy Lehne began her career as a clerk at an oil company. By founding Sun Coast Resources, her own oil wholesale distributor company, she filled a niche her employer had decided to abandon. She turned it into one of the *Working Woman* top woman-owned companies.

She went to work for Jasper Oil Company in Houston as a work-study high school student, beginning as a clerk, then receptionist, then sales person. When Jasper Oil decided to cease their local distribution business in 1985, Lehne looked at her loyal customers and decided that she could keep them and build her own business. The main obstacle was getting financing, so she persuaded Jasper to sell her oil on credit.

Sun Coast Resources Company buys petroleum from independent refineries and sells it wholesale to school districts, trucking and railroad companies, corporate fleets, convenience stores, and companies with fleets of vehicles. With less than one hundred clients and three employees, its first year's sales were $787,000. Soon refineries other than Jasper were extending it credit. In 1990 she hired a consultant to write a business plan and a proposal for bank credit, resulting in a $1.5 million credit line from a bank. This was a major turning point for the company, allowing it to hire more sales staff and expand into a larger territory encompassing Kansas, all of Texas, Louisiana, and Oklahoma. By 1991 sales were $86 million, doubling by 1994. Two years later it had seventy-five employees, sales were $217 million, and it was the top woman-owned company in Houston. It is a cutthroat business with very thin margins. To deal with this it is expanding into other products, trying to buy in higher volumes, cutting overhead, and continuing efforts to buy from the very lowest-cost suppliers.

Lehne credits her success to four elements: good credit, excellent employee relations, computerization of office functions, and knowing the business. Firmly believing that happy long-term employees are a key to success, she not only pays better than competitive salaries and supplies better benefits than her competitors, but also has on-site day care where her own two daughters were raised. She has, on occasion, hired massage therapists to come into the company. She always promotes from within the company, going outside only for entry-level positions.

When she started Sun Coast Resources, Lehne was a single mother with one daughter. She is now married and has two daughters.

See also: Energy Industry

Further Reading
De Rouffignac, Ann. "Kathy Lehne Takes Sun Coast Resources, Inc. to the Top."
"A New Kind of Oil Dynasty."

Lepore, Dawn G. (1954–), Investment Advisor

Dawn Lepore is vice chairman of technology and administration for Charles Schwab, the online investment company. She has been ranked on the *Fortune* lists of the most powerful women in corporate America since 1999.

She was born and raised in San Francisco, earned a music degree from Smith College in 1977, and that year started work at Cincinnati Bell as a computer programmer. Two years later Lepore joined the San Francisco information consulting firm, Informatics. In 1981 she moved to Charles Schwab, where she volunteered to become involved in redesigning their computer system from a mainframe to a client/server system. Although she didn't have much information technology background, she was one of the leaders of this massive two-year project and recruited experts to help. In 1989 she was promoted to senior vice president of development and, in 1993, to executive vice president and chief information officer (CIO).

She was the first woman to hold the CIO position at the company, responsible for all systems, applications, development, and telecommunications activities. In 1995 Schwab began their online investment business, treating it as a separate unit. Now, 42 percent of their assets are invested in online trading accounts. In 1999 Lepore became vice chairman and CIO and, in October 2002, took her present position. She is a member of the executive management committee, and the CIO now reports to her. She is developing two new tools, an online search tool and an online screening tool.

Self-described as "competitive and a warrior by nature" ("Executive Profile," p.10) she is hard-working, risk-taking, charismatic, and competent. She focuses on customers and company growth but believes that employees must feel that they make a valuable contribution to the corporate vision. She firmly believes in teamwork and is said to be very patient, particularly in explaining new technologies. She credits her three bosses as mentors who believed in her and took an interest in her development. She is married and has a stepdaughter and a son. When their son was born in 1997, her husband quit his job as a programmer for Visa and became the stay-at-home parent. They share both household chores and parenting.

She has served on the corporate boards of eBay, PointCast, Times Mirror, Viador, and Wal-Mart. *Network World* called Lepore one of the "25 most powerful people in networking" in 1995; she was one of the "Top CIOs of 1996" according to *Information Week*; she received the Lattanze Information Systems Executive of the Year Award in 1998, the same year that the

San Francisco Chronicle named her one of the Bay Area's most powerful corporate women. Recently, she was named by Money one of the "50 smartest women in the money business," by Future Banker one of the "10 hottest CIOs," and, by San Francisco Women on the Web, one of the "top 25 women on the Web."

See also: Finance Industry

Further Reading
DiDio, Laura. "Corporate Strategist: Dawn Lepore."
"Executive Profile."
"Schwab Tech Group Focuses on Client Support."

Leslie, Miriam Follin (1836–1914), Magazine Publisher

Miriam Leslie, one of the foremost publishers of the nineteenth century, began her life as the owner of a publishing empire after her husband, Frank Leslie, died in 1880. Having spent many years learning about publishing, she was prepared when she took over his bankrupt publishing empire and paid his debts, eventually becoming an even better publisher than he was. She was known as the "Empress of Journalism."

She was of French Creole heritage, born in New Orleans to a sometimes-wealthy common law family. Her father tutored her at home, particularly in languages: French, German, Latin, Italian, and Spanish. Due to financial troubles, the family moved to New York City, where her brief marriage to a jeweler, David Peacock, was annulled. She then went on the stage in Albany, Providence, and Pittsburgh as a protege of Lola Montez, a friend of her brother's.

She met Ephraim Squier, a noted archaeologist, and married him in 1857. He contributed articles to Frank Leslie's Illustrated Newspaper and was accepted socially in high places. They first met Frank Leslie at Abraham Lincoln's first inaugural ball and began their lengthy association with him. The three began to go everywhere together, including Lincoln's second inaugural ball, where they were pictured together. Ephraim continued to write for the newspaper and she helped him translate books, learning both the editorial and business aspects of publishing from him. In 1861 she also began a series of editing assignments for Frank Leslie beginning with Leslie's Lady's Magazine. In 1865 she inaugurated Frank Leslie's Chimney Corner, which soon circulated to 80,000 readers.

In 1867 Miriam, Ephraim, and Frank went to Europe together. By this time, Frank had separated from his wife and was living with the Squiers. He and Miriam embarked upon an affair, and in 1872 his wife divorced him and Miriam divorced Ephraim, who later went insane. Miriam and Frank married in 1873 and began an opulent life of pleasure. She was thirty-eight, he was fifty-three. They built a ninety-two-acre estate in Saratoga, New York, where they entertained royalty and prominent politicians They also used their $35,000 Palace Pullman car for a trip to the West. Miriam interviewed Brigham Young, went down into the Bonanza Mine in Nevada, and roundly criticized Virginia City, Nevada, in articles that her husband published. As they traveled extensively, she wrote about their travels with wit and interest.

The panic of 1877 caused problems for the Leslie publishing empire, which by then consisted of sixteen different entities. The article about Virginia City came back to haunt them, for a reporter there researched and published all the old scandals about the Squier *ménage a trois*. Frank was given three years to pay his debts, but he had throat cancer and died in 1880. Miriam claimed that he asked her on his deathbed to save the publishing business and pay his debts. So she did.

She used her diamonds to secure a $50,000 loan and not only paid the debts but enabled the paper to report extensively on President Garfield's assassination. This was her first journalistic coup; she was first and best with the news. The report was dramatic and sensational. She added more information to the Tuesday edition and published an extra edition three days later. She hired artists, printed pictures, and provided coverage that was incredibly complete. When Garfield died three months later, she provided the same treatment, including pictures of the autopsy and embalming. Nothing escaped her reporter's eye, and it sold papers.

She legally changed her name to Frank Leslie to establish her ownership. She was involved in seventeen lawsuits over the years, including one from Frank's sons contesting the will. She also examined every aspect and department of the company, pruning the publications down to six, and concentrating on *Frank Leslie's Illustrated Newspaper* and *Frank Leslie's Popular Magazine*. She looked at every contract, every page that was published, and every other piece of the business. She introduced new methods of production and hired women reporters and editors. She was highly respected in the publishing world for her business acumen and reporting skill. At its peak, the company had a combined circulation of 250,000, employed 400 persons, and had a weekly payroll of $32,000. There were sixteen presses, thirty engravers, and fourteen artists.

In 1889 she sold the *Illustrated Newspaper* and other weeklies, keeping only *Frank Leslie's Popular Magazine*. After leasing that to a syndicate, she returned to her exciting social life. In 1891 she married 39-year-old Charles Kingsbury Wilde, the older brother of Oscar Wilde. Two years later the marriage was dissolved. When the panic of 1893 caused financial problems for the leasers of the publishing company, the magazine reverted to her. She soon put it back on its feet and began publishing fiction by American writers including William Dean Howells, Frank Stockton, and Bret Harte, building the circulation to 200,000 in four months. Money again became a problem in 1900, and she had to surrender half of the stock and was supplanted as editor by Ellery Sedgewick. She sold the magazine to him, and he eventually turned it into

American Magazine. By 1905 the Frank Leslie Publishing House no longer existed.

She died at age seventy-eight with a $2 million estate, leaving half to Carrie Chapman Catt to use for women's suffrage. With that money, the *Woman's Citizen*, the official organ of the National Woman's Suffrage Association, was established in 1917, giving new life to the movement.

See also: Publishing Industry

Further Reading

Cheney, Lynne Vincent. "Mrs. Frank Leslie's Illustrated Newspaper."

Fischer, Christiane. *Let Them Speak for Themselves; Women in the American West, 1849–1900*, p. 313–325.

Ross, Ishbel. *Charmers and Cranks*, p. 61–88.

Stern, Madeleine B. *Purple Passage; The Life of Mrs. Frank Leslie*.

Lewent, Judy C. (1948–), Pharmaceutical Industry Executive

Judy Lewent is the chief financial officer and an executive vice president of Merck, the pharmaceutical company. She has been on the *Fortune* list of most powerful corporate women since 1998. She is famous for her complicated financial model that measures the future value of new drugs.

She was born and grew up in New York City. Her mother was an accountant, and her father an executive with an import-export company. During her childhood, she read the stock quotes in the newspaper to her grandfather, and dinner table conversations included debates on important issues dealing with the economy. After graduating from Hunter High School, Lewent went on to receive a BA from Goucher in 1970 and an MS in management science in 1972 from the Sloan School at MIT, where she was the only woman majoring in finance. She and her husband decided not to have children because of their demanding careers.

Her first summer job was transferring manual accounts to a computer at a large New York department store. After earning her masters, Lewent went to work at E.F. Hutton's corporate finance department. She then worked as an assistant vice president of strategic planning at Bankers Trust and a senior financial analyst at Norton Simon, each for one year, before becoming a division controller at Pfizer from 1976 to 1980. Then executive headhunters recruited her for Merck as the director of acquisitions and capital analysis.

She moved into increasingly responsible positions there until 1990 when she was appointed vice president of finance and CFO, first woman CFO in the pharmaceutical industry, responsible for the treasury, finance, and tax issues. She was also the highest-ranking woman at Merck and served on the operating review committee, which is closely aligned with the CEO. In 1993 Lewent was appointed senior vice president and CFO, responsible for joint ventures and partnerships, in particular with Medco for distribution and Schering-Plough for respiratory and cholesterol medications. She was also responsible for the acquisition of the biotech firm, Sibia. Two of her accomplishments were a financial training program and the establishment of the Merck Women's Network, an in-house mentoring program. In 2001 she was promoted to executive vice president and CFO, responsible for all the financial aspects of the company as well as a subsidiary, Merck Capital Ventures, LLC. In 2002 her responsibilities included marketing and sales in Asia.

Lewent used her complex financial model to convince Merck's upper management of the wisdom of researching and marketing new drugs. This system showed that the more drugs were developed, the more profitable the company would be. Under her watch, Merck produced medicines for baldness, migraines, and AIDS because she proved that additional spending on research and development would eventually prove beneficial to the company. She is known as a tough boss who is extremely well organized.

Lewent has served on the boards of Quaker Oats, Motorola, and Dell as well as the board of trustees at Goucher and the advisory board of Sloan Management School. In 1992 she was named one of the fifty top women in business by *Business Week*; the following year she was on *Working Woman*'s list of the ten most admired women managers in the United States. She co-authored a chapter in Robert Kolb's book, *The International Finance Reader*.

Further Reading
Kohn, Ken. "Are You Ready for Economic-Risk Management?"
Lewent, Judy C. and A. John Kearney. "Identifying, Measuring, and Hedging Currency Risk at Merck." In Kolb, p. 305–314.
Nichols, Nancy A. "Scientific Management at Merck: An Interview with CFO Judy Lewent."
Weber, Joseph. "I am Intense, Aggressive, and Hard-Charging."

Lewis, Harriet Gerber (1919–), Plumbing Fixtures Executive

Harriet Lewis took over her father's plumbing fixtures company in the mid-fifties and built it into one of the top woman-owned companies in the United States. Gerber Plumbing Fixtures Corporation manufactures and sells plumbing fixtures to wholesalers.

She was born in Chicago and received a BA from Northwestern University in 1941. In 1940 she married Maurice Lewis and later had two daughters and a son. After her father died in 1935, she took over the company, becoming president, CEO, and chairman of the board. Eventually her son and daughter joined her; Alan became CEO (much later) and Ila became head of marketing.

The plumbing fixtures business has changed over the years with Fashionable or decorator fixtures becoming popular. Regulations affected the company positively; the emphasis on low-water use plumbing caused sales to rise as did the need for disabled-accessible plumbing. In 1995 sales were so good that it was difficult to keep the wholesalers stocked. Lewis has expanded the business through new lines of fixtures and attempts to build up the export business. However, it is a business that is very dependent on the amount of construction.

Gerber Plumbing Fixtures is a true family-owned company with the probability of becoming a third generation company. One of their new infant's potty seats is a case in point; it is named the "Eli" after Harriet's great-grandson. She is active in the Jewish United Fund, Finch Medical School, the American Israel Chamber, Board of Philanthropic Funds, and the Jewish Federation.

See also: Manufacturing

Further Reading

Schmuckler, Eric and Harris Collingwood. "The Top 50 Women Business Owners," p. 66–67.

Lewis, Loida Nicolas (1942–), Food Executive

After a traditional year of mourning, Loida Lewis took over her late husband's company, TLC Beatrice, and made it one of the top woman-owned businesses in the United States. Reginald Lewis, the Jackie Robinson of business, was a legendary black businessman who died in 1993 from a brain tumor. His wife, Loida, a Filipino American immigration lawyer as well as his business confidante and informal advisor, became the chairperson and CEO of the company in 1994.

She was born in the Philippines to a wealthy family. Her father owned the largest furniture company on the island as well as numerous other businesses. She was the oldest of five children, all of whom were raised to be entrepreneurial. After graduating cum laude from St Theresa's College in Manila, she received her law degree from the University of the Philippines College of Law, ranked in the top ten in her class. In 1967 she passed the bar exam and received a world tour as a gift from her father, having fulfilled his dream by becoming a lawyer. While in New York City, she met Reginald Lewis, a Wall Street lawyer, on a blind date, and they married one year later. This decision was a difficult one for her, for it meant leaving her home in the Philippines and living in New York City.

In 1975 she passed the New York bar exam, one of the first Asian women to pass without having studied law in the United States. That year she also became a citizen. While studying for the bar exam, she published a political magazine very critical of Ferdinand Marcos, then the president of the Philippines. She attempted to get a job as an attorney with the U.S. Immigration and Naturalization Service (INS), but was turned down. Later she discovered that they had hired someone with inferior qualifications. She sued and won the suit, back pay for three years, and a job. She worked for INS until 1987, when her husband bought Beatrice and they moved to Paris. In Paris she wrote three booklets to help immigrants with the green card process required by the United States.

In December 1992 Reginald was diagnosed with brain cancer and died in January. She mourned for a year, a tradition among Filipino Catholic families. At the end of the year spent largely in ordering his estate and finishing his autobiography, she took over TLC Beatrice from her brother-in-law, a move they both say was agreed upon from the beginning. The largest black-owned company in the United States, it manufactured ice cream and snack foods and owned two supermarkets in Europe. According to *Black Enterprise,* this was justified after Lewis' death by the statement that the Lewis family and company board of directors were black. Unfortunately, at this time, it was also in financial trouble due to an unwieldy set of subsidiaries, a recession in Europe, lagging sales and profits, management uncertainty, and a minority stockholder revolt.

Loida Lewis turned the company around by cost cutting, selling the company jet, abandoning her husband's opulent office, getting rid of the leased company fleet of cars, cutting the New York staff, and selling money-losing subsidiaries. She also hired a new chief financial officer and refinanced a $170 million bank loan. A deeply spiritual and religious woman, she began her first board meeting with a prayer, ending with a quote from Isaiah, "and I know that I will triumph." She has said she heard snickers at that point, but she refused to be upset and proceeded to follow her plan for getting the company financially solvent. The Lewis family owned 51 percent of the closely held stock at this time with one of their two daughters, Leslie, sitting on the board of directors. Some of the stockholders were unhappy and sued the company for mismanagement; she felt they were trying to force her to go public. She resolved this by making a secondary offering so they could cash out.

The first year she spent putting out fires. The second year she consolidated, sold under-performing subsidiaries, beefed up the top management team, and began to expand the French supermarkets from nineteen stores to 250. By 1997 TLC Beatrice was one of the world's largest multinational food companies with over 600 stores in France. She had turned it around. In September of that year she sold the two French chains with their $2 billion in sales to a French company, Groupe Casino, for $573 million. She felt that the time was right for the sale, and she needed to reduce debt and give some value to the shareholders. Sales for the company were reduced to $344 million per year, but the company was financially solvent.

In May 1999, with mixed feelings, she began to sell the rest of the company. She had met with her management team and investment bankers, and they concluded that liquidation was the only way to ensure shareholder value. She had not planned to sell, but going public was not feasible, and the time was again right for selling. The board approved a plan of liquidation, and the ice cream business was sold to Iberian Beverages group for $191 million and Tayto to Cantrell & Cochrane Holdings Ltd. of Ireland for $116.5 million. Distributions totaling $42 per share were made to shareholders. She also approved a $1 million distribution to the employees of Tayto after their union negotiated for a cash bonus payout. Since 1997 TLC Beatrice has realized $924.5 million for its shareholders. She feels that, with the sale, she has completed Reginald Lewis' legacy.

Lewis' management style was very different from that of her husband, who tended to be volatile though charismatic. She characterizes herself as opinionated, demanding, and as ambitious as he was, but a better listener, more intuitive and empathetic. She believes in listening carefully to all options before making a decision and created a collegial atmosphere with lots of hugs. She also found that her lawyer skills matched the skills needed by a CEO, that of fact-finding, asking for good advice, making decisions, and making sure that employees do their jobs. She quickly gained the respect of her European managers and employees who complimented her for her common sense, knowledge of European habits, and ability to talk the local language (she is fluent in French, Italian, Spanish, Filipino, and English). Her real mission was to finish what Reginald had begun; getting the company on its feet was the priority.

She calls her keys to success the same as his: love your neighbor, give your customers a quality product, be attentive to their needs, and give back to the community. She was unfortunate in that she was always operating under several mythologies: her husband's status and accomplishments as an African American man making it in the white world; the company's status as the largest black-owned company; her celebrated status in the Filipino community, and the company's ranking in the world of woman-owned businesses. Her devout spirituality helped her as well as her will to finish the job her husband had begun.

Loida Lewis did not accept honorary degrees while she was running the company; she said she was too busy. She did sit on the steering committee of MOPAC (Mobilization for Economic Opportunity Political Action Committee), however, which financially supports candidates and attempts to stop the backlash against affirmative action programs. She also runs the Reginald Lewis Foundation and has reenergized it, giving millions to a variety of educational, civic, and civil rights organizations. Recently, with the money gained by the sale of the company, the Lewis family gave $1 million and the Foundation another $1 million to begin the National Federation for Teaching Entrepreneurship, whose mission is to teach inner-city young people how to run businesses. It is totally in keeping with her philosophy of always giving back to the community. In this case, it was Reginald Lewis' community and a fitting memorial. She also created the Runners Club, an advisory group focused on transforming African American businesses into major players in the business community and gave money to NAACP to endow youth camps in eight cities. In June 2002 the Foundation pledged $5 million to endow the Reginald F. Lewis Maryland Museum of African American History and Culture in Baltimore.

See also: Asian American Businesswomen; Food Industry; Immigrant Businesswomen

Further Reading

Chappelle, Tony. "Time to Take the Spotlight at TLC."
Dingle, Derek K. "TLC's Final Act."
"Lewis, Loida." *1997 Current Biography Yearbook*, p. 321–324.
Solomon, Jolie. "Operation Rescue."

Liang, Christine (1959–), Computer Components Importer

Christine Liang is the founder, president, chief coordinating officer, and majority owner of Asian Source, Inc. (ASI), an importer of computer components from Asia, one of the top fifty companies in the *Working Woman* list of woman-owned companies. It was first listed in 1996 at number 17 and was number 20 in 2001, the last year of the list.

She was born in Taiwan and received her BA there from Tang Ming College in 1979. She ran a jewelry business but moved to the United States in 1986 to accompany her husband, Marcel, who represented a computer maker. Her brother, James, persuaded her to import computer components for the reseller and clone-maker markets. He encouraged her by selling monitors and components to her at his cost. Because she owns over half of the company, it also qualified for minority and woman-owned business programs funded by the federal government. In the beginning, her husband helped during his off hours but joined the company full-time in 1989. He oversees strategy as chair and CEO while she is the major owner, president, COO, and takes care of purchasing, finance, and some parts of sales. She thinks this division of labor and titles is just fine.

The company now imports motherboards, cases, power sources, monitors, keyboards, video cards, and other components and sells them to their 10,000-plus customers, 70 percent of whom are system integrators and 30 percent are resellers. They had an early setback when their largest customer, Gateways 2000, who was responsible for half their revenue, went elsewhere, but they survived and, by 1996, had sales of $326 million and 340 employees. This was the year they were first listed in the *Working Women* top woman-owned companies. In this industry, however, there is a lot of competition and profit margins are very, very thin. ASI tries to differentiate itself with superb customer service and knowledgeable salespersons. Its shipping and inventory accuracy is 99 percent, and it offers same-day orders and free delivery to local customers. The company eschews voice mail and boasts an 85 percent live-answer rate. Its technical support department is well staffed with a strong enlightening development component. Salespeople are also urged to stay current. It has a Web page but still believes that good human help is far superior.

In 1996 ASI made both the *Working Woman* list and the *Inc.* 500 list of best entrepreneurial companies. Liang was also a finalist for Entrepreneur of the Year. In 1998, the company was one of the top fifty distributors in the United States.

While the business was beginning and building, she was married with two small children and was always worried about keeping the balance between family and business. The company has grown from one office to eight. All the facilities have been expanded including a headquarters for manufacturing their own computer system.

See also: Asian American Businesswomen; Immigrant Businesswomen; Information Technology Industry

Further Reading
Rivera, Eddie. "Christine Liang: Going for Broker, Owner of Asia Source Inc."
Schmuckler, Eric and Harris Collingwood. "The Top 50 Women Business Owners," p. 36–37.

Line and Staff Managers

Line and staff managers differ chiefly in their contribution to the central mission of the organization. Line managers have profit-and-loss responsibilities, and the authority to command and give orders. They are in the direct chain of command from the CEO. Promotions to executive vice-president and higher ranks usually come from line managers. These positions are most often in sales or marketing, production, or high-level finance, directly concerned with profit-making.

Staff managers are responsible for support departments such as human resources, public relations, or corporate communications. Women have traditionally been over-represented in staff positions for several reasons: successful line managers have been described as aggressive and risk-taking; staff jobs are seen as more supportive of work/life balance; women's skill sets have not included engineering, which has been used for evaluating job candidates.

Most companies do not move managers from staff positions to line positions. A woman who wishes to enter into the higher realms of management needs to obtain experience as a line manager.

See also: Management

Further Reading
Catalyst, Cracking 2000, p. 30–31
Schneider, Dorothy and Carl J. Schneider, pp. 150, 252

Livermore, Ann (1958–), Electronics Executive

Ann Livermore is the president of HP Services at Hewlett-Packard, the division that brought in $15 billion in revenues in 2002. Her position has ranked her on *Fortune*'s list of the most powerful women in business since 1999. In 2002 she was number 23.

She was born and raised in Greensboro, North Carolina, the middle child with two sisters. She received a BA in economics from the University of North Carolina in 1980 and went on to Stanford for an MBA. While there, she devised the winning plan for running the student snack bar. She bought doughnuts for five cents and sold them to corporate recruiters for fifty cents, using the profits, which she was able to keep, to pay for her MBA, earned in 1982.

Her first job was for Hewlett-Packard, working on processes and systems. She rose through the ranks in research and development, marketing, and managerial positions of ever increasing responsibility and challenges. In 1997, as senior vice president and general manager of software and services, Livermore reorganized the global sales force and restructured the services. She was a contender in the 1999 search for the new HP CEO but lost to Carly Fiorina; however, she is an important part of Fiorina's executive council, and became CEO and president of one of the divisions, Enterprise Computing. Her goal was to turn HP into an Internet power. After the 2002 merger with Compaq Computer, she became the president of HP Services, one of the four HP business groups. That year she initiated and signed a $1.3 billion services contract with CIBC, the largest contract in HP's history.

Livermore is reputed to be a straight shooter who can listen. She is widely respected and manages through a combination of compassion and competence. Sales, costs, and profits are important to her, but so are customer and employee satisfaction. She is very focused on the customer and ambitious for the company more than for herself. She also strongly believes in gender, ethnic, and social diversity and says it's good for the company as well as for society. Her motto is from her father: "It's amazing how much you can get done when no one is worrying about who gets the credit" ("All smiles and mantra," p. 13).

She sits on the board of directors of UPS. She is married with one daughter and seems to balance career and family successfully.

See also: Information Technology Industry

Further Reading
Burrows, Peter. "The Hottest Property in the Valley?"
Kornblum, Janet. "She's Sitting on Top of the High-Tech World."
Markoff, John. "Private Sector; Trailblazer in the Silicon Jungle."

Loans, *see* Financing

Longaberger, Tami (1962–), Home Accessories Executive

Tami Longaberger is the president and CEO of Longaberger Company, maker of baskets and other home accessories. Her company had 8,700 employees and $1 billion in sales in 2001, enough to rank number 18 on *Working Woman's* list of the top woman-owned companies.

She grew up in the Longaberger Company. Her grandfather began working for the Dresden Basket Factory in 1918. He bought it in 1936 for $1900, enlarged it, changed the name several times, and left it to his son Dave, Longaberger's father. He built a new thirty-four-acre manufacturing campus in 1990. The home office building in Newark, Ohio, is a huge seven-story replica of a Longaberger basket (www.longaberger.com), and the company makes baskets, pottery, fabrics, wrought iron furniture, home décor, and accessories. They sell through in-home sales and shows by independent sales associates as well as on the premises.

By 1998 it was the largest maker of handmade maple baskets in the United States. That year Dave stepped down and his daughter became CEO. He died of cancer the following year.

Longaberger had several different jobs at the company while in high school, ending as official tour guide for the company. After earning a BA in marketing at Ohio State University in 1984, she became Longaberger's first head of customer service. At that time, the company employed 300 persons and had annual revenues of $6 million. She became president in 1994 and diversified into furniture. In 1997 she initiated the basket-collectors club; that year, they sold 7 million baskets.

After becoming CEO, she built Longaberger Homestead, a complex with six restaurants, shopping, and entertainment as well as the Longaberger Golf Club and a hotel in Newark. She also focused on increasing the market and on improving employee diversity. By the end of 1999, there were 50,000 sales associates, and the headquarters was the largest tourist draw in central Ohio. The company is one of the 500 largest privately held companies in the country.

Longaberger has said she learned the art of decision making from her father as well as a sense of judgment. She firmly believes in maintaining balance between company demands and her family. She is divorced with a son and a daughter; her ex-husband runs the golf club. She is in the Ohio Women's Hall of Fame and has won the Women Means Business Award. She has served on the Greater Columbus Workforce Leadership Council and as chair of the board of the Direct Selling Association. She is the driving force behind Longaberger's Horizon of Hope breast cancer awareness fund-raising effort, raising over $3 million for research.

See also: Manufacturing

Further Reading
Kanner, Bernice. "The Weaver."
Longaberger, Dave. *Longaberger: An American Success Story.*
Longaberger, Tami. "Diversity: It's Right, It's Here, Embrace It."
www.longaberger.com

Love, Gay McLawhorn (1929–), Packaging Executive

Gay Love is the chairman of PrintPack, a packaging company that was in the top twenty on *Working Woman*'s list of the largest woman-owned companies from 1996 to 2001, the list's final year. In 2001 the company had sales of $999 million and 4,000 employees.

She grew up on her family's tobacco farm and earned her BA from Duke University in 1951. After college she moved to Atlanta as a management trainee for Rich's Department Store. There she met and married J. Erskine Love. He started PrintPack in 1956 with one client (Herman Lay) and loans against the car, the house, and his life insurance. She was appointed to the board of directors.

By the time Love took over the company after her husband's death in 1987 at age fifty-eight, it had several clients, including Frito-Lay, and revenues of $200 million. Because she had been on the board from the beginning, she was familiar with the management, customers, and suppliers. She appointed her son Dennis president, and the company thrived. By 1996 sales had tripled due to the expansion of Frito-Lay, as well as new customers Eagle Foods, Hershey, M&M/Mars, and Hormel. PrintPack moved into flexible packaging as well as other new materials and techniques. In 1997 it acquired the James River Corporation and began packaging personal care products and diapers. It also built a new plant in Mexico. As of 2002 the company employed 4,300 people at twenty manufacturing facilities in the United States, England, and Mexico and packages a large variety of products.

In 1999 Gay Love was nominated for the Leading Women Entrepreneur of the World Award. Five of her six children are involved in the company while all six plus four outside directors comprise the board of directors.

Further Reading
Bamford, Janet and Jennifer Pendleton, p. 38–39.
Schmuckler, Eric and Harris Collingwood, p. 35.
www.printpack.com

Lukens, Rebecca Pennock (1794–1854), Iron Manufacturer

Rebecca Lukens was the first woman ironmaster in the United States; she and her husband established the first mill to manufacture rolling iron boiler plate. She was on the leading edge of the Industrial Revolution that saw the iron industry move from primitive, small local crafts operations to a large-scale industry.

She was born in Chester County, Pennsylvania, the eldest surviving child of a Quaker family with nine children. Her father had abandoned farming to begin the Federal Slitting Mill just before she was born. In 1810 he bought the Brandywine Mill that eventually belonged to Rebecca. In 1813 at age 19, she married Dr. Charles Lukens who gave up medicine to join her father. Four years later they leased the dilapidated Brandywine Mill from her father for $420 per year and began the task of converting it to a plant that had the capability of rolling charcoal iron boiler plates. Charles was convinced that this was the future. Their first large order was for iron plates to gird the first metal-hulled ship in the United States, the steamship Codurus. Just after finishing the plates, he died, leaving her with five children and expecting another. Her father had died the year before and left an ambiguous will. Although he had promised to leave the Brandywine Mill to her, he left it to her mother during her life. Charles died intestate, but Lukens continued with the mill as he had wished. Legal complications dragged on until 1853 when the mill finally became hers.

Meanwhile she continued operations, hiring her brother-in-law, Solomon, as manager of operations and assuming the executive management herself. She had learned the techniques of ironmaking from her father, and now she learned about the commercial end, getting supplies, price setting, the ins and outs of contracts, and marketing and sales. She also kept aware of pertinent legislation. Lukens encountered many problems: difficult transportation that depended on the river, upstream competitors, and heavy debts incurred by having to pay her mother and rebuild most of the mill. Fortunately, however, she was an exceptional marketer and saleswoman and, despite all the problems, the mill was a success. All steam engineers knew her plates for their quality.

> Rebecca Pennock Lukens was on the leading edge of the Industrial Revolution that saw the iron industry move from primitive, small, local crafts operations to a large-scale industry.

During the panic of 1837, Lukens worked on maintenance when the market was slow. Tariff reductions of 1837 were also a problem, but she never laid off a worker. During the trouble, they worked on the farm and she paid them in produce. She also built substantial tenant houses for her mill workers and offered premiums for increased output. When the railroad arrived, the market expanded, and the mill supplied boilermakers in Boston, Baltimore, Albany, New York, and New Orleans. Shipments were also made to England and used in building some of the earliest steam locomotives. By 1844 she was worth over $60,000, had paid all the various debts, and had rebuilt the mill.

In 1847 Lukens signed articles of co-partnership with her son-in-law Abraham Gibbons Jr. and went into semi-retirement. The business was renamed for him. In 1849 another son-in-law joined, and by 1850 the company had two heating furnaces and a train roll and employed seventeen men and boys. She died in 1854 with an estate valued at over $100,000, an enormous amount for that time. In 1859 the ironworks was again renamed the Lukens Iron Works, and in 1890 it was incorporated as the Lukens Steel Company. In 1994 it was number 395 on the *Fortune 500* with revenues of $862 million and the oldest continuously operating steel mill in the United States. Rebecca was named to the National Business Hall of Fame in 1994, the second woman to be so named. She could be proud of her legacy; the *Fortune* article says of her, "She took over an ailing iron mill and forged the foundations of a modern steel giant" (Nulty, "The National Business Hall of Fame," p. 126). They called her America's first female CEO of an industrial company.

See also: Manufacturing

Further Reading
Drachman, Virginia G., pp. 33–40.
Nulty, Peter. "The National Business Hall of Fame."
Stern, Madeleine B., pp. 237–250.
Wolcott, Robert Wilson. *Woman in Steel: Rebecca Lukens (1794–1854)*.